NEIGHBOURS AND STRANGERS

Literary and Cultural Relations in Germany, Austria and Central Europe since 1989

Edited by

Ian Foster and Juliet Wigmore

Rodopi

Amsterdam - New York, NY 2004

ISBN: 90-420-1891-7 (Bound)
©Editions Rodopi B.V., Amsterdam - New York, NY 2004
Printed in the Netherlands

NEIGHBOURS AND STRANGERS

Literary and Cultural Relations in
Germany, Austria and
Central Europe since 1989

GERMAN MONITOR No. 59
General Editor: Ian Wallace

Table of Contents

Acknowledgements

The inspiration for this volume was a conference held in Salford in July 2002 under the title 'Neighbours and Strangers: Germany, Austria and Central Europe: Literary and Cultural Relations since 1989'. The editors would like to thank the staff of the European Studies Research Institute at the University of Salford for their help in running this event smoothly. While not everyone who gave a paper at the conference was able to contribute to this volume, we are particularly pleased that colleagues who did so found time to expand and revise their papers and responded patiently to our editorial promptings to produce the present volume. Their work is presented here alongside other commissioned essays. We would like to thank all of our authors for their contributions. In addition, we would like to thank our colleague Andy Hollis for his advice and support and Ian Wallace for his editorial guidance.

We are grateful to Professor Norman Davies for allowing us to reproduce the map in Brigid Haines's essay on p. 13 and also to his publishers Pimlico Press and Oxford University Press (New York) for the US rights.

Ian Foster would like to thank Sally, Sarah, Daniel, Samuel and Rachel Foster for being tolerant of his hours at the lap-top and desk.

Ian Foster and Juliet Wigmore

Salford, January 2004

Juliet Wigmore and Ian Foster

Introduction

Following the events which culminated in the unification of Germany in October 1990, much has been written about the historical relationships between Germany and its neighbours to the east. Discussions have also arisen on topics which, in 1989, could not have been anticipated, any more than could the shape that events would take nor the speed at which attitudes would change and new allegiances be forged. Not least among these issues, for instance, is the increased mental freedom which has finally begun to allow discussion and debate of the Germans' role as victims of war and expulsion, topics which hitherto had been largely taboo because of the rigidly polarised positions that prevailed. One might contrast the debate over Daniel Goldhagen's *Hitler's Willing Executioners* in 1996 with the recent success of Jörg Friedrich's popular historical account of the Allied bombing of Germany in *Der Brand*.[1] Whereas the debate on Goldhagen's book exhausted itself largely in restating established positions with regard to the collective guilt or innocence of average Germans and what that might entail, Friedrich's book presented the German civilian population as victims of Allied bombing and thereby ran the risk of accusations that he was relativising Nazi war crimes. Similar phenomena may also be observed in the controversies that surrounded the touring exhibition 'Vernichtungskrieg. Verbrechen der Wehrmacht 1941–1944', popularly known as the 'Wehrmachtausstellung', which toured 33 German cities from March 1995 to November 1999.[2] Established authors, such as Günter Grass, have also recently turned to writing on similar formerly taboo topics. The question is whether it is simply the elapsing of time and the distance from the events themselves that render a topic such as the sinking of the German ship *Wilhelm Gustloff* by a Soviet submarine in 1945 and the resulting deaths of 4,000 children sufficiently 'manageable' as subject matter; and to what extent it is the result of the improved relations established between Germany and Poland as a result of the ratification of their shared border. Undoubtedly, the ensuing reduction in tension between neighbouring countries is at least partly responsible for allowing a more measured approach to repressed horrors and old resentments.

This volume presents some of these issues as they have been addressed particularly in literature in German since 1989. In this sense it complements other recent publications, such as Keith Bullivant's *Germany and Eastern Europe*,[3] with its stronger focus on cultural as well as literary relationships, and Steven Tötösy de Zepetnek's study of comparative literature.[4] *Neighbours and Strangers* includes essays devoted not only to prose fiction, but also to a wide range of literary and artistic production, a reflection of the pervasiveness of the changes in perception which have taken place. For whilst discursive genres, fiction in particular, offer the most obvious scope for discussing ethical issues, these recent topics have been taken up in other contexts, including drama (Birgit Haas), film (Alexandra Ludewig) and the life and work of a poet (David Rock). Above all, the period since 1990 has seen a removal of political constraints which has been mirrored in many different ways by writers. On the one hand, the opening up of European boundaries has enabled the meeting of different cultures across formerly largely impermeable borders. With this new mobility has come the potential for debate and conflict, especially as those who were kept apart come face to face with new and unfamiliar viewpoints. To this extent, the significance of the title of the present volume, 'Neighbours and Strangers', at one level reflects an actual geographical dimension, which has ethical implications.

The beginnings of the development of a new European identity, which has come about as a result of the redefinition of political and geographical boundaries, has been accompanied by concerns on the one hand about loss of identity but also by the emergence of new concepts of identity, often regional, but sometimes transnational. These include identities defined by, for instance, historical connections, lifestyles, gender or cultural identities of various kinds, including those based on race and religion. These 'globalised' identity issues have occurred at the same time as the 'new Europe' has been coming into being and undoubtedly would not have proceeded at such a pace had it not been for the political changes in Europe. Now, the geographical east-west alignment has been replaced by a new sense of engagement between countries which were formerly estranged.

In literature, this period has also seen a revisiting of the past, particularly the Holocaust and the Nazi period. These topics are now treated in the context of a discussion in which the generation which actually experienced that period directly is in decline, whilst the post-Cold War generation is shaping contemporary Europe. As was noted at the time, the fall of the Berlin Wall finally marked the end of the post-war era. Writers who tackle the war or the Third Reich now look back on those periods of history very differently and with altered horizons. But examining the past also means, for some writers, reflecting on the division of Germany and re-examining the role of GDR writers in the new European context.

The reshaping of the European map, with Germany at its centre, both geographically and in many respects also culturally, the latter applying also to Austria, has both forced and enabled German-language writers and artists to re-assess their perceptions of their countries. It is therefore understandable that, in this period, too, the concept of *Heimat* has undergone a resurgence,[5] as the German-speaking peoples look both at their own countries and over the fence at their neighbours, including German-speakers in other countries, notably those of the former 'east'. The quest for *Heimat* is often associated with the search for identity, as Arthur Williams shows in his essay on W. G. Sebald's *Austerlitz*. For others, it has allowed issues relating to the 'east' to be raised, whereas during the Cold War such topics had been too fraught, either with the sense of loss or indeed with fear because they were too closely associated with the political Right, owing to the claims of German *Vertriebene* and *Aussiedler*. Only in this recent period has the veteran Günter Grass taken up the story of the *Gustloff*, (see the essay by Julian Preece in this volume, who also examines how the Jewish writer Edgar Hilsenrath revisits the eastern homeland). So too, discussing the liberating effects of the political change, Alexandra Ludewig shows how German films can now be located on the Baltic, without any implication of reclaiming lost territory for Germany. These examples suggest perhaps that in the 'new' Europe, regions which were once off-limits, not only physically but also culturally, are once again legitimately regarded as part of the greater European neighbourhood. For many, including writers who have left or lost their homeland, but not only for them, it is a case of 'Heimat in der Sprache' as Stefan Hermlin put it.[6] Geography has become less important, culture more so.

The idea of 'good relations' has also undergone a change with regard to relations between the GDR and eastern Europe. For here old alliances have had to be revised. As Keith Bullivant has expressed it:

> the ties to other Warsaw pact countries had constituted a sort of enforced brotherhood that papered over the cracks inherent in German relationships with those countries. (Bullivant, 1999, p. 6)

And yet even as the old allegiances were being revised, the fear was also expressed that West Germany would colonise the GDR and destroy its values and culture (Heiner Müller, cited by Martin Kane).[7] In this volume, two contributions address GDR issues from contrasting perspectives: looking back to the time when it was unusual for GDR citizens to travel beyond the eastern bloc, Ricarda Schmidt analyses Irmtraud Morgner's *Hochzeit in Konstantinopel*, which offers a perspective on the GDR, including the taboo subject of the Nazi period, from the relatively 'neutral', 'brotherly' and 'southern' position of Yugoslavia. Renate Rechtien, on the other hand, examines Irene Böhme's highly successful novel *Die Buchhändlerin* (1999) about different generations of women in the GDR.

Neighbours and Strangers does not focus exclusively on German and Austrian views of the east, but also presents other variations on cross-border perspectives. The decreased sensitivity towards the issue of *Aussiedler* and expropriation has meant, for instance, for the Romanian Germans, Herta Müller and Richard Wagner, a wider audience in the west as well as a need to speak about their 'German' identity and affiliation to German culture (Mariana Lăzărescu, David Rock). Other perspectives are offered by migrant writers writing in German and looking back at their countries of origin and other locations in Europe. These include the Czech Libuše Moníková, who wrote in German and reflected continually on the position of her homeland (Brigid Haines). Irena Brežna, a Slovak who left Czechoslovakia in 1968 and lives in Switzerland, presents perspectives on Slovakia and on Russia, which are concerned but also distanced (Dagmar Košťálová).

At times, place has metaphorical or symbolic significance (as suggested by Nicole Immler's contribution) and may be associated with sites of commemoration (Ian Foster). The question is how significant locations of these kinds can be transformed into places representing good neighbourly relationships without deliberately suppressing the past beset by conflicts. In Austria, the removal of boundaries has led to renewed discussion of the Habsburg lands. Here, as in Germany, there is no sense of reclaiming lost territory, although re-establishing productive cross-border relations can perhaps benefit from reminders of previous cultural ties. Above all, the removal of artificial boundaries has enabled the opening up of a new metaphorical geography, suggested by 'Böhmen am Meer', the topic explored in Brigid Haines's contribution. During the Cold War, Austria, despite its neutrality, was only too conscious of the many non-porous borders with the countries which surrounded it. Geographical proximity was indeed a source of alienation, rather than one that prompted a sense of connection.

Against this background, the concepts reflected in the title of this volume, *Neighbours and Strangers*, are to be seen as two sides of one coin. Since 1990, it has become imperative for those countries and peoples who were estranged by circumstances to become aware of their neighbours and to treat them as such. This means paying attention to them, not least in cultural enterprises. However, the present cannot merely overlook the past and that includes the way neighbours within the boundaries of Austria or Germany were made into strangers by the politics of the time; most notably, this meant the exclusion from mainstream society of the Jewish population, before the Nazi period the 'quintessential of Central European culture',[8] but it also applied to other ethnic and social minorities. This volume contains explorations of the aftermath of this process and some attempts to overcome its effect. Increased mobility has meant that some 'strangers' from beyond the borders of Germany and Austria have migrated or returned to these countries, and this has not been without its problems. These events have shown up tensions endemic in German and Austrian society and have influenced both official and illegal political movements: these include the rise of the FPÖ in Austria (see Anthony Murphy, this volume), on the one hand; and on the other hostility to foreigners, which has emerged as a topic in German theatre (see Birgit Haas's essay).

Returning refugees or their offspring have met with mixed receptions and various responses to their attempts to re-integrate, such as in Anna Mitgutsch's *Haus der Kindheit* in which a Jewish returnee acts as a catalyst for attitudes towards the Jewish community in Austria to emerge (see Anthony Bushell's essay). Elisabeth Reichart's *Nachtmär* (discussed by Juliet Wigmore) suggests parallels between generations and between the processes of persecution displayed in the past and among the postwar generation.

Notes

[1] The German edition of Daniel Goldhagen's book, entitled *Hitlers willige Vollstrecker. Ganz gewöhnliche Deutsche und der Holocaust* (Siedler Verlag: Berlin, 1996) provoked a popular debate that transcended the academic sphere, but the question of collective or individual guilt was certainly nothing new.

[2] The exhibition was suspended after controversies regarding the labelling of some exhibits.   See http://www.verbrechen-der-wehrmacht.de/, consulted 22 December 2003.

[3] Keith Bullivant, *Germany and Eastern Europe*, Rodopi: Amsterdam, 1999.

[4] Steven Tötösy de Zepetnek, ed., *Comparative Central European Culture*, Purdue University Press: Lafayette, Indiana, 2002.

[5] Elizabeth Boa and Rachel Palfreyman, *Heimat. A German Dream*, Oxford University Press: Oxford, 2000.

[6] Stefan Hermlin, 'Wo sind wir zu Hause?' in: *Gespräch mit Klaus Wagenbach. Freibeuter 1. 'Auseinandervereinigung. Bitte weitergehen!'*, Verlag Klaus Wagenbach: Berlin, 1979.

[7] Martin Kane, *Legacies and Identity. East and West German Literary Responses to Unification*, Peter Lang: Oxford, Bern, 2002, pp. 7-8.

[8] Tötösy de Zepetnek, *Comparative Central European Culture*, p. 14.

Brigid Haines

'Böhmen liegt am Meer', or When Writers Redraw Maps

This paper traces the productive use of Shakespeare's 'mistake' in ascribing Bohemia a coastline in texts by Franz Fühmann, Volker Braun, Ingeborg Bachmann and Libuše Moníková. While the German/Austrian writers' play with the concept is inspired by their reflections on twentieth-century history and ideology, where Prague has repeatedly signified rupture, the Czech-born Moníková's embracing of 'Böhmen am Meer' is a way of claiming ownership of a wider European identity and registering the trauma of her country's fractured history. Thus for these writers, as for Shakespeare, the relationship between real and imaginary 'Bohemias' is complex.

> **Antigonus:**
> Art though perfect, then, our ship hath touched upon
> The deserts of Bohemia?[1]

> *[W]ir alle, die wir Böhmen, diesem innigsten Binnenland, entstammen, lieben das Meer, diese Wüste aus Wogen und Wolken, mit einer verzehrenden Liebe, und ich stamme aus Böhmen und hatte zwölf Jahre nicht mehr das Meer gesehn.*[2]

Can there be anything more fanciful or oxymoronic than an imaginary sea coast? A coast is, after all, so very real. A natural boundary, it represents to the landlubber openness, infinity, perhaps danger, but to the sailor who spies it from afar it signals geographical certainty, orientation and safety. Crucially though, neither landlubber nor sailor, nor indeed the asylum seeker attempting to swim from Morocco to Gibraltar, will be in any doubt about its empirical reality. Coastlines pre-exist and outlast national borders, which seem transitory and permeable by comparison. Whether as holiday destinations or sites of ecological disasters such as oil spills, they serve to remind us of our closeness to the elements.

We do not need cartographers to tell us that coastlines occupy a privileged place on maps: they are 'that elemental separating line between land and sea and at first sight the most fundamental and obvious boundary on any small-scale map'.[3] The increasingly accurate mapping of coastlines is a measure of the progress of science, for mapmaking has always been associated with Enlightenment and modernity. Mapping as part of the Enlightenment project was figured as 'a form of literacy, a sign of civilization',[4] and can also be seen, with the benefit of hindsight, to have always functioned as an inherently political activity: what could be mapped and navigated could be controlled. As my asylum seeker knows, coastlines are also easier to defend than internal borders, and this factor has played a huge part in the self-definition of the British people, for one. And as the barbed wire on the north coast of East Germany showed, the reverse of keeping other people out can be keeping one's own people in. Conversely, for those countries lacking a coastline, their distance from the sea can be a cause of wistful yearning or of jocularity. A European identity, if there is such a thing, derives in part from our shared and complex coastline, which, as Norman Davies points out, was delineated far sooner than our land frontier.[5]

But perhaps coasts are not as real or as fixed as we think. We do perhaps need cartographers to tell us that maps not only have the capacity to lie but, for a variety of technical reasons, they in fact always lie.[6] The representation of coasts on maps is not an exception to this: a coast is not a line at all but a zone, even with non-tidal seas.[7] This might seem a pernickety point to make – though it wouldn't for inhabitants of the soon-to-disappear islands of Tuvalu – but mapmaking has entered the postmodern age in more ways than one. Postmodernist international relations theorists point towards the possibility of 'a global politics of difference, a politics of deterritorialized flows across a smooth world, free of the rigid striation of state boundaries'.[8] We are told that it is the multi-dimensional maps of cyberspace that matter now:

> In the opinion of many observers, it is the spacialities of connectivity, networked linkage, marginality and liminality, and the transgression of linear boundaries and hermetic categories – spatial 'flow' – which mark experience in the late twentieth-century world. Such spatialities render obsolete conventional geographic and topographic mapping practices while stimulating new forms of cartographic representation, not only to express the liberating qualities of new spatial structures but also the altered divisions and hierarchies they generate.[9]

Having raised these thoughts of the elements and of borders, of impregnability and breaching, of countries and continents, of facts and fictions and of national identity and the exercise of power I turn now to an enduring and paradoxical literary topos, that of the 'irredeemably landlocked' Bohemia[10] having a sea coast. 'Böhmen am Meer' starts, traditionally, with Shakespeare, though he inherited the 'mistake' from his source, Robert Green's *Pandosto: The Triumph of Time*. His late play, *The Winter's Tale*, is set in Sicilia and Bohemia. Sicilia is a wintry land where misplaced passion and patriarchal values hold sway. The tyrannical king, Leontes, accuses his faithful wife, Hermione, of adultery with his friend Polixenes, the King of Bohemia, and sends their baby daughter Perdita away to be exposed, thinking wrongly that she is Polixenes' child. Bohemia, by contrast, is an idyllic place, associated variously with Arcadia, the pastoral, or Eden, at least until such time as corruption and violence intrude here too. Famously, neither location has much to do with Sicily or Bohemia as real geographical places. Shakespeare's Bohemia has deserts and a rocky sea coast: though Perdita, abandoned here by Antigonus on the order of Leontes, is rescued and grows up and finds love here, the poor Antigonus is savaged by a bear and his crew members shipwrecked. Was Shakespeare making a gaffe? Was he really so ignorant? The *Wordsworth Dictionary of Shakespeare* glosses the matter thus:

> Shakespeare's attribution of a seacoast to Bohemia has inspired much comment, for that land does not in fact have one. It has been argued that the discrepancy points to the playwright's ignorance and provinciality, or to his carelessness in simply accepting the notion from *Pandosto*. The 18th-century scholar Thomas Hanmer substituted Bithynia, a region of Asia Minor, for Bohemia, and many later editions of the play followed his lead. Other commentators hold that Shakespeare may legitimately have thought Bohemia bordered the Adriatic Sea, since after 1526 it was part of the Hapsburg Empire, which did so. Also, medieval Bohemia had briefly controlled a stretch of the same coast.[11] However, the actuality of Bohemia's coast is irrelevant; *The Winter's Tale*, as one of the romances, was expected to dazzle its viewers with exotic locales. Bohemia was very little known in England during Shakespeare's lifetime, for it was small and deep within continental Europe, in an age of difficult travel and communication. Most of *The Winter's Tale*'s original audience doubtless accepted a Bohemian coastline without thinking about it; *it was a satisfying image, providing a dramatic approach to a fabulous land.* For those who knew the truth, probably including Shakespeare himself, the anomaly may have been mildly amusing, like modern jokes about the Swiss Navy.[12]

Other commentators contest the view that Bohemia was little known in Shakespeare's day, pointing out that as a stronghold of Protestantism, it was a subject of great interest.[13] Indeed James I's daughter, Princess Elizabeth, later married the future king of Bohemia, Prince Frederick the Elector Palatine. But for whatever reason, Shakespeare felt at liberty to recreate Bohemia, to untie it from its geographical location; he thereby started a trend which has continued to this day.[14]

I move now to a short story by Franz Fühmann from 1962 but set in the mid 1950s, which sees the narrator, a young writer, on holiday on the Baltic coast, where he becomes absorbed by the melancholic behaviour of his landlady, Hermine Traugott. A refugee from the Sudetenland, she has made a home in this new community but remains traumatised by undisclosed events in the past. It is odd that she stays here, because she is terrified of the sea; she refuses all offers to relocate and no one can understand why. Back in Berlin the narrator, who is also from the Sudetenland, attends a *Heimattreffen* of Sudeten expellees where he is shocked by the nationalistic spectacle and the sentiments expressed, which he had thought long consigned to the past. He comes to realise that a prominent member of that community, Baron von L., was responsible for Hermine Traugott's continued distress as she had borne his child after he had raped her. Visiting her again, the narrator solves the mystery of her continued stay: 'es war die menschliche Gemeinschaft, in der sie sich geborgen fühlte trotz der fremden Landschaft, vor der ihr schauderte'.[15] The message is clear, perhaps too clear: the humane values of the GDR act as salve to heal the wounds of the past.

My next literary exhibit is a play by Volker Braun published thirty years later in 1992; it is 'ein heiteres Trauerspiel'[16] set on the Adriatic coast.[17] A Czech émigré couple, Pavel and Julia, invite an American industrialist, Bardolph, and a Russian journalist, Michail, to stay with them. Pavel stage-manages a debate between these representatives of East and West, in which it becomes clear that he holds the ideologies of capitalism and communism, both equally bankrupt, in contempt. In an apocalyptic ending Pavel is murdered by marauding refugees from the hungry South. The message here is less clear: ideology in its two forms has failed but who can say what will replace it?

These two works have much in common. Both are set by the sea and have a loose connection with Czechoslovakia, as it was then. Both feature Czechs as displaced people, as émigrés who have lost their *Heimat* (for different reasons: Frau Traugott and the narrator of the story are displaced Sudeten Germans, while Pavel and Julia left after the Prague Spring). Both are clearly of their time: Fühmann's 1962 story seeks to justify the expulsion of the Sudeten Germans from Czechoslovakia after the war, that still controversial act of ethnic cleansing, which forcibly removed three million German-speakers, many but by no means all of whom had been Nazi supporters, from their homes. In black and white terms Baron von L. is painted as the epitome of evil, the GDR as the way forward. Braun's play, by contrast, with its references to chaos theory, the crisis of ideology and the environmental legacy of the Cold War, is unmistakably a product of the unsettled early 1990s and of the disillusionment of GDR intellectuals. But the most obvious thing the works have in common is their title: both bear the name *Böhmen am Meer*.

Arguably better known and more influential than either of these works is Ingeborg Bachmann's late poem, *Böhmen liegt am Meer*, published in 1968, and celebrated by, among others, Erich Fried, Thomas Bernhard, Hans Magnus Enzensberger and Barbara Köhler.[18] The poem was also one of her own favourites; she described it as 'das Gedicht, zu dem ich immer stehen werde'.[19] It is a complex and ambiguous poem about a crisis of faith, a search for identity in a world of collapsing certainties. It gives a positive value to rootlessness, to 'bohemianism': 'Wollt ihr nicht böhmisch sein, Illyrer, Veroneser, / und Venezianer alle'. The poem ends thus:

> Ich grenz noch an ein Wort und an ein andres Land,
> ich grenz, wie wenig auch, an alles immer mehr,
>
> ein Böhme, ein Vagrant, der nichts hat, den nichts hält,
> begabt nur noch, vom Meer, das strittig ist, Land meiner Wahl zu sehen.[20]

The title, with its constatation that Shakespeare's 'mistake' produced what is on some level at least a truth, is an assertion of the power of the imagination, and the ending seems to be upbeat: the loss of *Heimat* can mean being at home everywhere, though Erich Fried, who knew Bachmann and her state of mind, reads despair in the poem, pointing out that the 'noch' in the last line shows the utopian hope to be unsustainable.[21]

All three exhibits show the enduring appeal of 'Böhmen am Meer', but I would like to argue that while they in part continue the tradition of the romance, the exotic and the utopian set up by their Shakespearean source, they also relate in complex ways to the realities of 'Bohemia' in the twentieth century. They do not, in other words, simply invoke the Bohemia which belongs on the same map as Atlantis, El Dorado and King Solomon's mines,[22] or the Bohemia associated with the German phrase 'Das sind mir böhmische Dörfer' ('it's all Greek to me'). The distinction matters, of course, because studied ignorance of 'the real Bohemia' was used to gloss over the Western powers' shameful refusal to defend Czechoslovakia in 1938 against Hitler's advances, in Neville

Chamberlain's declaration that he had no interest in 'a quarrel in a faraway country between people of whom we know nothing'.[23] The resulting Munich Agreement is one of the starkest realities of 'Bohemia' in the twentieth century – but I should perhaps pause here to comment on the inverted commas which have appeared around my subject.

One of the best frameworks for exploring the problems of locating and defining 'Bohemia' in the late twentieth and early twenty-first centuries is the conceptual map in Norman Davies's *Europe* (1997), which depicts various historical fault lines within Europe.[24] The map resembles a set diagram, though the rounded shapes which represent the countries, which are roughly the right size and in roughly the right position relative to one another, do not intersect like sets or border each other as the countries do in reality; rather they are intersected by the lines, which, by cutting through them in various ways, divide them into intersecting groups. Bohemia as such does not appear because the term 'Bohemia' is not the Czechs' own name for their land, which is Čechy.[25] The name Bohemia comes from Roman name for Celtic people, Boii, who were replaced in the Czech lands in the sixth century AD by Slavonic tribes, whose mythical leader was called Čech. The area known as Bohemia or 'Böhmen' lies today in the Czech Republic, which was born shortly after midnight on the morning of 1st January 1993 when the old Czechoslovakia split into its component parts. (I shall continue to use the term Bohemia to distinguish the historical continuity from its various political manifestations.) Line 1 on Davies's map shows the geographical divide between East and West: both Bohemia and most of Slovakia lie on the Western side of this because Davies is most insistent that Russia belongs in Europe. (He is concerned to correct the historiography of earlier historians who have omitted so much from the big picture in privileging certain aspects and certain countries.) But Bohemia lies north of the Roman line (line 2), as it was never colonised. Line 3 shows the Catholic-Orthodox divide, and line 4 the Ottoman line: Bohemia lies West of those. Davies does not represent a Protestant / Catholic divide in Europe, perhaps because it has moved too often, not least in relation to Bohemia: Jan Hus (1370-1415), like John Wycliffe in England, was in the vanguard of religious reform in Europe, enunciating 'many tenets of what was to become the Protestant Reformation a century before Luther',[26] and the Catholic Counter-Reformation was fought in Bohemia and Moravia in the course of the seventeenth century. The success of this can be judged by the fact that, while at the beginning of the seventeenth century the large majority of Czechs were probably Protestant,[27] by the later eighteenth century most were again Roman Catholics.[28] Today, 39% of the population are Catholic and less than 5% Protestant, with 40% declaring themselves atheist.[29]

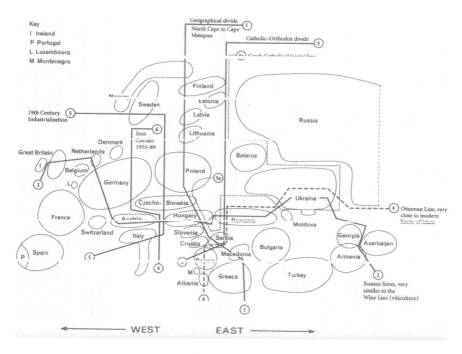

Norman Davies, Map of East-West Fault Lines in Europe[30]

   Line 5 shows nineteenth-century industrialisation; it separates the relatively industrialised Czech Republic from the still largely agricultural Slovakia.   This line highlights the artificiality of the very concept 'Czechoslovakia'.   Up until 1918 the Czech lands (Bohemia and also Moravia) were part of Austria, while Slovakia was part of the Kingdom of Hungary.   (They were all part of the Habsburg lands.)   In 1918 Czechoslovakia was born, a late product of the nineteenth-century nation-building process which occurred all over Europe.   It was a parliamentary democracy, and it lasted until the Munich Agreement of 1938 gave Hitler the go-ahead to annexe the Sudetenland.   On 15 March German troops entered Prague and the Reich Protectorate of Bohemia and Moravia was set up from 1939.

So far, so Western. But the most crucial divide in terms of recent history was the Iron Curtain: line 6 on Davies's map. The Red Army arrived on 9 May 1945 and from then until the 'Velvet Revolution' in the winter of 1989-90, Czechoslovakia was a Soviet satellite state, and belonged, in the consciousness of most Westerners, in the East. This reinforced the 'extrusion of Bohemia from "Europe", "the West", and "modernity"'[31] and continued its remoteness in the mind for Westerners, though not for other central Europeans caught behind the Iron Curtain. But the curious thing about Bohemian history from an outsider's perspective is its tendency to disappear from view for long periods of time, only then to reappear at the vanguard of change: this happened in 1620 with the Battle of the White Mountain, in 1938 and, in the second defining moment for twentieth-century Czech history, 1968, when the Soviet Union sent in the troops to crush the reform movement of the Prague Spring. Thus Prague became synonymous with a new phase in the Cold War and signalled for many in East and West conclusive proof of the failure of the Soviet experiment. From then until the 'Velvet Revolution' it functioned for many as a site of identification and of mourning for a lost hope.

Václav Havel's Civic Forum slogan 'Back into Europe' set the tone for the post-communist era. On one level this slogan was a nonsense, in that Bohemia has never been marginal to Europe but central. I mean this in a geographical sense, for it is always instructive to remember that Prague lies north-west of Vienna, but also in the historical sense already mentioned, namely that, 'in reality Bohemia has been a frontier zone, over which the armies of competing European modernities – Reformation and Counter-Reformation, empire and nation, fascism and democracy, capitalism and communism – have repeatedly rolled back and forth'.[32] But on another level the slogan gave voice to the widespread desire to catch up with and become part of the capitalist West. The Czech Republic is set to join the EU in 2004, though the entry is still subject to discussions on the status of the Beneš decrees, the legal grounding for the post-war expulsion of the Sudeten Germans from Czechoslovakia, which the Sudeten Germans would like repealed. The wounds of the past are, in this respect, still very much open.

It would not be appropriate to finish this historical digression without a comment, implicit in what I have said so far, on the meanings of the term 'Bohemian'. The obvious definition is 'a native of Bohemia', but this could of course historically mean either a German or a Czech. Germans had been a presence in Bohemia since the influx of German miners and other colonists in the twelfth and thirteenth centuries. Jewish and German exclusion from Bohemia as a result of the Holocaust and the 1945 expulsion is a comparatively recent phenomenon, and the expellees still lay legitimate claim to a Bohemian identity. The second principal meaning of 'Bohemian', however, has little to do with geography and everything to do with rootlessness and art: the 'gypsy of society' invoked by Puccini, the Bloomsbury Group and free spirits the world over.

Let me now return to my texts. All are in some sense consciously rewriting Shakespeare in intratextual ways. The Fühmann story has structural parallels with *The Winter's Tale*, with the emotionally dead Hermine Traugott a reincarnation of the petrified Hermione, the statue who comes alive after sixteen years, and Baron von L., the Nazi representative of the Sudeten Germans, a modern-day redrawing of the tyrant king Leontes. Time heals in Shakespeare, a just society in Fühmann. There are direct references too: the evil Baron von L. dismisses Shakespeare's concept of 'Böhmen am Meer' for nationalistic reasons: 'Der große Shakespeare läßt Böhmen einfach am Meer liegen […] da können Sie mal sehen, mein Lieber, welche Meinung er von diesem Volk gehabt hat!'[33] For him, the idea of 'Böhmen am Meer' is an insult. But he has his own sinister version of the motif too: the narrator remembers him envisioning a greater German Reich which would stretch to the Arctic Ocean, and when he sees him again at the *Heimattreffen* the Baron is still speaking of freedom, self-determination and the right to a *Heimat*, indicating the perceived expansionist aims of the West even after 1945. The tale thus functions as an anti-*Heimat* story: those who prove themselves unworthy of their *Heimat* deserve to lose it. But the Bohemian refugees have found a place to be safe: 'Böhmen am Meer' (now transposed to the Baltic) also represents the idyll of a just society, a really existing socialism. A simple moral is drawn: 'in dem einen Deutschland gab man den Umsiedlern ein Stück Land und eine Wohnung und eine ehrliche Arbeit, und in dem anderen Deutschland steckte man ihre Kinder in tote Trachten und speiste sie ab mit einer Hoffnung, die mörderisch war'.[34]

Braun's play also has echoes of Shakespeare. Pavel is a modern-day Prospero: an elderly exile, stage-managing the lives of and the debate between his visitors, although, true to the lessening of moral certainties of

the late twentieth century, he does not have the wisdom, the magical
powers or the natural authority of Prospero. The storm which rages in the
play is another echo of *The Tempest*. This Bohemia by the sea is a
dystopia, representing the chaos of modernity in every sphere. Sexual
chaos is rampant: the woman here is, unlike Shakespeare's Hermione,
unfaithful: she has slept with both her husband's guests, and her son is
clearly Bardolph's, not Pavel's. When Pavel compares her constancy with
that of the sea to its coastline ('Du hast zu mir gehalten, ja. Das Meer /
Zu seiner Küste'),[35] it is a moment of deep irony. There is also ideological
chaos: while Fühmann's story unmasked the ideology of the capitalist
West in the name of (socialist) truth, Braun's play sees ideology as a curse
on both sides and expresses disillusionment. Pavel's judgement is: 'A
plague o' both your houses!',[36] to borrow again from Shakespeare. Chaos
also threatens the environment: the Adriatic is polluted, filled with green
algae, as a result of man's bad stewardship, and the tourists have been
scared off. Finally, social and geopolitical chaos also looms: the social
order is threatened by the hunger of the masses. There is '*nothing* to hold
on to',[37] for '[d]as Chaos ist die Summe der Vernunft'.[38]

Bachmann's poem invokes Shakespeare's comedies with references
to Bohemians, Illyrians and so on. The genesis of the play makes the
importance of Shakespeare for Bachmann clear: when she was asked, as a
representative of German literature, to write a poem for a Shakespeare
festival in Stratford-on-Avon, she declined:

> Dann ist mir etwas aufgefallen, nur ein einziger Satz von Shakespeare,
> nämlich: 'Böhmen liegt am Meer'. Nun gibt es einen Streit zwischen
> Shakespeare und einem seiner allergescheitesten Zeitgenossen, Johnson, der
> ihm vorgeworfen hat, er sei ungebildet, ein schlechter Dichter, er wisse nicht
> einmal, daß Böhmen nicht am Meer liegt. Wie ich nach Prag gekommen bin,
> habe ich gewußt, doch Shakespeare hat recht: Böhmen liegt am Meer.[39]

'Böhmen am Meer' for Bachmann means a new, poetic topography in
which, as Sigrid Weigel argues, the 'absolute Metaphor' of 'Grenze' and
'Grund' are deconstructed. As elsewhere in her work, Bachmann is
overcoming the division between logical thought (philosophy) and
metaphorical language (literature). In the poem, the I and the word, the
sea and the land border each other. The poet trusts words not because they
represent reality but because they are creative. This means that 'das Ich
sich niemals im Besitz von Welt und Sprache befindet, sondern immer in
die Stellung des Angrenzens verwiesen bleibt'.[40] With 'Grund' she is

playing on material ground and logical ground (cause), for example the line 'ich will zugrunde gehn' signifies both 'zugrundegehen' and also 'zum Grunde gehen'.[41]

Her new topography keeps alive a certain utopian hope. Fried, as we saw, denied this, though Bachmann's own comment indicates that she saw the poem positively:

> Es ist gerichtet an alle Menschen, weil es das Land ihrer Hoffnung ist, das sie nicht erreichen werden. Und trotzdem müssen sie hoffen, weil sie sonst nicht leben können. (…) Es ist das *Gedicht meiner Heimkehr*, nicht einer geographischen Heimkehr, sondern einer geistigen Heimkehr. Deswegen habe ich es genannt: 'Böhmen liegt am Meer'.[42]

As is becoming clear, all three works not only rewrite Shakespeare but are also rooted in the recent history of the Czech lands, and thus have a complex relationship with the real. Franz Fühmann was himself from the Sudetenland and was therefore a Bohemian writer. As a young man he had been a supporter of the Nazis and he claimed that his conversion to Marxism was the defining moment of his life. But it has been argued that the real turning point for him was the loss of his *Heimat*, unacknowledged as a trauma until late in life.[43] In his eagerness to proclaim a new *Heimat* based on the community values of the GDR, he overlooks his own trauma. He came closer to acknowledging this in later life, for example in 1977 when he visited Salzburg and commented on the complexity of his roots:

> Meine Kindheit war fünfzig Jahre fern und war mir, das so unbegreiflich Andere, nun jählings näher als mein Heute, aus dem ich in die Vergangenheit trat: Meine katholische Kirche, meine fromme Kindheit, meine Kindheit mit Schutzengel und Jungfrau Maria, meine österreichische Kindheit, meine böhmische Kindheit, meine deutsche Kindheit, meine abendländische Kindheit, meine Kindheit im Gebirge, meine Kindheit in den Wäldern.[44]

This opens the way for a reading of his story as based on the denial of own trauma, in which Frau Traugott's rape figures the personal trauma occasioned by the loss of *Heimat*.

Volker Braun had more detachment from 'Bohemia' in a personal sense but his play can be read as a working through of his own thoughts about the Prague Spring. In his poem 'Prag', written as a response to the Soviet invasion in 1968, 'Böhmen am Meer' had become transformed into:

Böhmen
Am Meer
Von Blut?[45]

as Prague, the 'Goldene Stadt / Die wir uns versprachen' became
'Durchdröhnt / Aber von schwarzen Panzern'. The poem did not
condemn the invasion but registered the pain and the shock it occasioned
and, as the question mark after 'Von Blut' indicates, gave expression to
the sense of anticipation and the agonised questioning of the onlooker
about how to respond. The sense of involvement, particularly in the lines
'Da lag ich / Überrollt und blühend / Aus eigenem Mund', is very
different from the weary detachment expressed in the 'end of ideology'
play of over twenty years later.
    Bachmann's poem arose from a trip to Prague in 1964. She had
been living in divided Berlin and she described her visit to Prague as
being like a homecoming. Her earlier poem 'Prag Jänner 64' described
this visit; it creates a topography in which various places, Prague, Vienna
and Carinthia, represented by the Vltava, the Danube and 'mein
Kindheitsfluß', come together to enable a return to language:

Seit jener Nacht
gehe und spreche ich wieder,
böhmisch klingt es,
als wär ich wieder zuhause.[46]

As the use of the term 'böhmisch', meaning here but not substitutable by
'seltsam', indicates, real and imagined topographies come together. This
poem was unwittingly topical, as, though written earlier, it was published
in 1969 when Czechoslovakia was in the news.
    One might expect that Czech Bohemians (as opposed to German
Bohemians like Fühmann, or would-be 'Bohemians' like Bachmann)
would give these exoticised images short shrift and object to the
highjacking of their country as an image of utopian longing or dystopian
gloom. But the concept of 'Böhmen am Meer' plays a prominent part in
the work of the Czech-born German writer Libuše Moníková (1945-98).
Though she chose to write in German, which for her was a foreign
language, her most enduring concern was the trauma occasioned by Czech
history, and in particular the great betrayals of the twentieth century: 1938
and 1968. A defining moment for her was when 'der brennende Jüngling'
of Braun's poem about the Prague Spring, Jan Palach, set himself alight in

protest against his countrymen's passive response to the Soviet invasion: Moníková cannot forget that she was yards away at the time, in a cinema.[47] Time and again in her works she rehearses the facts of Czech history and explores aspects of Czech culture; for example, in her early novel, *Pavane für eine verstorbene Infantin* (1988), she plays with the myth of Libuše, the founder of Prague, and rewrites parts of Kafka's *Das Schloss*. Historiography itself is her theme in the sprawling, Švejkian 'Schelmenroman', *Die Fassade* (1987), while exile is explored in *Treibeis* (1992): two Czech exiles, one of whom left after the Second World War and one of whom left after 1968, discuss their memories of Prague and cannot make their memories correspond, so slippery is Prague. An attempt is made at reconciliation between Czechs and Germans in *Verklärte Nacht* (1996), her last completed novel, which deals with a love affair between a returning Prague émigré and a Sudeten German. Finally her unfinished novel, *Der Taumel* (2000), confronts what had hitherto been a blind spot in her *oeuvre*: the traumatic period of 'normalisation' immediately after the Prague Spring.

Many of these ideas are present in her 1994 volume of essays, *Prager Fenster*, which contains amusing and less amusing anecdotes on the interrelationship of German and Czech culture and on relations between Germans and Czechs, for example when, in the Protectorate of Bohemia and Moravia, her father's dog, adopted from an emigrated Jewish family, attacked and killed the dog of a Gestapo man; fearing for his life, her father was relieved when the Gestapo man offered to buy the dog, admiring its aggression.[48] *Prager Fenster* also includes an essay entitled 'Kirchfeste: Über die Annexion Europas an Böhmen anläßlich des 50. Jahrestages des Münchner Abkommens' (1988). As the paradoxical title makes clear, Moníková here reverses the usual balance of power and muses on which countries she would allow into her ideal Europe based on their record of violence and aggression in the past. Despite Chamberlain's betrayal of Czechoslovakia in 1938 she decides to allow England (by which she means the United Kingdom) into her ideal Europe because of Shakespeare's productive mistake, for 'Dichterische Entwürfe erweisen sich auf die Dauer als die zäheren "Haupt- und Staatsaktionen"'.[49] This faith in literature is further elaborated in an essay on Bachmann's poem 'Böhmen liegt am Meer'. Moníková, who incidentally wrote her PhD on the figure of Coriolanus in Shakespeare and Brecht, was also fond of Shakespeare's 'mistake' and finds that in Bachmann's poem, 'ist auch Heiterkeit spürbar, "böhmisch" als Synonym für losgelöst, ungeschützt, unverankert […] Böhmen als Verheißung der Ungebundenheit, wo man nicht geprüft wird und doch besteht'.[50] She concludes by giving her assent to 'Böhmen am Meer' as 'das unerreichbare Reich der Poesie am Horizont'.[51] When said by someone from the continent, 'Böhmen am Meer' belongs to 'den dringlichen Verbesserungen von Mitteleuropa'.[52]

Moníková places her faith in imaginary cartography and lays claim to a share in Europe's coastline because national borders are for her associated with anxiety: they may not protect, they can be breached and redrawn and have been in living memory. This causes trauma: she writes that after 1968, she experienced 'ein Land, ein Böhmen, das nicht mehr am Meer lag – die Armeen kamen und rückten es dorthin, wohin es gehören sollte, an den Rand der Steppe'.[53]

But the redrawing of borders can also be liberating, if still always traumatic: here I wish to cite as my last literary exhibit, Jáchym Topol's *City Sister Silver* (1994). This chaotic novel invokes life in post-'Velvet Revolution' Prague from the standpoint of a group of young people trying to make a living on the new black market in 'the Klondike […] of the Wild East'.[54] The hero and his friends experience time as strictly divided into the time before, which was ordered and slow and watched over by 'the Monster',[55] and the time after, which is fast, chaotic and unpredictable. This is a world in which historical forces and the forces of globalisation vie with each other to produce daily a new reality. The order of the day is confusion. Early in the novel, in the 'old time', the group watch the East Germans piling into the West German embassy in Prague in the summer of 1989 and then leaving in their buses: a scene many readers will remember, and another example of Prague being in the international spotlight at a time of crisis. Topol captures this extraordinary moment when the East Germans faced freedom but the Czechs still feared that their protests could turn 'Chinese-style'[56] – obviously a reference to the Tiananmen Square massacre of 4 June 1989:

> A hand reached out one of the bus windows holding a can of Coke, a German no longer squatting on the cold cobblestones, handing down from on high the shiny greeting of capitalism. […] the driver of one of the buses honked […] In the quiet of that historical moment it sounded out of place, like a fart during Mass. The Germans in the last bus smiled happily and wearily, some flashing the V-sign, now they looked like sightseers. And the Czechs in the streets, the ones blocking the route, the ones who took a few steps after the last departing bus, furtively filling in the space from which you could clear the iron hurdle with a turn of the key in the ignition, not that you'd want to, maybe not … but the possibility was there … to disappear, *suddenly the border was just a few*

steps over the cobblestones, nothing out of the ordinary from an everyday pedestrian point of view … maybe they felt the wings of time, maybe now time was like an angel, or a dragon, here and there its feathers grazing a person or two in the crowd, knocking someone's hat off maybe, shattering a window somewhere.[57]

Let me return, finally, to life, literature, and real and imagined Bohemias. In imagining Bohemia by the sea, Franz Fühmann was wrestling with history and ideology, Volker Braun expressing disappointment in them, Ingeborg Bachmann perhaps trying to transcend them; Libuše Moníková subscribed to 'Böhmen am Meer' because, like her fellow Czech, Jáchym Topol, she was working through the trauma resulting from the breaching of borders. Literature as a reaction to historical and political change is not new: *The Winter's Tale* ultimately upholds the tyrannical Leontes where Lear or Othello, similarly passionate and wrong-headed individuals, are brought down. Kingship is not challenged as it is in Shakespeare's earlier history plays either: Leontes' right to rule is not questioned. But Leontes is not the moral victor. The flexible genre of the romance allows for reconciliation. But why did Shakespeare turn to the romance towards the end of his life? Perhaps because the unpopular James I was now on the throne and was invoking the Divine Right of Kings, talking of his subjects' 'fear and subjection' in contrast to his predecessor, Queen Elizabeth I's, talk of her subjects' 'love and good affections'.[58] James I actually liked the play and had it performed at court repeatedly because it does uphold the right of the king to rule; but his audiences may have questioned just this and considered Leontes lucky. Shakespeare's drama then, like my various German and Czech literary exhibits, is seeking solutions in literature to political problems that seem intractably difficult in life and showing that mapmaking is too important to be left to the cartographers and the politicians and (in the era of global capital) the business interests they serve.

Notes

[1] William Shakespeare, *The Winter's Tale*, Act 3, scene 3.

[2] Franz Fühmann, 'Böhmen am Meer', in: *Erzählungen 1955-1975*, Hinstorff: Rostock, 1993, pp. 285-318 (here: p. 285).

[3] Denis Cosgrove, 'Introduction', in: Denis Cosgrove, ed., *Mappings*, Reaktion Books: London, 1999, pp. 1-23 (here: p. 7).

[4] Cosgrove, p. 8.

[5] Norman Davies, *Europe*, Pimlico: London, 1997, p. 8.

[6] 'Not only is it easy to lie with maps, it's essential.' Mark Monmonier, *How to Lie with Maps*, University of Chicago Press: Chicago, 1996, p. 1.

[7] Cosgrove, p. 7.

[8] Michael Hardt and Antonio Negri, *Empire*, Harvard University Press: Cambridge MA, 2000, p. 142.

[9] Cosgrove, pp. 4-5.

[10] Derek Sayer, *The Coasts of Bohemia: A Czech History*, Princeton University Press: Princeton, 1998, p. 11.

[11] Under Otakar II in 1270 the Bohemian kingdom briefly stretched from the Baltic to the Adriatic.

[12] 'Bohemia', in: *The Wordsworth Dictionary of Shakespeare*, Wordsworth Editions: Ware, 1996, pp. 67-68 (my emphasis).

[13] Sayer, p. 8.

[14] The Royal Shakespeare Company's latest production at the Roundhouse in London continues this poetic licence by setting the play in the US. The production draws on motifs from films, with the Sicilian parts set among mafia bosses and the Bohemian scenes invoking the hillbilly Appalachia of the Coen brothers film, *Oh Brother, Where Art Thou?*. The production met with mixed reviews, but at least the setting gave the notorious man-eating bear (see the stage direction: 'Exit. Pursued by a bear.' in Act 3, scene 3) more credibility than it usually has.

[15] Fühmann, p. 317.

[16] From the blurb to the first edition: Volker Braun, *Böhmen am Meer*, Suhrkamp: Frankfurt am Main, 1992.

[17] References will be taken from the second, revised edition: Volker Braun, *Böhmen am Meer*, in: *Texte in zeitlicher Folge*, volume 10, Mitteldeutscher Verlag: Halle, 1993, pp. 61-116.

[18] Thomas Bernhard, *Auslöschung. Ein Zerfall*, Suhrkamp: Frankfurt am Main, 1986, p. 511. Erich Fried, *Ich grenz noch an ein Wort und an ein andres Land. Über Ingeborg Bachmann – Erinnerung, einige Anmerkungen zu ihrem Gedicht 'Böhmen liegt am Meer' und ein Nachruf*, Friedenauer Presse: Berlin, 1983. Hans Magnus Enzensberger, 'Epilog: Böhmen am Meer', in: *Ach Europa!: Wahrnehmungen aus sieben Ländern. Mit einem Epilog aus dem Jahre 2006*, Suhrkamp: Frankfurt am Main, 1989, pp. 449-500. Barbara Köhler, 'Paperboot III' and 'Meer im Sicht', in: *Deutsches Roulette*, Suhrkamp: Frankfurt am Main, 1991, pp. 54 and 83.

[19] Quoted in Kurt Bartsch, *Ingeborg Bachmann*, Metzler: Stuttgart, 1988, p.132.

[20] Ingeborg Bachmann, 'Böhmen liegt am Meer', in: *Werke I: Gedichte, Hörspiele, Libretti, Übersetzungen*, 2nd edition, Piper: Munich, 1982, pp. 167-168.

[21] Fried, p. 9.

[22] Sayer, p. 6.

[23] BBC radio broadcast of 27 September 1938, reported in the *Times* (London), 28 September 1938. This was followed by the Munich Agreement signed by Chamberlain, Edouard Daladier, Adolf Hitler and Benito Mussolini on 29/30 September 1938, as a result of which Germany annexed 37% of the Czech Lands.

[24] Davies, p. 18.

[25] Much of the historical explanation which follows is based on Sayer.

[26] Sayer, p. 36.

[27] Sayer, p. 43.

[28] Sayer, p. 50.

[29] 'Czech Republic', CIA, *The World Factbook*, http://www.odci.gov/cia/publications/factbook/geos/ez.html, accessed 21 November 2002.

[30] Davies, p. 18.

[31] Sayer, p. 8.

[32] Sayer, p. 16.

[33] Führmann, p. 294.

[34] Führmann, p. 313.

[35] Braun, 1993, p. 69.

[36] William Shakespeare, *Romeo and Juliet*, Act 3, scene 1.

[37] Theodore Fiedler, 'Apocalypse Now? Reading Volker Braun's *Böhmen am Meer*', in: Margy Gerber and Roger Woods, eds, *Changing Identities in East Germany: Selected Papers from the Nineteenth and Twentieth New Hampshire Symposia, Studies in GDR Culture and Society*, 14/15, University Press of America: Lanham, 1996, p. 100.

[38] Braun, 1993, p. 63.

[39] Quoted in: Sigrid Weigel, *Ingeborg Bachmann: Hinterlassenschaften unter Wahrung des Briefgeheimnisses*, Zsolnay: Vienna, 1999, p. 356.

[40] Weigel, p. 361.

[41] Weigel, p. 362.

[42] Quoted in: Bartsch, p. 132 (emphasis in the original).

[43] See Louis Ferdinand Helbig, 'Ein deutscher Dichter aus Böhmen. Franz Fühmann', in: Frank-Lothar Kroll, ed., *Böhmen: Vielfalt und Einheit einer literarischen Provinz*, Duncker & Humblot: Berlin, 2000, pp. 109-126 (here: p. 111), and Denis Tate, *Franz Fühmann. Innovation and Authenticity: A Study of his Prose Writing*, Rodopi: Amsterdam, 1995, p. 77.

[44] Quoted in Helbig, p. 118.

[45] Volker Braun, 'Prag', in: *Texte in zeitlicher Folge*, volume 4, Mitteldeutscher Verlag: Halle, 1990, pp. 99-101.

[46] Ingeborg Bachmann, 'Prag Jänner 64', in: *Werke I: Gedichte, Hörspiele, Libretti, Übersetzungen*, 2nd edition, Piper: Munich, 1982, p. 169.

[47] Libuše Moníková, 'Die lebenden Fackeln', in: *Prager Fenster*, Hanser: Munich, 1994, pp. 104-113 (here: p. 113).

[48] Libuše Moníková, 'Zwetschgen: Über Deutschland', in: *Prager Fenster*, pp. 72-90 (here: p. 72).

[49] Moníková, 'Zwetschgen', p. 17.

[50] Moníková, 'Böhmen am Meer', in: *Prager Fenster*, pp. 56-62 (here: p. 60).

[51] Moníková, 'Böhmen am Meer', p. 62.

[52] Moníková, 'Böhmen am Meer', p. 58.

[53] Moníková, 'Böhmen am Meer', p. 57.

[54] Jáchym Topol, *City Sister Silver*, translated by Alex Zucker, Catbird: North Haven CT, 2000, p. 70.

[55] Topol, p. 28.

[56] Topol, p. 21.

[57] Topol, p. 28 (my emphasis; ellipses not in square brackets are Topol's).

[58] Lord Thomas Howard in 1611, quoted in: Stephen Orgel, 'Introduction', William Shakespeare, *The Winter's Tale*, Oxford: Oxford University Press, 1996, 1-83 (here: p. 14).

Julian Preece

The German Imagination and the Decline of the East: Three Recent German Novels (Edgar Hilsenrath, *Jossel Wassermanns Heimkehr*; Hans-Ulrich Treichel, *Der Verlorene*; Günter Grass, *Im Krebsgang*)

Three recent German novels address the theme of the return of Central and Eastern Europe: Edgar Hilsenrath's *Jossel Wassermanns Heimkehr* (1993), Hans-Ulrich Treichel's *Der Verlorene* (1998) and Günter Grass's *Im Krebsgang* (2002). It is striking that all three focus in their different ways on the discontinuities in the transmission of cultural identity and personal history across the generations. Where Hilsenrath evokes the tragic loss of the narrative of Yiddish communities in Central Europe in the journey of the fictional residents of Pohodna to Auschwitz, Treichel focuses on the discontent and fractured identities of Germans moving East to West and Grass on the fateful legacy of unresolved personal and political trauma.

The pub which belonged to Jossel Wassermann's grandfather in the shtetl called Pohodna on the river Pruth in the crown land of Bukovina was quite likely to run out of drinking water but never of schnaps. The young Emperor Franz Joseph who, according to Edgar Hilsenrath in *Jossel Wassermanns Heimkehr*, paid an unexpected visit in 1855, is advised that he can choose between 'rumänischen Cuika, serbischen Sliwowitz, russischen und polnischen Wodka'. There is also, says grandfather Wassermann 'jüdischen Schnaps', but 'keiner weiß, was das ist'. Jossel's grandmother defines it like this:

> ein bißchen polnisch, ein bißchen rumänisch, ein bißchen serbisch und ein paar Gewürze aus Ungarn und anderen Ländern, so obendrauf, um den goiischen Schnaps wie jüdischen schmecken zu lassen - mit ein bißchen Witz [...] und Pfeffer, so daß man zugleich lachen und weinen kann. Natürlich auch niesen und husten.[1]

On the Sunday afternoon of the Emperor's visit, the clientele is a touch more varied than the alcoholic bill of fare, a fact most obviously apparent in the different languages they are speaking among themselves and to each other. The Poles of course speak Polish, the Ruthenians, who are really Ukrainians, speak Ruthenian (which the Russians would claim is a dialect of Russian), the Romanians, Hungarians, Armenians, and Bulgarians all speak their national languages, as do the handful of Turks, left over from the time of Turkish rule which ended in 1774 with the first partition of Poland, while the Lemkos communicate with each other in a Lippo-Russian dialect, and the Hutsuls in a Hutsulian version of Ruthenian. Everybody, on the other hand, knows some German, but the Jews speak it the best, for two reasons: they do business with the ruling Austrians, and Yiddish is related to Middle High German. This is not the only linguistic advantage enjoyed by the Jews, as they are also the best speakers of the 'Kauderwelsch' which serves as the Bukovinian *lingua franca*, perhaps because Yiddish, like Jewish schnaps, is such a hybrid, 'vermischt mit der Sprache der Thora und des Talmuds - also Hebräisch und Aramäisch - und den Sprachen ihrer Umwelt, vor allem Polnisch, Rumänisch und Ruthenisch' (p. 112).

The ethnic multiplicity in the mid-nineteenth century was matched by the variety of rulers and regimes which had been known to this region through history: 'Mal waren's die Russen, mal die Polen, mal die Rumänen, mal die Türken, mal die Osterreicher' (p. 48). As the novel opens, it is, for the first time, the Germans who are in charge. On the first page of Hilsenrath's first post-*Wende* novel, which he would presumably have written exactly the same way had Eastern European communism not collapsed in 1989, two soldiers, one Polish, one Ruthenian, discuss the fate of the shtetl's inhabitants, after the shtetl itself has been looted by its non-Jewish neighbours. There is one thing the soldiers are sure about: the Jews have left traces of their wealth hidden somewhere. This is the winter of 1941-42. The Soviets, who had invaded eastern Poland in September 1939, have been overrun by the Nazis on their forward drive to Stalingrad; the Jews who remained behind have been rounded up in cattle wagons. Ninety years ago the only German in the vicinity of Pohodna was called Heinrich Müller, who owned a saw-mill five kilometres away. At the end of the novel we encounter another German, Anton Krüger, a *Volksdeutscher* from the area of Lemberg, a predominantly Ruthenian city, capital of Galicia, with a strong Jewish presence (Polish Lvov between the wars; Ukrainian Lviv since 1991). Krüger stumbles into the deserted Pohodna, six days after it was cleared, as its inhabitants are still waiting on a length of track somewhere on the way to their final destination. He has deserted from the *Wehrmacht* and is on the run. As looters have slit open every item of bedding trying to find the Jews' hidden wealth there are so many feathers in the air that he at first thinks it is snowing. After hiding for two nights at Jankl Wassermann's old place, Krüger is caught by two Polish auxiliary policemen who are at a loss as to what to do with him. Picking up one of the novel's leitmotifs, that a Jew only knows two possibilities, they point out to him that he has two choices. Either he can give himself up as a deserter, in which case he will be shot, or he can pretend to be Jewish, as they initially assumed him to be, and join the train carrying the Pohodna Jews to their fate. A Jewish joke to end all Jewish jokes. They cannot let him go because he will surely be caught and then they will then be for it. Krüger chooses to join the train, and so the Lemberg *Volksdeutscher* disappears with the Bukovinian Jews. Hilsenrath here presents anti-Semitism as a universal east European phenomenon; the cowardice of subalterns 'just obeying orders' is here the cowardice of Polish subalterns.

In the days of the Habsburgs, Austria's most easterly provinces formed 'ein Bollwerk gegen Unsittlichkeit, gegen Aberglauben und Hexerei', a *cordon sanitaire* no less against the mixture of pre-modern perils which all originated further eastwards. Bukowina's capital, Czernowitz, 'war der Arsch Europas, die letzte Festung seiner kaiserlichen Majestät [...]. Hinter Czernowitz fing der russische Winter an, dort lauerten eisige Schneestürme, asiatische Steppen, Cholera, Typhus, Läuse, die Pest, Kosaken und wer weiß was noch' (p. 105). The problem for the Jews, set to guard their gentile neighbours from these dangers, was that should any of the pests or plagues cross the border, the Jews would either be the first to suffer, as they suffered from the grasshopper swarm in 1866, or the first to be blamed by those who did suffer. Pohodna's Jews thus live in a state of tension with the *goyim* who surround them, their relations with them, even if sometimes friendly, are underlain by mutual suspicion. But the Jews were Emperor Franz Joseph's most loyal subjects, just as they had loyally served the Polish kings and landowners in the late Middle Ages. While all the other peoples wanted their own state (and the Czechs deserted *en masse* to the Russians in the World War), the Emperor could trust his Jews. They had no one else to protect them.

In Günter Grass's *Im Krebsgang* the two characters responsible for violence against Germans have ethnically rich east European backgrounds. David Frankfurter, who assassinates the Nazi functionary, Wilhelm Gustloff, after whom the celebrated but doomed *Kraft-durch-Freude* cruise ship was subsequently named, was born five years before the beginning of the First World War in the Serbian town of Daruvar, the son of a rabbi. His fractured identity is indicated through the several languages he is obliged to know: 'Zu Hause sprach man Hebräisch und Deutsch, in der Schule lernte David serbisch sprechen und schreiben, bekam aber den täglichen Haß auf die Juden zu spüren'.[2] The captain of the Soviet submarine who fired the torpedoes at the *Wilhelm Gustloff* on 30 January 1945, causing the deaths of more than 4,000 children, was not Russian, but half Ukrainian, half Romanian. Born four years after Frankfurter in 1913, he grew up in Odessa, which is why he spoke 'ein Mischmasch aus vielerlei Sprachen', since Russians and Ukrainians, Romanians, Bulgarians and Greeks, Turks and Armenians, Jews and gypsies all lived in close proximity:

> Sosehr er sich später bemühte, Russisch zu sprechen, nie wollte es ihm ganz gelingen, sein von jiddischen Einschiebseln durchsupptes Ukrainisch von seines Vaters rumänischen Flüchen zu säubern. Als er schon Maat auf einem Handelsschiff war, lachte man über sein Kauderwelsch; doch im Verlauf der Jahre wird vielen das Lachen vergangen sein, so komisch in späterer Zeit die Befehle des U-Bootkommandanten geklungen haben mögen. (pp.13-14)

Eastern Europe pre-1939 fairly pullulated with ethnic difference, but neither Grass nor Hilsenrath allows false sentimentality about multi-racial harmony in this lost world. On the contrary, their novels are about conflict.

In the prologue to *Jossel Wassermanns Heimkehr* the Jews are heading east for the second time in their history, but what awaits them, they are unsure. The 'East' has a number of connotations:

> Arbeit soll es dort geben [...] Weiß jemand, wo das im Osten ist? (p.15);

> Der Osten liegt dort, wo die Sonne aufgeht, auch wenn es zum letzten Mal ist (p.19);

> Ein geflügeltes Wort. Aber lag der Osten wirklich im Osten? Könnte es sein, daß der Osten im Norden liegt? Ist so was möglich? Es schien aber so zu sein, denn der Zug machte eine lange Kurve, irgendwo, und fuhr dann wieder geradeaus. In eine ganz andere Richtung. (p. 22)

The 'East' is both where they are going and where they come from, it is a real and a metaphorical place, and its location dependent on where one is standing. As it is where they have always lived, they associate it with poverty and backwardness which contrasts with the progress and wealth of the West. Franz Joseph's civilising mission had evidently not been entirely successful. If the train is taking them in the direction of a sanatorium, for instance, then Jankl Wassermann's services as water carrier will not be required because there will be running water and toilets: 'Du bist hier zwar im Osten, aber die freundlichen Leute, die all die Wunder für uns gebaut haben, die kommen aus dem Westen' (p. 29), he is told.

The first Jewish journey east was the result of a mistake. When the Jews were blamed for the Black Death and fled Western Europe in the mid-fourteenth century, God commanded them in Hebrew, '*Po-lin!*', which apparently means: 'here you shall stay'.   But because most of the Germanised Jews had already forgotten their Hebrew, they thought he meant them to cross the Oder to Germany's eastern neighbour: 'Und so zogen sie, die vorher keiner Himmelsrichtung mehr getraut hatten, in Richtung Osten. Und sie kamen nach Polen. Und dort ging es ihnen gut. Dort regierte der König Kasimir' (p. 85). Another Jewish joke.

Jossel Wassermanns Heimkehr recounts the life story of the title character, the childless owner of a Zurich matzo factory, who wants to bequeath nine-tenths of his fortune to the community of Pohodna and the remaining tenth to his nephew, Jankl, his sole heir to remain in the shtetl. As Jossel lies on his death-bed on 31 August 1939 he narrates his story to his two lawyers whose secretaries commit it to paper.   Stories are about the past, and Jossel's autobiography begins - after an invocation of Adam, his ancestor - with the first Jewish migration eastwards.   Stories are also about the future: the history of the Jews, which is the history of Pohodna, must be passed on, re-told, transferred to the next generation, like Jossel's money, and like his body which he wants to be transported to his home for burial. One theme of the novel is the generations and the traditions and stories which link them. Jossel was the youngest of six brothers and sisters and the decline in the prospects of Pohodna, if it ever really had prospects in that sense, are signalled by his having to choose Jankl, whose job marks him out as the lowliest citizen, as his heir. The Pohodna Jews appear to be dying out before the Nazis finish them off. As Jankl and his neighbours are packed into the wagon, they decide the only safe place for their history is the roof of the train.

Generations, the ruptures between them, and the transfer or non-transfer of cultural identity from one to another, are also the underlying themes of two recent best-selling novels, Grass's *Im Krebsgang* and Hans-Ulrich Treichel's *Der Verlorene*.[3] Both chronicle the legacy of the German expulsion from East and West Prussia and both turn on an event from January 1945. On 30 January 1945 the *Wilhelm Gustloff* was sunk by Soviet torpedoes. Yet even though the number of casualties make it the worst maritime disaster in German history and several times worse than the *Titanic*, the sinking is not well known, even in Germany, despite a 1958 film (*Nacht fiel über Gotenhafen*) and several books. Grass himself, however, had mentioned the sinking in his first novel, *Die Blechtrommel* (1959), and again in *Die Rättin* (1986). Several of Oskar Matzerath's neighbours are drowned on the night of 30 January 1945. From *Hundejahre* (1963) Walter

Matern's parents die in the Baltic evacuation, from *örtlich betäubt* (1969) Eberhard Starusch's mother. But in his earlier fiction Grass never dwelt on the *Gustloff* sinking or similar catastrophes. In his anti-Cold War apocalyptic satire, *Die Rättin*, sinking ships, in analogy to the stricken spaceship earth, are a leitmotif, but while he cites the details of the *Gustloff*, it was the *Cap Arcona*, sunk off the coast of Schleswig-Holstein by British bombers in the last week of the war, now mentioned in passing in *Im Krebsgang*, to which he devotes his attention. On board the *Cap Arcona* were several thousand concentration camp evacuees. While the British involvement complicates the war-time narrative of good and bad, the victims of the British were first victims of the Nazis, who did their best to finish off any survivors as they struggled to the shore.[4] The *Gustloff* victims, however, who included military personnel, could have served the same literary purpose in Grass's earlier novel.

In *Die Blechtrommel*, it is an imaginary disaster subsequent to the *Gustloff* sinking which claims the lives of 4,000 children. They are said by the doctor who treats Oskar after his fall into his father's grave to have been part of a *Kindertransport* from East Prussia, and to have been killed as they tried to cross the river near a place called Käsemark. 4,000 is roughly the number of children estimated to have drowned on the *Gustloff*, a figure which would have been as well known to Grass in 1959 as it is in 2002, when he spends some time trying to get the figures straight. The imaginary Käsemark catastrophe feeds into Oskar's nightmare of the infernal merry-go-round, kept going by Goethe and Rasputin, the false metaphysical poles of an inadequate world view, taking turns to slot coins in the machine. The passage is one of many prose *tours de force* in *Die Blechtrommel*. What strikes us now after *Im Krebsgang* is that in 1959 Grass ducked apportioning blame. As the children scream for the merry-go-round to stop, the reader is left with the impression that this godless world is randomly cruel and systematically malign. We might compare the merry-go-round with the equally rich imagery of the 'Weihnachtsmann' who turned out to be the 'Gasmann' which surrounds the narration of the *Kristallnacht* in the last chapter of book one of *Die Blechtrommel*, 'Glaube Liebe Hoffnung'. Here the persecutors are named and their names attached to deeds. Grass's approach to Soviet atrocities was different, which was surely not from reluctance to offend East-bloc sensitivities.

In *Im Krebsgang* one of the *Gustloff* survivors is Tulla Pokriefke, the leading female character from *Katz und Maus* and *Hundejahre*. At the moment of catastrophe, according to one version of the story (history usually happens in at least two ways in Grass's fiction), as the scream of the doomed passengers fills the icy air and the ship disappears into the deep, Tulla gives birth to a baby boy.[5] *Im Krebsgang* is narrated by Paul Pokriefke, who recounts the story of his mother, his own birth, and their lucky escape. What preoccupies him at the age of fifty when he sits down to commit the story to paper is the legacy passed down to the next generation, born half a lifetime after the events of 30 January 1945. It is this which gives *Im Krebsgang* its impetus, as Pokriefke's own son, Konrad, born in 1980, acts out a bloody revenge fantasy on behalf of his aggrieved grandmother, Tulla, the victim of which is an adolescent his own age, who in an act of historical compensation assumed the identity of Wilhelm Gustloff's Jewish assassin, just as Konrad Pokriefke took on the role of Gustloff. Paul Pokriefke, who does not know the identity of his father, as his mother was famously promiscuous as a teenager, nominates both Wilhelm Gustloff and David Frankfurter as substitute fathers because, he believes, they were authors of his life story. He himself turns into a failed husband and an inadequate father who cannot communicate with his own son, named after Tulla's drowned brother. Paul is also a refinement of a character type which has populated Grass's fiction since his first novel, the type which switches from one ideological extreme to the other. While Paul writes one minute for the Springer Press, one minute for the *tageszeitung*, he has allegiance to neither.

The reason the *Gustloff* catastrophe is not well known is that revanchists and expellees from the lost territories exploited German suffering at the hands of the Soviets in order to de-legitimise the post-45 map of Central Europe and Germany's new Eastern borders in particular. Writing about Germans as victims gave succour to the bigots of the *Landmannschaften*, in whose side the author, the most famous of all twentieth-century West Prussians, had always been a thorn. In *Im Krebsgang* Grass edges in the direction of the truth through a series of sideways, crab-like movements and disentangles the many strands of the story, most of which ignore significant facts which do not fit their self-serving purpose. Grass knew he was stepping onto a minefield: the explosive devices might have been planted a long time ago but they were still primed and ready to go off. For this reason he is punctilious in including all points of view: the Soviet narrative is more complex than one might expect as the submarine captain found himself in a Siberian labour camp shortly afterwards, though for actions which had little to do with his naval prowess. As far as the Soviets were concerned, the *Gustloff* was a legitimate military target; they did not know most of its passengers were civilians. The German crew, or rather its several captains, were also not without fault, a fact which complicates the matter of deciding guilt. The life-boats were too few and badly maintained, the course steered was foolish, and the decision not to black out the ship's lights proved fatal. The strategy of closing off one part of the ship in case of torpedo strike in order to slow down a possible sinking not only meant that more than 1,000 passengers had no chance of escape, but also that crew trained in the procedures for abandoning ship were fatally trapped below decks. Perhaps the most shameful details of all are that all three captains survived and that the ratio of men saved to men drowned was much higher than that for women and children. Children had the least chance of getting off alive.

While the historical narrative of the sinking is compelling and handled deftly, the contemporary plot played out in 1996-97 is highly contrived. Grass makes Gustloff himself and Frankfurter, his assassin, a Jewish student who had suffered under Nazi racial laws, into key characters, not only in the 1930s but in the 1990s when the pair of teenage Germans, Konrad Pokriefke and Wolfgang Stremplin, first re-tell their story in an internet chatroom and then re-enact its fatal final episode. Only this time the Neo-Nazi Konrad, who plays 'Wilhelm', shoots the philo-Semite Wolfgang, who plays 'David'. Konrad has fallen under the spell of his grandmother because she is worthy of his respect in ways neither of his parents were. Because she settled in the Mecklenburg capital of Schwerin, for no other reason than that it happened to be Gustloff's birthplace, her only grandchild, born in the Federal Republic, did not meet her until the year of reunification. Thus if Tulla is a child of Hitler's Germany and her son embodies the uncertain and self-effacing West Germans of the post-war state, Konrad comes of age in the Berlin Republic. He is seventeen, so often a key age for Grass's characters, when he commits his pointless murder. While the re-enactment of past conflict in the 1990s shows that the legacy of the past is alive, the historical Wilhelm Gustloff and his assassin are insignificant figures. Gustloff may have been the NSDAP's highest representative in Switzerland and second to Horst Wessel in Nazi martyrology, but the link between him and the ship named after him is accidental. Grass misses out the suffering on the winter treks to the West. Konrad and Wolfgang do not mention the lost Eastern territories at all, or the Soviet invasion and annexation in 1945, nor do they dwell on the mass rapes, which pertain far more directly to the sinking of the ship than the history of how the ship came to have its name. Grass still appears to be evading key issues.

Ten days before the sinking of the *Gustloff*, on 20 January 1945, as most of the civilian population of East Prussia fled west on foot, the mother of baby Arnold in Treichel's *Der Verlorene* passed her starving son to another woman in a moment of panic when their trek ran into a group of Russian soldiers. The mother, like Arnold's younger brother who now narrates the family's story, does not get a name, fearing that she and Arnold's father, Arnold senior, would be killed, or that 'etwas Schreckliches' (p. 15) would happen. She miscalculated:

> Wohl sei ihr etwas Schreckliches zugefügt worden von den Russen, aber die Russen hätten es gar nicht auf ihr Leben oder das ihrer Familie abgesehen gehabt. Die Russen hätten es immer nur auf eines abgesehen gehabt. (p. 16)

This traumatised woman, who mourns the lost Arnold more than she cares for her second son born after the war, was raped by the Russian soldiers. This is not stated, but, as the mass rapes of German refugee women are so much a part of the narrative of expulsion, Treichel relies on his readers' ability to pick up allusive hints. As the giving away of Arnold and the rape happened in very quick succession, the mother appears, in mourning Arnold and neglecting her other son, to be coping with the trauma of rape. Perhaps she even emotionally associates her second son with the rape, feeling that he is - metaphorically - a product of it.

Der Verlorene spans a little more than a decade, a decade of economic recovery and emotional retardedness, during which the nameless mother of the nameless narrator at one point suffers a mental breakdown and at another throws a bundle of her husband's proudly earned 100-mark notes into the oven. Like her husband, she is unable to enjoy her leisure time, making Sunday-afternoon outings with the parents into a trial for their second son; unlike her husband, she cannot sublimate her unhappiness into economic activity, which sees the family slowly acquiring all the accoutrements of material success in the Federal Republic of the *Wirtschaftswunder*.

Arnold is the brother who was born 'zuhaus'. 'Zuhaus, das war der Osten' (p. 7) we are told in the third sentence on the first page. In their new home in *Ostwestfalen* they try, like émigrés and expatriates everywhere, to recreate their old home.[6] The former agricultural outhouses and pieces of derelict equipment remind Arnold senior of the lost East Prussian farm he was intended to inherit. In a single week he flattens the lot to build new cold-storage facilities, an ostentatious symbol of his flourishing new meat-distribution business. Economics takes precedence over memory. The father moves from rearing animals for meat (in his original East Prussian home) to selling meat and meat products to retail outlets (in his new East Westphalian *ersatz* home). The move from East to West is thus a move away from nature. The tales of slaughtering animals in the East which he exchanges with his fellow expellees and their rapturous consumption of such delicacies as pig's brains at bi-annual feasts contrasts with the mean-mindedness demonstrated in the meat-buying habits of the customers in the shops which his business supplies. The customers' personalities express themselves in the niggardly but precise quantities of sausage they purchase from shopkeepers whose mental equilibrium is upset by the conflicting demands made on them: the need to stock enough of each product not to run out clashes with the knowledge that the product will go bad if it is not sold. The narrator feels in two minds on the subject of collecting the pig's blood, an essential component in his father's veritable pig-cult, from the local small-holders in East Westphalia. He is squeamish at seeing the pig squeal in its death throes, the blood spurt from the fatal neck wound into a carefully positioned bucket. He also finds little pleasure in consuming the pig's brains. On the other hand, these feasts are the only occasions he sees his parents happy, 'heiter und ausgelassen':

> Besonders wenn die Bekannten des Vaters zu Gast waren, die ebenso wie er aus dem Osten stammten und eigentlich hätten Bauern werden sollen, konnte das Essen von einem unermüdlichen Gelächter begleitet sein, ohne daß ich, der ich die weichliche Hirnmasse so schnell und unzerkaut wie möglich die Speiseröhre hinunterzubringen suchte, begriff, warum hier eigentlich gelacht wurde. (p. 43)

That the present has not yet escaped the past is signalled when it turns out that the rediscovered 'Arnold' or Foundling 2307 is training to become a butcher. When the authorities from the Red Cross inform Arnold senior and his nameless wife that a boy who could be their own first-born has been found in an orphanage, the parents' hopes of being reunited with their lost son are rekindled. And on the face of it for good reason. Foundling 2307, re-christened Heinrich by the end of the novel, was on the same trek and the woman who took him from his real mother did not see the mother's face because it was covered almost completely by a cloth, just like Arnold junior's mother's face. *Der Verlorene* could have been entitled 'Das Verlorene' or perhaps 'Verlorenes', as there is always something missing, always a search for lost wholeness. The photographs of the narrator as a boy only ever show a part of his body, which he takes to be a sign that his parents who took the photographs were not sufficiently interested in him to make sure they snapped him in full. Needless to say, in happier times they captured all of baby Arnold. At the 'Gerichtsanthropologisches Laboratorium', where the family have casts made of their feet to compare with the feet of Foundling 2307, the narrator realises that he has never previously seen his father's body in its entirety, never even glimpsed his naked feet. He knows only his father's head, neck, hands, and parts of his forearms. He is now forced to notice that his father's feet are very different from one another, a fact ignored by the doctor and his assistant, with consequences which will render their test, which already rests on pseudo-scientific foundations, quite worthless even in its own terms.

The missing Arnold is perhaps more the empty sign of a lack than the lack itself. That would help to explain why, when finally able to meet Foundling 2307, who looks so much like the narrator that the chances of the pair not being brothers appear infinitesimal, the mother signals for Herr Rudolph, whom she seems likely to marry after Arnold senior's death, to drive on rather than begin the long-delayed and now officially sanctioned adoption proceedings. The narrator is himself astounded by his resemblance to the adolescent behind the butcher's counter and leaves his readers to speculate on his mother's actions. Could it be that the mother does not want the limited closure which reunion with Arnold junior would bring? Her other loss, that of her home and the life she would have led there, cannot after all be made good.

Bodies might be the key underlying theme of *Der Verlorene*: there is Arnold's missing body, and the attempts to identify the body of Foundling 2307. There are the bodies of the dismembered pigs. Society has not yet evolved new ways of understanding human bodies: when the Anthropological Institute asks for photographs of the narrator's head, from back, front, and each side, his father is delighted for a reason to make his son have a crew cut, 'die mich zu einer Art Lagerinsassen machte' (p. 66). The father is obsessed with the length, or rather shortness, of his son's hair and it is not until after the father's death that his would-be step-father intervenes to persuade the mother to permit her son to grow his hair a little. Bodies cannot always be controlled. The narrator's mother cannot watch human bodies kissing on the newly acquired television and has to turn it off and leave the room if she and her son are watching together. The narrator develops travel sickness as a child, which is a reaction against enforced proximity to his parents on those painful Sundays, and can be brought on by the smell and texture of a new car, in turn the symbol of material success and emotional repression. His father's body cannot withstand the double blow of learning from the Institute that, according to their 'scientific' comparisons, the probability that Foundling 2307 is not his son is 99.73% and, on returning home, that his new cold-storage facilities have been burgled and their uninsured contents stolen. He suffers a heart attack and dies. Earlier that day the talkative hearse driver they meet at the Heidelberg laboratory tells the family about the city's new crematorium which burns bodies so effectively that the director has been known to place a bone in his mouth to demonstrate the cleanliness of the operation. Lurking unmentioned in the collective memory are the millions of other bodies also burnt in crematoria for reasons associated with a conception of 'hygiene'. It is ultimately because of these bodies that East Prussia was evacuated and Arnold was lost.

Science, or the pseudo-science practised by the institutes who try to establish whether Foundling 2307 is related to the family, dismembers bodies by taking prints and measurements from feet, fingers, heads. This science disengages common sense from theory and ignores evidence which is plain to behold. It is ham-strung, in other words, by the assumptions of its own dogma, which, the novel repeatedly hints, are those of the Nazi racial theorists. There are a number of quite comic indications. The narrator is obliged to conclude that the evidence which shows that Foundling 2307 is so unlikely to be his parents' son renders it equally unlikely that he is their son either. When he sees his father's naked feet for the first time, he is struck by the great difference in their size and shape. The professor's assistant, however, is only interested in taking the measurements of each person's right foot: as most people's feet do resemble each other, however, and both Arnold's feet are of the type exemplified by the father's left foot, then the whole exercise is invalidated.

It is here that the story links up with its East Prussian theme. The haughty specialist who oversees the foot comparison exercise turns out to be an expellee from the very same region as the family. His scientific methods are no more advanced than his social views, which insofar as they contain a racial component are consonant with his science. He confides to Arnold senior that his maternal grandfather 'ebenfalls aus dem Kreis Gostynin stamme und dort ein großes Gut besessen habe, daß dieses Gut aber wie alles andere auch verloren sei. *Vorläufig* jedenfalls' (my italics, p. 109). To the father's remark on the high quality of the soil in Gostynin, the professor replies that the soil is only as good as the people who work on it and that the Russians, to whom Gostynin presumably now belongs, 'noch jeden Boden zuschanden gemacht hätten'. Arnold senior, unwilling to broach a taboo and talk about injustice inflicted by Russians, then recounts the experiences of his community with the local Poles. While his own village had been called Rakowiec, the Poles, who had lived in the adjacent village called Rakowiec II, had moved there only once the Germans, the narrator's own forbears, had made the land fit for agriculture. The two communities, the Poles and the Germans, then expressed their characters in the ways they looked after the twin villages, according to the unwritten principles of separate development:

> Während man Rakowiec I schon von weitem ansehen konnte, daß dies das Dorf der Deutschen war, konnte man Rakowiec II schon von weitem ansehen, daß es von Polen bewohnt wurde. Alles Kraut und Rüben. Abfälle im Garten, Schlammlöcher auf den Wegen, löchrige Zäune, offene Ställe, Gänse und Hühner, die im ganzen Dorf herumstreunten. Am Ende seien die polnischen Bauern aus Rakowiec II so verarmt gewesen, daß sie sich als Knechte bei den Deutschen in Rakowiec I verdingen mußten. Und alles wegen der Unordnung. 'Die Russen', sagte der Professor [...] 'konnte man nicht mal als Knechte gebrauchen'. (pp. 110-11).

The impoverishment of most of rural Poland gave rise to the phrase 'polnische Wirtschaft', first mentioned in print by Georg Forster in the 1780s.[7] The cultural fault-line which divides Eastern from Western Europe has divided rich from poor since the decline in the Polish-Lithuanian Commonwealth in the sixteenth century.

It is tempting to read *Der Verlorene* allegorically, in the way that Bernhard Schlink's *Der Vorleser* has been read as a commentary on contemporary Germany.[8] Both narrators then 'stand for' the truncated West German nation, their troubled and unfulfilled personalities embodying the legacy of National Socialism. While Michael Berg in *Der Vorleser* will never integrate into society because of his under-age love affair with a woman who turned out to be a concentration camp guard, Arnold's younger brother lives in the shadow of his parents' overwhelming loss. Unlike Michael he typifies his generation: his allergic reaction to outward signs of material wealth and his underperformance at school mirror the behaviour of 1960s student radicals. How then do we interpret the ending, when his now widowed mother refuses to get out of her car to meet the all but grown-up Foundling 2307 even though (or is it precisely because?) he resembles her second son so closely. He describes him as 'mein eigenes, nur um einige Jahre älteres Spiegelbild' (p. 174). Foundling 2307's reaction is no different to his younger brother's: they both turn pale as they stare into each other's face. Their mother meanwhile shows no interest, does not go into the butcher's shop, and gives the word to get going. Her emotional refusal to get what she claims to want above all else matches the failure of the science practised at the Anthropological Institute to demonstrate the obvious. Why is it that the mother and the authorities do not want to accept that Foundling 2307 is Arnold? Do they not really want a resolution despite the pain, the father's heart attacks, and the mother's inability to fulfil herself? If we take Foundling 2307 to be Arnold then it is with this question that Treichel leaves his readers. Other readings of this ambiguous novel are possible. Stuart Taberner, for instance, does not believe Foundling 2307 is Arnold and implies that the similarities between him and the narrator are to be understood only metaphorically. The mother must ignore the resemblance of the two boys because to do otherwise would be 'to concede the legitimacy of German pain and to establish a link between a despicable past and the present'.[9] The problem with this view, which affords valuable insights into the narrator's own unacknowledged and unwanted links with the national German past, is that the evidence pointing to Arnold and Foundling 2307 being the same person is not presented as metaphorical by the narrator. He asks of his mother: 'Erkannte sie ihr eigenes Kind nicht mehr wieder?' (p. 174). He clearly recognises his brother, while their mother, who averted her gaze from intimate scenes on television, appears to prefer the pain of her continued loss, to which she has grown accustomed, to a 'reunion'. The ties are by now after all only those of blood. It will be impossible to create the emotional closeness, the bonding between parent and child, which can only come from shared family experience. The narrator's reactions are involuntary: his body takes over as he is suddenly overcome with an allergic reaction to the new car and has to wind down the window to take deep breaths, which prevents him from speaking: 'Ich wollte der Mutter sagen, ich wollte sie anflehen, daß sie endlich aussteigen und endlich hineingehen solle zu ihm. Doch ich mußte atmen und konnte nichts sagen' (pp. 174-75). Thus, he too ducks a confrontation with the truth, which like his mother he looks likely to repress.

Jossel Wassermann wanted his life history to be transmitted to posterity and his money to be passed on to the next generation. He wanted his body to be transported to the shtetl where he was born. He died too late for the second and third of these requests to be carried out, but we do have his story in all its squalid glory. All that Emperor Franz Joseph's loyal Jews left behind were the disembodied voices whispering to each other on the roof of the train. The Germans' engagement with the East, their own lost

East, of course continues, and like Treichel, Grass ends ambiguously. Konrad destroys the model of the *Wilhelm Gustloff* in his prison cell and appears to be recovering from his obsession, but his father is disturbed to note that his son the murderer has already inspired an internet cult, reminiscent of Gustloff's own. 'Nie hört das auf', is the novella's last line.

Notes

[1] Edgar Hilsenrath, *Jossel Wassermanns Heimkehr*, Piper: Munich, 1993, p. 122.

[2] Günter Grass, *Im Krebsgang*, Steidl: Göttingen, 2002.

[3] Hans-Ulrich Treichel, *Der Verlorene*, Suhrkamp: Frankfurt a.M., 1998.

[4] See D. G. Bond and Julian Preece, '"Cap Arcona"' 3 May 1945: History and Allegory in Novels by Uwe Johnson and Günter Grass', *Oxford German Studies* 20/21 (1991-1992), 147-63.

[5] In this she resembles the narrator's mother in Hilsenrath's *Das Märchen vom letzten Gedanken*, whose baby son, according to one version of what happened, is cut out of her womb by an Ottoman soldier on the Armenians' death march in 1915. The relationship of that surviving baby to his past is the subject of that novel too. See Edgar Hilsenrath, *Das Märchen vom letzten Gedanken*, Piper: Munich, 1989, pp. 10-14.

[6] Rhys Williams notes the autobiographical basis for the novel and that, for Treichel, '*Ostwestfalen*, whose geographical components 'Ost' and 'West' seem almost to cancel each other out, [is] not a geographical place so much as a psychological condition of exposure to a sense of guilt that has no specific cause'. See Rhys W. Williams, '"Mein Unbewusstes kannte ... den Fall der Mauer und die deutsche Wiedervereinigung nicht": the Writer Hans-Ulrich Treichel', *German Life and Letters* 55:2 (2002), 208-18.

[7] Georg Forster, Letter to Therese Heyne 24.01.1785, *Werke in vier Bänden*, edited by Gerhard Steiner, vol. 4, *Briefe*, Frankfurt a.M., 1970, p. 331.

[8] Bernhard Schlink, *Der Vorleser*, Diogenes: Zurich, 1997.

[9] Stuart Taberner, 'Hans-Ulrich Treichel's *Der Verlorene* and the Problem of German Wartime Suffering', *Modern Language Review* 97 (2002), 123-34 (here: p. 134). For Taberner, 'Arnold, who embodies familiarity, even intimacy, and continuity, must be repressed. *Heimat*, etymologically related to *heimlich*, meaning that which is familiar yet must also be kept secret, thereby becomes *unheimlich*. Yet German identity will always be incomplete without Arnold' (p. 133).

Mariana-Virginia Lăzărescu

Rumänität in den Büchern eines Deutschen

Hans Bergel is a German writer born in Transylvania, Romania, who has lived as a writer, journalist and editor in Munich since 1968, but who has never ceased to think and write about the country of his birth. He has an interesting biography. For the younger generation in Romania he is an important witness: his texts sensitise the reader to common cultural perspectives and the growth of European integration. They make possible a better mutual understanding by highlighting the habits of life, including the differences and similarities between the representatives of the multicultural region Transylvania, where Romanians, Hungarians, Germans, Ukrainians and Gypsies have lived together for centuries.

Der deutsche Romanist Klaus Bochmann bemerkte sehr treffend in einem Aufsatz, dass die moderne rumänische Kultur in einem selbst für Mitteleuropäer ungewöhnlichem Maße von der Frage nach der eigenen Identität und dem Verhältnis zu den Anderen diesseits und jenseits der Grenzen bestimmt ist.[1] Diese Frage nach der Identität hat, wie erwartet, nicht nur die Kultur, sondern zu gewissen Zeiten auch die Politik beeinflusst. Der Mythos der Identität hat einen konstanten Vorrang vor jedem kulturellen und ideologischen Problem gehabt.

Eine erste Erklärung dafür ist die Tatsache, dass Völker mit einer relativ jungen Geschichte im Rahmen eines eigenen Nationalstaats ein besonders großes Interesse an Fragen von Identität und Alterität haben. Eine zweite Erklärung ist die historische Tatsache, dass Rumänien immer wieder in der Geschichte fremde Herrschaften hatte. Eine dritte Erklärung ist die besondere Lage Rumäniens als romanische Insel im slawisch-griechisch dominierten Südosten, zwischen Balkan, Osteuropa und Mitteleuropa gelegen, die an allen diesen drei Kulturzonen teilhat.

Diese drei Erklärungen, die der Leipziger Germanist anführt, werden auch von anderen Kulturwissenschaftlern vertreten, denen ich mich als Germanistin anschließen möchte. Die rumänische Historiographie stellt die Geschichte ihres Volkes und seiner Staatsformen oft als eine Geschichte von Märtyrern dar, die sich für die Verteidigung des christlichen Europa geopfert haben. Darauf baut das moderne rumänische Geschichtsbewusstsein auf. Erfahrungen von Verrat und Auslieferung an fremde Interessen haben zur Folge, dass Rumänien oft kritisch auf Europa und die großen und kleinen Mächte jenseits der veränderlichen Grenzen der jeweiligen rumänischen Staaten blickt

(Abtretung der Bukowina 1775, Annexion Bessarabiens 1812, Wiener Schiedsspruch und Molotow-Ribbentrop-Abkommen 1940, erneuter Verlust von Bessarabien und Nordbukowina 1944 usw.).

Eine weitere Tatsache ist die, dass das Ausland das Spezifikum und die Originalität der rumänischen Kultur als Mischung von Archaismen und Modernismen, von Aberglauben und Mythen, nicht genügend zur Kenntnis nimmt und sich nicht wirklich bemüht, das Land und seine Kultur zu entdecken.

Im Rahmen der imagologischen Untersuchungen zum Eigen- und Fremdbild in der rumänischen Literatur kommen mehrere Bereiche in Frage. Einer davon ist, so Gabriella Schubert und Wolfgang Dahmen,[2] die nationalkulturelle Identifikation nach der Entstehung 'Großrumäniens' im Gefolge des Ersten Weltkriegs. Die Literatur aus den hinzugekommenen Gebieten Siebenbürgen und Bukowina hat diesbezüglich eine große Bedeutung. Lucian Blaga und andere rumänische Autoren beschäftigten sich mit der Verherrlichung der Symbiose von Latinität und byzantinisch orthodoxer Spiritualität.

Hans Bergel ist den meisten rumänischen Germanisten und Germanistinnen sowie in der Auslandsgermanistik als der deutsche Schriftsteller bekannt, der aus Siebenbürgen, und zwar Rosenau bei Brasov/Kronstadt in Rumänien stammt, seit 1968 als Schriftsteller, Journalist und Herausgeber in München lebt, aber keinen Augenblick sein Herkunftsland Rumänien vergessen hat. Als Erzähler, Essayist und Lyriker gilt seine Aufmerksamkeit und sein Interesse immer wieder dem Südosten Europas. Dass seine Bücher mehrmals in Deutschland, Österreich und Rumänien mit bedeutenden Preisen ausgezeichnet wurden, zeugt von der hohen ästhetisch-literarischen Qualität seiner Werke. Seit April 2001 ist er Doctor honoris causa der Universität Bukarest.

In den letzten Jahrzehnten hat Hans Bergel bei seinen Landsleuten und nicht nur bei diesen heftige Dispute ausgelöst. Die einen loben ihn als bedeutenden Schriftsteller und Vertreter der Siebenbürger Sachsen, die anderen stempeln ihn zum mittelmäßigen Regionalautor und selbstherrlichen Journalisten. Bergel ist somit oft Anlass zur Kontroverse. Wegen Hochverrats wurde er 1959 im 'Kronstädter Schriftstellerprozess' zu 15 Jahren schweren Kerkers verurteilt. Nach fünf Jahren Haft wurde er im Zuge der allgemeinen Amnestie für politische Häftlinge aus dem Gefängnis entlassen und 1968 emigrierte er infolge der Unterstützung von Günter Grass in die Bundesrepublik Deutschland.

Hans Bergel ist in allen literarischen Gattungen produktiv gewesen, hat sich als ein guter Kenner der Musik und der bildenden Künste, als ein begabter Übersetzer aus dem Deutschen und ins Deutsche erwiesen. Für die meisten Rumänen ist der Schriftsteller Hans Bergel heute ein Zeitzeuge, seine Texte stellen unter anderem ein informationsreiches Kapitel der siebenbenbürgischen Geschichte dar.

Der Essay 'Die Begegnung mit dem anderen. Gedanken über die Gestalt des Rumänen in den Büchern eines Deutschen' (1978)[3] lässt ein vielschichtiges Bild von rumänisch-deutschen Beziehungen, Mentalitäten, Vorurteilen entstehen und kann zum Beispiel interkulturellen Lernens werden. Der Essay 'Rumänität in den Büchern eines Deutschen' (2000)[4] klärt den Leser über die Wechselwirkung zwischen rumänischem und deutschem Kulturverständnis auf. Diese beiden Texte lassen sich meines Erachtens als Ausgangspunkte für eine Auseinandersetzung mit Bergels Werk gut verwenden. Vor- und Hintergrundwissen, vor allem landeskundliche Kenntnisse, Einfühlungsvermögen, aber auch Freude am Verstehen des literarischen Textes und Lust an der Interpretation werden bei der Lektüre der Bergel-Texte gleichermaßen aktiviert.

In meinen Ausführungen stütze ich mich im folgenden zunächst auf den Artikel 'Rumänität in den Büchern eines Deutschen', gehe dann aber auch auf andere Texte von Hans Bergel ein, die der Veranschaulichung dieses Themas dienen sollen. Es stellt sich von Anfang an die Frage nach der angewendeten Terminologie: der Rumäne und die Rumänin sind bekanntlich Bewohner des Landes Rumänien, die Rumänisch als offizielle Landessprache sprechen.

Bergel spricht in seinem Essay von 'rumenitá', das meiner Meinung nach als Synonym für Rumänität oder Rumänentum verstanden werden muss und das so in einer italienischen Hülle verpackt eine besondere Resonanz aufweist und beim Leser eine tiefere Wirkung erzielt. Die Definition des Begriffes 'rumenitá' könnte in Anlehnung an die Definition des Begriffes 'Deutschtum' im Duden[5] folgendermaßen lauten: a) die Gesamtheit der für die Rumänen typischen Lebensäußerungen; rumänische Wesensart; b) Zugehörigkeit zum rumänischen Volk; c) Gesamtheit der rumänischen Volksgruppen im Ausland. Es ist nicht zu verwechseln mit 'Rumänischtümelei', was abwertend für eine übertriebene Betonung rumänischer Wesensart steht.

Bergel hat Recht, wenn er behauptet, dass die Generation der im 19. Jahrhundert geborenen deutschen Autoren zum Beispiel in Siebenbürgen aus der historischen wie kulturellen Situation heraus rumänischen

Daseinsformen und -stilen weitgehend fremd gegenüber gestanden hat. Für sie waren diese eine geographieimmanente Kulisse in ihrem Werk. Den später geborenen Autoren erscheint die 'rumenitá', so Bergel, auch innerlich in einem Maße vertraut, das vorher undenkbar gewesen wäre.

Ein Grund für die gesellschaftliche und persönliche Annäherung zwischen Deutschen und Rumänen waren die neuen politischen Verhältnisse in Siebenbürgen nach 1918, vor allem die geistige Auseinandersetzung der dort lebenden Deutschen mit der Kultur der Rumänen.

Nicht nur ein einziges Mal hat Bergel behauptet, dass er alles, was seit der Kindheit von außen an Rumänität in seine 'angeborene wie anerzogene Germanität' einfloss, im Grundsatz nur bedingt als ein Fremdes, viel eher als das *alter ego* seiner selbst verstanden hat. Die Erklärung dafür ist die, dass ihn das Fremde in der Sprache, in der Nationalität und in der religiösen Konfession so sehr fesselte, dass es sich ihm dank seiner physischen Unmittelbarkeit auch als ein Teil seiner Persönlichkeit aufdrängte. Bergel glaubt an die Gemeinsamkeit der europäischen Verwurzelung beider Seiten, der rumänischen und der deutschen. Dieser Gedanke, der gleichzeitig zum wesensbestimmenden Gefühl wird, ist seine These über die Rumänität in seinen Büchern als Deutscher. Ein sprechender Beweis dafür ist die am 26. April 2001 gehaltene Dankrede bei der Verleihung der Ehrendoktorwürde durch die Universität Bukarest, die unter dem Titel 'Am spirituellen Kosmos der Rumänen teilhaben', veröffentlicht wurde.[6] Darin hob Bergel hervor, dass er trotz über dreißigjähriger Abwesenheit ein Mensch mit den Wurzeln in den Landschaften nördlich und südlich der Karpaten, der Donau, der Schwarzmeerküste und der moldauischen Landstriche ist.

> Und ich bin und bleibe bis ans Lebensende eine weitgehend von den Kulturmanifestationen dieser Landschaften determinierte geistige Individualität.

Was bindet Bergel, den Deutschen nach Geburt, Muttersprache, Erziehung und Bildung, an den spirituellen Kosmos der Rumänen und lässt ihn aktiv an ihm teilhaben? Seine Antwort lautet:

> Das Rumänische in seinen reinen, historisch gewachsenen Ausprägungen von der Volks- bis zur modernen Kunst, von der Musik über die Literatur bis zur Philosophie erscheint mir als eine jener Ausdrucksformen Europas, die den Kulturverständnissen des mittleren und westlichen Europa strukturell fehlen.

Damit sage ich zugleich, was auch mir als Individuum in jenen Teilen Europas fehlt, in denen ich seit 1968 lebe. Das hat nichts mit Nostalgie zu tun. Es ist vielmehr eine Feststellung von kulturdefinitorischer Relevanz, über die sich vieles sagen ließe.[7]

Eine der vielleicht schönsten und treffendsten Definitionen der sogenannten Rumänität stammt ebenfalls aus der Feder von Hans Bergel:

> Eine Geistigkeit, die sich philosophisch im Banne in sich selber widersprüchlicher Konstellationen von Sehnsucht nach Geborgenheit im Autochthonen, existenzieller Verzweiflung und egozentrischer Weltsicht, jedoch immer im Zeichen der Humanität bewegt, eine Literatur, die den vitalsten Impuls ihres Selbstbegreifens von der Lyrik bis zur Prosa aus den Schichtungen einer an Mythen unerschöpflichen Volkspoesie bezieht, eine Malerei, der die aus Landschaft und Geschichte erwachsene Melancholie in den Muttergottesaugen ostchristlicher Ikonen vorgezeichnet ist, und eine Musik, in deren bedeutenden Schöpfungen sich die Archaik südöstlicher Diktion mit der Geste avantgardistischen Okzidentalismus mischt - dies alles ist als Kulturakzent durch und durch und nur rumänisch. Es ließe sich an Namen veranschaulichen von Eminescu bis Culianu, von Arghezi bis Blaga, Cioran bis Noica, von Grigorescu und Andreescu bis Enescu oder Vieru und vielen anderen.[8]

Bergel hegt nicht nur Gefühle, wenn er an sein Heimatland zurückdenkt, sondern er philosophiert auch mit besonderem Einfühlungsvermögen über den Gedanken der Rumänität:

> Das Universum einer Nationalkultur, deren Polarität auf der einen Seite das unerschütterliche In-sich-selber-Ruhen seiner ländlichen Volksmasse in introvertierter byzantinischer Frömmigkeit aufweist, auf der anderen das bis zum zynischen Exzess erregbare extravertierte Raffinement seiner lebhaften intellektuellen Komponente [...].[9]

Bergel stellt bei der Übersetzung der Gedichte eines großen rumänischen Dichters die Tatsache fest, dass es kein 'rumänisches', 'französisches', 'deutsches' oder 'italienisches' Gedicht gibt, sondern dass im Grunde allein das stilistisch gelungene zählt, oder wie er es anschaulich formuliert: 'das inspirierte oder das nichtinspirierte'.[10] Es gibt einen gemeinsamen Nenner der Kulturen. Indem er von der geistigen Haltung spricht, bezieht er sich auf die europäische Relevanz, die in demselben Maße die französische, deutsche oder englische Lyrik bestimmt:

Es eignet uns, im Bild gesprochen, jenseits der Nationalsprache eine
Muttersprache, so daß etwa Blaga mit Goethe eine stärkere Bruderschaft
verbindet als Blaga mit dem rumänischen oder Goethe mit dem deutschen
Anonymus. [11]

Es gibt, so Bergel, eine Sprache europäischer Lyrik, die von
Walther von der Vogelweide bis García Lorca, von Charles Baudelaire bis
Odysseas Elytis, von Friedrich Hölderlin bis Tudor Arghezi, von Arthur
Rimbaud über T. S. Eliot bis Paul Celan die eine gemeinsame Sprache des
Gedankens, des Gefühls und des Geistes der Poesie ist, 'wie sie auf
diesem Kontinent ungeachtet der nationalen Idiome seit jeher die
vornehmste Verbindlichkeit der Besten war'.[12]   Pathetisch, doch
eindrucksvoll, meint Bergel weiter:

Die Dichtung ist nicht auf die Kontur der nationalen Region limitierbar, wir
sind zur Freiheit idealler Maßeinheiten aufgerufen, die nationale Region kann
dieser immer nur die Farbe anbieten.

Der Text 'Die Begegnung mit dem anderen. Gedanken über die
Gestalt des Rumänen in den Büchern eines Deutschen' drückt wie bereits
gesagt ein komplexes Bild von den rumänisch-deutschen Beziehungen
aus. Er wird von einem Motto Arthur Schopenhauers eingeleitet:

Wer also die Menschheit ihrem inneren, in allen Erscheinungen und
Entwicklungen identischen Wesen, ihrer Idee nach erkennen will, dem werden
die Werke der Dichter ein viel treueres und deutlicheres Bild vorhalten, als die
Historiker je vermögen.

Auf einige Hauptideen des Textes werde ich im folgenden eingehen.
Die Problematik von der Existenz des Rumänen in den Büchern eines
Deutschen, in unserem Fall Hans Bergels, ist eine Tatsache und hat
zeitsymptomatischen Charakter. Geistige und historische Dimensionen
des Rumänen können in den meisten bereits geschriebenen und
veröffentlichten Arbeiten Bergels nachvollzogen werden.

Alles Vergangene als gelebtes Leben hat laut Bergels Auffassung
erst dann einen Sinn, wenn es organischer Teil unseres Selbst in einem
solchen Maße wurde, dass wir es jeden Augenblick als bewusste
Gegenwart in uns tragen können - als Individualität und Persönlichkeit, als
Verhalten und Haltung.

In Hans Bergels Büchern tritt der Rumäne nicht nur als Anatomie
oder Kolorit, als Komparse oder Statist, nicht nur als historische

Erfahrung seines Lebens auf. Die Gestalt des Rumänen ist als Teil der Individualität in den Arbeiten des Autors immer gegenwärtig. Die Begegnung mit der geistigen Dimension Rumänien ist eine Bereicherung der geistigen Existenz des Autors. Es ist eine Begegnung, die sich auf den vielbödigen Ebenen des Geistigen abspielt. Die Gestalt des Rumänen ist in Bergels Belletristik, in Novelle, Erzählung, Roman, kultur- und geistesgeschichtlicher Monographie, im kulturphilosophischen Essay, in der Porträtstudie gegenwärtig. Kennzeichnend ist Bergels Suche nach den Wurzeln der Geistigkeit des rumänischen Volkes, nach seiner Spiritualität und deren innerem Duktus.

Die historische Dimension des Bildes vom Rumänen in den Werken eines Deutschen wird von Hans Bergel auf der Zeitachse verfolgt. Phänotypisches und Genotypisches[13] werden in der Gestalt des Rumänen, der bald als Hirt, bald als Widerstandskämpfer, bald als politischer Häftling und viel mehr vorkommt, untersucht.

Die geistige Dimension des Bildes vom Rumänen äußert sich darin, dass er als analphabetischer und zugleich weiser und lebenserfahrener Hirte, als Kulturphilosoph, als Musiker, Künstler, Dichter, Politiker auftreten kann. Er erscheint in sozialer Präsentation und ebenso differenziert in der geistigen Manifestation vom Hirten zum Bauern über den Offizier und Universitätsprofessor, vom Flößer über den Techniker bis zum Staatssekretär und Prinzen.

Andere Charakteristika der Rumänität sind: Die geschichtliche Kulturlandschaft von Siebenbürgen als multikulturelle Region Rumäniens, wo Rumänen, Ungarn, Deutsche, Juden, Ukrainer und Roma seit Jahrhunderten zusammenleben; und der anthropologisch angesetzte Vergleich zwischen Deutschen und Rumänen, nämlich die Deutschen als Volk, dessen Kulturbegriff in der Daseinsformel der Sesshaftigkeit gründet, während die Rumänen ihre Existenz an die Jahreszeitenwechsel verbinden.

In diesem Sinne unterscheiden wir folgende Aspekte in Bergels Werk, die auf seine Rumänität hinweisen:

1. Der Hirte als geschichtliche Urgestalt des menschlichen Daseins, als Urgestalt des Rumänen.
2. Der Tanz als eine Konstante in Bergels Werk, als Aufschrei oder Liebeserklärung, als Ausbruch und abgründige Selbstversenkung, als Jubel und zugleich Erinnerung.
3. Die Frau als Verkörperung des Schönen, als Liebende, als Mutter, als Verführerin, als Weissagerin - das facettenreiche Bild

als Synthese zwischen dem Romanischen und dem Orientalischen, als Porträtstudie.

Die Frauen, so wie sie in den Romanen *Der Tanz in Ketten* und *Wenn die Adler kommen* bzw. in einigen Erzählungen erscheinen, fanden nicht nur als belebende Kulisse oder als abwechslungsreicher Dekor Eingang in seine Texte, was in Äußerlichkeiten steckenbleibende Rumänität hieße, sondern weil die spirituelle Substanz der Aussageabsicht dies erforderlich machte. Diese läuft darauf hinaus, ein Stück Europa, in diesem Fall deren südöstliche rumänische Region, in der Komplexität der Existenz festzuhalten. Die sogenannten 'Ränder' Europas sind im Vergleich zu den europäischen Zentralen durch die Dichte und Intensität ihrer ethnischen Gruppierungen und daher ihrer kulturellen Schnittpunkte unendlich reicher. Sie veranschaulichen auf konzentrierte und reifere Weise, welches die europäischen Probleme der Gegenwart und der Zukunft sind. Sie bewegen sich - Spannungen und Konflikte eingeschlossen - auf Ebenen der Erlebnis - und Erfahrungsvorgänge, denen die kontinentale Mitte nichts an die Seite zu stellen hat.

> Die Spannungsweite und -tiefe dieses Reichtums nur aus der schmalen Perspektive eines sich selber ghettoisierenden nationalen Weltverständnisses zu sehen, führt hier zwangsläufig zum falschen Bild nicht nur der Welt, sondern auch seiner selbst.[14]

Im Roman *Der Tanz in Ketten*, eine Metapher allen menschlichen Seins, wie ihn Bergel selbst nennt, wird der Tanz von einem Rumänen getanzt. Das muss so sein, weil der Tanz als Element des Ausdrucksbedürfnisses im Leben der Rumänen - anders als bei den deutschen und den übrigen Romanprotagonisten - in ungleich größerer Vitalität präsent ist. Er ist ein Bestandteil existentieller Kulturmanifestation. Auch diesmal ist Bergel bestrebt zu zeigen, dass, obwohl der Tänzer eindeutig rumänischer Herkunft ist, sein Tanz als eruptives Freiheitsbekenntnis über die spezifische nationale Situation hinaus zur Demonstration jener menschlichen Unbesiegbarkeit wird, die Albert Camus mit dem Sisyphos bezeichnete.

Die rumänische Hirtenfamilie in dem Roman *Wenn die Adler kommen* ist mit allen Attributen der Rumänität ausgestattet, und das Schicksal, das sie erleidet, ist so bei keinem der anderen Völker des Romans - Deutschen, Ungarn, Juden, Zigeunern - denkbar. Die elementare Dimension der rumänischen Tragödie hat ihre Wurzeln in der uns Europäern allen gemeinsamen Vorstellungswelt der griechischen

Antike: jenseits der divergierenden historischen Konditionsreflexe sind wir Brüder und Schwestern.

Die Rumänität in den Büchern des deutschen Schriftstellers Hans Bergel ist ein Begriff von tiefgründiger Bedeutung: sie wird über das Exterieur des nationalen, ethnischen oder ethnographischen Moments hinaus zum konstitutiven geistigen Bestandteil der Aussage.

Eine Erklärung dafür ist die Tatsache, dass Bergel als Prosaautor aus einer der kulturell facettenreichsten Randgeographien Europas, aus einer Vielvölkerlandschaft stammt, was er auch sehr früh erkannte. Er ist kein Anhänger der Phrasen und Theorien. Er belächelt die Idyllenkonstrukte zentraleuropäischer Ideologien, die sich bei diesem Thema auf unheilvolle Weise in den Abstrakta hoffnungslos realitätsfremder, dessen ungeachtet penetrant besserwisserischer Messianismen verlieren.

In der reichhaltigen Essayistik, die sich auf zehn Bände beläuft, ist Bergel auf der ständigen Suche nach der 'rumenitá' seiner belletristischen, kunst- und kulturhistorischen sowie kulturphilosophischen Perspektive. Er sucht nach der gültigen Formulierung, folgt ewig neugierig und wissbegierig über das deutsche Elternhaus hinaus ins 'Faszinosum des gleichzeitig lateinischen wie byzantinischen Kosmos der Rumänen'.

Ein wichtiger, wenn nicht der wichtigste Text diesbezüglich, ist der Essay 'Über die Zerrissenheit und Einheit Südosteuropas', der 1994 als dreiteilige Serie für den Bayerischen Rundfunk konzipiert wurde. Südosteuropa gehörte über viele Jahrhunderte hindurch in den Herrschaftsbereich von Großreichen, des Osmanischen Reiches einerseits und des Habsburger Reiches andererseits und erlebte eine historisch diskontinuierliche politische, soziale und kulturelle Entwicklung, Kriege, Vertreibungen und Migrationen. All dies führte zu einem Neben- und Miteinander verschiedener Ethnien und Konfessionen sowie zu einem kulturellen Synkretismus. Es galt oft bei den sich neu bildenden Nationen, das Erbe der imperialen Vergangenheit zu überwinden, doch gerade dieses Erbe wurde zum Ausgangspunkt neuer Identitäten und Alteritäten. Die Gleichzeitigkeit von Ungleichzeitigkeiten: eine ständige Verschiebung der Grenzen, ethnische und kulturelle Inhomogenität, Kampf um das Erbe der zerfallenen Großreiche, Hinwendung nach Europa und Modernisierung einerseits, Rückwärtsgewandtheit und Glorifizierung der eigenen Größe von einst andererseits, sowie ein ständiger Wechsel von Solidarisierung zu Abgrenzung führten in Südosteuropa zu jenen komplexen Kulturüberlappungen und Mehrfachidentitäten, die im postkolonialen Milieu unter dem Aspekt der Hybridität und des kulturellen Missverstehens untersucht wurden. Solche zwischen Mythisierung der 'nationalen' Vergangenheit und Eurozentrismus oszillierenden Selbstzuschreibungen werden in der Literatur immer wieder sichtbar.[15]

In dem genannten Essay gelingt es Bergel, mit dem klassischen Instrumentarium deutscher Essayistik den Grundlagen der rumänischen Volkskultur völkerpsychologisch, entwicklungs- und brauchtums- geschichtlich als eines der Segmente des großen, in die Antike zurückreichenden südosteuropäischen Kulturkomplexes nachzugehen. Das Ergebnis der Recherchen zur kulturtheoretischen und -kritischen Arbeit bestand nicht nur in der Erkenntnis, dass die Gesamtheit der rumänischen Kultur einer weitergefaßten Exegese bedarf, als sie bisher im Umlauf ist, sondern dass der zentral- und westeuropäische Kulturbegriff in größerem Maße als üblich zur Einbeziehung der südöstlich-byzantinischen Welt in sein Selbstverständnis bereit sein müsse. Mit anderen Worten flossen Elemente der 'rumenitá' korrigierend in die 'germanitá' seiner literarischen Textur ein. Über die vertraute griechisch-orthodoxe Komponente der rumänischen Gedankenräume wurde Bergel der Zugang zum Byzantinismus etwa in dessen Athos- oder Osios-Lukas-Dimension erschlossen, was eine substantielle Bereicherung darstellte. Solche Horizontausweitungen sind ein Merkmal der Rumänität Bergels und schlagen sich im Roman *Wenn die Adler kommen* nieder. Vor allem dort, wo die Rumänität als integrierender Teil des Romanganzen zur Sprache kommt. Ähnliches gilt für den Roman *Der Tanz in Ketten*, für die Schilderung des Donau-Deltas 'Dunja, die Herrin', aber auch für Gedichte wie 'Donausteppe', 'Brief aus den Südkarpaten', 'Auf den Tod einer rumänischen Freundin' und andere mehr. Alle Texte kennzeichnen sich durch die Offenheit ihres deutschen Autors angesichts der spezifischen kulturellen Vibrationen der Rumänität: sie wären nicht entstanden ohne das Zugehen auf das 'Fremde', das sich, aus der Nähe betrachtet, nicht mehr als fremd, sondern lediglich als nationaltypische Ausdrucksform dessen herausstellte, was Goethe das 'allgemein Menschliche' nannte. In diesem Sinne war Bergel als deutschem Autor die Rumänität als einer der europäischen Dialogbeiträge niemals fremd. Er empfand sie als Aufforderung, die Grenzen der eigenen Individualität neu zu überdenken.

Dass das Interesse für die Rumänistik an den Universitäten des Auslands leider immer noch relativ gering ist, ist natürlich entmutigend und enttäuschend, zumal sich die Vertreter der rumänischen Kultur immer mehr bemühen, sich in die westeuropäische Kultur zu integrieren, ohne die eigene Identität dabei aufzugeben. Es gibt die Gefahr in der rumänischen Kultur, dass einige Stereotype oder Fremdbilder immer wiederkehren oder sich leicht verändert erhalten. Die Auseinandersetzung mit dem Fremden ist eine Konstante im Bewusstsein des rumänischen Volkes. Bergel liefert mit seinen Texten eine eher kulturgeschichtliche Auseinandersetzung mit dem Thema der Rumänität, keine nationalistische oder ethnizistische oder antieuropäische. Wegen der vielschichtigen aktuellen Problematik und der stilistischen Klarheit eignen sich viele Texte von Hans Bergel für die Aufnahme in ein Lehrbuch für Deutsch als Fremdsprache. Sie sensibilisieren nämlich die rumänischen Leser, die Deutsch sprechen, lesen oder lernen, für kulturelle Gemeinsamkeiten und für die Beschleunigung der europäischen Integration. Sie ermöglichen ein besseres gegenseitiges Verständnis durch das Kennenlernen der Lebensgewohnheiten, der Unterschiede und Ähnlichkeiten zwischen den Völkern in der multikulturellen Region Siebenbürgen/Transsilvanien, wo Rumänen, Ungarn, Deutsche, Ukrainer, Roma seit Jahrhunderten zusammenleben.

'Als Europäer haben wir alle miteinander keine andere Wahl', lautet die fast wie ein Aphorismus klingende Schlussfolgerung am Ende des Textes von Bergel über die Rumänität. Durch Bewusstmachung imagologischer Strukturen können die Texte zur interkulturellen Verständigung beitragen. Das positive Ergebnis der Lektüre seiner Texte liegt in der Vertiefung und Erweiterung des authentischen Dialogs zwischen verschiedenen Kulturen. Deutscher oder Rumäne zu sein, ist eigentlich eine Äußerung desselben Kulturwillens, 'der europäischen Grundform unserer Kulturexistenz, in der wir alle in unserer Zeit mehr denn je auf Gedeih oder Verderb gemeinsam eingebunden sind'.[16]

Anmerkungen

[1] Klaus Bochmann, 'Die Rumänen und die anderen. Kritisch-historische Betrachtungen über das Verhältnis der Rumänen zu sich selbst, ihren Minderheiten und ihren Nachbarn', in: Mircea Anghelescu, Larisa Schippel, Hrsg., *Im Dialog: Rumänische Kultur und Literatur*, Leipziger Universitätsverlag: Leipzig, 2000, S. 49-60 (hier: S. 49).

[2] Gabriella Schubert, Wolfgang Dahmen, 'Identität und Abgrenzung im Donau-Balkan-Raum. Das Eigene und das Fremde im Spiegel der Literatur', in: Mircea Anghelescu, Larisa Schippel, Hrsg., *Im Dialog: Rumänische Kultur und Literatur*, S. 149-160 (hier: S. 158).

[3] Hans Bergel, 'Die Begegnung mit dem anderen. Gedanken über die Gestalt des Rumänen in den Büchern eines Deutschen', in: Hans Bergel, *Gestalten und Gewalten*, Wort und Welt: Innsbruck, 1982, S. 183-190.

[4] Hans Bergel, 'Rumänität in den Büchern eines Deutschen', *Zeitschrift der Germanisten Rumäniens*, 8 (1999), Heft 1-2, 274-277.

[5] *Duden. Deutsches Universalwörterbuch*, Dudenverlag: Mannheim, Leipzig u.a., 1996, S. 337.

[6] Hans Bergel, 'Am spirituellen Kosmos der Rumänen teilhaben', *Allgemeine Deutsche Zeitung für Rumänien*, 9 (2001), Nr. 2112, S. 4.

[7] Ebenda.

[8] Ebenda.

[9] Hans Bergel, 'Rumänität in den Büchern eines Deutschen', S. 275.

[10] Ebenda.

[11] Ebenda.

[12] Ebenda.

[13] Laut *Duden. Deutsches Universalwörterbuch* (s. Anm. 5, S. 1146) versteht man unter Phänotypus das Erscheinungsbild des Organismus, wie es durch Erbanlagen und Umwelteinflüsse geprägt ist, während der Genotypus die Gesamtheit der Erbfaktoren eines Lebewesens bedeutet.

[14] Hans Bergel, 'Rumänität in den Büchern eines Deutschen', S. 276.

[15] Gabriella Schubert, Wolfgang Dahmen, 'Identität und Abgrenzung im Donau-Balkan-Raum. Das Eigene und das Fremde im Spiegel der Literatur', S. 152.

[16] Vgl. Hans Bergel, 'Am spirituellen Kosmos der Rumänen teilhaben', S. 4.

David Rock

'A German comes home to Germany': Richard Wagner's journey from the Banat to Berlin, from the periphery to the centre.

The article offers a brief introduction to Richard Wagner as a writer from the German minority in Romania. It examines the reasons why he left for West Germany in 1987, and explains the significance of Vienna as 'Habsburgischer Sockel' and Berlin as cultural centre of Germany for Wagner. His Banat roots are always inherent in his prose works written in the West: the past (for him invariably associated with his earlier life in Eastern Europe) lives on in the present in often curious ways. His choice of Berlin as place of residence is also explained: it represents for him the nearest thing to a cultural home.

Richard Wagner was born on 10 April 1952 in Lovrin in the Banat region of Romania.[1] When I asked him in 1997 whether he had experienced any problems of identity as a member of the German minority in Romania, his reply was unequivocal: that he sees himself as a German writer with a strong sense of his German identity:

> Ich hatte keine Identitätsprobleme, sondern eine klare Identität. Auch unter meinen Landsleuten, unter denen ich in einem Dorf aufgewachsen bin, das bis 1945 noch ganz deutsch, danach ungefähr zur Hälfte deutsch war, gab es eine sehr starke deutsche Identität. Das ließ auch mich nicht daran zweifeln, daß ich Deutscher war. Hinzu kam, daß wir auch von den anderen Bevölkerungs-gruppen in der Region, also von Ungarn und Serben und von den Rumänen, die die Staatsnation bildeten, als Deutsche angesehen wurden. Deutsch war nicht nur meine Muttersprache, sondern auch die Sprache meines kulturellen Selbstverständnisses. Ich habe auch eine deutsche Schule besucht und dort deutsche Sprache, deutsche Literatur und deutsche Literaturgeschichte gelernt. Es sind also die Komponenten einer deutschen Identität vorhanden gewesen, und deshalb habe ich mich auch von Anfang an als deutscher Schriftsteller gesehen und in dieser Sprache geschrieben.[2]

Wagner started writing whilst he was still at the grammar school and at the age of 17 he published his first poems in local German newspapers. He went on to study German at the university in Timisoara where in 1972 he joined the Communist Party of Romania and helped to found the 'Aktionsgruppe Banat' to which his future wife Herta Müller also belonged. The group had both political and literary aims: to reform socialism and to produce literature which was 'bewußtseinserweiternd',[3] with political and social influence. The Banat Action Group consisted of young intellectuals from German-speaking Banat families who had been inspired by the Prague Spring and by the idealism of the 1968 student movements in Paris and particularly West Germany, for, as Wagner explained in an interview which he gave in 1993, 'die Deutschen in Rumänien haben sich immer auf die Geschehnisse in der Bundesrepublik bezogen'.[4] Young Romanian-German writers thus focused their attention not on the issues of concern to ethnic Romanian writers who, writing in the 'Staatssprache', represented for Wagner the 'Staatskultur'; instead, they looked to what was being written in contemporary West Germany. Wagner was in this respect quite typical: 'Für mich war immer wichtig, was in Deutschland passiert, in der deutschen Gegenwartsliteratur, in der Moderne. Mich interessierte auch immer das Westliche' (Keele, 1997).

Although like many other authors in Eastern Europe he was eventually turned into an opponent of the system by the system itself, the young Richard Wagner was initially prepared to give communism a chance. The relaxed atmosphere prevailing in Romania in 1968 meant that Romanian-German writers were much less restricted than, for instance, their GDR counterparts, as Wagner explained: 'Als ich anfing zu schreiben, konnte man schreiben, was man wollte'.[5] Young ethnic German writers, with their interest in Germany as their cultural centre, were also under less pressure than critical ethnic Romanian writers who saw themselves as having a cultural role to play, with opposition to the dictatorship necessary for the survival of Romanian culture. On the other hand, this did not mean that Wagner identified with the culture represented and practised by the German minority in the Banat which he regarded as a 'konservative bis reaktionäre Bevölkerungsgruppe' (Keele, 1997). Indeed, when he started out as a writer, Wagner was more concerned with the sinister nationalistic tendencies of the people in the small German village communities in Romania than with the repressive Romanian state itself: 'Wenn sie betrunken waren, haben sie Landserlieder gesungen, die Generation meines Vaters war zu 90 Prozent in der Waffen-SS, die pseudo-intellektuelle Schicht, das waren die reaktionären Dorflehrer. [...] Gegen diese Leute, dieses Milieu habe ich geschrieben'.[6] The young members of the 'Aktionsgruppe' therefore took every opportunity to parody the German 'Heimatliteratur' of the region, and their provocative public performances led to their being denounced as 'Nestbeschmutzer' by their fellow Germans. Only later did Wagner adopt what he called 'eine kritische Grundhaltung' towards the political system in Romania, but early on, these young, mostly twenty-year-old intellectuals in the Banat Action Group were not so much interested in political tactics as in simply adopting an insolent stance, making no attempt to keep their activities secret. Initially, even the feared *Securitate* was disconcerted by the Group's policy of 'kritische Offenheit'.

As its title suggests, Richard Wagner's first volume of poetry, *Klartext* (1973),[7] exploits the poetic potential of concrete language. With this he was very much going against the prevalent tendency at that time when young Romanian poets, struggling to rehabilitate aesthetic values from the formal tyranny of Socialist Realism, were seeking to produce 'higher' forms of poetry, remote from real life. The big early influence on Wagner had been Bertolt Brecht, and the words 'Lakonie', 'Sachlichkeit', 'Understatement' and 'Ironie' are the ones most frequently used by Wagner to describe Brecht's lyric poetry, but they are also terms applicable not only to Wagner's own poetry written in Romania but also his later prose works. In *Klartext,* then, as he has commented, his aim was twofold: 'Ich suchte einen Ton gegen das Pathos der Heimatliteratur aber auch gegen das Pathos des Sozialistischen' (Keele, 1997).

Wagner had joined the Romanian Communist Party in 1972 in the hope that, by opposing what he mockingly called 'den real existierenden Schwachsinn', he could help to work towards a socialism which was more than 'nur das verzerrte Gesicht der Mächtigen'.[8] Yet any high flying political hopes were soon brought down to earth, and in his second volume of poetry *die invasion der uhren* (1977),[9] his 'Frühlings-hoffnungen' give way to scepticism about all utopian thinking. Ceauşescu's move away from his policy of pseudo-pragmatic socialism to despotic autocracy had been driving Romania to economic ruin and social chaos. By 1975, the 'Aktionsgruppe Banat', with its programme of open discussion of problems inherent in the sociopolitical system, was regarded as a group of dangerous dissidents, and Wagner was arrested but released after the intervention of the Federal Republic. This marked the end of the Group, and Wagner's activities during his remaining time in Romania were under continual pressure from increasingly repressive measures. By the end of the 70s, the disillusioned Wagner realised that what was being practised in Romania under the guise of socialism was not reformable, 'daß mit dem System nichts mehr zu machen war'.[10]

Politics was always a very important dimension in his work, for, as he explained: 'In einer Diktatur ist überall Politik. Ich stelle sie nicht ins Gedicht, sie kommt von alleine hinein'.[11] Being able to publish was also vital, and this became more and more difficult in Romania after Wagner lost his position as Banat cultural correspondent for the German newspaper, the *Karpaten Rundschau,* in 1983 as a result of huge pressure from the editorial office. In 1984, an open letter to the Party and the Writers' Union led to 'Berufs- und Publikationsverbot' for Wagner and other Romanian-German writers, many of whom applied to leave for the German Federal Republic as a result. Now effectively unemployed, he thus also experienced a sense of increasing personal isolation. An attitude of resignation permeates his works written just prior to this time, such as *Gegenlicht* (1983)[12] and *das auge des feuilletons* (1984).[13] Depressed by the conformity all around him, he now had to concede 'daß die Menschen alles mitmachen, daß sie bereit sind, diesen ganzen Wahnsinn, dieses Absurde mitzutragen',[14] and so Wagner, too, decided to leave, knowing now that he would only be allowed to publish 'Nebensächliches' and that such publications could have been used to legitimise the regime by making it appear to Western eyes to be more liberal than it actually was. He also realised, though, that his application for an exit permit would mean the loss of his public for a writer who had received several prizes and published seven volumes of poetry and prose in Romania. The last few volumes of poetry to be published in Romania, the two cited above and the earlier *Hotel California* I and II (of 1980 and 1981)[15] which had adopted an aggressively defiant, rebellious tone, had been aimed specifically at his Romanian-German readership.

Wagner's next two stories were aimed at different readers. They were published in the West and have as their theme his departure from Romania in 1986 and his arrival in the West. Both feature the same central characters drawn from Wagner's biography: a journalist and writer called Stirner, and his German teacher-wife, Sabine; and both stories give an anecdotal, discontinuous account of events narrated in the third-person yet from the exclusive perspective of Stirner, emphasising both the latter's isolation and his disconnection from the world around him.

Ausreiseantrag (1988*)*,[16] set in a town in the Banat in the 1980s, records the effects of the Ceauşescu dictatorship on everyday life which eventually drive the couple to leave the country. The external social decline of the world around Stirner is relentlessly accompanied by his complete isolation and inner paralysis. Faced with the interminable monotony of each day, he gradually loses his ability to think and to write. Stirner's capacity for recalcitrance (his name is a pun on the idiom 'jemandem die Stirn bieten') is gradually eroded by the cumulative effect of a repressive totalitarian society. As he roams the streets, searching in vain for some sense in his existence, Stirner's ultimate state of bitter resignation comes when he recognises the submissive lethargy which this repression has produced in the Romanian people: 'Er hatte den Sinn der Welt auf der Straße gesucht und dabei die Gosse in den Köpfen entdeckt' (A, p. 75).

Begrüßungsgeld (1989)[17] follows Stirner and his wife to West Germany. The story recapitulates the first six months which they spend after arriving at the transit camp in Nuremberg and then later in Berlin, and portrays the process of migration to Germany, above all in terms of its psychological effects upon the German *Aussiedler* from Romania. Stirner experiences a crisis of identity which stems from cultural and linguistic disorientation. Here, in his experiences in the capitalist, democratic society of the West, Stirner finds a grotesque counterpart to the deprivation of the right to self-determination which he experienced in the totalitarian state: interminable overstimulation, the dictates of fashion and the latent tyranny of 'the economy'.[18] The contrast between the fluid, transient arbitrariness of the West and the world of single meanings in the dictatorship, the 'Eindeutigkeiten' of the points of reference which he has left behind, threatens him with loss of his intellectual identity. Symptomatic of this is the increasing discrepancy which he experiences between the 'centre' and the 'periphery', between the German language spoken every day in the Federal Republic and the German which he speaks and writes. He had expected to feel linguistically at home in Germany, but his Banat German accent marks him out as 'einer der von außen kommt' and which is now becoming 'fremder', isolating him from those around him: 'Er war jetzt mit seiner Sprache allein' (B, p. 159), comments the narrator. And Stirner's inner turmoil and social disorientation are given striking expression in the form of the work: the sequence of events is sharply broken up, with fragments of experiences and memories intermingled with bits of dialogue, dream sequences and brief reflective passages, as the past is interwoven into the present.

Stirner had hitherto lived in a world where things had one centralising meaning in the dictatorship: 'Er kam aus einem Land, wo alles noch seine bestimmte Bedeutung hatte' (B, p. 249). In Berlin, Stirner finds himself above all in the capitalist world of advertising and the mass media, where words and images are manifold and everywhere, with their fluid, multiple meanings threatening to overwhelm the Romanian-German *Aussiedler*: 'Es waren zu viele Wörter um ihn. Überall war er mit Wörtern konfrontiert' (B, p. 212); 'Er mußte sich daran gewöhnen, daß alles zur Verfügung stand, Bilder, Ideen. […] Es fiel Stirner schwer, sich daran zu gewöhnen, da er bisher mit Eindeutigkeiten gelebt hatte' (B, p. 211). Yet despite the difficulties of attuning to the plurality of the city's signs, images and words and their meanings, pre-1989 West Berlin does suit Stirner in one respect: it corresponds to his way of thinking, for the existence of the Wall is a reminder of the clear polarities, the old 'Eindeutigkeiten' - the transit route, the border controls - with which he was familiar in Romania: 'Da kam Berlin seinen Vorstellungen entgegen: jedesmal die Transitstrecke, die Grenzkontrollen. Das hatte etwas von seiner bisherigen Reiserealität' (B, p. 170).

Since coming to the West, Wagner has published numerous literary texts in diverse forms: prose pieces and short stories such as *Der Mann, der Erdrutsche sammelte* (1994);[19] collections of poetry such as *Rostregen* (1986)[20] and *Heiße Maroni* (1993);[21] novels such *Die Muren von Wien* (1990)[22] and *In der Hand der Frauen* (1995),[23] and also collections of essays such as *Mythendämmerung. Einwürfe eines Mitteleuropäers* (1993)[24] and *Sonderweg Rumänien* (1991)[25] which are aimed at enlightening West German readers' ignorance about what has gone on in South Eastern Europe over the last 100 years. As he explained in Keele in 1997, in the truncated, post-1945 Germany of today, people are unaware 'daß es auch außerhalb Deutschland Deutsche gibt. […] Was die Angehörigen dieser Minderheiten heute stört und worunter sie auch leiden, ist, daß sie in Deutschland nicht als Deutsche anerkannt werden'.

Wagner now sees another of his tasks as being 'über und gegen das politische Verbrechen in unserem Jahrhundert zu schreiben' (Keele, 1997). His first attempt to do this began with his story *Ausreiseantrag*. Literature thus also has a commemorative function for Wagner: 'Sie beschreibt Lebensräume und tut dies sehr konkret, weshalb sie anschaulicher ist als wissenschaftliche Texte'.[26] Texts such as *Ausreiseantrag* give us an understanding of the things that went on under communism by transforming them in all their everyday dimensions into literature. Yet Wagner is not only concerned with the past but also the way it lives on in the present: 'Bei mir verzahnt sich alles', he commented in Keele (Keele, 1997), and so his roots as a Banat Swabian are always inherent in his writing, sometimes explicitly as a central theme, for instance, in his novel *Die Muren von Wien* (1990), in which he explores the question of Banat-German identity. Although *Die Muren von Wien* does not feature the two recognisably autobiographical central characters of the previous two stories, a writer and a teacher, this novel, published just one year after *Begrüßungsgeld*, is a continuation of the previous two stories in terms of themes and style. It is, as Hannes Krauss has argued,[27] an attempt to tell a story, an attempt that fails: a story of Benda, a man from the Banat now living in Munich, who, after his girlfriend leaves him, sells his car, gives up his flat and goes to Vienna, where he roams aimlessly around the city, gaining fleeting impressions which intermingle with sudden memories of Romania. At the end of the novel, he suddenly returns to Munich, alone. The attempt to tell a third-person story falters almost from the outset as the narrative disintegrates into a disconnected, often fragmentary protocol of momentary impressions and distanced observations, sudden associations and fleeting memories as Benda himself becomes increasingly disconnected from the life going on around him in the city, finally losing all sense of direction in his own life:

> Er hätte aufstehen wollen und gehen, das Haus verlassen, die Stadt. Er tat es nicht. Er blieb liegen, dachte nach. Er fühlte sich in lauter Konjunktivsätze hinein, er trieb von einer Möglichkeit zur anderen, er lebte, er schwebte, die Gedanken eilten ihm davon. [...] Tag um Tag könnte so vergehen, aber es war der Gedanke da, daß er nicht weiterkam. (M, p. 132)

His life becomes an aimless wandering from place to place: 'Ich flaniere mit geringem Interesse durch mein Leben, ich wechsele die sich wiederholenden Orte. Ich bin und ich weiß nicht wohin' (M, p. 40). Benda is a *flâneur* who is unable to stroll through the city in the leisurely fashion of Walter Benjamin's 'stroller' but roams restlessly through the suburbs of Vienna. As his German girlfriend points out shortly before she leaves him, and some eleven years after his flight from Romania, he now lives in a state of perpetual homelessness:

> Du hast die fixe Idee, nirgends dazuzugehören, sagte Eva. Du hast nicht ganz zu deinen Schwaben gehört, nicht zu den Rumänen, und auch hier gehörst du nicht dazu. (M, p. 18)

The central experiences portrayed in his two earlier stories are now intermingled: the outsider figure with the observant but distanced gaze, whose behaviour and language marked him out as outsider in *Begrüßungsgeld*, now finds himself in the old centre of the Habsburg Empire, Vienna, a city which everywhere evokes memories of the past and his former home in Romania, the theme of *Ausreiseantrag*:

Wien ist ein Wort für Vergangenheit, sagte er. Du sagst "Wien", und schon
befindest du dich in deiner Kindheit, obwohl du in deiner Kindheit nie in Wien
gewesen bist. Wien ist die erdabgewandte Seite deiner Kindheit. (M, p. 44)

The choice of Vienna as the setting for his novel is thus significant: the
Banat is, for Wagner, not the territory of the German minority but:

ein Territiorium, auf dem eine Vielzahl von Völkern lebt. Der kulturelle
Hintergrund des Banat, den ich meine, ist mehr der Habsburgische Sockel, der bis
heute in der Alltagskultur der Region nachwirkt. (Keele, 1997).

Yet this region is also indelibly marked not only by the Habsburg
legacy, but also by the more recent communist past. In the novel, one
episode from the summer of 1989 reveals the significance of the puzzling
imagery of its title: 'die Muren von Wien' is the moraine of the past, and it
remains a formidable obstacle for refugees from all over the the Eastern
Bloc trying to escape this past:

In jenem Sommer, in Wien, wuchs die Hitze ins Unerträgliche, wie in der
Kindheit. Die Tage hatten mehr Vergangenheit als Gegenwart. Nachts stürmte es,
das Radio sprach von Muren und Verschüttungen. Die Flüchtlinge versammelten
sich am Plattensee zu Tausenden. Ich sah die ganze Bevölkerung des Ostblocks
vor mir, wie sie sich auf die Westgrenzen zu bewegte. Wie seinerzeit ich. Die
Muren gehen, die Menschen rennen los. […] Die rennen jetzt, und sie sind
überzeugt, sie rennen um ihr Leben. Und danach werden sie graben müssen. Denn
auch wer davongekommen ist, bleibt verschüttet. Die Mure bleibt. Jeder muß sich
irgendwann selbst ausgraben. Die wenigsten schaffen es. (Q, p. 57)

Benda too is struggling to dig himself out of this moraine: he has fled
from the repressive dictatorship in Romania in the hope that he will find
his true home in the German-speaking world in the West, but here, even
though he is a native speaker of German, he is still regarded as an
outsider: not only does he speak with a strange accent ('Bis an mein
Lebensende bin ich durch meine Aussprache gezeichnet sagt er' (M, p.
30)), his behaviour too carries the mark of his Romanian past: 'Er hatte in
einer Gesellschaft der Zurechtweisungen und Maßregelungen gelebt, und
das hatte bei ihm eine unsichere Gestik erzeugt' (M, p. 104). And so he
comes to realise that a Banat Swabian is neither a Romanian nor a German
and that he is split between two completely separate lives:

Benda hatte ein Leben aus dem Banat und eines aus München. Sie berührten sich nicht. Er war zusammengefügt aus diesen beiden Leben, aber sie berührten sich nicht. Es hätte ein Marx-Brothers-Witz sein können, dachte er. Den Trennstreifen bildeten die zwei ersten Jahre im Westen an die er, wie er immer wieder überrascht feststellte, kaum Erinnerungen hatte. (M, p. 104)

Even his idea of the West itself proves to be an illusion, invented to counter the deadening banality of everyday life under the dictatorship but now impeding his life in the West:

Sein Westen war eine Illusion gewesen, die er sich gegen die tötende Banalität des Lebens in Rumänien ausgedacht hatte. Sein Bild vom Westen hatte ihm im Osten genützt, im Westen behinderte es ihm. (M, p. 107)

If elsewhere in Wagner's works the Banat Swabian issue is not an explicit theme, it is there, implicitly, in everything that he writes, as he explained in his Frankfurt Poetics Lecture at the Goethe University, comparing it to Bobrowski's Sarmatia:

Das Rumäniendeutsche ist das Abwesende, das immer präsent ist. Es schreibt mit. [...] Ich war in dieser Minderheit zuhause aber nicht heimisch, ich trauere ihren Lebensformen nicht nach, aber sie geht mir nach. Jetzt, in Berlin, geht es mir wie Johannes Bobrowski mit seinem Käuzchen. 'Das ist nicht ausdrückbar,' schreibt Bobrowski, 'und ist der Ort, wo wir leben.' Schreibt er. Das Banat zieht sozusagen sarmatische Kreise.[28]

And even though, as we have noted, Wagner adopted an oppositional stance towards them, his background was and remains the German minority: 'ohne sie ist diese Region für mich nicht existent'. Now, though, living mainly in Berlin and a long way from the Romanian reality of his childhood and youth, this part of his identity exists only 'in meinem Kopf als Bestandteil von mir und meiner Literatur'.[29]

Berlin is the setting for the last two works discussed here. In the novel *In der Hand der Frauen* (1995), a first-person narrator who possesses a biography not unlike that of Wagner and of Stirner in *Ausreiseantrag* and *Begrüßungsgeld,* again portrays the painful and negative experiences of a Romanian immigrant in a city like Berlin. One of the central concerns of this novel is the narrator's relationship to post-*Wende* Berlin, a predominantly Western city, but one in which the divided past is still in evidence: 'Berlin war der einzige Ort in Deutschland, an dem die Teilung wirklich war, und Berlin ist der einzige Ort in

Deutschland, an dem die Vereinigung wirklich ist' (F, p. 41). 'Berlin ist ein Chamäleon' (F, p. 61), comments the first-person narrator who strolls through the city, from the Kurfürstendamm to Kreuzberg to Prenzlauer Berg. We see Berlin from its many, varied and changing sides as he visits its cafes, its 'Kneipen' and its cinemas and we experience with him not only a kaleidoscope of everyday images of Berlin, its streets, its different newspapers in its different suburbs, its underground stations, advertising signs, slogans and graffiti, but also something of the current time and situation in passing references to the rapidly changing face of East Berlin since unification, with houses being renovated all over Prenzlauer Berg, and to people in the news such as Mayor Diepgen and the criminal Dagobert.

Occasionally this Banat German narrator gives the reader the impression that, after some eight years' residence in Berlin, he is more integrated than his predecessor Stirner in *Begrüßungsgeld*. Yet his claims that he feels at home in the city are unable to convince even himself:

> Ich fahre durch die Stadt, in der ich seit acht Jahren lebe. Es ist die Stadt, in der ich zu Haus bin, wie ich sage. Ja, ich sage das. Ich rede wie ein Heimatist, während mir die Gedanken munter durch den Kopf springen. Wie diese Schwachköpfe, die herumlaufen und rufen: Berlin ist Hauptstadt, Berlin ist Weltstadt. Als müßten sie es sich einreden. (F, p. 139)

Despite his ironic air of self-assurance and self-mocking irony, his sense of identity remains unstable, just as Stirner's was. Although he adopts the seemingly untroubled pose of the *flâneur*, as Graham Jackman has shown,[30] his ultimately unstable sense of identity again belies the decided resemblance to Walter Benjamin's figure of the 'stroller'. Both the narrator and his text lack a sense of direction: like *Die Muren von Wien*, the text is episodic, drifting with its narrator from place to place and from thought to thought. And the narrator himself remains an immigrant in Berlin, identified by his East European origins: 'Osteuropa ist tief eingegraben im Kopf' (F, p. 14), he says at one point. And early on in the novel, he even admits to a paranoia deriving from his earlier experiences, as he reflects on the possibility that the sudden, seemingly inexplicable death of an acquantance in America might be linked to his work on Palestinian emigrants: 'Meine osteuropäische Paranoia dachte lauthals mit. Ich wußte es und würgte den Gedanken jedesmal ab' (F, p. 13).

As with Stirner in the earlier story, the stable meanings in his life have gone, they exist only in the past, in the narrator's earlier life in Ceauşescu's Romania, and it gradually becomes apparent that the narrator is no more at ease amid the indeterminacy of Berlin than Stirner was. Even the old East-West polarities which reassured Stirner in *Begrüßungsgeld* are now disappearing in East Berlin, as the narrator wryly remarks when he drinks a Coca-Cola in the Café *Tati*: 'Im Osten trinke ich immer Cola. Um Volker Braun zu ärgern' (F, p. 179). Yet many of his own friends, indeed most of the many women who feature in the novel, come from the east; as he explains early on, 'in der Regel begegnet man in Berlin ja nur Zugereisten' (F, p. 24). Hence Berlin is a substitute home for the narrator in so far as it is made up of people like himself: migrants and 'foreigners', a floating and constantly changing population without long-term roots there. Not only is he familiar with, and a keen observer of, the many cafes and Kneipen in Berlin, they become, as Jackman has shown, 'the signposts within the labyrinth of the city by which the immigrant first charts his way, the havens from which he constructs a familiar world amid the initial strangeness of the city'.[31] Yet even though he may, in one sense, feel at home in Berlin, he is unable to escape his origins, as two unrelated incidents illustrate: once, when he is awoken by an anonymous telephone call, he comments, 'Für einen Augenblick ist die Vergangenheit wieder da' (F, p. 63), and later, the sinister Romanian past is again momentarily evoked when he catches sight of a man in a trenchcoat getting up from his seat in the U-Bahn and the word 'Securitate' suddenly comes to mind:

> Ich denke es nur für eine Sekunde, und dann denke ich darüber nach und bin erstaunt. Nach so vielen Jahren. Es war nur ein winziger Augenblick, und er bedeutete so gut wie nichts. Und doch. (F, p. 144)

The one theme present in most of the works discussed already in this paper is absent in the novel *In der Hand der Frauen*, for its narrator, though he has his problems as 'Aussiedler', experiences no difficulties as a result of his strange German accent. Yet the relationship of minorities to their language remains of central concern to Wagner for, as he has explained: 'Ich bin der Meinung, daß Minderheiten eine andere Beziehung zu ihrer Sprache haben, da sie ihre Sprache immer gefährdet sehen'.[32] This is one reason why, in Romania, Wagner and other Romanian-German writers focused on Germany as their cultural centre. Wagner defines this relationship as 'das Spannungsverhältnis zwischen Peripherie und

Zentrum', a tension which Wagner believes has been productive, with the German minority from its position on the periphery in Romania being the only one since the Second World War to produce noteworthy writers in contemporary German literature such as Oskar Pastior, Herta Müller, Werner Söllner and Wagner himself.

And although he now lives at the German 'centre', in Berlin, Richard Wagner prefers to see himself as a Central European.[33] When I asked him if he felt at home in Berlin, he replied:

> Zu Hause ist nicht der richtige Begriff. Ich bin nach Deutschland ausgewandert, habe aber mit dem Territorium Deutschland nichts zu tun, da ich mich die ersten 35 Jahre meines Lebens nicht in Deutschland aufgehalten habe. (Keele, 1997)

This is one reason why his relationship to the past plays such an important part in his work, as he commented in 1994: 'Jenseits davon schreit die Vergangenheit und ruft die Gegenwart nach vertrackter Beschreibung'.[34] For Wagner, then, writing involves giving literary shape to the interwoven complexity of the past and the present. The multifarious material for *Der Mann, der Erdrutsche sammelte* (1994), for instance, is drawn from Wagner's critical awareness of both the past and the present, from memories of the past, but also from humdrum events in the present, everyday experiences in pubs, in the street and in shops, and newspaper, television and radio reports. *Der Mann, der Erdrutsche sammelte* is a collection of 66 'Kalendergeschichten', short, often witty, usually humorous anecdotes in the tradition of Johan Peter Hebel, Bertolt Brecht and Günter Eich. The diversity of these little pieces and parables (most are less than one page in length) is indicated in the range of titles, from the everyday 'Der Mann, der in Westberlin lebte' to the seemingly fantastical 'Der Mann, der durch die Luft gehen konnte'. The collection is divided into four parts, each of which bears the title of one of the stories, indicating loose thematic connections between them, as the author as literary *flâneur* meanders between past and present. The first section, 'Der Mann, der in Westberlin lebte' features life in Berlin east and west, reflecting Berlin as the city of Wagner's residential choice, Berlin as the 'centre' of the German cultural world, but also Berlin as unique, like no other city in Germany because of its cosmopolitan character, because of its links with socialism and the east and the 'periphery' of German culture, and because it is the only place in Germany where unification, convergence between East and West, can be experienced directly.

Recollections of life in the Banat intermingle with life in Germany after the demise of Socialism, and Berlin forms the focal point, a city full of contradictions as in the story 'Der Mann, der mit einer Ananas über den Potsdamer Platz ging'. Here, it is as if the 'periphery' is now at the very centre: 'Es war so leer auf dem Potsdamer Platz, als wäre der Potsdamer Platz das Mitteleuropa von Berlin' (E, p.18); the man with the pineapple, though, is undaunted and carries on across the Square, proudly displaying his pineapple and looking as if he is walking through Central Europe, ready to be photographed at any moment by some news agency. Yet suddenly, the humorous atmosphere changes to one of threat at the end as the past, too, seems to come alive, for 'es war ihm, als höre er vereinzelt Schüsse' (E, p. 18).

For Wagner, the journey from the periphery to the centre, from the Banat to Berlin, has been one fraught with all manner of personal difficulties. He has experienced the quandary of all Romanian-German *Aussiedler*, articulated in the laconic words of his protagonist Stirner in *Begrüßungsgeld*: 'In Rumänien haben sie immer gesagt: Du Deutscher, sagte Stirner. Hier bin ich der Rumäne' (A, p. 205). In the Banat, even though Wagner had been critical of it, he had also been conscious of belonging to the minority German culture and not in any way to the Romanian one:

> Auch wenn ich den Rumäniendeutschen kritisch gegenüberstehe, bin ich natürlich auch ein Produkt dieser Bevölkerungsgruppe gewesen. Wir hatten als Minderheit immer eine Distanz zur rumänischen Kultur und Nation und zum rumänischen Staat und fühlten uns nicht dazugehörig. (Keele, 1997)

Consequently, in Germany Wagner has been able to give unique expression to the difficulties of a writer with a strong sense of German identity, but whose Germany is not a territorial concept but a cultural one:

> Mein Deutschland ist ein kultureller Begriff - die Kulturnation. [...] Und was Rumänien betrifft, Rumänien war für mich immer der Staat. Womit ich mich in Beziehung gesetzt habe, das ist das Banat, die Region. In Ostmitteleuropa sind die Regionen wichtiger als die Staaten, sie sind auch älter als sie. Für die Minderheiten ist es selbstverständlich, sich zuerst mit der Region zu identifizieren. [...] Zum Banat, wo ich aufgewachsen bin, habe ich also diese territoriale Beziehung, die ich zu Deutschland nicht habe. (Keele, 1997)

This explains, too, his choice of Berlin as place of residence, precisely because it is not a quintessentially German city, but rather a cosmopolitan

meeting-point between East and West; and so it represents for him the
nearest thing to a cultural home:

> Berlin habe ich ja nicht gewählt, weil es so wunderbar deutsch ist, sondern weil
> es das eben nicht ist, und weil es eine kosmopolitische Stadt ist. Andernfalls
> hätte ich ja in eine richtige deutsche Stadt im damaligen Westdeutschland
> ziehen können. (Keele, 1997)

Richard Wagner is, then, a German writer in a unique sense, which
he briefly defined in his Frankfurt lecture:

> Ich saß in meiner isolierten Region Banat und baute mir einen Rand aus
> Wörtern. [...] Die Herkunft aus einer Minderheit im Osten beschreibt mein
> Verhältnis zur Sprache und zur Welt als Rand. Die deutsche Herkunft
> ermöglicht mir den Blick von Ost nach West als Sehnsucht nach der Mitte.[35]

He has been forced to recognise, too, the danger of this longing for the
centre: for a writer such as himself, it is a linguistic danger that threatens
his own independent voice - and thus also his very identity: 'Doch wer die
Mitte erreicht, schreibt nicht mehr. Er verläßt die Sprache der Literatur
und findet die Sprachregelung der Gesellschaft'.[36] So for Wagner, the
journey from the Banat periphery to Berlin, his German cultural centre,
has, paradoxically, been a journey back to the periphery in the recognition
that, in modern western societies such as that of the new Germany, the
writer, especially a German one from Romania, frequently remains on the
fringe as critical outsider and *flâneur*: 'Literatur der Rand des
Wirklichen'.[37]

Notes

[1] Many of the details about Wagner's life in Romania were explained by the author in
an interview, in several conversations and in three short presentations at Keele in
November 1997. For an English translation of the hitherto unpublished interview, see:
'"...a form of literature which was intentionally political." Richard Wagner in
conversation with David Rock and Stefan Wolff', in: David Rock and Stefan Wolff,
eds, *Coming Home to Germany? The Integration of Ethnic Germans from Central and
Eastern Europe in the Federal Republic*, Berghahn: Oxford/New York, 2002, pp. 139-
144.

[2] Unpublished interview, Keele 1997. Later references to this interview are included
in the text as (Keele, 1997).

[3] Csejka, Gerhard, 'Richard Wagner', in: Heinz Ludwig Arnold, ed., *Kritisches Lexikon zur deutschsprachigen Gegenwartsliteratur,* edition text + kritik: Munich, 1991, pp. 1-5, (here: p. 3).

[4] Susanne Broos, 'Richard Wagner: Politik ist immer eine Dimension in meinem Schreiben', *Börsenblatt*, no. 87, 2. November 1993, pp. 18-20, (here: p. 18).

[5] Susanne Broos, p. 18.

[6] Susanne Broos, p. 20.

[7] Richard Wagner, *Klartext. Ein Gedichtbuch,* Albatros: Bucharest, 1973.

[8] Csejka, Gerhard, 'Richard Wagner', p. 2.

[9] Richard Wagner, *die invasion der uhren. Gedichte,* Kriterion: Bucharest, 1977.

[10] Susanne Broos, p. 20.

[11] Richard Wagner, 'Die Bedeutung der Ränder oder vom Inneren zum Äußersten und wieder zurück', *neue literatur: 'Ideen in Not'*, vol. 1, 1994, 33-49 (here: pp. 44-5). (This essay is the published version of Wagner's 'Frankfurter Poetik-Vorlesung').

[12] Richard Wagner, *Gegenlicht. Gedichte*, Facla: Temeswar (Timişoara), 1983.

[13] Richard Wagner, *Das Auge des Feuilletons. Geschichten und Notizen.* Dacia: Cluj-Napoca, 1984.

[14] Susanne Broos, p. 20.

[15] Richard Wagner, *Hotel California I. der Tag der mit einer Wunde begann. Gedichte,* Kriterion: Bucharest, 1980; and *Hotel California II. Als schliefe der Planet. Gedichte,* Kriterion: Bucharest, 1981.

[16] Richard Wagner, *Ausreiseantrag. Eine Erzählung,* Luchterhand: Darmstadt, 1988, hereafter abbreviated to A followed by the page numbers.

[17] Richard Wagner, *Begrüßungsgeld. Eine Erzählung,* Luchterhand: Darmstadt, 1988, hereafter abbreviated to B followed by the page numbers.

[18] See Armin M. Huttenlocher, 'Richard Wagner' in: Walter Jens, ed., *Kindlers Neues Literatur-Lexikon*, Kindler: Munich, 1998, pp. 345-347 (here: pp. 346-7).

[19] Richard Wagner, *Der Mann, der Erdrutsche sammelte. Geschichten,* DVA: Stuttgart, 1994, hereafter abbreviated to E followed by the page numbers.

[20] Richard Wagner, *Rostregen. Gedichte*, Luchterhand: Darmstadt, 1986.

[21] Richard Wagner, *Heiße Maroni. Gedichte*, DVA: Stuttgart. 1993.

[22] Richard Wagner, *Die Muren von Wien. Roman*, Luchterhand: Frankfurt, 1990, hereafter abbreviated to M followed by the page numbers.

[23] Richard Wagner, *In der Hand der Frauen. Roman*, DVA: Stuttgart, 1995, hereafter abbreviated to F followed by the page numbers.

[24] Richard Wagner, *Mythendämmerung. Einwürfe eines Mitteleuropäers. Essays*, Rotbuch: Berlin, 1993.

[25] Richard Wagner, *Sonderweg Rumänien. Bericht aus einem Entwicklungsland. Essay*, Rotbuch: Berlin, 1991.

[26] Susanne Broos, p. 20.

[27] Hannes Krauss, 'Fremde Blicke. Zur Prosa von Herta Müller und Richard Wagner', in: Walter Delabar, Werner Jung, Ingrid Pergande (eds), *Neue Generation - neues Erzählen. Deutsche Prosa-Literatur der achtziger Jahre,* Westdeutscher Verlag: Opladen, 1993, pp. 69-76 (here: pp. 74-76).

[28] Richard Wagner, 'Die Bedeutung der Ränder oder vom Inneren zum Äußersten und wieder zurück', p. 46.

[29] Susanne Broos, p. 20.

[30] See Graham Jackman, '"Alone in a crowd": The Figure of the "Aussiedler" in the Work of Richard Wagner', in: David Rock and Stefan Wolf, eds, *Coming Home to Germany? The Integration of Ethnic Germans from Central and Eastern Europe in the Federal Republic*, Berghahn: Oxford/New York, 2002, pp. 157-170.

[31] Graham Jackman, '"Alone in a crowd": The Figure of the "Aussiedler" in the Work of Richard Wagner', p. 164.

[32] Susanne Broos, p. 20.

[33] Ibid.

[34] Richard Wagner, 'Kulturbrief aus Berlin', *Literatur und Kritik*, April 1994, vol. 283/4, pp.11-12 (here: p. 11).

[35] Richard Wagner, 'Die Bedeutung der Ränder oder vom Inneren zum Äußersten und wieder zurück', p. 36 and p. 37.

[36] Ibid.

[37] Ibid.

Dagmar Košťálová

Die Migrantenschriftstellerin Irena Brežná

The Slovakian writer and journalist, Irena Brežná, lives in Switzerland, writes in German and, like many migrant writers, has left behind both her homeland and her native language. Since 1989, she has again visited her former home country, now Slovakia and the Czech Republic. This article discusses her collection of articles *Falsche Mythen. Reportagen aus Mittel- und Osteuropa nach der Wende* (1996), written during her first return visit after the *Wende*. As the title suggests, it presents a complex, amended image of Central and Eastern Europe, as she contends with the feelings of longing that had developed over the period of her enforced absence.

Im Sommer des Jahres 1968, unmittelbar nach dem Einmarsch der Armeen des Warschauer Paktes in die ehemalige Tschechoslowakei, wird nach dem kurz davor bestandenen Abitur ein 18-jähriges Mädchen, meine damalige Mitschülerin, von ihren Eltern gezwungen, in die Schweiz zu emigrieren. Gegen ihren Willen, wie sie später behaupten wird. Ein Jahr später, als ich den Sommer in London als Hilfskrankenschwester verbrachte und als immer noch große Lastkraftwagen mit Alexander Dubčeks Namen in riesigen Buchstaben durch England fuhren, wo ich, weil aus der besetzten Tschechoslowakei stammend, einen Wintermantel beträchtlich billiger kaufen durfte, traf ich in einem Vorstadtzug plötzlich die ein Jahr älter gewordene Irena Brežná. Ich fuhr am Wochenende aufs Land, um meine Tante zu besuchen. Irena arbeitete während der Ferien als Sozialhelferin irgendwo außerhalb Londons und war umgekehrt gerade in der Großstadt unterwegs. - Ein uns beide total überraschendes flüchtiges Wiedersehen, Kreuzen von zwei Lebenswegen, die später nicht unterschiedlicher sein konnten. Im Herbst 1990, während eines Studienaufenthaltes in Basel, wo Irena Brežná seit ihrer Ankunft im 'Westen' lebt, traf ich sie wieder. Ich Germanistin, sie deutschschreibende Schriftstellerin und Journalistin.

Irena Brežná studierte in Basel Psychologie, Philosophie und Russistik und arbeitete später als Lehrerin und Psychologin. Sie wurde Mitglied der Amnesty International und begann sich an vielen Orten der Welt - immer wieder in der ehemaligen Sowjetunion und in Afrika - für Entrechtete und Dissidenten zu engagieren. Ihr zweiter Sohn entstammt der Beziehung zu einem afrikanischen Intellektuellen. Tschetschenien zeichnete sie für ihren Einsatz im ersten tschetschenischen Krieg mit einem Verdienstorden aus. Seit 1989 besucht Brežná nach 21 Jahren erzwungener Enthaltsamkeit neben vielen anderen 'Problemorten' der Welt auch wieder ihre alte Heimat, Tschechien und die Slowakei.

Sie gehört zu der weltweit merklich ansteigenden Zahl der Migrantenschriftsteller, die mit der Heimat auch die eigene Kultur und Muttersprache verließen. Für Brežná bedeutete der Kampf um das angetroffene fremde Deutsch den Kampf ums Überleben, um eine neue Identität. Heute versteht sie sich als 'Fremde unter Fremden, heimisch in der Vielfalt',[1] wie sie sagt. Sie schreibt deutsch, spricht jedoch außer Russisch auch Französisch und Englisch, am Telefon beinahe jedes Mal in einer anderen Sprache. Die Schweiz ist zwar der feste Wohnsitz, zugleich jedoch nur einer der vielen Orte, wo sich ihr Leben und Wirken abspielen. Eigentlich ist sie seit 1968 nur noch unterwegs: eine Nomadin, in deren Texten viele Kulturen zueinander finden und gegenseitige Vergleiche wagen. Aber nicht nur das. Die Mitgliedschaft in der Amnesty International hat ihre Denk- und Schreibweise tief geprägt. Sie reist mit wachen Augen, liefert sich an die bereisten Orte aus, um zu erkennen und kritisch Stellung zu nehmen. Dass ihr Engagement mehr beinhaltet als das, was im journalistischen Beruf, auch im Kriegsjournalismus üblich und alltäglich ist, das scheint der ihr verliehene tschetschenische Verdienstorden unter Beweis zu stellen.

Von ihren bisher veröffentlichten fünf Büchern - eines davon, ein Kinderbuch, schrieb sie zusammen mit dem Vater ihres schwarzen Kindes - möchte ich auf den 1996 erschienenen Band *Falsche Mythen. Reportagen aus Mittel-und Osteuropa nach der Wende* näher eingehen. Er enthält 13 Reportagen, von denen die ersten sieben der komplizierten und vielschichtigen Auseinandersetzung mit dem Heimatland während der ersten Besuche nach der Wende Ausdruck verleihen. '[...] ein überzeugendes, oft erschütterndes Psychogramm des osteuropäischen Umbruchs',[2] schrieb man über dieses Buch, auch, dass es zu den interessantesten und stilistisch eindrucksvollsten Arbeiten zähle, die über den Epochenumbruch von 1989 erschienen seien.[3] Das Besondere an dem Buch ist, dass es zweifach interessant und auch zweifach erschütternd ist: einmal für Leser im einstigen Westen, einmal und ganz anders für jene Menschen, von denen Brežnás Buch erzählt. Als ich selbst das Buch mit slowakischen Studenten behandelte, kamen mitunter Widerstände auf, Ausdruck der Erschütterung des tradierten Bildes des 'Eigenen' von sich selbst, Ausdruck auch des womöglich überhaupt nicht erwarteten Verletztwerdens, ja des sich Beleidigtfühlens durch den inzwischen distanzierten Blick einer Landsmännin. Ich kann mich nicht entscheiden, welchen von den beiden Wirkungsaspekten dieser Art von Literatur ich mehr schätzen möchte. Zwölf Jahre nach dem Zusammenbruch des totalitären Sozialismus zeigt sich, dass beide Seiten, sowohl der Osten wie auch der Westen in einem Trugbild vom gegenseitigen Verhältnis lebten, folglich auch im Trugbild des je Eigenen und Fremden. Brežnás versprachlichter Blick in beide Richtungen stellt eine Art Schneewittchens untrüglicher Spiegel dar. Mit beiden Welten vertraut ist sie zugleich in keiner mehr zu Hause. Der Ort, wo sie sich in ihrer Entwurzeltheit immer wieder neu zusammensucht, ist die Welt der aufgesammelten fremden Wörter, die immer von neuem zu einer intensiven Konfrontation des verlorengegangenen Kultureigenen mit der angetroffenen Fremde herausfordern. Diese Konfrontation ist das konstitutive Element ihrer Texte.

In den *Falschen Mythen* geht es, wie der Titel bereits andeutet, um eine Art heilsame Entmythisierung, versuchte Objektivierung und Richtigstellung des Bildes Mittel- und Osteuropas nach der langen Abwesenheit der Autorin und angesichts ihrer mit der Zeit gewachsenen Sehnsucht danach. Indem Brežná die von ihrer Phantasie produzierten inneren Wunschbilder der verlassenen Heimat an der vorgefundenen Wirklichkeit misst, erschmuggelt sie dem nach Libuše Moníková Klarheit verschaffenden Deutsch (FM, S. 47) ein ganz besonderes Bild einer für alle Beteiligten ganz besonderen Konstellation: des allmählichen Zusammenkommens zweier nicht nur ökonomisch sondern auch, wie sich zeigt, in ihrer Mentalität sehr unterschiedlichen Welten: des konsumverwöhnten und daher ökonomisch und politisch triumphierenden kapitalistischen Westens mit dem in vielerlei Hinsicht zusammen-gebrochenen verarmten posttotalitären Osten.

Die erste der sieben Reportagen ('Meine kleine revolutionare Zelle. Reise in die samtene Revolution') ist der Rückkehr Brežnás in die ehemalige Tschechoslowakei unmittelbar nach Ausbruch der Wende gewidmet. Ihr ganz persönliches Problem dabei, das sie in mehreren Texten, sehr eindrücklich in den späteren tschetschenischen Reportagen behandelt, ist das in ihrer Erinnerung hängengebliebene schlechte Gewissen ob des 'feigen' Geflüchtetseins vor den russischen Panzern im Sommer 1968, das für sie dem Verrat an der Heimat gleichkam. Daher der Entschluss, diesmal zum erst möglichen Zeitpunkt zurückzueilen, um sozusagen selbst Hand anzulegen. Trotzdem ging, wie Brežnás selbstironischer Ton verrät, die Emigrationszeit nicht spurlos an ihr

vorbei: sie schreibt, wie sie sich 'einen dunkelgrünen, langen Mantel im
Stil der russischen Revolutionäre' kauft, und fährt fort:

> Ich fahre in die Revolution [...] Ankunft in Prag: [...]. Mein ersehnter
> osteuropäischer Geliebter trägt einen dicken, graumelierten Pullover [...]. Er
> sieht darin wie ein Wesen mit ungekämmtem, vor Kälte abstehendem Fell aus,
> er riecht nicht nach der Wildnis der Revolution. (FM, S. 12ff.)

Der durchästhetisierte westliche Lebensstil, dem so schwer zu widerstehen
ist, zumal für die Menschen aus dem schmuddeligen, grauen
sozialistischen Osten, ist jenes Unterscheidungsmerkmal, wo zuallererst
der Kulturschock stattfindet. So heißt es über das tschechoslowakische
Flugzeug auf dem Flug in die Heimat:

> Brüchig ist die dünne Plastik auf den Klapptischen, schäbig sind die
> Sesselüberzüge, vergilbt die Polyestervorhänge. [...] Der Übergang aus der
> sogenannten ersten in die zweite Welt beschäftigt zunächst die Sinnesorgane.
> [...] Glatt, glänzend, geebnet, glorreich ist die Hülle des Westens. Gut
> geschützt der Inhalt. Gut bezahlt die Fassadenbauer. Aus dem Mund
> wohlüberlegter Anstand. Nicht angreifbar. Der Flug von Zürich nach Prag ist
> ein drastisches Bremsen der galoppierenden Euphorie der letzten Tage. Hier
> stockt der Rhythmus, eine neue Melodie wird zaghaft eingeübt. (FM, S. 13)

Mit 'Rhythmus' und 'Melodie' gelingt der Autorin eines von einer
ganzen Reihe von Vergleichsbildern der beiden Welten. Je weniger es in
ihrer Heimat zu sehen gibt, umsomehr verzaubert sie die lieblich
klingende, sanfte Melodie der Muttersprache (FM, S. 16), wie sie schreibt,
deren Weichheit, welche der Beherrschbarkeit, etwa durch den die Zeit
streng einteilenden Sprachrhythmus trotzt: '[...] kein Kleid war sie'-
immer wieder vergleicht Brežná Fremdsprachen mit von ihr oft und gerne
gewechselten Kleidern -, 'sondern ein Subjekt, ein zu verführendes
allerdings' (FM, S. 16), heißt es. Als ob das rhythmische Ordnen der
Sprache - in diesem Fall der fremden deutschen - ihr tatsächlich mehr
Klarheit verleihen würde, Genauigkeit, außerdem eine in der emotionalen
Distanz begründete Unbefangenheit des Gebrauchs - in diesem Sinn wird
von Brežná ihre schon erwähnte Schriftstellerkollegin und Freundin
Libuše Moníková zitiert (FM, S. 47ff.) - kurz, als ob der Rhythmus das
rationale Ausdrucksvermögen der Sprache steigern würde, wogegen ihre
Melodieführung eher intuitiver Ausdruck der Kollektivseele der
jeweiligen Sprachbenutzer wäre.

Im Text 'Sprachbilder. Über Sprachen, Körper, Schreiben' geht die Autorin noch einmal ausführlich auf das sie stets besonders berührende Thema der Sprache ein. Mit 18 Jahren in einer unbekannten Sprachwelt angekommen, musste sie zuerst gegen die eigene Stummheit ankämpfen. 'Das Schreiben fing dort an' (FM, S. 58), bemerkt sie dazu. Für sie ist ihr eigenes Deutsch eine geschichtslose Sprache (FM, S. 61), wie die 'Fotos von weiblichen Akten eines blinden Fotografen', meint sie (FM, S. 57). Umso aufmerksamer geht sie damit um, jedes Wort gleichsam riskierend, in völliger und vereinsamter Eigenverantwortung, 'ohne den Schutz einer Sprachgemeinde', heißt es (FM, S. 59). Der mühsame, wohl bewusste Spracherwerb im Erwachsenenalter wurde für Brežná ein wesentlicher Bestandteil ihres Individuationsprozesses, der sie von der unbedächtig und zweifellos die Sprache verwendenden 'Sippe', wie sie meint, zwar unwiderruflich trenne, den sie jedoch nicht mehr aufgeben könne:

> Ich wache allmählich auf, begreife, dass ich so nicht mehr sprechen kann, nicht mehr sprechen will. Ich [...] ziehe meine Muttersprache aus, falte dieses [...] Kinderkleidchen zusammen, [...] kurz und verwaschen scheint es mir jetzt. (FM, S. 59)

Das Migrantendasein ergibt eine besondere sprachliche Konflikt-konstellation: einerseits erbrachte das erlebte Sprachtrauma eine nie mehr aufhörende Sehnsucht nach heimatlichem Sicheraufgehobensein, in welcher Sprache auch immer, andererseits führte es zu einem Grad an Sprachwachheit, an Sprachzweifel, der jedes Zugehörigkeitsgefühl von vorherein unmöglich macht. Migranten, umso mehr die schreibenden, sind nicht nur Kultur- sondern auch Sprachnomaden:

> Meine deutsche Stimme ist hoch wie die Stimme der Kastraten. Ich habe bei ihr Zuflucht gefunden vor der klebrigen, verführerischen Muttersprache, von der ich mich jedes Mal mit viel Kraft losreißen muss [...] ich fliehe vor dem Dämmerlicht der Kindheit [...], wo ich so heimisch bin, dass ich dort keine Augen brauche. Ich renne zu Worten ohne Geschichte. Das neue Haus hat luftige, nach nichts riechende, lichte Räume. (FM, S. 61)

Die zu Beginn als erzwungen erlebte Trennung von der Mutter-sprachengemeinschaft wird von Brežná später als eine Art Entbindung in individuelle Unabhängigkeit wahrgenommen, die, um bestehen zu können, lernen müsse, meint sie, 'Eigenwärme zu erzeugen' (FM, S. 62). Diese Eigenwärme ist meines Erachtens bei Brežná und ihresgleichen die eben nur ihnen eigene Quelle eines freieren, unabhängigeren und daher

objektiveren Blicks und Urteilens. Uns Muttersprachlern und Daheim-
gebliebenen - auf allen Seiten der überschrittenen Kultur- und Sprach-
grenzen - hat sie, haben Menschen wie sie Beides voraus.

In diesem Artikel ist es nicht möglich, auf die Sprachproblematik in
Irena Brežnás Texten im Detail einzugehen. Ich möchte nun noch einmal
kurz auf ihre Besuche in der Heimat zu sprechen kommen. Erfahrungen,
die ihre Texte wiedergeben, sammelte sie, wie gesagt, unmittelbar nach
dem Aufgehen des Eisernen Vorhangs, in einer Zeit, die sehr neu, sehr
kurz und sehr intensiv war und mittlerweile unwiederbringlich vorbei ist.
'Sind wir, die Emigranten und Emigrantinnen, das zukünftige "Ich"
Mittel- und Osteuropas?', lässt sie einen slowakischen Landsmann
einführend zum Text 'Das mitteleuropäische Gesicht, nur für den Westen
osteuropäisch' fragen (FM, S. 20). Sie zielt damit auf einen den aus dem
Westen nach langer Zeit zurückkehrenden Landsleuten ins Auge
stechenden Mentalitätszug der Slowaken, auf ihr, wie sie meint, sich mit
dem Individualismus schwertuendes monolithartiges Zusammenleben
(FM, S. 20). Als ein sich der Totalität widersetzender solidarischer
Protest aller ist dieses Phänomen auch aus anderen Ländern des
ehemaligen Ostblocks bekannt. Bei den Slowaken hängt er darüber hinaus
mit ihrer besonderen kulturellen Überlebensgeschichte zusammen und
macht sich bis heute auf vielfache Weise vor allem negativ bemerkbar.
Die, glaube ich, zum Teil auch nur scheinbare Solidarität vor der Wende
verwandelt sich mit den wachsenden sozialen Unterschieden während des
Reprivatisierungsprozesses nach 1989 in ein kollektives Hass- und
Neidgefühl aller gegenüber allen, während offiziell kollektiver
Nationalstolz auf Erreichtes vorgetäuscht wird. Individualisten haben es
immer noch schwer in der Slowakei: 'Eine an der Nähe kränkelnde Welt,
[...] Der inzestuöse Mief [...] Von der allzu warmen, gepressten Luft des
Clans bekomme ich Atemnot', heißt es bei Brežná dazu (FM, S. 26ff.).
Nicht weniger überrascht begegnen die heimkehrenden Emigranten der
hinter dem Eisernen Vorhang bis zum Schluss überlebenden Illusion vom
paradiesischen Westen. Nichts wurde so intensiv herbeigewünscht und zu
Hause je nach Möglichkeit präzisest nachgeahmt - umsomehr natürlich
von den privilegierten Parteibonzen, wie der westliche Konsumstil:

> Im Badezimmer stehen wie Wachposten oder Schutzengel [...] Produkte
> westlicher Marken. [...] Hat Ivana Potemkinsche Dörfer gebaut? [...] Hat sie
> ihre Würde in der importierten Fassade gefunden? Ist ästhetischer Genuss ein
> Menschenrecht? Mitteleuropa vermutet unter dem Hochglanzpapier des
> Westens Würde, Schönheit, Leben an sich. (FM, S. 20)

Dass somit absurderweise der kapitalistische Westen selbst am Aufrechterhalten des Eisernen Vorhangs beteiligt zu sein schien, ist eine wohl
überraschende doch logische Schlussfolgerung:

> Meine Generation hatte den Rückzug ins behaglich Private angetreten. Fenster
> zu, draußen herrschte die hässliche Hydra […]. Die Klage meiner Landsleute
> war immer da, seit ich mich erinnern kann. Ihr monotoner Redefluss der
> Belanglosigkeiten übertünchte das Wesentliche. (FM, S. 22f.)

Quer durch die anderthalb Jahrhunderte slowakischer Emanzipations-
geschichte hört man Schriftsteller immer wieder über dieses 'Fenster zu'
der Slowaken klagen, zugleich jedoch ihre Überlebenskunst hervorheben.
Möglicherweise ist beides eine antrainierte Verhaltensweise angesichts der
tausendjährigen Unterdrückung. Die 40 Jahre Totalität waren in diesem
Zusammenhang nur deren fatale Fortsetzung. Fatal, weil die Slowaken
inzwischen eine relativ sehr gut ausgebildete und fähige junge
Industriegesellschaft geworden sind, wie sich zeigt, doch mit
beträchtlichen Versäumnissen im sozialen Bereich sowie in Weltoffenheit
und der Fähigkeit zu kritischer Selbstreflexion.

Brežná findet für die unterschiedlichen Aspekte des slowakischen,
vielleicht auch mitteleuropäischen Charakters noch mehr Bezeichnungen.
Auf die Frage des Sohnes, warum die Slowaken - nach der Wende,
versteht sich - wie im Traum wandeln, wie nach einer Katastrophe,
antwortet sie im Text 'Flüssiger Fetisch. Rückkehr nach Trenčín': 'Das
ist Mitteleuropa. Die Region der Melancholie' (FM, S. 30f.), eines sich,
meine ich wiederum, stets weiter fortsetzenden Gefühls, Opfer der
Verhältnisse, gleichzeitig ein Held in deren Erdulden zu sein. Jetzt, wo
die Menschen mit der demokratischen Öffnung ihres Landes umzugehen
lernen, wird dieses Lebensgefühl paradoxerweise viel häufiger und lauter
zum Ausdruck gebracht. 'Das Geschwür dieses Landes ist sein
Negativismus', lässt die Autorin eine in ihrer Heimatstadt Trenčín
angetroffene ehemalige Klassenfreundin behaupten, die inzwischen den
amerikanischen Lebensstil ausprobieren konnte:

> […] alles ist schon gedacht, geschrieben, gedruckt worden. Und wir haben es
> nicht gewusst. Je mehr ich davon erfahre, um so blinder hasse ich die
> Kommunisten, dass sie uns diese Welten vorenthalten haben. Schau uns an,
> seelische Analphabetinnen und Analphabeten. (FM, S. 36)

Es geht nicht darum, Ihnen ein negatives Bild meines eigenen Landes zu vermitteln. Wie bereits gesagt, es schlängelt sich durch unsere ganze Literaturgeschichte neben Liebesbezeugungen wie ein roter Faden eine ähnlich schroffe Kritik der slowakischen Schriftsteller selbst an ihrem Volk, die vor allem eines im Sinn hat: den kritischen Selbst-erkenntnisprozess einer Nation vorwärtszutreiben, die während der tausend Jahre Fremdherrschaft letztlich doch erfolgreich ums Überleben kämpfte, und die allein im 20. Jahrhundert beinahe alle zwanzig Jahre einen ideologischen und politischen Regimewechsel erlebte. Brežná vergleicht die Slowakei nach 1989 mit jener vor 1968. Ich, die ich mich auch mit älteren Entwicklungsepochen der slowakischen Kultur befasse, glaube, das sich neben den von der Totalität angerichteten Schäden heute auch Entwicklungstendenzen bemerkbar machen, die älteren Datums sind und nach deren Deutung daher weiter zurück in der Vergangenheit gesucht werden müsste.

Der Titel der letzten der sieben Reportagen lautet: 'Das Reich des unendlichen Provisoriums. Die Slowakei am Vorabend ihrer Unabhängigkeit'. In diesem mittlerweile 10 Jahre alten Text setzt sich die Autorin mit der Zeit unmittelbar vor dem letzten, zugleich eminent wichtigen politischen Wechsel auseinander - vor dem Zerfall der Tschechoslowakei in zwei selbständige Staaten. Ihre Beobachtungen sind auch deshalb interessant, weil sich noch heute beiderseits der neuen Grenze viele Tschechen und Slowaken fragen, wie es dazu überhaupt kommen konnte. 'Die Slowakei wartet auf die Tat, die von außen auf sie zukommen mag oder auch nicht', schreibt Brežná,

> Der slowakische Staat kommt auf die Menschen zu […]. Sie stehen im fatalistischen Nebel wie diese fünf Arbeiter […], die sagen: Was können wir schon tun? Wir sind klein, wir wissen nichts […], die Politiker da oben entscheiden über unsere Köpfe hinweg […]. (FM, S. 68f.)

Ich glaube, dass dieser 'fatalistische Nebel' und jenes 'Fenster zu' zusammen gehören und diese Mischung ein wesentliches Merkmal des slowakischen Volkes ist, die schon erwähnte lange genug trainierte Überlebensfähigkeit angesichts der Fremdbestimmung und drohenden kulturellen Entwurzelung. 'In der Slowakei ist der Mensch vor der Endstation ausgestiegen, denn er glaubt nicht an die Chimäre eines Ziels' (FM, S. 65), meint Brežná,

> Hier fängt der slawische Raum an, hier unterscheidet man bei jedem Tätigkeitswort den vollendeten und unvollendeten Verbaspekt [...]. Der unvollendete Verbaspekt bedeutet in den slawischen Sprachen Kontemplation, Wiederholung [...]. Der Mensch steht inmitten der Zeit, einbezogen ins Geschehen, das sich ohne Anfang, ohne Ende über ihn wälzt.- Die Slowakei ist das Reich des unvollendeten Verbaspekts, daher der Eindruck des Statischen, der leisen Bewegung im Kreis in einem [...] Provisorium, das jedoch ewig zu dauern scheint. (FM, S. 67)

Interessanterweise gibt es bereits in älterer deutscher Reiseliteratur über Pressburg (Bratislava), die heutige Hauptstadt der Slowakei und Umgebung, ab und zu die Bemerkung, hier fange bereits der Orient an!

In diesem Zusammenhang würde sich ein Vergleich mit jenen Texten anbieten, die von Brežnás Besuchen Russlands berichten. Mit dem mächtigsten der slawischen Völker verband die Slowaken früher eine leidenschaftliche Sehnsucht nach brüderlicher Hilfe im Kampf gegen die Unterjochung. Die Geschichte lehrte uns inzwischen eines Besseren, trotzdem kann - auch in Bezug auf die so oft diskutierte Frage, wo eigentlich Europa zu Ende ist - von manchen Wesenszügen der Slowaken ausgehend auch auf allgemeinere - slawische Züge geschlossen werden, wie Brežná es tut. 'Europa ist eine Treppe. Je weiter nach Osten, um so tiefer steigt man hinab', lässt sie einen ehemaligen slowakischen Bauern, nun Schweißer in einem ostslowakischen Eisenwerk, behaupten, 'Böhmen und Mähren sind westlicher, eine Stufe höher. Daher wird es den Leuten dort besser gehen als uns' (FM, S. 72). Über die frühere Sowjetunion heißt es ein Stück weiter:

> Die alte Sehnsucht Mitteleuropas nach dem Westen, das Unbehagen vor dem Osten, die Angst, dass in diesem Zwischenraum wieder die Vertikale umkippt, zur Horizontalen wird. Die ukrainische Grenze ist nicht weit von Kaschau. Dahinter das unüberschaubare Russland, dubisko, die alte, mächtige slawische Eiche [...]. Ein besseres Bild wäre die russische Steppe als Inbegriff der Horizontalen. (FM, S. 72f.)

Die als unaufhaltsam erscheinende aktivistische westliche Zielstrebigkeit, der die Menschen voneinander entfremdende, den Individuationsprozess fördernde Konkurrenzgeist streben nach Brežná, einer Vertikalen gleich, immer weiter in die Höhe - das bergige West-, Mittel- und Südeuropa könnten als deren geographischer Ausdruck gelten, während die weite Steppe umgekehrt der passivistisch anmutenden kontemplativen Horizontalen gleicht, wo es die Menschen - einer Herde gleich -

zusammentreibt und nach kollektiver Wärme suchen lässt. In der
Slowakei, wo der Westbogen des Karpathenmassivs die Grenze zwischen
beiden Regionen zu verkörpern scheint, haben wir es, wie sich nach der
Wende zeigt, mit beiden Denk- und Lebensweisen zu tun.
Tschechoslowakisten auf der einen, Nationalisten auf der anderen Seite.
Die Einen wünschen sich nach Brežná ein Land des vollendeten
Verbaspekts, 'eine Abfolge von eruptiven Taten […], die immerfort neue
Taten hervorbringen, […] das Machertum, […] schnelle Annäherung an
den Westen' (FM, S. 68). Dagegen, meint sie, versprach Vladimír Mečiar,
der populistische Ministerpräsident, den anderen 'den unvollendeten
Verbaspekt, die Langsamkeit, das Verharren in der sozialen Gemeinde'
(FM, S. 68). 'Der Westen und der Osten', schreibt sie, 'die westliche
Arroganz, das Besserwissertum und die östlichen Minderwertig-
keitskomplexe mit ihrer Suche nach dem nächsten Feind, an dem reibend
man wachsen kann' (FM, S. 73). Dass Herdenwärme und Suche nach
dem Feind zwei Seiten einer Medaille sind und daher zusammengehören,
bezeugt die Tatsache, dass der slowakische Ultranationalismus neben den
westlich orientierten Tschechoslowakisten zugleich 'juden-, ungarn- und
intellektuellenfeindlich ist' (FM, S. 76). Ich glaube, dass trotz der
überwiegenden Mehrheit jener Stimmen in der Slowakei, die eindeutig auf
dem 'westlichen' Weg des Landes bestehen, der lodernde Konflikt im
Land mehr symbolisiert als nur den innenpolitischen Wirtschafts- und
Machtkampf. Er ist die durch konkrete Menschen verkörperte, lebendige
Grenze zwischen West und Ost, die zugleich übernational und
überstaatlich zu verstehen ist.

Zum Schluss möchte ich noch einen letzten Aspekt von Brežnás
Konfrontation der beiden Regionen Europas erwähnen. Für das Verstehen
der bestehenden Unterschiede ist er umso interessanter, als er nur im
übertragenen Sinne als ein Aspekt des West-Ost-Verhältnisses
wahrgenommen werden und nicht anhand ethnischer, geographischer,
klimatischer oder kulturgeschichtlicher Gegebenheiten interpretiert
werden kann. In der schon erwähnten Reportage 'Sprachbilder' unterzieht
sie westdeutsche und ehemalige DDR-Schriftstellerinnen einem
Vergleich. Diesmal stellt sie in erster Linie Folgen der gelebten
politischen bzw. ideologischen Unterschiede fest, die zwar mit den schon
erwähnten zum Teil gleichzusetzen sind, die jedoch nach 40 Jahren
unterschiedlicher Realität sogar bei einem und demselben Volk
anzutreffen sind. Auch diesmal gelingt es ihr, die beobachteten
Unterschiede mit grammatischen Kategorien zu fassen.

> Im Berliner Schriftstellerhaus sitzen literaturproduzierende Frauen. Aus Ost und West. Nur eine zieht mich an. Der schwere Busen drückt sie zu Boden, fünf Kinder hat sie gestillt. Für diesen Literaturanlass hat sie ihre Haare nicht gewaschen. Ihre Tage in der Küche trägt sie als ranzigen Geruch im blauen Pullover auf sich. Eine Intellektuelle aus Ostberlin. Vertane Möglichkeiten. In ihrem Körper hat sich der Konjunktiv niedergelassen […]. Wenn die Umstände anders gewesen wären, wenn […]. Ich kann die Augen von dieser Frau nicht abwenden. Wenn sie in ein Schaumbad steigen würde, wenn sie Haarbalsam auf die verklebten Haare auftragen würde […]. Der Osten der verpassten Möglichkeiten wühlt mich auf. Nicht das Ergebnis der Waschung abwarten, […] nur die Möglichkeit […] denken, das Aufblühen […]. Ich will sie ihr nicht nehmen, die Poesie des Konjunktivs. (FM, S. 54f.)

Dazu im Vergleich heißt es über eine Frau aus dem Westen:

> Ihr gegenüber sitzt eine gepflegte, schöne Westlerin, ruhig gealtert im Indikativ, geworden wie geworden, zur ebenmässigen Form gegossene, erschöpfte Möglichkeiten. Das könnte Prosa sein. Das wühlt mich nicht auf. (FM, S. 55)

So mögen sich die zwei gelebten politischen Systeme von außen, dem 20 Jahre lang trainierten westlichen Blick der Autorin darbieten. Als Konjunktivform der kommunistischen Utopie gegenüber der Indikativform der in Tat umgesetzten Möglichkeiten der kapitalistischen Marktwirtschaft. Für uns zu Hause jedoch besaß der real gelebte Sozialismus keine Möglichkeiten mehr, der Alltag war nüchternste perspektivloseste Prosa. Indikativ als Zwangsjacke. Den Konjunktiv herbeigesehnter Möglichkeiten verbanden wir dagegen in unserer Phantasie mit der Welt hinter dem Eisernen Vorhang, mit dem Westen. Daraus ist nun ebenfalls der Indikativ des auch für uns nun real Verwirklichbaren geworden, auch wieder Prosa. Insofern hat Brežná recht, wenn sie behauptet: 'Die Utopien verlassen die Sprache. Der Indikativ wartet im Flur, Berichte von Taten drängen sich vor, Träume, Alpträume hinter sich lassend' (FM, S. 56). Für uns war die Totalität ein Alptraum, der Gottseidank zu Ende ist. Doch mit der Ankunft im realen Kapitalismus verloren wir auch den utopischen Traum an eine wahrhaft gerechte und humane Welt. Dass wir uns nicht von vornherein einen neuen, dritten Weg überlegten, was sich viele Menschen im Westen von uns gewünscht hätten, zeugt von unserem Müdegewordensein vom Umgang mit dem theoretisch Möglichen und von unserem Ausruhenwollen im praktisch Verwirklichbaren. Von Menschen wie Irena

Brežná jedoch, die zwischen den zusammenkommenden Welten stehen, erhoffe ich mir auf jeden Fall mehr: eine keiner von beiden Seiten tributpflichtige objektivierende Sicht, möglicherweise die Quelle künftiger Utopien.   Immerhin hat Brežná 5 Millionen ihrer Landsleute zwei Jahrzehnte kritischen Vergleichenkönnens voraus.   Eine nützlichere Lektüre kann ich mir für die Slowaken daher kaum vorstellen.

Anmerkungen

[1] Irena Brežna, *Falsche Mythen*, eFeF-Vlg: Bern, 1996, S. 29. Im Folgenden bezeichnet als FM und Seitenangaben.

[2] Robert Elstner: *Brežná, Irena: Falsche Mythen*, ekz-Informationsdienst.

[3] Vgl. DeutschlandRadio am 29. September 1996.

Anthony Bushell

**The Return of the Native, or the Neighbours are back: Anna
Mitgutsch's novel *Haus der Kindheit***

Haus der Kindheit explores the issue of relationships between neighbours not at the
point of frontier, as between sovereign states, or even different linguistic groups, but at
a point within the state. Mitgutsch's depiction of the return to Austria of a successful
Jewish American who seeks out his mother's former home in provincial Austria raises
questions of identity, exclusion, acknowledgement and the ownership and control not
only of physical property but also of a community's collective history and memory.
Mitgutsch draws a dark picture of a society's ability to recognise its past actions or to
avoid repeating those attitudes which gave birth to them.

In the United Kingdom geography has ceased to be a compulsory subject
at secondary school level. It comes as something of a revelation to many
British students of German, therefore, to be shown a map of Germany and
to be asked to count how many countries share a border with Germany.
When that question is slightly amended and the concept of the German
Sprachraum replaces the idea of Germany and when, instead of other
countries, the idea of other linguistic communities is used, then these
students, often for the first time, realise to their surprise that German-
speakers can be defined as a nation of neighbours.

These neighbours come in many forms: ancient and well-
established states on the one hand, such as France or Denmark, or entities
created or restored within the last few years, such as Slovakia or the Czech
Republic. The nature of these neighbouring communities has not
remained static. Until recently the Frisians of North Germany and the
Slovenes of Austria shared a similar status: both minority linguistic
communities with fellow-speakers in an adjacent state who also
constituted a linguistic minority, in the Netherlands and Yugoslavia
respectively. But that status can change suddenly, and Austrian Slovenes
now find that their language has been raised to the privileged status of the
national language of an independent and sovereign state just across their
border. It will still require some time to gauge how that change of status
will impact upon the consciousness of Slovene speakers within Austria
itself.

I mention these facts because they all serve to remind us that locked
into our concepts of neighbours are diachronic and synchronic dynamics
which are never wholly at rest.

Sometimes a relationship between neighbours can undergo profound but almost unexamined transformations. Germany's most troubled relationship with its neighbours has probably been that with Poland, yet for the first forty years of its existence the Federal Republic of Germany enjoyed, if one may use a sporting expression, a period of 'time out' with its frontier with Poland, and a physical proximity was suspended in temporal terms. It is difficult to measure how this absence of direct contact might have helped heal deep wounds and allowed these two post-war states to re-establish themselves initially free from the frictions of daily dealings.

Germany's relationships with its neighbours are not simply replicated in miniature by Austria. There is of course one immediate and profound difference. In all its contacts with its neighbouring states Germany remains, and this surely cannot be overstressed, by far the larger element, all the more so since its population was increased upon reunification with East Germany after 1989. Not only is Austria significantly smaller than its larger German and Italian neighbours to the north and the south, but also relatively moderately sized neighbouring states such as the Czech Republic and Hungary have larger populations than Austria. Size will have very tangible political consequences in an expanded European Union when we recall how voting power is coupled to size of population. And it colours and shapes the way in which a state such as Austria regards those who surround it.

So far I have been content to define neighbours in political or linguistic terms. A political boundary or a different language is a traditional and familiar marker of those concepts of difference, of 'otherness' with which we often acknowledge and denote ourselves and those whom we consider to be somehow different – in other words, markers to show where our world finishes and somebody else's begins. And no doubt some of these concepts have deep, almost atavistic roots in concepts of family, kin, tribe or community.

But these are not the only ideas of neighbours that reside in our consideration of Germany's - and Austria's - relations to those who are to be found close to them but are not necessarily identical or synonymous with them.

What I wish to do here is to examine a text by the Austrian writer Anna Mitgutsch, because it raises a number of issues which I believe to be central to our discussion of the idea of neighbours and strangers in the German and Austrian context and because Mitgutsch's text plays out many of those arguments that will claim our attention. I have also had in mind that the writer of fiction operates with different criteria to those who at first sight might prove more reliable guides. In his biography of the French war-time Vichy leader Marshal Pétain, Professor Richard Griffiths wrote: 'It is not the duty of the historian or biographer to accuse or to justify, but to describe and to attempt to explain'.[1] But sometimes, as we shall see, neutrality is not enough, it is not adequate to the situation under discussion and it is left to creative writers to offer something more than documentation.

Haus der Kindheit, Mitgutsch's sixth novel, appeared in the year 2000.[2] It received extensive critical coverage in Germany and Switzerland and praise from leading literary figures such as Erich Hackl and Karl-Markus Gauß, but rather more restrained attention in much of Mitgutsch's native Austria, so much so that Mitgutsch has claimed that the book's success has been in the face of media coverage in Austria: 'Das Buch hat sich […] gegen die Absicht der Wiener Mediengewichtung gut verkauft'.[3] It is indeed an uncomfortable work for Austrian society. By the standards of Mitgutsch's previous novels, *Haus der Kindheit* has a marked clarity and simplicity of narrative technique, and for once it offers a male character at the heart of the story. That story is at first sight uncomplicated and quickly retold: Max, the central character, left his native Austria for America as a child along with his Jewish parents and brothers in time to escape the deportations and liquidation that were to engulf the rest of the family and their Jewish community during the Second World War. The mother's only hold on her past is a photograph of the house which Max's grandfather had had built for her on her marriage, a symbol of a once prosperous, successful, cultivated and far from rigidly orthodox Jewish family in the Austrian provinces.

The novel traces the descent into near poverty in New York of Max's family and Max's mother's inability to find a secure financial or emotional hold in her new world. Max's mother, Mira, clings for many years to the dream of returning to her house, and of being restored to a society and a European culture from which she has been torn. Mitgutsch places that house clearly in the Austrian provinces, 'in einer österreichischen Kleinstadt' (p. 8). It echoes Mitgutsch's own background: she herself was raised and lives for much of the year in her native Linz in Upper Austria.

Max grows up to be an extremely successful and fashionable architect and interior designer in New York. He is very comfortable in

American society; his financial success is matched by his sexual conquests. Only a reluctance to father children betrays the scars of his unsettled childhood. He is very much at home in this new world and it certainly is not failure to integrate that turns his thoughts back to Austria, it is his mother's photograph and her silent longing that do not leave him. She has ensured that Max speaks German, her native language, although it is that of those who forced her to leave her home in Austria. As a result, the idea does not quite leave Max that he should return one day to Austria and claim the home that had been his mother's property and the house of his own near forgotten childhood. The novel reminds us that our affinities are not always elective and that our relationships to our neighbours may not be our own but may have been acquired or inherited:

> Es war, als hätte Miras Sehnsucht sich in seiner Phantasie eingenistet, eine
> leise, beharrliche Sehnsucht, die sich betäuben ließ, aber die nie verstummte.
> (p. 46)

The novel dwells for the most part on Max's ever more frequent visits to Austria, his attempts to make good his legal claim to the house after his mother's death in the face of a hostile and unyieldingly insensitive Austrian bureaucracy, his decision upon his retirement to settle in that house and his encounters with the fragile remnants of the town's Jewish community.

In this brief synopsis we see immediately how many themes raised by the topic 'Neighbours and Strangers' are at work in Mitgutsch's *Haus der Kindheit*. These issues revolve around ideas of space, of shared history, of memory or denial of that history, of recognition both at a legal and a moral level, and recognition also at an institutional and at a personal level, of restitution and the right to be accommodated. In focusing on the Jewish community, Mitgutsch places this debate not in the more obvious context of linguistic or national confrontation, as say between Czechs and Germans, but at points of ethnic, religious and racial frictions, and thus Mitgutsch reminds us that the meeting point between neighbours and strangers can take place not only at the very edge of sovereignty – that is at a frontier – but also just within those lines of demarcation that we call international boundaries.

The problems raised by *Haus der Kindheit*, and in particular the issues of dispossession and restitution, are not limited exclusively to the fate of Austria's Jewish community. Similar issues became immediately apparent in Germany after the fall of the Berlin Wall in 1989 when the question of ownership of former private property in the GDR became very urgent, and today we are witnessing the revival of an acrimonious debate concerning the Beneš decrees and the legal rights and claims of the German-speaking community that once lived in what is now the Czech Republic and Slovakia.

Mitgutsch places this debate in the tangible context of the fate of a particular house, a building and in the lives of those who possess it. The novel begins with an image, however, of dispossession. On the first page Max recalls how in his earliest New York childhood his mother would take her children to the Atlantic coast: 'Mira […] wies mit dem Finger auf jene graue, manchmal unsichtbare Linie, die den Himmel vom Wasser trennte: Dort drüben liegt Europa' (p. 7).

But Mira does not possess the quiet grandeur we associate with Anselm Feuerbach's portrait of the gazing Iphigenia.[4] And Goethe's Iphigenie reminds us that even in her physical exile she was linked by invisible bonds to her homeland and confidently expected these feelings to be replicated by those from whom she was parted. We recall Goethe's familiar words in Iphigenie's opening speech:

> Denn ach mich trennt das Meer von den Geliebten,
> Und an dem Ufer steh ich lange Tage,
> Das Land der Griechen mit der Seele suchend.[5]

It is clear that no one will set out from Europe and cross the water to restore Mira to her home and to those whom she loves, for no one is looking for her, and this raises a concept at the heart of the idea of neighbours and belonging. It is not a one-sided act. To be a neighbour, to be a part of a community, requires not only that we see ourselves as someone else's neighbour, as entities that are recognised as impinging upon the world of others, but that others acknowledge our existence and our presence.

It is a recurring theme in post-war Austrian studies that, in contrast to Germany, there was a noticeable reluctance and reticence in Austria to seek out those who had gone into exile and to encourage them to return. Peter Eppel, in his study of the dilemma facing Austrian émigrés in the United States who were considering returning after 1945, noted the many discouragements that held them back from returning:

> vor allem […] weil die Erinnerungen an das in der alten Heimat erlittene Unrecht mit der Angst, zumindest erneut auf Ablehnung zu stoßen, verbunden war, und diese Angst durch das Fortleben des Antisemitismus, die halbherzige

Durchführung der Entnazifizierung, negative Erfahrungen bei Besuchen und durch den Mangel an Aufforderungen zur Rückkehr eher verstärkt wurde.[6]

In being denied a place as accepted neighbours and fellow-citizens within Austrian society, Jews had a number of ways, they could scarcely be deemed choices, to respond, and these are worked out in Max's own family history.   As the family, robbed of its own sense of place and purpose in Austrian society, disintegrates in New York each member responds differently.   Max's father, now estranged from his mother, becomes a passionate Zionist and Max's elder brother eventually resettles in Israel, the middle brother fails to establish himself in the new world and, tortured by schizophrenia, ultimately descends into madness and an early death.   Max's mother, unable to master English adequately, passes her days on the fringes of New York's Jewish community, lapsing into Yiddish and ceasing to speak German, irredeemably displaced both linguistically and socially.   She and those that suffered her fate are lost between these two worlds and are at home in neither.   Max observes to himself as he visits his mother and her ageing Jewish acquaintances in New York:

> Da saßen sie dann in winzigen, muffigen Stuben, die mit dem bunten Kitsch aus Osteuropa und mit Familien- und Hochzeitsfotos überladen waren.   Die nach außen zur Schau gestellte Verachtung für *The Old Country*, das ihnen das Lebensrecht entrissen hatte, schien in diesen Wohnzimmern und Küchen in nostalgische Sehnsucht umzuschlagen. (p. 22)

Only in more recent times has the state of Austria admitted the reluctance of the young Second Republic to call back the artists and intellectuals that had been driven away.   In the words of Kunststaatssekretär Franz Morak on a visit to Israel to attend the opening of a Sigmund Freud exhibition in Tel Aviv in 2002: 'Es ist eine zutiefst tragische Tatsache, dass die junge Zweite Republik nach 1945 kaum Anstrengungen unternommen hat, diese Künstler und Intellektuellen wieder nach Wien einzuladen'.[7]

Max alone of the family becomes the successful American citizen. He is not obliged to seek re-entry into Austrian society but his return represents a challenge to that society.   Linguistically and socially secure in his American identity, Max is in many respects a free agent in his decision to discover the house of his childhood, a property that had subsequently passed into local hands under the terms of the Aryanisation laws.   (We later discover that once Max's grandfather had been removed to a death camp the family property was squabbled over by Austrian Nazis as they enjoyed the first fruits of the Anschluss.)

How would post-war Austrian society respond to those who once were its neighbours? Austrian society had of course changed dramatically since the exile to America of Max's parents. It has been estimated that over 27% of Austrian Jewry perished between the years 1939–1945.[8] Over 128,000 Jews had fled Austria or were expelled, leaving the once thriving Jewish community virtually wiped out.[9] Having removed Jews as neighbours, the National Socialist state had systematically eradicated their physical and legal presence by the whole-scale re-allocation of Jewish property to loyal Nazi supporters. In Vienna alone it has been calculated that seventy thousand dwellings were Aryanised, a popular move in a city with a notoriously acute housing shortage, and well-known Jewish properties such as the Herzmansky department store were taken over by Austrian or German rivals, often at a fraction of their commercial value.[10]

Although Austria was ultimately to pay the price for the role of many of its citizens in the Third Reich by being subject to Allied occupation for a decade, the effects of the Jewish pogroms could not be reversed and in this respect Austria had become and remained in many districts, especially outside of Vienna, virtually *judenrein* from 1945. But, as has been seen not only in Austria, homogeneous and apparently successful societies are particularly ill-equipped to cope with any social phenomenon that is perceived to threaten that homogeneity. As the sociologist Bülent Diken has observed in his study of Turkish migrant communities in Denmark:

> cosy Denmark has another side, and this is illustrated by its problem with the way it has tackled immigration and with its fear of "strangers". Denmark remains one of the most culturally homogeneous countries in Europe and thus experiences social and cultural heterogeneity rather traumatically.[11]

Max's first visit to Austria and the family home is brief and takes place immediately after the end of the Second World War. In the uniform of an American corporal he snatches a few moments to visit the family house of which he has only a photograph and a distant recollection. It is occupied and showing signs of neglect. Max encounters a young woman in the garden of the house and addresses her in perfect German: 'Sein fehlerfreies Deutsch rief nicht die geringste Spur freundlichen Erstaunens hervor' (p. 36). Instead she buries her face, runs into the house and bolts the door, refusing to make any contact with Max. This is a fictional encounter which takes place in 1945. At exactly the same time, but in reality, someone in a rather different type of uniform is recalling a similar response. Primo Levi, in his book *The Truce* (*La Tregua*), the sequel to *If this is a Man* (*Se questo è un uomo*), describes the days immediately following his release from a German concentration camp in 1945. On the tortuously slow return to his native Italy, Levi is delayed in Munich in the October of 1945. It is his first opportunity to walk amongst the people who had once been his captors. Still in his prison clothes, he goes in search of a response, convinced that he would be the object of some form of interest:

> As I wandered around the streets of Munich, full of ruins, near the station where our train lay stranded once more, I felt I was moving among throngs of insolvent debtors, as if everybody owed me something, and refused to pay. I was among them, in the enemy camp, among the *Herrenvolk*; but the men were few, many were mutilated, many dressed in rags like us. I felt that everybody should interrogate us, read in our faces who we were, and listen to our tale in humility. But no one looked us in the eyes, no one accepted the challenge; they were deaf, blind and dumb, imprisoned in their ruins, as in a fortress of wilful ignorance, still strong, still capable of hatred and contempt, still prisoners of their old temple of pride and guilt.[12]

What Levi experienced on the streets of Munich is replicated in what Max encounters in the fictional town of H. His existence is denied, his would-be neighbours refuse to acknowledge his very presence, his suffering or even his right to claim their attention. They shut Max out physically, hiding behind their doors, which were ironically but pointedly once his childhood doors, and, as Mitgutsch shows at a later point, denying him his place in their midst by means of the law and with the full authority of the Austrian state.

As Max begins his more frequent returns to Austria he has to acknowledge that the history that he carries within him is not necessarily one shared by others, and that the passage of time has not brought enlightenment to others. Again it is at the personal and private level that Mitgutsch wishes to work. On Max's second visit in 1974 he finds himself in a railway compartment listening to two mature ladies in conversation. As the two women peer out of the train window they recall with considerable fondness the outings into the Austrian countryside on which they had gone as young girls and as members of what must have been a Nazi-approved organisation:

Die Mädelführerin, warf die andere ein, wie hat sie doch schnell geheißen, weißt du, die mit der Gretlfrisur, die hat uns so begeistert. Kannst du dich an das Lied erinnern? [...] Das war achtunddreißig, sagte sie, mein Gott, und es ist, als wäre es gestern gewesen. (p. 63)

There is no interregnum of wisdom or repentance to separate the memory of events from the events themselves, and Max must realise painfully that his past is not automatically that of those who were once his parents' neighbours and those who will be his again when he re-establishes his home in Austria. Whilst these women were enjoying the Austrian landscape as young girls, a landscape from which incidentally they have never been dislodged and to which therefore a continuity of experience exists, Max and his family were moving from one poor rent to another in the less agreeable districts of New York. The concept of neighbourhood for Max has been ruptured and it cannot be shared with those whom he faces in the railway carriage.

Max's dilemma is brought vividly to his own consciousness by his encounters with the landlord of the first non-descript hotel he chooses to live in when he returns to the town of his birth. The landlord tries to place his new guest into some scheme of identity. An air of provincial hostility to the outer world is evident in his attitude. The problem exists for both parties and the landlord's initial curiosity exposes the paradox of Max's position:

Besuchen Sie hier Verwandte, fragte der Wirt, als Max sich an den Frühstückstisch setzte.
Nein, antwortete Max, ich kenne keinen Menschen hier.
Aber Sie sind doch hier geboren, es steht in Ihrem Paß, beharrte der Wirt.
Max schwieg. (p. 65)

Is Max laying claim to an affinity to which he has no right? The landlord's curiosity is finally quenched by Max's question:

Sagen Sie, fragte Max, gibt es hier eine jüdische Gemeinde?
Wieso, fragte der Wirt verblüfft zurück. Er schaute Max minutenlang forschend an. Dann schien ihm ein Licht aufzugehen, und ein pfiffiges, verstochenes Grinsen huschte über sein Gesicht [...] und der Wirt stellte keine Fragen mehr. (pp. 65-66)

Revealingly both exchanges end in silence. Good neighbourly relations, be it between sovereign states or simply those conducted over the garden fence, require dialogue and Mitgutsch is preparing the reader in *Haus der Kindheit* for the failure of that dialogue.

Following his arrival in Austria, Max does attempt to enter into dialogue with the local authorities in the matter of the restitution of the family property. He discards advice to employ a good lawyer, seeing his own position so clearly as one that is based on morality and natural justice that the services of a lawyer appear to him to be superfluous. His initial contact, however, quickly establishes that his dealings are not to be circumscribed by good neighbourly relations but by a cold officialdom. Max is asked to produce the death certificates for his missing relatives, an uncle and aunt who had shared the family home and who had not escaped the holocaust. Max asks where he is to find certificates for people who have been murdered:

> Das zu beantworten liege nicht in seiner Kompetenz, erklärte der Beamte ungerührt. Wie wollen Sie denn wissen, daß sie umgebracht wurden, wenn Sie es nicht beweisen können, fragte er. (p. 72)

Max is also reproached for being so tardy in making a claim and for good measure is told that in purely legal terms he has no valid claim at all, that the present ownership of the house is perfectly legal and above board. Indeed the property had been transferred at some point after the war and is now 'im Besitz der Stadtverwaltung' (p. 69). The law then has made good the initial criminal act, for as Max is told when it is clear it will takes years for the house to be returned to him: 'Das Problem läge in der Unkündbarkeit von Mieterschutzwohnungen' (p. 103).

It is as if Max and his family had not existed for this small town in Austria, and it is in keeping with the historical record of Austria in the matter of restitution that Max encounters the state's marked reluctance to accept responsibility for actions it claimed had not been undertaken in the name of the state of Austria, a state which had ceased to exist in the years between 1938 and 1945.[13] Austria had embarked upon a course of double denial: it denies Max an automatic claim to be restored to what is his, a step which would allow him to take his place in the Austrian community; but in addition Austria denies not only the existence of the victim but also the crime, because from its point of view no crime had been committed. Whatever outrages the Third Reich might have committed, they could not be attributed to the state of Austria.

If the state shows defiance, so do its citizens, and an air of latent aggression emerges as Max tries to reclaim his family's past. It is demonstrated by Mitgutsch in a series of minor incidents, anecdotes and very private turmoils. Max hears how a thriving Jewish shop had been Aryanised and continues to be in the hands of a leading non-Jewish family in the town of H., where Max's house is situated. A distant Jewish relative of the original owners meekly arrives one day and asks if she might visit the property. As the wife of the present business owner relates to Max:

> Eine Unbekannte, die sich nicht auswies, eine Ausländerin mit schlechtem Deutsch wollte in die Wohnung. Man drohte ihr mit der Polizei [...] da flüchtete die Fremde. Eine Geistesgestörte, sagte die Besitzerin, wann immer sie davon erzählte. (p. 232)

Branding one's opponents as criminal or insane, or ideally both, is a resolute way of avoiding the issue of ownership. Such defiance is tangible when Max revisits his mother's house, still occupied by people who are strangers to Max. Max is struck by the injustice of those who have arrogated other people's property to themselves and have made themselves comfortable at his family's expense:

> Er sah darin eine Selbstbehauptung, die sich überheblich und wie selbstverständlich über zugefügtes Unrecht hinwegsetzte, als wäre dieses Unrecht nie geschehen. Max sah eine Frau in seinem Alter im Nachbargarten stehen, sie schaute direkt, ohne die Miene zu verziehen [...] die Hände in die Hüften gestemmt. (p. 68)

Far from being welcomed, Max is often made to feel an outsider, an unwanted intruder disrupting a homogeneous and prosperous community. The result is more than simply to prevent Max from making contact and becoming a neighbour, instead it kindles in him more keenly an awareness of his Jewish identity which hitherto had not been the all-defining factor in his make-up. Fear and mistrust, the very opposite of a sense of belonging, now enter his mind, feelings which, it can well be imagined, must have been experienced by his parents before they escaped from Austria: 'Es gab Tage, an denen flößten ihm die Gesichter der Menschen, die ihm begegneten, eine unbekannte Angst ein, er traute ihnen nicht, keinen von ihnen' (p. 81).

Almost by accident, Max enters the life of the dwindling Jewish community of the town, led by the wise, infinitely patient Spitzer, a man who befriends Max and guides him initially through the history of the Jewish community in the town. Max is often called upon to be present to make up the required number of Jewish male adults at religious occasions. Whereas the state of Austria or this particular provincial town has no pressing need for Max's presence, his place in the Jewish community awakes in him an unexpected sense of belonging, as he experiences at a Jewish burial service which he has been implored to attend:

> Ein warmes Gefühl der Zugehörigkeit durchströmte ihn, als er sich den anderen umwandte und dankbare Anerkennung in ihren Augen las. Warum sollte er auch darauf beharren, daß er nichts mit ihnen zu tun hätte, daß es reiner Zufall sei, jüdische Eltern zu haben, daß er ihnen nichts schuldig sei. Hier wurde er offenbar gebraucht, von diesen Menschen wurde er ohne Frage und Mißtrauen angenommen. (p. 94)

It is through his growing contact with Spitzer that Max learns to see differently. This seeing differently means that Max will never be absorbed wholly into the community of this Austrian town. Memory means he does not share the perception of the locals themselves. The present moment offers one reality but it is not the one he sees. Max and the Jewish community may share the same space as their gentile Austrian neighbours but it is not the same world: 'Er wußte, daß die Stadt […] eine andere war als die, die das Auge wahrnahm' (p. 187). At one point Spitzer tours the town, pointing out shops and offices with their unmistakable Austrian gentile names and recalls the Jewish names of their former owners. The locals themselves do not exercise this memory as Spitzer recounts from his own return after the war, a rare survivor in his own family of the holocaust:

> Als Spitzer nach dem Krieg aus Palästina zurückkam, hatte das Geschäft einen neuen Namen. Viele Geschäfte hatten neue Namen. Die Zeugen des Namenwechsels hatten keine Erinnerung an den Zeitpunkt der Veränderung. Sie hatten Schlimmeres mitgemacht, davon erinnerten sie sich genau, an die Bombennächte, die Sirenen, oft mehrere Male in der Nacht, den Zusammenbruch, den Hunger nach dem Krieg. Vorwurfsvoll hätten sie ihm davon erzählt, erinnerte sich Spitzer. Das können Sie sich gar nicht vorstellen, hätten sie gesagt, was wir mitgemacht haben, seien Sie dankbar, daß Sie das nicht haben mitmachen müssen. (p. 231)

This response betrays not only an amnesia that is simultaneously collective and highly selective, it expresses a common belief among many ordinary Austrians who had remained in the country throughout the war years that they had in some way suffered far worse than the fortunate few who had been driven into exile.[14] Suffering, far from being a universal experience that unites people, has become a new marker with which to distance oneself from those who might, as in the case of the Jewish community in Austria, have some claim upon Austrian society and whose re-admittance into that society might not be congenial.

In time, the house of his mother does pass back into Max's possession. He begins to restore it but discovers that it is not the house alone that he is compelled to restore. He begins to research and write a chronicle of the Jewish community in the town of H. before the memory of it is completely lost. He is conscious of how the remaining traces of a Jewish presence in the town have been all but obliterated. Not only have the facades been changed, such as the replacing of Jewish business names after 1938, so has the very presence of the Jewish community itself been removed. With his architect's eye, Max seeks out the now disused and forgotten Jewish prayer houses in the town. Their presence has virtually disappeared: 'Wie eine Grasnarbe, die sich im Frühjahr über den Wunden des Vorjahrs schließt und so unsichtbar macht, so standen diese Häuser zwischen den anderen, ihre Geschichte verleugnend' (p. 192).

It is the great irony of the Jewish place in Austrian life that they, of all the people who made up the Austro-Hungarian Empire at the beginning of the twentieth century, were most committed to that state. As Ritchie Robertson has noted: 'Unlike Czechs, Poles, or Magyars, they had no other political identity available', or as the Viennese liberal Jewish newspaper *Österreichische Wochenschrift* bluntly put it in 1917: 'The Jews are not only the most loyal citizens of the Monarchy, but are also the only unconditional Austrians in this state'.[15] The fate of Austrian Jewry after 1918 demonstrated that a tolerated minority is only a part of a community so long as the majority wishes it. It was and is a contract that can be unilaterally terminated by the majority community.

Research into the history of the local Jewish community is not easy. It defines both the problem and the function of Max's chronicle:

> Das Problem dabei ist, sagte er, daß die Stadtschreiber die Juden kaum jemals erwähnten. Sie gehörten einfach nicht zur Geschichte dieser Stadt. Es ist die ausgeblendete Geschichte von H., die ich schreiben möchte. (p. 272)

Jews have no place in the town's history because the earlier chroniclers, who controlled the collective memory, have accorded them no place in that society or in the record of that society. It is a holocaust that takes place on paper, but Max soon discovers that the real thing has happened on numerous occasions, in an endless cycle of violence and pogroms.

What emerges from Mitgutsch's narrative quickly becomes more disturbing than the painful recollection of distant events. Here we see Max describing one particularly virulent spate of attacks on the Jewish community in the fifteenth century: 'Die Überfälle waren von Mitgliedern der Stadtverwaltung angezettelt worden, vollstreckt von einem zornigen Proletariat' (p. 247). The expression seems to beg for the use of the term 'Volkszorn', and once the town has been become an important centre for the Catholic Church, local Christians are forbidden to purchase from the Jewish community, who can only live by trade. These prohibitions echo the 'Kauft nicht bei Juden' familiar to us from the 1930s in Nazi Germany and later in annexed Austria, whilst premonitions of the gas chambers are unmistakably awakened when Max recounts in his chronicle the burning alive of Jews during the Plague years if they refused to convert to Christianity. Max's chronicle is more than a history, for it has a far more painful message. It demonstrates that the brutality and intolerance of National Socialism, which has often been portrayed as a twelve-year aberration in the history of Germany and Austria, is in fact a recurring and constant feature. Max looks at the papers he has amassed on his study table:

> der Tisch war mit Fotokopien und Zetteln übersät, die Jahrhunderte gerieten ihm durcheinander in ihrer Wiederholung des immer Gleichen, im Kreisen um vorsehbares Unheil, vorhersehbar und dennoch unabwendbar. (pp. 229-230)

Max's growing awareness of the town's past and its treatment of Jews down the centuries lead him to a sobering assessment of what the town is now. He is confronted by its stark immutability:

> Es war nicht die Stadt, die seine Mutter gekannt hatte, auch nicht die, aus der man einst seine Verwandten abgeholt hatte, aber sie war das Gehäuse, das alle diese unsichtbaren weiterlebenden Städtebilder umschloß. Und etwas Unverwechselbares war ihr geblieben. Nie würde sie sich von Grund auf, in ihrem Wesen ändern. (p. 187)

It was perhaps the most crushing remark about Austria, by an author whose life's work was devoted to making crushing remarks about Austria, when Thomas Bernhard in his play *Heldenplatz* allowed Anna to say of post-war Austria, and almost as an aside: 'Die Zustände sind ja wirklich heute so wie sie achtunddreißig gewesen sind'.[16]

Max comes to see that his relationship with the population of his maternal home is an approximation of a relationship. Writing back to a

close Jewish friend in New York, who has no intention of ever returning
to Europe, Max confesses:

> Ich lebe nicht eigentlich unter ihnen [...] ich sehe sie auf der Straße, ich kenne
> nur ein paar von ihnen, eigentlich lebe ich in der Vergangenheit dieser Stadt, an
> ihrer Oberfläche habe ich mich nur vorläufig eingerichtet. (p. 240)

We are aware that in a relationship between neighbours space is not only a
factor in physical terms, it also inhabits a time dimension and Max grows
closer to the depressing realisation that the space he inhabits is not that of
the majority of those who live as his neighbours in the town of H.

Mitgutsch's novel *Haus der Kindheit* partly reverses our notion of
majorities and minorities by creating a novel where most of the characters
presented are Jewish and the majority population are viewed as if they
were on the outside. Those Austrians that do enter Max's world are
tormented or assertive but are certainly not at peace with themselves.

There are attempts at reconciliation in the course of the novel. The
young non-Jewish librarian and local historian Thomas is touching in his
earnestness to get to know the town's Jewish community. We later learn
that Thomas's grandfather had been a prominent Gauleiter. Thomas helps
Max in his search for documents and even writes an article in the local
newspaper about Max and his research:

> Er war gut gemeint. Er war auch mutig. Es war ihm sicher nicht
> leichtgefallen, von Max' ermordeten anstatt von seinen umgekommenen
> Verwandten zu schreiben, von Raub und Diebstahl zu sprechen, wenn es
> Wörter wie Arisierung und Enteignung gab. (p. 245).

In this debate on neighbours and strangers we see Mitgutsch raising key
questions such as the very vocabulary we use to talk of one another. And
here she touches on a central issue: to what extent does one community
have the right to take possession of the depiction of a neighbouring
community for its own purposes and in order to bury its own demons?
Does one part of the community become no more than illustrative material
to allow others to work out their guilt complexes? And Mitgutsch seems to
be asking if a dialogue can be forced or manufactured when there is little
or no common ground to be entered?

Towards the end of the novel, Thomas organises a painfully
embarrassing podium discussion, 'Wie lebte man in einer christlichen
Gesellschaft', and Max agrees to be one of three Jewish platform speakers,
each of whom has different political or religious leanings, one more

secular, and one more orthodox than Max. He does so reluctantly and only so as not to give offence to the well-meaning Thomas, who has omitted to ask Max if he feels such a meeting is an appropriate means of reconciliation. A few of the small Jewish community attend but show a reluctance born of experience to expect much from such encounters. The exchange with the audience is minimal. Questions from the non-Jewish audience come uneasily and sparingly. What is revealed in the few questions that are asked goes beyond the words used and has a sinister undertone: 'Ob er sich als Österreicher betrachte, wurde Max' weltlicher Nachbar gefragt. Was dagegen spräche, fragte er zurück. Das Publikum lachte höflich' (p. 260).

If Thomas represents a form of stumbling good-will towards the Jewish community, there are others who are less eager to seek an understanding. The Jewish community in the town of H. makes no attempt to proselytise but receives occasional visits from those who believe they may be of partial Jewish extraction and who find it difficult to be at home in provincial Austrian society. (Mitgutsch feels none of the compunction to impartiality on this point that the historian quoted early in this paper felt when describing the life and works of Marshal Pétain. Her views on life in the Austrian provinces are unmistakable in all her works.)

One of these Austrians of partial Jewish descent is a young woman called Diana, now married to the son of a well-established family and a pillar of the local Roman Catholic community. Her mother-in-law's contempt is barely concealed as she makes clear to Max:

> Und die Schwiegermutter rätselte, woher die Neigung ihres Sohnes zu Fremdartigem komme, von ihr jedenfalls nicht, denn sie hätte sich nie zu *Andersrassigen* hingezogen gefühlt. (p. 235)

Diana reaches the point of a nervous breakdown as she tries to reconcile her place between these two communities. After undergoing a period of therapy – and here there is an uncomfortable suggestion that to have tried to enter Max's world was akin to an illness – Diana reappears but has now been stripped of her natural humanity. She has become mechanistic and lifelessly self-conscious in her actions. In the private tragedy of this minor life Mitgutsch seems to be suggesting that a third way, a symbiosis, is not possible. Diana must inhabit one orbit or the other, and the overwhelming gravitational pull of social habit returns her to the family of her in-laws.

Haus der Kindheit acts out the public tragedy of Europe in the twentieth century as experienced in the German-speaking world and it looks in particular at the after-shocks in provincial Austria. In 1897 the Zionist pioneer Herzl had depicted the fate of modern Jews in his play *Das neue Ghetto*, which has been described as 'emancipation without assimilation'.[17] A century later, and after the destruction or removal of most of European Jewry, as in the case of Austria, Anna Mitgutsch offers no more an optimistic picture and certainly no resolution. She has, however, rehearsed in fictional form many of the incidents that inform the debate concerning neighbours and strangers. In particular she brings out the significance of dispossession and restitution, of repression and suppression of memory, of the public and private acts of acknowledgment and recognition that would allow others to share space. She exposes the hollowness of empty political and civic gestures and institutional obstructionism, and she reminds us that historical forces are played out in individual human lives.

At the end of the novel Max flies back to New York, and a sense of warmth rather than loss reaches out to him the closer he gets to America. And Mitgutsch, perhaps unintentionally or perhaps with grim humour, has one last act of detachment from Austria waiting for us. On the first page of *Haus der Kindheit* Max's mother had waited in vain for her Greeks, as it were, to sail the seas to find her. Max recalls on the flight back to America all those who will be pleased to see him on his return to New York. Amongst them will be, as he remembers on the final page of the novel, an old Greek workman who carries out the repairs in his apartment block. It seems as if Greeks did make it after all but they do not appear to be in a hurry to return.

Mitgutsch's novel is a sombre and sober investigation of communal relationships. I believe it deserves our attention because of its paradigmatic presentation of the nature of community and the forces for inclusion and exclusion. In its specifically Austrian context the novel has a profound, if wistful, pessimism. The issues at stake have gone beyond questions of emancipation and assimilation, of communities leading parallel but separate lives. The presence of America fulfils the role of a utopian safety valve, but it is not one available to all, and the idea of departure as a resolution, be it to America, to Israel or any other place, which appears to be the fate of the small Jewish community in the Austrian provinces, is as much an expression of failure as it is a promise of a new future.

Notes

[1] Richard Griffiths, *Marshal Pétain*, Constable: London, 1994, p. xii.

[2] Anna Mitgutsch, *Haus der Kindheit*, Luchterhand: Munich, 2000. All page references after quotations from the text refer to this edition.

[3] Günther A. Höfler, '"Ideologie interessiert mich nicht…" Gespräch mit Anna Mitgutsch', *Deutsche Bücher*, 1 (2002), 5-17 (here: p. 5).

[4] Staatsgalerie Stuttgart.

[5] Goethe, *Iphigenie auf Tauris*, Reclam: Stuttgart, 1987, I, i ll, pp. 10-12.

[6] Peter Eppel, 'Bemerkungen zur Frage der Rückkehr österreichischer Emigranten aus den USA', in: Johann Holzner, Sigurd Paul Scheichl and Wolfgang Wiesmüller, eds, *Eine schwierige Heimkehr: Österreichische Literatur im Exil 1938–1945*, Innsbrucker Beiträge zur Kulturwissenschaft: Innsbruck, 1991, pp. 111-138 (here: p. 134).

[7] *Bundespressedienst Austria: Informationen aus Österreich*, 12/02, (10 June 2002), p. 6.

[8] David Vital, *A People Apart*, Oxford University Press: Oxford, 1999, pp. 897-898.

[9] Thomas Albrich, 'Holocaust und Schuldabwehr. Vom Judenmord zum kollektiven Opferstatus', in: Rolf Steininger and Michael Gehler, eds, *Österreich im 20. Jahrhundert*. Band 2, Böhlau: Vienna, 1997, p. 53.

[10] Ernst Hanisch, *Der lange Schatten des Staates: Österreichische Gesellschaftsgeschichte im 20. Jahrhundert*, Ueberreuter: Vienna, 1994, pp. 353-354.

[11] Bülent Diken, *Strangers, Ambivalence and Social Theory*, Ashgate: Aldershot, 1998, p. 4.

[12] Primo Levi, *If This is a Man* and *The Truce*, trans. by Stuart Woolf, Abacus: London, 2000, pp. 376-377.

[13] For a useful discussion of the history of post-war Austria's attitude to the vexed question of restitution see Hans Winkler, 'Österreich – die völkerrechtlichen Aspekte', *Österreich in Geschichte und Literatur*, 45 Heft 5-6 (2001), 341-359.

[14] See the experience of some of the returnees from exile collected in: Jochen Jung, ed., *Vom Reich zu Österreich: Kriegsende und Nachkriegszeit in Österreich erinnert von Augen- und Ohrenzeugen,* dtv: Munich, 1985.

[15] Ritchie Robertson, *The 'Jewish Question' in German Literature 1749 – 1939*, Oxford University Press: Oxford, 1999, p. 84.

[16] Thomas Bernhard, *Heldenplatz*, Suhrkamp: Frankfurt am Main, 1988, pp. 62-63.

[17] Robertson, p. 247.

Juliet Wigmore

Dreams on the Danube. Elisabeth Reichart's *Nachtmär*

Elisabeth Reichart's novel *Nachtmär* (1995), examines the legacy of guilt about the Nazi past in relation to the postwar generation. Prompted by the presence of a Jewish returnee, whose parents emigrated from Austria, members of the younger generation are forced to confront their own attitudes towards strangers in their midst. As a result, they reflect, too, on their parents' behaviour in parallel situations in the past. In the process of doing this, their perception of the past is extended from the immediate experience of a stranger in their own lives to considering Austrian attitudes towards other outsiders, including the country's relations with Slovene neighbours on their national border.

Like much of Elisabeth Reichart's fiction, *Nachtmär* (1995) concerns the legacy of guilt resulting from the Third Reich and the Austrians' failure to confront this period of history in a way which might initiate changes in attitudes towards it. Reichart has commented that, in contrast to earlier times, when Austrian society preferred to ignore these events, since the Waldheim affair in 1986 there has been extensive, and even obsessive, discussion in Austria about the problem of responsibility relating to the country's role during the Nazi period. Yet, says Reichart, airing the taboo topic has, paradoxically, become a ritual which has inured Austrians to genuine insight and contrition:

> Viele denken, "Ja, o.k.. Wir waren mitschuldig," aber daß keine Verbindungen zur Aktualität herrschen. Es gibt kein Geschichtsbewußtsein. Sonst wäre es auch nicht möglich, daß ein Teil der ÖVP wieder mit den Rechten zusammengehen will.[1]

The author explains that, in an attempt to find a means of breaking down barriers to an authentic confrontation with the past, she seeks to approach this topic from different angles. In *Nachtmär,* Reichart widens the scope of the issue by relating it to Austria's wider geographical and political location, particularly with reference to the country's southern neighbours, the Slovenes. The connections are drawn especially through dreams, which both occur in the form of literal experiences and are used metaphorically to represent aspirations and unfulfilled wishes. Through the dream, links are established between different time scales and contexts. The significance of dreams in the specifically Austrian context is alluded to by one protagonist who mentions that, since Freud, all

Viennese imagine themselves to be experts on the symbolism of dreams ('jeder Wiener glaube doch, erst mit ihm sei der wahre Freud geboren', p. 126),[2] an allusion which invites the reader, too, to treat the dream sequences as symbolic. Above all, it is in the dreams that links are established between the recurrent theme of guilt in relation to the Jews in the Nazi period and the less emphasised literary subject of the problematic relationship between Austrians and their southern neighbours, the Slovenes, and implicitly, the Slavic peoples more generally.[3] In hightlighting the relationship with Austria's southern neighbours in *Nachtmär*, I wish to redirect the emphasis towards a less familiar aspect of facing the 'uncomfortable past',[4] which has become relevant again since the upheavals in the central European region in the 1990s.

In *Nachtmär* dreams provide an important means by which the atrocities of the past are lent relevance to the situation in which the protagonists, members of the younger generation, find themselves. Dreams, both literal and metaphorical, represent another world, in which alternatives can be tested, aspirations expressed, and, above all, they represent nightmarish reminders of a distorted reality, a 'Nachtmahr' (a word which occurs in the text, p. 38). As in a dream, too, distinctions and conventional boundaries are frequently blurred in the narrative; in particular, the perspectives of the four main protagonists are mingled and are sometimes barely distinguishable from one another. So, too, their voices reflect shared or overlapping histories and past experiences. At the time of narration, they are isolated from one another, but they share a common background. As students of *Theaterwissenschaft*, they had all aspired to professions demanding creativity and believed they might make major contributions to the world of the theatre. However, these aspirations, referred to metaphorically as their 'Träume' (e.g. p. 126), have remained largely unrealised, and at the point at which the narrative begins, their illusions have been shattered. In the 15 or so years since they graduated, all have been forced to lower their expectations. Thus, one of them, Paula, contents herself with the role of *Regieassistentin* (p. 28), even though she might have become a theatre director and had earlier aspired to an acting career (p. 238); another, Marlen, intended to write plays, but abandoned her goals in order to meet the demands of married life, which has also proved unsatisfying; a third, Ingram, manages an advertising agency, while the fourth, Rudolf, works as a *Dramaturg*, but is plagued by self-doubt, which limits his success (p. 100). As a result of losing sight of their earlier dreams, they all suffer a sense of frustration.

It is in the final section of the narrative that the dream motif emerges most explicitly and highlights particular aspects of the earlier part of the text. Paula, probably the most self-aware of the four, experiences dreams which take her beyond the confined space of the theatre where she works. This episode begins with her waking up, an event that is itself apparently part of her dream: 'Gleißendes Sonnenlicht weckte sie, schien ihr direkt in den offenen Mund, der sich verdammt ausgetrocknet fühlte' (p. 214). Her dry mouth suggests that she is experiencing difficulty in expressing herself, and points to the symbolism of the passage. Paula finds herself on the bank of the Danube, whether in dream or in reality is unclear. Nevertheless, it is one of the few incidents in the novel which take place in a specific outdoor location, and as with the other such settings, the events that occur here prove to be threatening and confrontational. This aspect contrasts with earlier references to the Danube, when it was associated with happier times, as, for instance, a place where the protagonists went on outings.

The first part of Paula's dream takes her beyond the borders of Austria. She finds herself in a glider, flying not over the Danube but over the sea, an image implying that she is breaking out of the confines of her landlocked homeland, referred to as an 'eingegrenztes Land' (p. 64). In a panic and suffering thirst, she parachutes onto an exotic-looking, apparently lush island, only to find that the entire island consists of a giant cactus (p. 215). As in a normal dream, events represent transformations of waking reality, for early in the narrative it is mentioned that Paula tends a cactus which requires much watering and seems to grow continually (p. 32). Symbolically, the cactus in the dream suggests that Paula's thirst is not to be quenched and she is trapped without sustenance.

This dream introduces into the present a pivotal figure from the four narrators' shared past. The pilot of the plane in Paula's dream is the fifth member of the group of former fellow students, a Jewish American named Esther. The daughter of refugees from Vienna, she returned to her parents' country of origin to study, only to discover that people of her own generation, born after the war, are still deeply affected by reminders of the wartime past and conditioned by the experiences and attitudes of their elders. They are caught in cycles of repetition, as a result of which, even now, they are prone to a variety of destructive and life-denying impulses, including lapses into antisemitic thinking. By the time the novel opens, Esther has, indeed, removed herself from this circle of people, having departed without explanation. The narrators are left with feelings of guilt about the the way they behaved towards her, evoked repeatedly at the time of narration because they are anticipating their annual reunion, from which Esther will, as usual, be absent.   Over the years of re-enacting this occasion, the reunion has become a 'selbstgeschaffenes Ritual im Schatten der uneingestandenen Verluste' (p. 11).   Each protagonist has come to dread it, and on this occasion, for a variety of reasons, all absent themselves from it; even the host, Marlen, is relieved when the others fail to appear.   The group's sense of belonging, always fragile, the narrative suggests, was previously cemented by Esther, and after her departure their group identity is destroyed by obsessive guilt about the way they behaved towards her.

Through the narrators' memories and dream sequences, it emerges gradually that Esther's disillusionment with her friends surfaced when she became pregnant and was ordered to take extensive bedrest. Needing help in this predicament, she asked her Austrian friends to look after her: they, however, refused, for selfish reasons, and so, as they now interpret it, made her feel rejected.   Although their behaviour was not prompted primarily by explicit or latent antisemitic motives, their subsequent feelings of guilt have been exacerbated by the fact that she was Jewish. Indeed, when they first became acquainted with Esther, Paula, one of the more self-aware of the group, expressed her fears about the potential for the legacy of Nazism to undermine their developing friendship.   While Paula referred to her generation as 'Wir Eichmann-Kinder' (p. 187), Esther at this point expressed the more optimistic view that younger Austrians were not to blame for the past.   Nevertheless, Esther's Jewish identity always plays a role in the way the group interacts and the way it finally disintegrates. After Esther's plea for assistance has been rejected, the group attempt to defuse the hostile feelings that this caused by making an expedition to Prater.   Yet the ill-feeling is not dissipated; on the contrary, it surfaces again, especially when Rudolf, apparently annoyed by Esther's plans for him in her project, expresses antisemitic thought processes, in a statement which continues to haunt them all up to the time of narration. Standing under the Great Wheel, the *Riesenrad*, in Prater, Rudolf proclaimed, as retold through Paula: '[…] daß es ein alter Fehler der Juden sei, immer nur von denen Hilfe und Opfer zu verlangen, die ohnedies auf ihrer Seite stünden' (p. 208). This declaration suggests that Rudolf's attitude towards Austria's Nazi past is complacent, as well as displaying his insensitivity to Esther's pressing needs. The setting, under the Great Wheel, a potent symbol of Vienna, reinforces the idea of

recurrence, like the impending reunion at the time of narration; as this
'Nachtmahr' suggests, it indicates repetition of an inability to treat their
neighbours, especially those who are different, in a truly humane way.
Although this episode crystallises the fundamental insecurity of the
relationship between Esther and the Austrians, according to Ingram, and in
contrast to Paula's view, it was merely the repetition of a tension which
had repeatedly threatened to surface (p. 29). Immediately after the
episode in Prater, Esther disappeared without explanation, a symbolic re-
enactment of the disappearance of the Jews during the Nazi period. Then,
as in the re-awakened memories of the narrators, mere tolerance was not
sufficient to protect Jewish neighbours and friends, a parallel pinpointed
by Linda DeMerritt: 'Esther's safety, like that of innumerable Jews under
Nazism, requires the engagement, work and commitment of her friends'.[5]
Of course, even this is an understatement of the situation, since during the
Nazi period many Austrians actively worked against the Jews and literally
betrayed them. In Paula's dream, the nightmare of guilt resulting from the
episode in Prater is reflected when Esther, the pilot of the plane, flies off
alone over the sea, perhaps back to America, leaving Paula stranded on the
desert island, which might be interpreted as representing Austria.

It is their feelings of guilt in relation to Esther which provide the
motivation for the four protagonists to narrate. They relive not only their
own experiences but also their earlier memories of what they have gleaned
about the role played by their parents' generation during the war,
behaviour which the younger generation sense that they are in danger of
repeating. They make spontaneous connections between Esther, the
second-generation Jewish returnee whom they treated as a stranger in their
midst, and the way other neighbours, regarded as outsiders, but not
necessarily Jewish, were treated in the past by their parents' generation.
Above all, their unease about the past, triggered by Esther's
disappearance, focuses on relationships affected by historical relations
between Austria and the neighbouring country to the south, Slovenia.

All four narrators come from a village not far from Austria's
southern border, and their closeness and shared background is perhaps
what makes them appear to be a 'geschlossener Kreis' (p. 8); they are both
close to each other and closed to outsiders. They epitomise the
metaphorical insularity of Austria, the 'eingegrenztes Land' (p. 64). At
least part of the reason for their close identification with each other lies in
the fact that they share knowledge of their parents' earlier lives, or, at
least, as much as they have been able to piece together from fragmented

accounts, and that the older generation's experiences also overlap. Through the narrators' memories, the narrative reveals what the older generation suffered and how each of them died. Each individual narrator represents these past events as part of his or her own life, suggesting that the narrative is part of a collective memory shared by the wider community. This effect is intensified by the fact that it is frequently not immediately apparent which of the four is narrating, as both the content and the language in which it is conveyed converge.

The narrators' feelings about Esther at the time of narrating provide the link to another strand of the novel, which highlights the uneasy and guilt-ridden relationship between Austrians and their Slovene neighbours. The narrators' awareness of having failed Esther prompts memories of the more distant past to surface: this shared memory focuses on a Slovene girl called Neva, who was persecuted and eventually, we assume, killed by the Nazis. Although at least one reviewer assumed Neva was Jewish,[6] this is certainly not made explicit. It is at least as relevant to interpret Neva's story as an exploration of the upheavals that occurred between Austria and its southern neighbour, a tension which in turn has more general implications. In the early part of the novel, allusions to Neva, not always by name, occur mainly in the narratives and thoughts of Ingram and Paula. Only later does her story gradually emerge, allowing parallels between Esther and Neva to become more evident. The implied link between the two situations is based on the narrators' association of their own feelings of guilt regarding Esther with the guilt of their parents' generation, in relation both to the Jews and, more specifically, to their treatment of Neva. The parallel between these two contexts is suggested before Esther's name has even been mentioned, when Ingram recalls an earlier situation in which he experienced unease when faced with a foreign culture. Finding himself in the Philippines, on a fruitless mission to make a film, the poverty he witnessed there made him feel awkward, yet curiously detached. Like all the narrators, he is at least moderately self-aware and at this point acknowledges his own indifference to others' suffering ('was gingen ihm diese Menschen an' (p. 21)). This situation from his own earlier career, and the language in which he formulates it (or remembers having formulated it at the time), prompted him to recall the behaviour his father displayed in deliberately ignoring the suffering he had caused during the war. After the Slovene girl, Neva, had vanished, Ingram's father reproached his mother, in words echoed by Ingram's own, saying, as Ingram now recalls, 'Was geht mich deine Neva an? Hör auf, über deine mißglückte Lebensrechtfertigung zu lamentieren' (p. 21). As one critic has interpreted it, '[Ingram] has inherited a monstrous and all-encompassing indifference from his father'.[7] However, it remains an open question whether he has actually modelled his behaviour on that of his parent, or whether he simply acknowledges that his own attitudes are similar. The affinity between the generations in this respect highlights the idea that the younger generation are trapped in cycles of repetition.

The sense of conflict evident in Ingram's reflections is later clarified: his dying grandmother reminds him of how his mother constantly retold Neva's story 'als ewige Mahnung gegen das Unrecht, das in meinem Haus geschah' (p. 140). This warning, according to the grandmother, has gone unheeded: she now reproaches Ingram for behaving insensitively towards her, and thus she too implies that the younger generation are more inclined to repeat their elders' failings than to learn from them. In the events and feelings portrayed in *Nachtmär*, as in Ingram's family, the reproach of insensitivity towards other people, family, neighbours or foreigners, is shown to be a great 'Unrecht', especially if it means ignoring or mistreating those in difficulty instead of offering assistance.

Neva was a refugee sheltered by Ingram's family during the war; in this sense, on the one hand, she was their 'Lebensrechtfertigung', as Ingram's father suggests, their alibi at a time when most people shared in the collective process of persecution. However, the protection offered by the family was too limited. Neva gave herself up after being sexually abused by Ingram's father, for, as Paula now thinks, 'nicht um jeden Preis leben wollen, wird sich Neva gedacht haben' (p. 219). Even Ingram's dying grandmother, whose presence triggers memories of his parents and of Neva, admits that, in showing sympathy for Neva's plight, she was also responsible for what happened: she encouraged Ingram's father to make overtures to Neva when she was in hiding, thinking it would make her happier, and she too uses the 'dream' metaphor to represent hope: '[Neva] sollte etwas zum Träumen haben in ihrer Kammer' (p. 141). Like many other allusions to dreams in the novel, the grandmother's misjudgement turned out to be self-delusion and part of the process through which truth is evaded.

The constant presence of Esther in the minds of the four narrators, together with her equally pervasive absence in person, evokes parallel situations from the wartime past, in which not only Neva, the Slovene, but also other persecuted people, including dwarves among the families' neighbours, simply disappeared (pp. 3, 64, 80). Yet, the evocation of memories in this way, often conveyed through associative language, blurs certain differences between the various situations. Unlike Neva, for instance, Esther, for all her difficulties, is not actually a victim: she states emphatically that she never suffered discrimination as a Jew in America, and even in modern Austria, she has the power to remove herself from the situation in which she feels rejected and thus to act for her self-preservation. Although there is no indication of what has become of Esther by the time of narration, it seems probable that, like the protagonist in Anna Mitgutsch's *Haus der Kindheit*, she may have returned to America, where Jews can live a 'normal' life.[8] By contrast, it is her Austrian companions who are unable to move on in the same way, and who remain burdened with the past, evoked by Paula's dream of being trapped on the desert island. Their sense of guilt renders them unable to distinguish between different situations, as a result of which they feel trapped in a cycle of perpetual recurrence.

In the minds of the Austrian protagonists, the border village, too, from which they originate remains a site of mental conflict, a reflection of its role as a scene of actual upheavals and atrocities in wartime. For Ingram's mother, particularly, the suffering and conflict was a tangible reality. She came from the Slovenian side of the border and had left her village, as Ingram recalls in the words 'Ort der Schande. Die Schande mitgenommen auf der Flucht' (p. 150). Like the younger generation who are narrating, she experienced the effects of disgrace incurred by her parents, who were 'Verfluchte Kollaborateure' (p. 150). This shameful situation oppressed her so intensely that she never spoke to her parents again and eventually she committed suicide, apparently because she was first so troubled by her family history and then by her husband's treatment of Neva. The guilt incurred by the parents' generation during the war thus persists from one generation to the next; here it relates specifically to the uneasy relationship between Austrians and their neighbours across the border. That this situation was not confined to Ingram's family but was part of a more general picture is illustrated by Marlen's attempts in her youth to gain information about her mother. Her father forbids her to speak of it to her mother, but provides the insight:

> daß ihre Eltern den Nazis geholfen haben und sie deshalb fliehen mussten. Ich nehme an, es war die Sprache, nichts sonst. Sie sprachen Deutsch, die Nazis sprachen Deutsch. (p. 191)

This comment nevertheless underplays the significance of the language issue, at least as far as the Slovenes were concerned at the time. For, particularly in 1938-9, Slovene culture had been systematically undermined, by increasingly Germanising school education and other influential institutions. The language issue had therefore been a particular cause of resentment.[9]

The strong interconnection between historical upheavals and individual fates in the border region in particular is reflected in the language of the text. A passage comprising a single sentence and extending over more than three pages, for instance, contributes to the blurring of boundaries between different situations. Its starting point is Ingram's mother's location in the historical context: 'Glasauge, das nur spiegeln kann, eine Fremde spiegelt es, nachdem ein paar Jahre zuvor die Slowenen zu Fremden erklärt und entfernt worden waren' (p. 157). Ingram's mother arrived in the village in Austria from Slovenia as a stranger, at a time when the Nazi hostility to Slavic nations was causing rifts between neighbours within Austria as well as across its national frontier with Slovenia. The repetition of the word 'Fremde' with different referents highlights the fact that the notion of the 'alien' is a fluid one. Other 'Ausgesiedelten', Ingram notes, like his mother, continued to cross the border, as the communities became increasingly isolated from each other. Although his mother is a displaced German-speaker, the depiction of these events also evokes the fate of many Slovenes during the Nazi period:

> 1942 begann die Aussiedlung von mehreren Hundert slowenischen Bauernfamilien aus Kärnten. Ende Mai 1942 befanden sich 1217 ausgesiedelte Kärntner Slowenen in deutschen Lagern [...][10]

The connection between the German-speaking refugees and the persecuted Slovene minority does not simply blur distinctions between 'Opfer' and 'Täter' in order to evoke sympathy for Austrian suffering. Reichart's position is far more rigorous than such an interpretation would suggest. For the unacknowledged suffering of the parents' generation is part of the psychological blocking imposed by both the parents themselves and by the younger Austrians who cannot face up to these issues either. It is implied that such blurring, as is revealed also by the narrative structure, is the result of failing to face up to the past and to acknowledge both guilt and suffering. However, it is not only the older generation which incurred guilt: the attitudes of the younger generation mean that they repeat similar processes, if in different contexts.

Ingram reveals a strong attachment to his parents' village, suggesting inability to detach himself from the past. Reflecting on the time after the war, for instance, he refers to: 'Zeit […], in der das Dorf nur noch Dorf war, sich die Weltgeschichte verabschiedet hatte' (p. 157). His memory of a castle in the village is mentioned again when Paula reads that Ingram has bought a castle near the village and set up a script-writing college there. Faced with this information, Paula is initially jealous at what appears to be the fulfilment of his dream to become a 'real' writer. Nevertheless, she dismisses the idea of taking up such an opportunity to study, reminding herself that she has to forget in order for her life to take a more positive direction, with 'Erfahrungen, die nicht permanent das Leben aushöhlten' (p. 219). Ingram, by contrast, appears to be returning to the past, symbolised by the location; and the castle in which his academy is housed can be interpreted as an attempt to erect a defensive bulwark against moving forward. This situation echoes events in Reichart's earlier novel, *Februarschatten* (1984), where a largely innocent figure, tainted by the actions of her parents' generation, returns to the site of suffering, where guilt was incurred. In both novels, the outcome remains open regarding the extent to which the return is associated with any genuine insight or healing process. Nevertheless, in view of the dominance of Paula's perspective at this point in the narrative, the reader is inclined to share her suggestion that Ingram is trapped in the past.

In *Nachtmär*, certain problematic aspects of Austrian history, culture and the longer tradition are underpinned by many allusions and quotations from Austrian literature, particularly Grillparzer's plays. In the intervals between her phases of dreaming on the banks of the Danube in the last part of the novel, Paula, the theatre professional familiar with classical drama, cites several extensive passages from Grillparzer's drama *Libussa*, a play that she had once hoped to produce with her friend Esther, and thus it stands for one of her many thwarted ambitions. Like much of Grillparzer's work, this play concerns a legend from a territory of the Holy Roman Empire, beyond the boundaries of contemporary Austria. Certain parallels between the play and figures and events in the novel become evident: Libussa, the legendary founder of the royal house of Bohemia, Přemysl, inherited the throne but was forced out by nobles who insisted on a male ruler. The disappearance of the central female figure epitomises the situation of both Esther and Neva, who, in different ways, made the decision to remove themselves when the situation with which they were faced became intolerable. In the speech Paula recalls, Libussa addresses ideas about justice, fairness and entitlement, reflecting concerns of *Nachtmär*, especially the idea of justice invoked by Ingram's dying grandmother:

> Daß du dem Dürftigen hilfst, den Bruder liebst,
> Das ist dein Recht, vielmehr ist deine Pflicht
> Und Recht ist nur der ausgeschmückte Name
> Für alles Unrecht, das die Erde hegt. (p. 220)

Occurring towards the end of the novel, the lines quoted suggest that Paula is perhaps beginning to acknowledge her feelings of guilt about Esther, with whom she closely associates the play. She now accepts that she neglected her friend by failing to support her and, above all, by failing to go in search of her. The constant reminders of the person of Esther mean that Paula's guilt remains tangible; far from universalising, and so dissipating or even exonerating individuals, the many references to classical or universal situations, whether Grillparzer's historical myths or biblical allusions, such as the story of Cain and Abel (p. 10) contribute to intensifying the issue and suggesting that the guilt incurred cannot be overcome simply by restating it.

Paula's dreams and meditations on the banks of the Danube in the final part of the text also highlight her sense of inescapable guilt by associating it with her memories of the way she behaved towards Esther and suggesting how her feelings of guilt have ruined her own life. Her dreams and reflections evoke comparison with earlier, happier times when the Danube was the site of happy excursions, when the five friends were still on good terms, and the river itself was the source of joy and even sustenance, when Ingram caught fish for them to eat (pp. 7, 166), an event mentioned on the first page. Now, in Paula's dreams, allusions to issues that have burdened her and the others since then re-appear in transfigured form, often with threatening overtones. First, Paula dreams of the 'Friedhof der Namenslosen', a cemetery containing the bodies of those who have drowned, whether by accident or suicide, described by Claudio Magris as a place where, 'death is elemental, basic, fraternal in the anonymity that we all share'.[11] Like the imagined 'Friedhof der ermordeten Töchter' on the banks of a lake in the central dream chapter ('der dritte Mann') in Ingeborg Bachmann's *Malina*, which evokes the nightmare of the Third Reich, this cemetery too evokes the idea of a community where death is all-pervasive.[12] The mass graves are evocative of the anonymous deaths of concentration camp victims. Paula immediately thinks of Esther, imagining that she might have committed suicide after being rejected by her friends and is relieved to find that there is no gravestone from the year in which the incident under the Big Wheel took place. Facing the possibility of Esther's death, displaced into the dream, allows Paula to confront her fear, and having addressed it, potentially to leave it behind. By contrast with Ingram's mother, who committed suicide in the face of unbearable circumstances, Paula's dream suggests that Esther has survived. Nevertheless, Paula's acknowledgement that Esther has escaped seems only to highlight the fact that she herself is trapped by the sense of her own guilt.

Paula's dream contains a number of transfigurations, which suggest that roles and situations have the potential to recur in altered form. For instance, Paula meets a ship's captain, dressed in a yellow uniform, which then turns to normal blue when he enters the *Gasthaus* and downs a beer. The yellow uniform is theatrical, by comparison with which the blue one suggests reality. The tension between the two echoes Paula's own increasing unease about her work in the theatre. In the next stage of the dream, Paula is invited to join a ship's crew by a woman who at first seems magical and to resemble a water spirit. At first, the strange woman speaks 'ein singendes Deutsch im Rhythmus der Donauwellen' (p. 230), evoking the typically Viennese intonation. She then metamorphoses into someone much less genial, forcing Paula into slavery and threatening to abandon her to the sirens to kill, who, like Esther and Neva have 'die Länder gewechselt' (p. 231). Like Furies, they are agents of nemesis.

At this point, we are told, 'kam Paula wieder zu sich' (p. 231). However, even her consciousness appears to be a dream, as she envisages Esther emerging from the water of the Danube to accuse her: 'Laß mich in Ruhe und such dir ein anderes Opfer jenseits deines Horizonts' (p. 232). Paula, who at some point has suffered an injury or accident – whether in her dream or in reality is not clear[13] - now swims out into the river, towards the spot where Esther emerged:

> Sie schwamm hinaus – endlich hatte sie wieder ein Ziel vor Augen – die Mitte erreichen, den sonnenbeschienenen Teil des Flusses […]. Sie kam aus den Schatten nicht hinaus, wurde nur weiter und weiter abgetrieben, jener Grenze zu, die allein für den Strom passierbar war, und der Schmerz, dass nur die Auserwählten ungehindert die Länder wechseln konnten, verdunkelte einen Moment lang alles um sie […]. (p. 232)

The crossing of rivers as a means of escape echoes Ingram's mother's story, for whom, as he imagines it, fleeing her village meant crossing rivers:

> Durch reißende Flüsse schwimmen oder mit einem kleinen Boot gerade noch das Ufer erreichen [...], er sah sie vor sich, seine Mutter und die Großeltern [...]. (p. 150)

This passage, and others, echo Bachmann's *Malina*, and particularly the story of the Prinzessin von Kagran, a utopian tale within the novel which suggests nostalgia for a time before the Danube basin was divided into nation states with restrictive boundaries. However, *Malina*, published in 1971, when these political boundaries represented real divisions, occupies a very different context from *Nachtmär*, dating from 1995, a time since movement across the borders of the former Holy Roman Empire has once again become unrestricted. The contrast between these two situations highlights the fact that Paula's feelings of narrowness and confinement are self-imposed, as she fails to break out of the shadow area. It is as if she continues to experience the 'Mauer im Kopf', which in Germany was said to persist after the end of division by the Berlin Wall. Paula's sense of containment contrasts with Esther's greater freedom of movement, suggesting that only someone who has thrown off the past can be free.

The Danube is an essential part of Austria's sense of location, a connecting link to the rest of the old empire and also a boundary marker between some of its nations. It is of symbolic importance in defining the country's relations to its neighbours and it is appropriate that some of the salient ideas in the novel reach their climax there. In the final part of the narrative, the river is associated particularly with drowning, evoked through literary reminiscences, including repeated mentions of Berg's opera *Wozzeck* (pp. 164, 166), which on one occasion is mentioned specifically in the context of an acquaintance of the four protagonists in a village on the Danube, who drowned herself. Yet, Paula's immersion in the river at the end of the novel is ambivalent: perhaps it signifies her recognition that her inability to penetrate mental boundaries and reach out to others is her own responsibility. Nevertheless, the immersion in water also signifies movement towards a change of state, as in the image of water, traditionally a symbol of fluidity, process and a life-giving element. It may suggest the positive aspect of Paula's ability to dream. Yet, the ending allows for a less optimistic interpretation, in which the Furies transport her across the shadowy rivers of Hades, where she, like the 'Namenslosen' in the cemetery, is not waving, but drowning, as in Berg's *Wozzeck*, whose central protagonist drowns himself in despair.

Notes

[1] Elisabeth Reichart, Interview with Linda DeMerritt and Peter Ensberg, *Modern Austrian Literature* 29:1 (1996) 1-22 (p. 5).

[2] Elisabeth Reichart, *Nachtmär*, Otto Müller: Salzburg, 1995. All page references refer to this edition.

[3] A similar concern can be identified elsewhere in Reichart's work from the 1990s, including the novel *Fotze* (1993), which was given impetus by reports of atrocities in the Bosnian war, especially the rape of the women. The narrator expresses her awareness of the continuity between atrocities old and new, which are linked by the horrors of war: 'Früher habe ich noch unterschieden zwischen den Kriegen [...], habe Lehrern und Professoren geglaubt und den Historikern und Journalisten, die von gerechten und ungerechten, von Erbfolge und Dreißigjährigen und vom Ersten und Zweiten Weltkrieg sprachen, vom Beginn des Krieges und seinem Ende, immer wieder von seinem Ende, um nicht sehen zu müssen, wie der Krieg fortgesetzt wurde, ausgelagert aus meinem Land, ein paar Hundert Kilometer weiter südlich abgelegt, wie er mir die Männer raubt, ein Raubkrieg ist das'. *Fotze*, Otto Müller Vlg: Salzburg & Vienna, 1993, p. 108.

[4] See also, Juliet Wigmore, 'Elisabeth Reichart's *Nachtmär*. The Enduring Nightmare of Austria in the 1990s'. In: Helmut Schmitz, ed., *German Culture and the Uncomfortable Past*, Ashgate: Aldershot, 2001, pp. 103-118.

[5] Linda DeMerritt, '*Lebkuchenherz* and Cultural Identity: Elisabeth Reichart's *Nachtmär*', *Modern Austrian Literature* 32:3 (1999) 85-99 (here p. 89).

[6] Thomas Kraft, 'Geschichte eines Verrats. Elisabeth Reicharts *Nachtmär*', *Süddeutsche Zeitung,* 11. October 1995 Beilage p. L4.

[7] Linda DeMerritt, op. cit., p. 88.

[8] Cf. Anna Mitgutsch, *Haus der Kindheit*, Luchterhand: Munich 2000. See Anthony Bushell, 'The Return of the Native, or the Neighbours are Back: Anna Mitgutsch's novel *Haus der Kindheit*', this volume.

[9] 'Mit der Einführung von Deutsch als Amtssprache, dem deutschsprachigen Unterricht an Kindergärten und Schulen, dem Berufsverbot für slowenische Beamte, Lehrer, Ärzte, für Teile der Priesterschaft und mit der Ausweisung zahlreicher slowenischer Intellektueller leiteten die NS-Behörden die Germanisierung ein'. Karin

Berger, Elisabeth Holzinger, Lotte Podgornik & Lisbeth N. Trallori, eds, *Der Himmel ist blau. Kann sein. Frauen im Widerstand. Österreich 1938-1945*, Promedia: Vienna 1985, p. 162.   See also: Mirko Bogotaj, *Die Kärntner Slowenen*, Hermagoras: Klagenfurt, 1989, pp. 82-83.

[10] K. Stuhlpfarrer, quoted in: Gero Fischer, *Das Slowenische in Kärnten*, Sprache und Herrschaft. Zeitschrift für eine Sprachwissenschaft als Gesellschaftswissenschaft. Reihe Monographien Nr 1: Vienna & Klagenfurt, 1980, p. 45.

[11] Claudio Magris, *Danube*, translated by Patrick Creogh, Collins Harvill: London, 1989, p. 191.

[12] Ingeborg Bachmann, *Malina*. In: *Werke* edited by Christine Koschel, Inge von Weidenbaum & Clemens Münster, Piper: Munich and Zurich 1982, Vol. 3, p. 175.

[13] Linda DeMerritt interprets this episode as an indication that Paula dies as a result of the accident she appears to suffer earlier. However, the blurring of the timescale means that such linkage is far from certain. See DeMerritt, p. 94.

Arthur Williams

'immer weiter ostwärts und immer weiter zurück in der Zeit':
Exploring the extended kith and kin of W. G. Sebald's *Austerlitz*

At least two real lives inform W. G. Sebald's story of Austerlitz's search for an
identity lost in the flight from the Holocaust, which ends when he traces an old
neighbour in Prague. Exploring even a few of Sebald's other sources yields rewarding
insights, while juxtaposing some of the less obvious allows us to suggest that a
coherent view of knowledge and the continuities of life and death underpins this
further exploration of European history in Sebald's work. This essay discusses
Sebald's extensive circle of intertextual and intellectual neighbours in *Austerlitz*,
including, among others, Stephen Hawking, Dan Jacobson, R. S. Thomas, and Ludwig
Wittgenstein.

1. Neighbours

Since W. G. Sebald's tragic death on 14 December 2001 many people
have become aware of the broad features of his life: a German intellectual
who could not relate happily to the land of his birth, who preferred to live
in Switzerland and, for most of his life, in England, and whose principal
academic focus was not German, but Austrian literature. Within this latter
context, a factor common to all of the figures he wrote about is the loss or
abandonment of an original home. He thus appears an obvious candidate
for inclusion in any discussion of the theme of 'Neighbours and Strangers'
in contemporary German-language literature.

As with so much of that literature, the Holocaust is present
throughout Sebald's work, but it is not its exclusive focus. It is often
subliminally, rather than explicitly, present:[1] the greater part of the œuvre
for which he has become internationally known explores the lives of
cultural and political exiles with non-Jewish backgrounds. These are
individuals cast beyond the pale of society for some apparent abnormality,
incompatibility, or unaccountability.[2] Mental illness and the way society
approaches it is one of Sebald's real concerns,[3] as is similarly death.

Critics and commentators rarely miss an opportunity to mention his
own 'duality': his deliberate choice to be 'W. G.' for his formal writing
and 'Max' among friends and colleagues. They have often been
fascinated also by his preoccupation with death, the dead, and their role in
life.[4] The relevance of this is also clear from a short letter to me (1 July
1998), written when he was already working on *Austerlitz*: 'The presence
of the Dead is something that preoccupies me more and more'. It is one of

the keys to *Austerlitz*, the work I intend to concentrate on here, for Sebald uses Austerlitz's voyage of self-discovery deliberately to blur the boundaries between time and space:[5] 'Freilich [...] hat das Verhältnis von Raum und Zeit, so wie man es beim Reisen erfährt, [...] etwas Illusionistisches und Illusionäres' (p. 18); the journey can also take us across the divide between life and death: 'die Grenze zwischen dem Tod und dem Leben [ist durchlässiger], als wir gemeinhin glauben' (p. 397).

While aspects of Sebald's own life are an important motivation for and an overt component of his work, to overemphasise them is to assume a naiveté his work does not possess.[6] I shall refer sparingly to details of his biography, drawing mainly on the evidence of his published œuvre, his directly cited sources, and those he used to impart a potent intertextual charge to his literary world, the intellectual neighbours he cherished.

The ambivalence of the 'neighbourly' relationship in Sebald's work can be summed up by reference to two figures: Jean Améry and Paul Bereyter. Améry is the subject of a 1988 essay.[7] Bereyter is the eponymous teacher of the second story in *Die Ausgewanderten* (39–93) and, since we know that the photographs in that volume are 'genuine',[8] we can assume that Bereyter's story has been fictionalised only to the extent that the context and Sebald's literary objectives require.

Sebald cites Améry in *Austerlitz* when he brings home to us the dreadful torture Améry endured in Breendonk as his shoulder joints are slowly dislocated under his own weight (p. 38).[9] The torture chamber is a small room that reminds the narrator of the butcher's shop back in the village of his childhood: the hooks, the table and the drain (p. 37). There is a terrible intimacy here in the bodily closeness of torturers and tortured. In the essay Sebald had outlined how Hanns Mayer had become aware of the significance of his middle name, Israel, and fled the Nazis only at the last moment — in his provincial home people had drifted along, comfortably oblivious of the significance of political events. He acquired a new name and a new language. In the resistance in Brussels, a detail that all but undid him was the accent of the SS man who suddenly knocked at his door; it was the vernacular of his youth. In 1978, Sebald reminds us, Améry deliberately returned to Austria to commit suicide in a specific Salzburg hotel: the 'Österreichischer Hof'.

Paul Bereyter, whose suicide the narrator of *Die Ausgewanderten* (1992) is seeking to understand, had been a wonderful teacher. He had committed suicide in the village where he had made his home because he could not shake off the shadow of the past. He was a 'Dreiviertelarier', he had served in the *Wehrmacht*, and was someone loved by the whole village: everyone knew him simply as Paul; he was like an elder brother. But these are not the recollections that had caught up with him. Paul's story, as told by a friend, recalls rather how neighbours had become strangers and killers.

The scenario can be seen to be typical in *Die Ausgewanderten*.[10] By the time Sebald wrote *Austerlitz* (2001), there seem to have been some subtle adjustments in his relationship to the German past as a result of his preoccupation with the continuing 'presence of the dead' in life and, probably, of his engagement with the German victims of the war (*Luftkrieg und Literatur*, 1999), and of a growing confidence in his own ability to harness the power of literature.[11]

In *Austerlitz*, Sebald brings his meticulous research skills, his powerful imagination and his immaculate pen to bear to re-assert the bonds of neighbourliness and brotherhood, or sisterhood, smashed by his father's generation around the time of his birth — a motif he stresses in this book (pp. 37–8).[12] A further aspect of the evolution in his work is apparent in the teacher–storyteller duality that he himself embodied. It is reflected at many points in *Austerlitz* and it is the storyteller who increasingly assumes the life-giving role. It is reasonable to suggest that Sebald had completed the same shift in his own life.[13]

Austerlitz is a true successor to Paul Bereyter:

> Austerlitz ist ja für mich, der ich zu Beginn meines Studiums in Deutschland von den seinerzeit dort amtierenden, größtenteils in den dreißiger und vierziger Jahren in ihrer akademischen Laufbahn vorangerückten und immer noch in ihren Machtphantasien befangenen Geisteswissenschaftlern so gut wie gar nichts gelernt habe, seit meiner Volksschulzeit der erste Lehrer überhaupt gewesen, dem ich zuhören konnte. (pp. 47–8)[14]

Yet Austerlitz never 'teaches', he only ever tells his tale and weaves his tapestry of observations. Sebald deliberately re-draws the boundary between knowledge and fiction, allowing the creative seasoning of the latter greater scope in *Austerlitz* than in any previous volume.

Austerlitz himself owes his first discovery of pride in himself to a brilliant teacher who knows how to bring European history to life and who became a brother to him (pp. 101–109). And he owes the rediscovery of his lost identity to a woman who had been both a good neighbour and a sister to his mother. Věra Ryšanová, his old nanny, had helped Agáta to pack for the first stage of her final journey (pp. 255–256). Věra herself had never recovered from that, but she had preserved everything in her private life as it was then to ensure the survival of the memory (p. 220). It is a peculiarly ambivalent, but deeply humane moment. Věra, as it were, performs the last rites for Agáta and, at the same time, she preserves her from oblivion. And, as Věra and Austerlitz talk together, his Czech returns and with it his identity. This constitutes the essence of Sebald's literary project.

2. Intellectual neighbours and biographical models

The quotation in the title of this paper: '...immer weiter ostwärts und immer weiter zurück in der Zeit' (*Austerlitz*, p. 266) suggests a space–time continuum. Travel from west to east in Europe, especially during the Cold War, but also after the events of 1989–1990, was often an unsettling experience of journeying back in time. GDR landscapes and, more particularly, townscapes, where they were not just hideously anonymous, were always a reminder of conditions and smells from a past that had disappeared in the West. The train journey that Austerlitz undertakes at this point in his story traverses just such landscapes and leads him into just such townscapes (pp. 265–281). But the journey eastwards in the past times that Austerlitz is seeking to uncover was also, for many, a journey to torment and to death. His mother's first destination had been Theresienstadt (Terezín), until she was sent on the next stage, further east (p. 291), presumably to Auschwitz. And the book ends, completing its span from the Wales of Austerlitz's childhood to Lithuania, with the first-person narrator finishing reading Dan Jacobson's account (1998) of his visit to Fort IX in Kaunas,[15] like Terezín and Breendonk, a star-shaped fortress which found its place in history for inhumanity, not heroics. Jacobson, like Sebald, and by dint also of research combined with literary skill, strikes a blow against the falsification of history;[16] it is a deliberate tribute when Sebald concludes *Austerlitz* with a set of negative images which yet reconnect the author (and his reader) both with the dead Jacobson has rescued from oblivion and with the life Sebald has just resurrected.

Our eponymous traveller has by now taken his leave. Our first-person narrator has returned to Antwerp and Breendonk. Depressing echoes of earlier texts and earlier times return:

> Ich verbrachte eine unruhige Nacht [...] in einem brauntapezierten, häßlichen Zimmer, das nach rückwärts hinausging auf Brandmauern, Abluftkamine und flache, mit Stacheldraht voneinander getrennte Dächer. [...] bis in den frühen

> Morgen hinein [heulten] die Martinshörner und Polizeisirenen. [...] Als ich das
> [...] Hotel [...] verließ, lag drunten [...] eine aschfahle, etwa vierzigjährige Frau
> mit seitwärts verdrehten Augen auf einer hohen Bahre. [...] ein Kanal, auf dem
> gerade [...] ein langer Lastkahn [...] anscheinend führerlos dahinglitt, ohne eine
> Spur zu hinterlassen auf der schwarzen Fläche des Wassers. (pp. 412–413)

The most uncompromisingly negative image comes in the form of a
quotation from Jacobson's 'Prologue' to *Heshel's Kingdom* (p. 5). The
diamond mines in South Africa, where Jacobson had grown up, were now
massive voids; anyone who dared could:

> bis an den vordersten Rand dieser riesigen Gruben herantreten und
> hinabblicken in eine Tiefe von mehreren tausend Fuß. Wahrhaft erschreckend
> sei es gewesen, schreibt Jacobson, einen Schritt von dem festen Erdboden eine
> solche Leere sich auftun zu sehen, zu begreifen, daß es da keinen Übergang
> gab, sondern nur diesen Rand, auf der einen Seite das selbstverständliche
> Leben, auf der anderen sein unausdenkbares Gegenteil. Der Abgrund, in den
> kein Lichtstrahl hinabreicht, ist Jacobsons Bild für die untergegangene Vorzeit
> seiner Familie und seines Volks, die sich, wie er weiß, von dort drunten nicht
> mehr heraufholen läßt. (p. 416)

The quotation from Jacobson is accurate, but Sebald's selection and
siting are precise. He has accentuated the finality in order to then reach
out beyond the void — and Jacobson has provided the means: in the
notorious Fort IX, he had found the last messages the victims had
scratched into the walls (Jacobson, p. 161). Among them (and Sebald has
shortened but not otherwise altered Jacobson's record) is 'Max Stern,
Paris, 18. 5. 44' (*Austerlitz*, p. 417): Sebald's own date of birth, his
preferred first name, and one of the great symbols of his book. We can
only imagine the effect this combination of signals from the dead,
reaching him when they did, from a colleague, as a result of the activity in
which he placed more faith than any other: reading, must have had on
Sebald.[17] If he had not already woven the image of star-shaped fortresses-
cum-prisons into his *Austerlitz* tapestry, this name must have dictated that
he do so. And the sharing of another name from Jacobson's search for
traces of his family is almost equally unnerving: '"the last Jew in Varniai"
is a woman mathematics teacher, once married to a Lithuanian, who had
taught in the local high school and is now widowed and retired. Her first
name [...] was Vera; but her surname and address were not known'
(Jacobson, p. 183). Jacobson, however, did find her; she became an ally

in his search; and: 'In a recent letter Vera wrote to me (in German), "You are my brother"'. (Jacobson, p. 200)

We are reminded here of a number of aspects of Sebald's project, including his view of his own contribution: to read and to communicate (or to listen and communicate: Austerlitz comments 'daß er bald für seine Geschichte, hinter der er erst in den letzten Jahren gekommen sei, einen Zuhörer finde müsse, ähnlich wie ich es seinerzeit gewesen sei in Antwerpen, Liège und Zeebrugge'; p. 64).[18] Sebald plants Jacobson's book deliberately as an invitation to read it and also to reflect on it alongside his own. — Jacobson writes to take stock both of what happened then in Lithuania and of where he and his people are now. While the record will stand and his account bear re-reading, his is essentially a personal act of closure. Sebald, writing as a German, is fighting to prevent closure, to re-connect with that same past. Our narrator finishes reading the fifteenth chapter of *Heshel's Kingdom* 'und machte mich dann auf den Rückweg nach Mechelen, wo ich anlangte, als es Abend wurde' (p. 417). We sense the weight of responsibility on his retreating shoulders and we know that he will neither lie easy nor lay aside his rucksack for good.[19]

The difference between the two projects becomes clearer when we recall that diamond extraction has all but ceased in the mines of Jacobson's 'Prologue', while Austerlitz, having made his connection in Prague, takes up residence in Paris in the 'rue des cinque diamants' (p. 358).[20] This is the quincunx of *Die Ringe des Saturn* (p. 29), the lattice symbol of the interconnecting and complementary nature of all knowledge that stands at the head of Sebald's English pilgrimage through modern European history. Jacobson's *Heshel's Kingdom* is thus simply the last of an extended family of texts which have a place in the genealogy of *Austerlitz* and which are introduced to us explicitly. Other texts are not named, but are unmistakable; yet others can be discerned individually by readers with appropriate previous acquaintance. Set against this background, the real identities on whom Sebald bases aspects of his Austerlitz figure tend to shrink somewhat in importance. They were, of course, important to Sebald; the book could not have happened without them. The rich tapestry of *Austerlitz*, however, derives from the other texts from the realms of literature, history, architecture, painting, film, photography, maps, museums, and zoological gardens. They draw us into a re-examination of the European culture to which we, no less than the victims and the perpetrators of the Holocaust, belong.

These distinctions between the levels of intertextual presence are important, and it is the second group, the non-explicit sources, that I want to try and raise a little closer to the surface, in some cases somewhat speculatively. However, it seems helpful to indicate something of the real models and more explicitly acknowledged texts first.

3. Forebears

In his '*Spiegel*-Gespräch' (12 March 2001) Sebald indicated that he drew on 'zweieinhalb Lebensgeschichten' for Austerlitz's story; to Maya Jaggi he was less specific: 'two or three, perhaps three-and-a-half, real persons' (*The Guardian*, 21 December 2001). Although he protected these real identities, the two main sources are: the retired 'Gelehrten, der [...] Baugeschichtler war und in London unterrichtet hat' ('*Spiegel*-Gespräch'), and an 'English woman who [...] had come to this country with her twin sister and been brought up in a Welsh Calvinist household' (Jaggi). The latter is Susi Bechhöfer, whose own published account of her harrowing story does indeed provide details easily recognisable in Sebald's Austerlitz.[21] But there are also fundamental differences, since Sebald's object is not to re-tell these real lives as such. One crucial difference is his re-location of the minister's home to a Welsh-speaking environment, the step to that 'Nahtstelle zwischen Dokumentation und Fiktion[, an der] literarisch die interessantesten Dinge entstehen' ('*Spiegel*-Gespräch'), where the intellectual undercurrents also come into play.

Among the sources Sebald cites extensively and explicitly, apart from Améry's *Über die Tortur*, Simon's *Le Jardin des Plantes* (pp. 38–40) and Jacobson's *Heshel's Kingdom* (pp. 414–417), are H. G. Adler's account of the Theresienstadt ghetto (pp. 331–347) and Balzac's *Le Colonel Chabert* (pp. 260, 395–397). Austerlitz tells our narrator that Adler's work was new to him and that it had cost him much effort to study it, allowing Sebald to detail some of his factual discoveries. Note, however, also the pre-echo (lost in the English) of the 'Adler-Nebel in der Konstellation Schlange', with its

> riesigen Regionen interstellaren Gases, die sich zu gewitterwolkenartigen, mehrere Lichtjahre in den Weltraum hinausragenden Gebilden zusammenballten und in denen, in [...] ständig sich intensivierenden Verdichtungsprozeß, neue Sterne [entstehen]. (p. 167)

Reading Balzac's novel was a similarly new experience for Austerlitz (p. 395), but Sebald exploited it at two pivotal points: the re-discovery of the photograph of Austerlitz, which had been hidden among its pages (p. 260), and the discovery of a photograph in an American architectural journal of the room with the prisoners' files in Terezín. The latter is linked to Balzac's somewhat 'kolportagehafte' story because this had caused Austerlitz to reflect that the boundary between life and death is more permeable than is usually assumed (p. 397) and it was with this thought in mind that he is confronted with the records he had failed to explore on his previous visit to Terezín.

Among the other texts Sebald incorporates into his book, which I can do no more than mention here, are the contribution to evolution of Charles Darwin (pp. 123, 136) and the related divergences within the Huxley family (of whom the uncles Aldous and Evelyn and great uncle Alphonso at Andromeda Lodge, the mystic and the natural scientists, are clearly embodiments; pp. 123, 128), paintings by Turner (pp. 153, 158–160; the owner of Iver Grove is, perhaps significantly, one James Mallord Ashman, p. 151), Leni Riefenstahl's famous film *Der Triumph des Willens*: both the account by Austerlitz's father (pp. 241–244) and the important transposition when Austerlitz himself strays into the centre of Nuremberg (pp. 317–320), and Alain Renais' film *Toute la mémoire du monde* (pp. 367–368) about communications in the Bibliothèque Nationale. As with all of Sebald's work, Kafka and Benjamin are constant, undeclared presences. And there are, in *Austerlitz*, two undeclared presences and one declared travelling companion; it is on these that I intend to focus.

Wittgenstein, explicitly identified early in the text as an Austerlitz *Doppelgänger*, constantly carried a rucksack, linking him also to our first-person narrator and, implicitly, to Sebald himself (cf. the photograph on page 175 and, for example, the original cover of *Die Ringe des Saturn*):

> die [...] Ähnlichkeit seiner Person mit der Ludwig Wittgensteins [...]. Ich glaube, es war vor allem der Rucksack, [...] der mich auf die an sich eher abwegige Idee einer gewissen körperlichen Verwandtschaft zwischen ihm, Austerlitz, und dem 1951 [...] gestorbenen Philosophen brachte. (pp. 58–9)

The idea of a 'körperliche Verwandtschaft' may be 'abwegig', but the link is too strong to be left to chance:

> Mehr und mehr dünkt es mich darum jetzt, sobald ich auf eine Photographie von Wittgenstein stoße, als blicke mir Austerlitz aus ihr entgegen, oder, wenn ich Austerlitz anschaue, als sehe ich in ihm den unglücklichen, in der Klarheit seiner logischen Überlegungen ebenso wie in der Verwirrung seiner Gefühle

eingesperrten Denker, dermaßen auffällig sind die Ähnlichkeiten zwischen den beiden, in der Statur, in der Art, wie sie einen über eine unsichtbare Grenze hinweg studieren [...]. (p. 60)

If Austerlitz shares so many qualities with Wittgenstein (I have shortened the list), then it seems reasonable to assume a deeper stratum of kinship — in Wittgenstein's ideas about language, culture and identity. If the relevance to Sebald's project is not immediately obvious, especially why he chose a Welsh-speaking environment for Austerlitz's childhood, fortunately, we have an excellent source to hand which locates Wittgenstein's thought in a context very close to Sebald's main research field: Ernest Gellner's *Language and Solitude. Wittgenstein, Malinowski and the Habsburg Dilemma.*[22] Gellner himself was born in Paris in 1925, brought up in Prague and moved to London in 1939. Malinowski hailed from Cracow, in Gellner's terms (p. 123), 'a suburb of Vienna in those pre-1914 days', placing him in the same intellectual climate that produced Wittgenstein, whose two major contributions to twentieth-century thought Gellner deconstructs in favour of Malinowski's social anthropology and its foundation in ethnographic fieldwork. The Habsburg world, for which Gellner uses Musil's term 'Kakania', had taken to extremes two intellectual currents which Wittgenstein had espoused in turn, but never synthesised. These are characteristic, on the one hand, of the cultural nationalist (from Herder via Darwin and Nietzsche) and, on the other, of the atomised, isolated individual (traced back to Descartes[23]). Wittgenstein was isolated on both counts, but it is the Wittgenstein of the *Tractatus* who most closely resembles the early Austerlitz — I cite the opening of the chapter 'Ego and Language' (Gellner, p. 59), one of the innumerable, uncannily relevant, eminently quotable passages:

> The *Tractatus* was the simultaneous expression of two kinds of anguish: that of the solitary explorer of the world propelled into 'cosmic exile' [...] and that of the Man Without Qualities, without any attributes imposed on him by his roots: lacking roots, and so lacking any genuine identity [...]. But there is another duality which can also be discerned in the *Tractatus*: alienation through the solitude of the self, and alienation through the inert superficiality of language.

As his argument unfolds, Gellner (pp. 62–3) recalls Wittgenstein's 'Death is not an event in life' and counters with:

> If death is not an event in life, then at any rate it would seem that the death of others would be a part of life. But the *Tractatus* appears to be an autistic work

> [...]. It appears that this world had no other significant inhabitants. A single
> consciousness mirrored a single world and was co-extensive with it.

One ends in a 'solitary black hole'. While all minds are held to be the same, they never meet, they merely photocopy atoms and then aggregate them (Gellner, p. 65). Thus all men are essentially the same, any differences in language and culture are superficial and unimportant (Gellner, p. 69). Again, a response is to hand:

> What is wholly absent is the suspicion that an important part of what we
> understand by meaning might be intimately, inescapably, inextricably mixed up
> with the concrete and contingent activities of a given, specific and idiosyncratic
> culture; that meanings might be carried, not by individuals but, on the contrary,
> by on-going collectivities, by partnerships of the dead and the living and those
> yet unborn [...]. For such communities, death is — very much so — an event
> *in* life. (Gellner, p. 70)

And he moves quickly to the later Wittgenstein who notoriously abjured his earlier position and crossed to the opposite, equally untenable extreme: 'he deployed the communal-cultural vision of thought not for the solution of socio-political problems [...] but, instead, to solve or dissolve abstract problems' (Gellner, p. 77). Consequently this Wittgenstein, caught in a Kafkan world, is stripped by decree of all his personal qualities. The escape route from the Wittgensteinian prison cell, which 'contains not one but two prisoners, each condemned to solitary confinement' (Gellner, p. 81), runs via Malinowski's meticulous ethnological fieldwork with its emphasis on social and cultural interdependence (Gellner, p. 121).

Sebald, of course, endorsed absolutely the research ethic,[24] and there are several further points where Gellner's discussion seems uncommonly close to Sebald's. Thus Gellner suggests that Darwinism had brought a history into view that went beyond the documentary record and, as a result, British anthropology had become the 'Remembrance of Things Collectively Past' (Gellner, p. 115) through the evidence of surviving 'savages' gathered in the main by the ethnographic 'time machine' of missionary and similar reports of distant cultures. By contrast, Malinowski's approach, which eventually triumphed, was essentially ahistorical: history, however, had a value in a functionally interdependent present (Gellner, p. 134), the 'Malinowskian past was not an interference, it was a social function *in the observable present*' (Gellner, p. 135). And, as Gellner draws together his threads in a final paragraph before his concluding section, he refers back to the Habsburg dichotomy:

> it does represent [...] a kind of convergence of the two currents which have concerned us. It is only a partial convergence: by now the streams are no longer pure [...]. But, for all that, the two rivers, though by now fed by so many streams, have come together in the end. (Gellner, p. 177)

4. Time and space

It is time now to return to the siting of the first part of Austerlitz's story, for among Sebald's many mysterious, submerged inspirations drawn from Wales are the two 'Quellflüsse', Dwy Fach and Dwy Fawr, that flow in the depths through the length of Lake Bala without ever mixing with its waters (p. 116). The Welsh connection, at the very least, is about time suspended, disconnected language, loss of identity in the midst of a culture-based community. The extreme nature and origins of Austerlitz's isolation bring him uncommonly close particularly to Wittgenstein's early thought. And, should we need a further clue, then it is to be found in the poetry (and, to some extent, the figure) of R. S. Thomas:[25] Austerlitz's adoptive father lies on his death bed in a home for the geriatric in Denbigh 'mit dem Gesicht gegen die Wand' — it is a line from R. S. Thomas's 'Death of a Peasant': 'You remember Davies? He died, you know, / With his face to the wall, as the manner is / Of the poor peasant in his stone croft / on the Welsh hills'. This poem, and one called simply 'Evans', conveys much of the atmosphere that goes into the preacher's house and several of the deaths in *Austerlitz*. However, it is the poem 'Welsh Landscape' which furnished the central anchoring of Austerlitz in North (better Welsh) Wales, with its mountains, ruined castles and drowned villages:

> To live in Wales is to be conscious
> At dusk of the spilled blood
> [...]
> Of strife in the strung woods,
> Vibrant with sped arrows.
> You cannot live in the present,
> At least not in Wales.
> There is the language for instance,
> The soft consonants
> Strange to the ear.
> There are cries in the dark at night

[...]
There is no present in Wales,
And no future;
There is only the past,
Brittle with relics,
Wind-bitten towers and castles
With sham ghosts;
[...]

Sebald's Wales, the product of his imagination and research, has uncanny echoes of the Rhine of legend and saga (pp. 320–323; Austerlitz is like the 'Siegfried in Langs Nibelungenfilm', p. 10) and requires the heightened vision that sees in the twilight zones (like Sebald's philosophers and animals in the Antwerp nocturama; pp. 7–8). In his Welsh excursion, Sebald is out to challenge our received perceptions, particularly of time, by dint of the power of myth and the mystical. This is a place where time has a different pace and a different effect. Ghosts inhabit the drowned village of Llanwddyn at the bottom of Lake Vyrnwy (pp. 74–8) and sometimes they brush past you in the street or on a mountain path, sometimes singly, quite often in groups, particularly processions,[26] and all, in some way, reduced in stature. Old Evan, from whom Austerlitz learned Welsh 'förmlich im Flug, weil mir seine Geschichten viel besser eingingen als die endlosen [...] Bibelsprüche, die ich [...] auswendig lernen mußte', maintained that 'die Erfahrung des Todes verkürzt uns, gerade so wie ein Stück Leinen eingeht, wenn man es zum erstenmal wäscht'. Evan told of 'Verstorbenen, die das Los zur Unzeit getroffen hatte, die sich um ihr Teil betrogen wußten und danach trachteten, wieder ins Leben zurückzukehren' (pp. 78–9).

There is more to Sebald's unsettling of the boundaries of space and time than just his magical realism, his mystical exploitation of the *Märchen* model he deliberately invokes (p. 411). A little reflection on some of the issues raised in Stephen Hawking's *A Brief History of Time*[27] allows us to suggest that Sebald is exploiting scientific models as well as literary ones to shake up our received perceptions.[28] It can be no coincidence that Gerald, Austerlitz's young friend, pursues his ground-breaking researches into the birth of new stars at Cambridge (pp. 165–168), where Stephen Hawking holds the prestigious Lucasian Chair once held by Isaac Newton (and both, like Wittgenstein, at Trinity College). And Sebald's detailed description (pp. 144–148) of the Royal Observatory at Greenwich, Newton's former home, with its green arrows always pointing one way and its unique star-shaped room, especially when taken together with Austerlitz's extensive commentary on the subjective nature of time, must bring together Hawking's disquisition on time, Europe's infamous star-shaped fortresses and the traces of the individuals who perished there.   In *Austerlitz*, these latter are also buried beneath the buildings we now occupy and the roads we tread, they are inscribed in the language of the architecture of our great buildings and in the systems which organise our lives and allow us to call ourselves civilised, be these our railways, our fortifications, or our clocks.

From the outset, Sebald reminds us how arbitrary, how imprecise and how recent is our organisation of time.[29] The chance first meeting of our narrator with Austerlitz takes place in a railway waiting room, where the whole setting is dominated by a massive clock, representing the 'neue Omnipotenz' facilitated by the advent of the railways (p. 17), a 'Gleichschaltung' after which time dominated the world, we are 'gezwungen, [unsere] Handlungsweise auszurichten nach ihr' (p. 18). Austerlitz, who never owned a watch (p. 147), described time as 'von allen unseren Erfindungen weitaus die künstlichste und, in ihrer Gebundenheit an den um die eigene Achse sich drehenden Planeten, nicht weniger willkürlich als etwa eine Kalkulation es wäre, die ausginge vom Wachstum der Bäume oder von der Dauer, in der ein Kalkstein zerfällt [...]' (pp. 145–146). Stephen Hawking reminds us that clocks close to the surface of the earth run more slowly than clocks at a distance from it, at the top of mountains, for example, or if one travelled through space at close to the speed of light. Hawking puts it this way:

> Newton's laws of motion put an end to the idea of absolute position in space. The theory of relativity gets rid of absolute time. [...] [E]ach individual has his own personal measure of time that depends on where he is and how he is moving. [...] Space and time are now dynamic quantities. (Hawking, p. 33)

The one thing that scientists still hold to be impossible, Hawking tells us, is reverse travel through time (all other laws of science hold good for both the positive and the negative, e.g. matter and antimatter). There are three arrows of time, at least (Hawking, pp. 143–145): the thermodynamic (entropy), the psychological (human perception based on memory) and the cosmological (expanding universe). The first determines the second and they always point in the same direction: things break and do not then remake themselves and we know this because our memory allows us to compare the first with the second state. When Hawking first discusses entropy, he uses the image of billiard balls which are initially contained in a defined (or ordered) space but then, as their motion and collisions increase, break out and dissipate their energy over a larger space (Hawking, p. 102).   Sebald (pp. 153–157, immediately after the Greenwich discussion) uses the image of a billiards room which has remained untouched since 1814 to suggest the idea of a 'time capsule', a space where time has been suspended and can be revisited.

5. Anti-hegemonic uncertainty

Entropy, or 'disorder' as Hawking calls it (pp. 102–104), expresses the movement from an ordered state to one less ordered, involving a loss of energy, a diminished state.   All of Sebald's ghosts, the illnesses and deaths in *Austerlitz*, involve a diminished state (and Hawking is never embarrassed by his own physical condition; cf. pp. 49, 99).   These figures shimmer at the edges, they move at a different pace from the living and their voices have a different pitch (p. 79).   In Sebald's world, these shades have the ability to move back out of the state of 'Abwesenheit', which seems to reflect the behaviour of matter and antimatter in movement around the edges of black holes, which Hawking compares to the edges of shadows (pp. 99–100).   This is an area of apparently 'empty space' in which uncertainty reigns (Hawking, pp. 105–106): 'Für mich aber, sagte Austerlitz, war es zu jener Zeit, als kehrten die Toten aus ihrer Abwesenheit zurück und erfüllten das Zwielicht um mich her mit ihrem eigenartig langsamen, ruhlosen Treiben' (pp. 191–192).

We are always aware in *Austerlitz* of the world that exists alongside our own, which, like the moths that appear out of the darkness in Wales (pp. 131–134), we do not normally see, but which is as necessary to our existence as are antiparticles to particles.   There are areas where all of the boundaries we normally observe begin to merge and become permeable (p. 139).   For Austerlitz, who often doubts the reality of his own existence, this complementary world and the uncertain boundaries that separate it from us may be his best hope: 'dann wieder meinte ich, ein unsichtbarer Zwillingsbruder ginge neben mir her, sozusagen das Gegenteil eines Schattens' (p. 80).[30]   When Austerlitz suggests that 'die Zeit' has always been 'ungleichzeitig' (p. 147), he is again resisting the order imposed on our perceptions by our human situation and by history.   He takes the view that 'die Toten seien ja außer der Zeit', and is aware that 'es genüge doch schon ein Quantum persönlichen Unglücks, um uns abzuschneiden von jeder Vergangenheit und jeder Zukunft' (p. 147) and hopes that he 'hinter [die Zeit] zurücklaufen könne, daß dort alles so wäre wie vordem oder, genauer gesagt, daß sämtliche Zeitmomente gleichzeitig nebeneinander existierten' (p. 148).

Sebald stresses the narrow band of conditions within which life is possible and the 'magische Schwelle' of 36°C (p. 134) when moths cease to be 'totenstarr' and begin to fly, a body temperature shared by 'Säugetiere [...], Delphine und Thunfische in voller Fahrt'. We know by now that his intention is to cross thresholds, even those between the different forms of life, all of which have 'memories' (cf. the circus group and the apparently intelligent goose; pp. 383–387). This perhaps reflects the scientists' search for one grand theory to explain the whole of the universe (Hawking, p. 11) and Darwinian theories of evolution (Hawking, p. 11; *Austerlitz*, p. 123), but it can also be seen as an attack on the anthropic principle (cf. Hawking, pp. 124–126) which sees a purpose in everything because it sees humanity as the pinnacle of creation, the be all and end all![31] In historiography, this view determines the significance of events retrospectively in the light of the currently prevalent product of that past; in Gellner's analysis of Wittgenstein, it perhaps corresponds to the 'autistic' traits he detects (e.g. Gellner, pp. 63, 65), the world limited in extent to the visual field (Gellner, p. 92). In *Die Ausgewanderten*, Sebald had explored the vanishing point that takes us beyond our horizons of expectation,[32] now he seems to be challenging the anthropic principle head on. His approach to knowledge, that it cannot be subdivided into discrete modules,[33] is at one with a view that resists hegemonic interpretations that arise from the accidents of history, especially where such hegemony is constituent of West European colonialism, be it political or cultural. In *Austerlitz*, while he is refusing to let the past be buried for good, he is also challenging the way we organise our readings of that past and the information we access in the process.

Advances in science have brought uncertainty and relativity to the apparently most reliable factors in life, liberating them from what are essentially our own limitations. Sebald would apply the same lesson of modesty and reflection to all our claims to knowledge. He would urge us to see beyond our immediate horizons, or at least to accept that they are 'our' horizons. In *Austerlitz*, he has enlisted the support of some eminent intellectual friends and neighbours to bring this home to us.

Ultimately, it is Sebald's belief in literature that allows him to combine real biographies and historical accounts with literary quotations and readings of cultural texts from the realms of architecture, painting and film and with reflections on the discoveries of science in our time in order to restore life to characters whom history otherwise would have condemned to oblivion and irrelevance. For literature, as Sebald knew, is much more than simply a 'Nahtstelle' where 'die interessantesten Dinge entstehen' ('*Spiegel*-Gespräch'):

> Wozu also Literatur? Soll es werden auch mir, fragte Hölderlin sich, wie den tausenden, die in den Tagen ihres Frühlings doch auch ahnend und liebend gelebt, aber am trunkenen Tag von den rächenden Parzen ergriffen, ohne Klang und Gesang heimlich hinuntergeführt, dort im allzu nüchternen Reich, dort büßen im Dunkeln, wo bei trügerischem Schein irres Gewimmel sich treibt, wo die langsame Zeit bei Frost und Dürre sie zählen, nur in Seufzern der Mensch noch die Unsterblichen preist? Der synoptische Blick, der in diesen Zeilen über die Grenze des Todes schweift, ist verschattet und illuminiert doch zugleich das Andenken derer, denen das größte Unrecht widerfuhr. Es gibt viele Formen des Schreibens; einzig aber in der literarischen geht es, über die Registrierung der Tatsachen und über die Wissenschaft hinaus, um einen Versuch der Restitution.[34]

Notes

W. G. Sebald's works referred to are (in chronological order): *Die Beschreibung des Unglücks: Zur österreichischen Literatur von Stifter bis Handke*, Fischer Taschenbuch Verlag: Frankfurt am Main, 1994 (1985); *Nach der Natur: Ein Elementargedicht*, Fischer Taschenbuch Verlag: Frankfurt am Main, 1995 (1988); *Schwindel. Gefühle.*, Fischer Taschenbuch Verlag: Frankfurt am Main, 1994 (1990); *Unheimliche Heimat: Essays zur österreichischen Literatur*, Fischer Taschenbuch Verlag: Frankfurt am Main, 1995 (1991); *Die Ausgewanderten: Vier lange Erzählungen*, Fischer Taschenbuch Verlag: Frankfurt am Main, 1994 (1992); *Die Ringe des Saturn: Eine englische Wallfahrt*, Fischer Taschenbuch Verlag: Frankfurt am Main, 1997 (1995); *Logis in einem Landhaus: Über Gottfried Keller, Johann Peter Hebel, Robert Walser und andere*, Hanser Verlag: Munich, 1998; *Luftkrieg und Literatur. Mit einem Essay zu Alfred Andersch*, Hanser Verlag: Munich, 1999; *Austerlitz*, Hanser Verlag: Munich, 2001.

[1] In a most informative '*Spiegel*-Gespräch' (*Der Spiegel*, 12 March 2001, 228–234), Sebald said: 'das, was von deutschen Autoren nichtjüdischer Herkunft über dieses Thema der Verfolgung und der versuchten Ausrottung des jüdischen Volks geschrieben worden ist, [ist] im Allgemeinen unzulänglich und [besteht] über weite Strecken aus Peinlichkeiten, auch aus Usurpationen'. To the comment: 'bei Ihnen [...] wird das Entsetzliche sehr vermittelt erzählt', he responded: 'Das ist gewollt, weil ich das Umkippen ins Melodramatische fürchte [...]. Dabei geht die ästhetische Authentizität verloren, die auf eine untergründige, intime Weise mit dem Ethischen verbunden ist'. Similarly he said to Maya Jaggi (*The Guardian*, 21 December 2001): 'So you would have to approach [this topic] from an angle, and by intimating to the

reader that these subjects are constant company; their presence shades every inflection of every sentence one writes. If one can make that credible, then one can begin to defend writing about these subjects at all'. Thus, what Benjamin Kunkel says of *Vertigo* ('Germanic Depressive', *Voice Literary Supplement*, June 2000) holds good for the whole of Sebald's œuvre: 'One unspeakable event is never mentioned. But as a result of this heartrending tact, the Holocaust casts its shadow across all of Sebald's pages'.

[2] Many critics, and particularly the hasty obituary writers of December 2001, have tended to miss this point. More aware commentators have understood the range of authors, intellectuals and artists Sebald 'spoke with', as Andrea Köhler put it ('jemand, der nie *über* seine Gegenstände, sondern immer nur *mit* seinen Gegenständen sprach'; 'Verabredungen in der Vergangenheit. Zum Tod des Schriftstellers W. G. Sebald', *Neue Zürcher Zeitung*, 16 December 2001). Köhler lists a few figures from *Schwindel. Gefühle.* and *Logis in einem Landhaus*. Sebald's 'Gesprächspartner' in *Die Ringe des Saturn* are too numerous to even begin to list; see instead the review in the *Frankfurter Allgemeine Zeitung* (Patrick Bahners, 'Kaltes Herz', 9 December 1995, B5) which provides an excellent insight into both Sebald's associative method and his range of 'fellow pilgrims' on his 'englische Wallfahrt'.

[3] Literature and psychopathology was one of Sebald's main research interests. The first of his two volumes of essays on Austrian literature (*Die Beschreibung des Unglücks*) explores, in the main, the psychological field (the second, *Unheimliche Heimat*, focuses on the societal frameworks). See also the discussions of Ernst Herbeck (*Schwindel. Gefühle.*, pp. 47–59) and Jan Peter Tripp (*Logis in einem Landhaus*, pp. 171–188), both of whom are schizophrenic. Sebald specifically acknowledges his debt to Tripp, an old schoolfriend whose work inspired him (cf. W. G. Sebald, 'Rede zur Einweihung des Literaturhauses Stuttgart, 17. November 2001', *Stuttgarter Zeitung*, 19 November 2001, 12) and who has organised an exhibition of his paintings and short verses by Sebald (W. G. Sebald – Jan Peter Tripp, *Unerzählt*, Hanser Verlag: Munich, 2003).

[4] For example, Köhler (note 2) talks of Sebald operating in 'halluzinativen Regionen [...] die den Grenzverkehr zwischen den Lebenden und den Toten erlauben' and James Wood entitled his review of *The Rings of Saturn* 'A death artist writes' (*The Guardian Saturday*, 30 May 1998, 8), but 'He claimed no false intimacy with the dead' (Eric Homberger, 'W G Sebald. German writer shaped by the 'forgetfulness' of his fellow countrymen after the Second World War', *The Guardian*, 17 December 2001).

[5] As he had done on his walks through the English countryside just a few miles from his Norfolk home in *Die Ringe des Saturn* (*FAZ* review; note 2).

[6] Many commentators have picked up the relevance of Sebald's time and place of birth, e.g. Köhler (note 2). Notwithstanding the precision of the biographical detail he introduces into all of his works, Sebald's position was classical: 'Die bürgerliche Person ist etwas anderes als der Schriftsteller. Der Schriftsteller ist etwas anderes als

der Erzähler. Und der Erzähler ist wiederum etwas anderes als die Figuren, die er beschreibt' ('*Spiegel*-Gespräch', note 1).

[7] 'Verlorenes Land — Jean Améry und Österreich', in: *Unheimliche Heimat*, pp. 131–144.

[8] The photographs in *Austerlitz* are about 'halbe-halbe' found by chance and taken specifically, while: 'In meinem Buch "Die Ausgewanderten" waren fast alle Bilder historisch und authentisch in Bezug auf die dargestellten Biografien' ('*Spiegel*-Gespräch'; note 1).

[9] See *Austerlitz*, pp. 37–8; '*Spiegel*-Gespräch' (note 1).

[10] On the 'assimilated' Jews in Sebald's *Die Ausgewanderten* see Arthur Williams, '"Das korsakowsche Syndrom": Remembrance and Responsibility in W. G. Sebald' in: Helmut Schmitz, ed., *German Culture and the Uncomfortable Past: Representations of National Socialism in contemporary Germanic literature*, Ashgate: Aldershot, 2001, pp. 65–86; esp. pp. 76–81.

[11] In the '*Spiegel*-Gespräch' (note 1), he indicates that he was already working on a new project exploring the 'éducation sentimentale' of Germans of his father's generation. His personal itinerary seems to have brought him ever closer to his German roots (cf. Williams, note 10, p. 84) and to a full-time commitment to writing: the award of NESTA funding allowed him to devote substantial periods to his writing. I discuss Sebald's changing attitude to his German roots in 'W. G. Sebald, Weit ausholende Annäherungen an ein problematisches Vaterland' in: V. Wehdeking and A-M. Corbin (eds), *Deutschsprachige Erzählprosa seit 1990 im europäischen Kontext. Interpretationen, Intertextualität, Rezeption*, Wissenschaftlicher Verlag: Trier, [2003].

[12] As he did on other occasions: *Nach der Natur*, pp. 73–5 and *Luftkrieg und Literatur*, p. 5 are just two examples.

[13] The essay 'Summa Scientiae: System und Systemkritik bei Elias Canetti' (*Die Beschreibung des Unglücks*, pp. 93–102) is a most relevant text; see Arthur Williams, 'W. G. Sebald: A holistic approach to borders, texts and perspectives' in: Arthur Williams, Stuart Parkes and Julian Preece, eds, *German-Language Literature Today: International and Popular?*, Peter Lang: Oxford, 2000, pp. 99–118, esp. 110–111.

[14] A similar view of German academics can be found in 'Una montagna bruna — Zum Bergroman Hermann Brochs' (*Unheimliche Heimat*, pp. 118–130, esp. p. 127). See Williams (note 13), pp. 100–101.

[15] Dan Jacobson, *Heshel's Kingdom*, Penguin Books: Harmondsworth, 1999 (1998).

[16] cf. Jacobson, *Heshel's Kingdom*, pp. 164, 211 and the (largely negative) review of *Austerlitz* in the *Frankfurter Allgemeine Zeitung*: 'Dahinter verbirgt sich ein Angriff

auf jede Art von öffentlicher Geschichtsschreibung [...] — zu allerdings nicht ganz fairen Bedingungen' and concludes 'W. G. Sebald hat ein Buch über die Theorie verfaßt, wie man Geschichte zu schreiben hat' (Thomas Steinfeld, 'Die Wünschelrute in der Tasche eines Nibelungen', 20 March 2001, L18).

[17] The first-person narrator notes that it was a book 'das mir Austerlitz bei unserem ersten Treffen in Paris gegeben hatte. Es war von dem Londoner Literaturwissenschaftler Dan Jacobson (einem mir all die Jahre hindurch unbekannt gebliebenen Kollegen, hatte Austerlitz gesagt) und handelte von der Suche des Autors nach seinem Großvater' (414–415). I am prepared to believe that reading *Heshel's Kingdom* helped Sebald crystallise some aspects of *Austerlitz* ('I am trying to dig another hole. And the digging seems to get harder all the while', letter to me, 1 July 1998). Dan Jacobson has informed me (e-mail, 4 November 2002) that Sebald did not contact him at all and he had not read *Die Ausgewanderten* which seems to anticipate several elements in *Heshel's Kingdom*. Dan Jacobson expressed what many of Sebald's 'sources', most cited only obliquely, must have felt: 'I was deeply affected by Sebald's invocation of *Heshel's Kingdom* at the end of *Austerlitz*. I greatly admired the book, thought it rich and poignant from the first page on, and to come upon something of mine invoked within it, in so natural and thoughtful a manner, on equal terms as it were, was a moving and even eerie experience'.

[18] I can vouch for Max Sebald the sympathetic and attentive listener on the basis of a few elements from our conversations that found their way into *Austerlitz*. They inform parts of this discussion of his work.

[19] cf. note 11.

[20] Gastone Novelli, a victim of the same torture as Jean Améry whose story was told by Claude Simon in *Le Jardin des Plantes*, emigrated to South America to become a diamond and gold prospector (pp. 38–39). The motifs of diamonds and plants run throughout the book: just three examples: the moment when Austerlitz first hears of the transport of Jewish children to London (p. 203); his arrival in his old home (p. 217); the reading room of the new national library in Paris which makes him 'geistesabwesend' (pp. 392–393).

[21] Sebald told Jaggi (note 1) he heard the story of the *Kindertransporte* in a Channel 4 documentary; Austerlitz hears it on the radio (p. 203). Several poignant details of Austerlitz's life and voyage of discovery are unmistakable intertextual references to Jeremy Josephs with Susi Bechhöfer, *Rosa's Child. The True Story of One Woman's Quest for a Lost Mother and a Vanished Past*, I. B. Tauris: London; 1996. Bechhöfer has expressed her dismay that Sebald did not explicitly acknowledge her book and given some detail of the borrowing she deprecates ('Stripped of my tragic past by a bestselling author', *The Sunday Times*, 30 June 2002). It is not appropriate to debate these particular claims here. A response within the academic study of literature must embrace, at the very least, Sebald's methods and objectives. My view is that a tribute

was intended which ranges Susi Bechhöfer's moving life-story alongside a number of others to which Sebald responded with similar empathy and discretion.

[22] Cambridge University Press, 1998.

[23] Descartes is present in the Rembrandt painting *The Anatomy Lesson* (a public dissection) which is one key to *Die Ringe des Saturn* (pp. 20–5).

[24] In the '*Spiegel*-Gespräch' (note 1), he argues that all writers should first learn to be industrious and conscientious reporters.

[25] The poems cited here can be found in *Penguin Modern Poets I: Lawrence Durrell, Elizabeth Jennings, R. S. Thomas*, Penguin Books: Harmondsworth, 1962, pp. 98–9 and *The New Poetry* (sel. and intro. A. Alvarez), Penguin Books, Harmondsworth, 1962, pp. 56–8.

[26] cf. *Schwindel. Gefühle.*, pp. 7–10; *Die Ringe des Saturn*, pp. 150–154.

[27] Stephen W. Hawking, *A Brief History of Time. From the Big Bang to Black Holes*, Bantam Press: London, 1988.

[28] His project also questions the way we organise knowledge. Thus, when Gabriele Annan (*The New York Review*, 1 November 2001) claims that Sebald strays off track towards the end of the book in a long attack on the new Bibliothèque François Mitterand in Paris (pp. 387–395), she is wrong. The passage is precisely placed. Sebald's reading of the 'text' of the new national library is deliberate and exemplary: its hegemonic modularisation of knowledge (discrete columns and rationed access), defeats the researcher of the traces of the past (now buried beneath it!). It is the antithesis of his quincunx ideal (*Die Ringe des Saturn*, p. 31). Hawking (pp. 10–13) reminds us that all science aims towards one grand theory and sees hope in Darwin's evolution, while Gellner, the polymath, emphasises the opposed views of knowledge underpinning the Habsburg dilemma (p. 3) and the effects on society of the new modular man (pp. 26–7).

[29] cf. Hawking, p. 143.

[30] The whole of Sebald's œuvre from his analysis of Grünewald/Nithart (*Nach der Natur*, esp. pp. 16–9) through to the friendships and uncles in *Austerlitz* contains examples of figures who are in some way (twin) brothers.

[31] I have explored some of these ideas further in 'W. G. Sebald: Probing the Outer Edges of Nature' in J. Preece and O. Durrani (eds), *Townscapes and Countryside in Contemporary German Writing*. Peter Lang: Oxford, [2003].

[32] See Arthur Williams: 'The elusive first-person plural: Real absences in Reiner Kunze, Bernd-Dieter Hüge and W. G. Sebald' in: Arthur Williams, Stuart Parkes and

Julian Preece (eds), *'Whose story?'* — *Continuities in contemporary German-language Literature*, Peter Lang: Bern, 1998, pp. 85–113, esp. pp. 98–110.

[33] See note 28.

[34] W. G. Sebald, 'Rede zur Einweihung des Literaturhauses Stuttgart, 17. November 2001', *Stuttgarter Zeitung*, 19 November 2001, 12.

Anthony Murphy

Culture Clash: The Austrian Freedom Party (FPÖ) and the Austrian Avant-Garde in the 1990s

Since the early 1990s the Austrian Freedom Party, the FPÖ, has used the issue of culture as a political lever, claiming that the Left enjoyed hegemonic status in the arts in Austria. While drawing attention to the high level of subsidies for creative artists in Austria is a legitimate political tactic, the Freedom Party has also involved itself in acrimonious disputes over individual cultural figures and its assertion that there was a 'left-wing cultural mafia'. Attacks on Hermann Nitsch, Elfriede Jelinek and Claus Peymann are characteristic of Freedomite tactics, but the force of rhetoric cannot disguise the absence of a genuine positive cultural policy once in power.

This article explores the background, content and reasoning behind an overt inclusion of *Kultur* (understood as the production, support and consumption of art in all its forms) in the FPÖ's political strategy during the 1990s. In this period, *Kultur* was instrumentalised by Jörg Haider, the FPÖ's leading figure, to expose and challenge the cultural élite in Austria. He claimed this élite was receiving state money to produce unwanted 'experimental' art, variously described by the FPÖ as 'obscene', 'rubbish', 'provocative' or 'unpatriotic'. Although the party already had an ambivalent attitude to modern art, it took the unprecedented step of attacking individual artists and cultural figures about their artistic credentials and questionable political agendas. Haider's *Kulturpolitik* hoped to attract the votes of 'ordinary' people disillusioned with a corrupt political and cultural elite. In addition to investigating the political aims underlying Haider's *Kulturpolitik*, the article will discuss two further aspects of the FPÖ's cultural stance. Firstly, their *Kulturpolitik* reveals a party with a reactionary right-wing core who view art as the cultural production of a nation or 'Volk' rather than an individual act of 'self-expression'. Their view of modern art has clear parallels with National Socialism - which labelled such art 'degenerate' in the 1930s and pursued a state cultural policy of encouraging 'real German art'. Secondly, right-wing 'intellectuals' associated with the FPÖ, such as Andreas Mölzer, began to formulate an ideological stance on *Kultur* based on the theories of the Italian Marxist, Antonio Gramsci.[1] Their assertion was that the Austrian left had a political strategy of achieving 'cultural hegemony' as the basis for influencing and setting the entire political agenda. As a result, for the Freedom Party most contemporary artistic production was brimming with an overt left-wing agenda, of little artistic merit and usually provocative or obscene in its content.

Kulturkampf 1995

The 1990s saw numerous examples of conflicts arising between the FPÖ and the avant-garde in Austria. The most notorious and *public* example was a poster plastered around Vienna during the October 1995 general election campaign, which stated: 'Lieben Sie Scholten, Jelinek, Häupl, Peymann, Pasterk... oder Kunst und Kultur? Freiheit der Kunst statt sozialistischer Staatskünstler'.[2] It was a very public statement by the FPÖ in their ongoing clash with certain aspects of contemporary art production in Austria. With it, Haider wanted to promote populist policies in the cultural arena, notably to curb state subsidies for certain types of art and stop wasting taxpayers' money on 'meaningless drivel calling itself art'. As an FPÖ spokeswoman, Magda Bleckmann, stated in 1996:

> Vieles, was heute als Kunst ausgegeben, von der öffentlichen Hand gefördert und von deren Vertretern bejubelt wird, erregt Ekel und Ablehnung, die soweit führen kann, daß mancher Bürger gar nichts mehr von Kunst wissen will.[3]

The FPÖ positions itself here as the 'defender' of public morals and 'common sense' by highlighting works of art perceived as 'unacceptable' to ordinary people. Haider wanted to connect with a real and pervasive antipathy towards modern art which was already widespread amongst the general population.[4] Aside from its populist appeal, there were additional factors behind this poster campaign. Firstly, by putting certain artists, cultural figures and politicians in one basket and juxtaposing them against 'art and culture', the implication is that these people are supporting and producing something that is of no artistic merit. Exactly what is worthy of the label 'art' is not defined by the FPÖ, their main concern being to devalue and reject most of the contemporary artistic production in Austria with little effort to replace it with art that conforms to 'suitable' aesthetic criteria.[5] Secondly, the poster was part of a campaign of attacking individual artists that was unprecedented since National Socialism. Whether intentionally or not, Haider was politicising culture in a way which had direct parallels with the ferocious attacks on 'entartete Kunst' under Hitler. In line with other issues highlighted by Haider, there was the aim of breaking taboos in Austrian society in order to appeal to the wishes of ordinary voters.[6] Defaming and openly criticising artists and their works was, and is, unusual for normal political parties. Thirdly,

Haider was placating the far-right core of his party. He owed this small but active faction within the FPÖ a considerable debt for their role in his successful leadership contest in 1986. This pan-German core welcomed any 'defence' of Austro-Germanism – in this case against the subversive threat of contemporary Austrian modern art.

Finally, by attacking artists, the FPÖ targeted a societal group comprised of people almost unanimous in their opposition and resistance to Haider. He labelled them the 'linke Kulturmafia'. In effect, Haider was trying to expose them as a left-wing cultural elite, bent on producing art for specific political purposes and rejecting any association with 'proper' German cultural values. Haider makes his distaste for the cultural scene clear when he states ironically:

> Diesen Abschnitt in meinem Buch widme ich meinen speziellen Freunden. Den Kulturschaffenden, Kulturjournalisten, Kulturgenießern, Kulturpolitikern, Kulturkämpfern, Kulturlandschaftsmalern, Kulturgutbewahrern, Kultur-revolutionären, Kulturkritikern, Kulturverteidigern und all den anderen kultivierten Menschen, die in der Vergangenheit einen Kult betrieben, sich als Teil einer Elite im Lande von der Nicht-Elite abzusetzen. Und damit vor allem von den Freiheitlichen.[7]

Targeting 'Left-Wing' Culture

To give an idea of those targeted by the Freedom Party, three examples of people representing Haider's 'linke Kulturmafia' are given below:

Hermann Nitsch

Hermann Nitsch was one of the Viennese Actionists in the 1960s and is one of Austria's most famous contemporary artists. He recently summed up his political stance as follows:

> meine kunst war nie politisch, sie hat nur dann politisch gewirkt, wenn politische gruppen, selbst der staat, ihre tabus und ungerechtfertigten statische wahrheitsansprüche in gefahr glaubten.[8]

For the FPÖ, Nitsch's art epitomises the degenerate state of Austrian contemporary art. Its content is described as 'obscene', 'indecent' and 'disgusting'. The 'cruel' use of animals, sacrilegious symbolism and the 'stomach-turning' elements of blood, vomit and urine used in his work, make Nitsch the ideal and principal target of FPÖ attacks on the state of Austrian art. A leading *Kulturkämpfer* in FPÖ circles, Walter Marinovic, describes Nitsch as an 'orgy-artist' who produces 'vomit as art'.[9] Aside

from the content of Nitsch's art, the FPÖ highlights the support and
sponsorship he receives from the Austrian state. Due to the 'infection' of
the 'Linke Kulturmafia' in Austria since the socialist Kreisky era (1970-
1983), artists like Nitsch are now held up as 'state' artists, representing
Austria at international exhibitions. Nitsch has become the acceptable
face of Austrian art, which indicates how public morals and German-
Austrian *Kultur* have been 'dragged through the mud'. A type of
'crusade' is necessary to re-establish 'old' and 'decent' values.[10]

Elfriede Jelinek

Jelinek is a contemporary Austrian playwright and author. Her subjects
are, among others, women, sexuality, the taboo-ridden Austrian society
and anti-Semitism. Unlike Nitsch, Jelinek has been willing to take a
public stance on many political issues. In particular, she has worked to
expose the post-war myth of Austria having been the 'first victim' of
German National Socialism.[11] Jelinek sees her task as a critical artist as
being to expose and bring such themes up to the surface and in the
consciousness of ordinary people: 'Gerade in stärker autoritär
strukturierten Ländern wie Österreich ist die Kunst die einzige
gesellschaftskritische Institution'.[12] Jelinek was at the forefront of
'cultural resistance' to Haider since the early 1990s and became a prime
target of FPÖ attacks for several reasons.[13] Firstly, the content of her
works (particularly her plays) is condemned as 'pornographic', 'perverse'
and of low quality. She is accused of using 'obscenity' in order to be
'provocative' rather than producing 'quality' productions. Secondly, her
work is also seen by the FPÖ as unpatriotic. By focusing on themes such
as Austria's Nazi legacy, Jelinek is regarded as dredging up her own
'warped' version of the past in order to criticise and condemn the
credibility of the Second Republic. She is viewed as a typical
'Österreichbeschimpfer' intent on bringing Austria's reputation into
disrepute.[14] Thirdly, Jelinek is seen by the FPÖ as a 'darling of the left',
serving the left-wing agenda of Austrian cultural 'hacks' who want to
further their own political influence at the expense of the FPÖ. Her works
are staged for the sake of political provocation rather than on grounds of
artistic merit or popularity. Finally, Haider rejects artists intent on
political 'interference'; they should concentrate on producing 'works of
beauty' rather than wasting their time in political agitation.[15]

Interestingly, after the aforementioned poster campaign in Vienna
for the 1995 general election, the FPÖ gave a public and 'official' apology

to Jelinek for her inclusion in the poster's wording.[16] She was the only 'artist' named in the poster, all the others being politicians and cultural figures. Implicit in this act of contrition by the FPÖ is, as is often the case, the feeling by 'moderates' in the party that the radical right of the party had 'overstepped' the mark again. In this case, it was the unprecedented 'naming and shaming' of an internationally reputed Austrian writer by a political party.

Claus Peymann

The German Claus Peymann became director of the Vienna *Burgtheater* in 1988. He is the embodiment of the FPÖ's 'Linke Kulturmafia' - intent on pushing a radical-left agenda through a state-cultural institution and thereby 'radicalising' the political climate. Peymann's view is that: 'Theaterarbeit in vielen Punkten sozialistischer Kulturpolitik auch entsprechen müßte'.[17] The FPÖ go even further in their perception of Peymann as a 'danger' to Austria - naming him as having been associated with Gudrun Ensslin in the 1970s. Ensslin was part of the infamous 'Baader Meinhof Gang', the terrorist group responsible for a bombing campaign in West Germany during the early 1970s. Peymann is also attacked by the FPÖ for being responsible for bringing the audience figures down at the Burgtheater during his tenure (he left in 1999). They allege this was due to the obscurity and radical political content of his productions. They maintain that Peymann and others have no connection with ordinary people who want art to provide them with solace and entertainment rather than abstraction, indecency and agitprop. In a comment directed at Peymann, Haider stated after the prodcution of Thomas Bernhard's *Heldenplatz* in 1988: 'Hinaus mit diesem Schuft aus Wien!', echoing the famous remark by Karl Kraus.[18] These and many other representatives of the 'linke Kultur' in Austria were targeted by the FPÖ. However, once a political party takes such a distinct position on culture, the question arises as to their own definition of *Kultur*. In short, the Freedom Party made it clear what they disliked about contemporary Austrian art, but what culture do they sanction and promote?

A Freedom Party *Kultur*?

Rechtsextremisten reden viel von Kunst und noch öfter von Kultur. Weniger oft sprechen sie darüber, was sie darunter verstehen. Was keine Kunst und keine Kultur sei, darüber schreiben sie ganze Bücher, das eigene Verständnis der Begriffe ist - abgesehen von der offenen Anlehnung an Nazi-Terminologie - nicht sonderlich entwickelt.[19]

The observation offered here can be partly applied to the FPÖ and certainly to the far right of the party. In fact, defining concepts and formulating policies has been a constant problem for the FPÖ. They have presented themselves as a party of opposition and managed to construct, under Haider's leadership, an extremely effective critique of the 'corrupt' and 'outdated' Austrian political system of *Proporz*. However, as seen by their recent experiment of sharing executive power with the ÖVP, the actual policies presented by the FPÖ are vague and incoherent. The internal strife within the party, particularly pressure from the far-right faction, led to the resignation of three FPÖ ministers and the fall of the ÖVP/FPÖ government. In the field of cultural politics, a similar pattern can be traced. Condemnation of a 'left-wing cultural mafia' might score political points, but as soon as the FPÖ have to define what they mean by *Kultur* things become less straightforward.

In order to uncover what FPÖ *Kultur* actually entails there are three distinct sources of information one can turn to. Firstly, there is a chapter in the party political programme entitled *'Weite Kultur - Freie Kunst'*. Secondly, there are Haider's own writings on the subject and a few podium discussions organised by the FPÖ.[20] Finally, various *Kulturexperten* within the FPÖ have attempted to define a 'Freedomite Culture' in interviews, books and pamphlets. Drawing on these sources, I will piece together four main strands of what can be understood under the notion of an FPÖ *Kultur*.

Kulturdeutsch

The FPÖ specify in their political programme that the basic vehicle of cultural expression is 'language': 'The Freedomite movement emphasises the fact that all Austrians belong to different cultural communities based on their particular language; for the vast majority of Austrians that means German'.[21] The party advocates an Austrian identity inextricably linked to a German cultural identity. By emphasising the German aspect of Austrian identity, Haider wishes to instil a sense of belonging to a wider, historic, cultural community - rather than just Austria. More significantly he wishes to defend this Austrian-German culture from being infected and influenced by multiculturalism.[22]

The special identification with German culture stems from the ideology of 'Pan-Germanism'. The FPÖ was the only Austrian political party after the Second World War that continued to challenge the legitimacy of an 'Austrian' state and Haider has been a long-standing sympathiser with German-nationalist elements in his party. However, on achieving party leadership in 1986, he realised that the popularity of German nationalism in Austria was relatively small and it was certainly not a vote-winner. He steered the party away from overt pan-nationalism, with its implicit challenge to Austrian state legitimacy, and at one stage called on the party to stop 'harping on about the German issue'.[23] By emphasising the German dimension of Austrian *Kultur*, rather than addressing the relationship with the German nation in the political field, Haider reinforces an Austro-German cultural identity and avoids questioning the legitimacy of the Second Republic. He stated in 1995:

> Recognising that Austria forms part of the German cultural region, the cultivation of German culture and language is of special importance to us. We consider it our duty to provide an Austrian contribution to the development of German culture.[24]

Anti-modern, anti-avantgarde

After the FPÖ started attacking individual artists in the 1990s, a historic parallel with the National Socialist assault on modern art became inevitable. The quasi-religious zeal and brutality with which the Nazis attacked modern art cannot be compared with the present-day FPÖ. However, linking moral and social decline to cultural production reflects a distinct tendency of the party to reproduce National Socialist ideology in a contemporary setting. No other right-wing populist party in Europe has entered into the field of aesthetics to such an extent. For some within the FPÖ, the former scapegoat of 'cultural Jewish-Bolshevism' has been replaced with a new one - the 'left-wing cultural mafia'.[25]

The FPÖ's crusade against modern art has its roots in an adherence to a kind of German 'fundamentalism', involving a rejection of modernity due to the erosion of 'natural' cultural forces that takes place and a wish to reinforce more traditional 'healthy' attitudes in people.[26] Modern art represents a manifestation of 'pathological' tendencies that should be challenged and eventually eradicated for the sake of a people's psychic health. Marinovic claims that much of contemporary art in Austria does not even deserve the label of 'degenerate art':

Dennoch sollte man mit dem Begriff 'entartete Kunst' vorsichtig sein, denn immerhin muß es wenigstens Kunst sein. Vieles von dem aber, was uns heute vorgesetzt wird, hat mit Kunst überhaupt nichts zu tun. Es ist auch keine Entartung, sondern bestenfalls Anzeichen einer geistigen oder psychischen Störung.[27]

The FPÖ were convinced that by attacking certain artists they were merely representing the views of the majority of Austrians who were 'alienated' from the contemporary art scene. For most people *Kultur* is the music of Mozart or the architecture of the baroque - not the ritualistic blood splattering of Nitsch. Ernst Hanisch, an Austrian historian, has pointed to the role of the state since 1945 in 'restoring' the Habsburg legacy and pursuing cultural policies specifically aimed at marginalising experimental and critical art.[28]

Morality and Culture

Pan-nationalism was, as already mentioned, diluted and channelled into the cultural rather than political arena. Another party principle to come under scrutiny under Haider was 'anti-clericalism', entailing an antipathy to Catholicism and political opposition to the Catholic ÖVP.[29] Haider changed this party stance. His reasoning was simple; in order to increase the party's share of the vote it was necessary to cast a wider net amongst the general population. Certain strongly held principles, such as anti-clericalism, were off-putting to potential voters, especially those switching from the ÖVP.

This ideological shift made the FPÖ take a party political stance on public morality, in particular 'family values'. Haider's deeply conservative views on these matters - such as the role of women 'at home', draconian solutions for the drug problem and notions of 'public responsibility' - led to the FPÖ sharing the same platform as the Catholic Church.[30] Within the cultural arena the FPÖ's reactionary views on contemporary art, especially their criticisms of 'obscene' or 'pornographic' art, are shared by many in the ÖVP. Both political parties wanted to promote traditional forms of culture at the expense of modern, critical or experimental art. Thus, while differences remained on issues such as tax or Europe, they saw eye to eye on art and culture. Haider increasingly portrayed himself as a 'protector' of 'decency, honesty and proper behaviour' during the 1990s.[31] The party's distinct stance on *Kultur* reinforced these 'Austrian' values and facilitated the political marriage with the ÖVP and the support of the Austrian Catholic Church.

Artistic Freedom But...

FPÖ *Kulturpolitik* is played out mostly in the realm of party rhetoric or media posturing. There is a big difference between many of the utterances or polemics of hard-line Freedomite *Kulturkämpfer* and 'official' party policy. When scrutinising party documents, three key areas emerge that contain specific ideas for cultural policy in Austria: the question of state subsidies for cultural projects and artists; proposals for an 'art market'; and the notion of 'artistic freedom' and censorship. The policy proposal given the most public exposure was a call for the radical overhaul of the system of state subsidies for artists and cultural institutions. The FPÖ exploited the view held by many Austrians that taxpayers' money was being wasted on unpopular cultural projects. The FPÖ take this public perception further by claiming that the subsidies are politically motivated in order to support and nurture certain types of art, particularly contemporary critical art. An example of this bias in cultural matters are the policies of Rudolf Scholten (former SPÖ Minister of Arts and Science) who was accused of: 'der Aufbau einer sozialdemokratischen Gesellschaftskultur, abhängig vom Subventionssäckel des Herrn Scholten'.[32] For Haider, this state support has no relation to artistic quality or public popularity but is an example of the left extending its control over society:

> Und für mich wird daher also auch in Österreich in vielen Bereichen die Kunst immer mehr zu einer Art subventioniertem Behübscher kultureller Hegemonie, die von der Politik und von den Machtinstitutionen vorgegeben ist.[33]

Haider's use of the term 'kulturelle Hegemonie' is a crucial theoretical basis for the whole project of FPÖ *Kulturpolitik* in the 1990s. I shall expand on this later.

Haider believes that state expenditure on culture benefits only a small elitist minority of culture hacks who have their own agenda of marginalising Haider and the FPÖ. For the general public this entails the 'subsidisation of boredom', in which people become alienated from the art being presented in exhibitions, theatre plays and opera which is either meaningless or simply 'rubbish'.[34] The FPÖ link the subsidy issue to the question of state interference and the unyielding, bureaucratic nature of the modern Austrian state.[35] The effect of this on Austrian culture is that, unlike in most European countries, there is no real 'art market'. Instead, there is an artificial situation where the state 'props up' artists and cultural projects instead of allowing a 'free' art market to develop based on the principles of 'supply and demand'. Haider outlined his position in 1995:

> We stand for a culture which reflects the free development of the citizen and society. It is the state's responsibility to preserve our cultural heritage; contemporary art has to orient itself to supply and demand and not political influence and subsidies. State support should be limited to preserving plurality in education and arts.[36]

The FPÖ is not alone in criticising this aspect of cultural policy, and indeed the Austrian state subsidises the arts more than any other country in Europe.[37] For many, this overbearing influence of the state on Austrian culture is badly in need of reform (ibid., p. 179). For the FPÖ however, this 'reform' would be used as a tool for dealing with political enemies and marginalising critical art forms rather than any balanced policy reform package.

Another area of cultural policy pursued by the FPÖ relates to the vexed question of artistic freedom. The bulk of Freedom Party writing on this subject concerns the boundaries of artistic taste: 'Daß man nicht nur sagt, es darf jeder was machen, sondern es gibt für mich einfach auch eine Grenzziehung zwischen künstlerischer Tätigkeit und Pornographie zum Beispiel'.[38] The party believes that art should be supported and displayed within a system of 'collective responsibility' and not just as an excuse for individual expression. The public should be protected from indecency, political provocation, obscenity and 'irrational rubbish': 'Somit kann die Freiheit der Kunst, Kultur und der Medien immer im Zusammenhang mit dem Begriff Verantwortung gesehen werden'.[39] This notion of 'artistic responsibility' involves anchoring culture to the 'people' rather than catering for the tastes of a cultural elite. Peter Sichrovsky (former FPÖ cultural spokesman) takes this issue further by criticising artists who are 'resisting' the FPÖ's *Kulturpolitik*. This 'resistance' takes place within a liberal-democratic (rather than totalitarian) context and their calls for 'freedom' reflect more their own artistic redundancy than a genuine plea for 'artistic freedom': 'Schreit er beleidigt nach Freiheit in einer Demokratie, so spricht das für seine Unsicherheit, in einem gegebenen Rahmen künstlerisch zu wirken'.[40] In other words, according to Sichrovsky, a reformed FPÖ *Kultur* would include a fairer system of subsidies, a free art market and more artistic responsibility. He thinks that many contemporary artists and artistic forms would disappear from the

Austrian cultural landscape, not as a result of censorship but based on lack of artistic merit and public demand.

Attempting to define FPÖ policy on *Kultur* reveals the minefield a political party enters when trying to make a specific stance on cultural matters. Issues such as censorship, artistic freedom, aesthetic criteria and political interference all make it a grey area for politicians. The FPÖ *Kulturpolitik* of the 1990s was an attempt to make political capital by populist criticism of an easy target - modern art. However, in the process of doing this, the party unleashed its hard-line *Kulturkämpfer,* exposing itself to accusations of trying to 'purify' Austrian culture in a similar way to the National Socialist project of the 1930s:

> Wie in der Zeit des Dritten Reiches zählen Vertreter der modernen Kunst zu den erklärten Feindbildern. Mit ähnlichen rhetorischen Mitteln wie die nationalsozialistischen Hetzer beuten die 'Kulturexperten' des rechten FPÖ-Flügels die Tatsache aus, daß viele Menschen Schwierigkeiten haben, Zugang zu zeitgenössischer Kunst zu finden.[41]

In a declaration issued in 1989, a think tank within the FPÖ called the *Lorenzer Kreis*, which assisted Haider to power in 1986, set out their view on art and culture:

> Die direkte Kunstförderung muß sich auf Werke beschränken, die unserem abendländischen Kulturkreis angehören und gemeinhin als künstlerisch anerkannt sind [...]. Keineswegs dürfen Steuermittel für Erscheinungen wie 'Aktionismus', blasphemische Darstellungen, für jegliche Werke, die die Gefühle unserer Bevölkerung grob verletzen, unsere Heimat und Überlieferung verächtlich machen oder der Geschäftemacherei dienen usw. verwendet werden. Auch die Förderung von Werken, die fremdartige Ausdrucksmittel benützen oder die unserer abendländischen Tradition zuwiderlaufen (z.B. Primitivkunst, fernöstliche Moderiten, 'Subkultur') ist abzulehnen.[42]

The War of Ideas

Underpinning FPÖ rhetoric on *Kultur* is a theoretical basis that seeks to justify and explain the party's *Kulturkampf* in the 1990s. It borrows and adapts concepts from the writings of Antonio Gramsci, noted for extending Marxist theory from the economic-political to the cultural-political realm. Gramsci introduced the concept of 'hegemony', where political power is derived not just from economic control and ownership of the means of production but from a domination of the cultural sphere - encompassing art, media and education.

Andreas Mölzer took ideas from right-wing scholars in France, notably Alain de Benoist, who had formed a think tank called the 'New Right'.[43] These ideas involved a revised interpretation of Gramsci, whereby his theory of hegemony was applied to the political goals of the right. A central aspect of this reinterpretation was to use *Kultur* as a vehicle for obtaining political power. In the context of Austria in the 1990s, this entailed attacking the perceived domination of cultural institutions and ideas by the left: 'Und der Einsatz in diesen Stellungskrieg ist die Kultur, die als die Befehls- und die Ausgabestelle für die Werte und die Ideen betrachtet wird'.[44] Mölzer was a personal advisor to Haider in the early 1990s and it is of little surprise that for Haider a central task of the FPÖ cultural-political strategy became the fight against the cultural hegemony of the Left:[45] 'Kunst und Kultur sind für Haider der Angelpunkt, die politische Hegmonie zu erlangen. Als Kärtner Landeshauptmann hat er sich als ertes das Kunst- und Kulturressort geschnappt'.[46] The war of ideas that was needed to achieve political ascendancy involved, as already set out in this article, a *Kulturkampf* targeting the pervasive influence of the left in the cultural sphere and thereby placing the FPÖ in the position of creating a 'new symbolic arrangement for the Second Republic'.[47] Political power would stem from challenging the 'control' of *Kultur* by the left. Apart from taking on the avant-garde, Haider also promoted the FPÖ as a party able to embrace youth culture. The party staged events, a 'Haider Rap' was written and recruiting took place in discos.[48]

Underlying the whole *Kulturkampf* was the strongly held belief, which took on conspiratorial dimensions, that the left had 'taken over' cultural institutions and thereby achieved political power: 'Social and cultural life has become to a large degree separated. It is this factor which has given rise to intellectual domination by the left in the cultural sector of a system based on market economy'.[49] Haider traces this 'domination of the cultural sector' to the 1960s: 'For the generation of 1968 it was necessary to smash domination of bourgeois thought, to criticise capitalism, America and everyone over 30, to get cultural hegemony. Their march through the institutions was successful'.[50] The political strategy of the FPÖ therefore became not simply a competition between the Austrian political parties, but a campaign to re-conquer the institutions of Austria that were dominated by a 'linke Kulturmafia'.

In summary, the ideological basis for the FPÖ's *Kulturkampf* had four aspects. Firstly, it anchored the cultural politics and policies of the party during the 1990s in a specific vehicle through which the FPÖ would gain political power. Secondly, a (Germanic) fundamentalist strand of thought is revealed within the FPÖ, whereby the left is shown to have not only gained political power through 'the march through institutions' but has also manipulated and distorted people's minds in Austria by creating a 'Dictatorship of Ugliness': 'Man raubt ihnen die Bindung an Glauben, an Volk und an Heimat.   Man zerschlägt die Maßstäbe des Guten und Schönen.   Denn eine kulturlose Masse hat keine Kraft zum geistigen Widerstand'.[51] Thirdly, a *Kulturkampf* is justified as a 'counterattack' by the right in order to regain political and moral ascendancy in a society 'plagued' by left-wing influence.   Finally, the belief in a cultural 'takeover' by the left produced a paranoia in the party that explains why *Kultur* took prominence for the FPÖ in their oppositional strategy during the 1990s.

Conclusion

The FPÖ made the strategic political decision to enter the Austrian cultural arena in the 1990s.   Once Haider had led the FPÖ to the Holy Grail of executive power in February 2000, it became apparent that the *Kulturkampf* of the previous years would be restricted to influencing budgetary decisions on arts grants and an attempt to have more direct influence in the state media outlet ORF, Austrian Television.[52] The attacks on the avant-garde subsided as the party became absorbed into the Austrian political class. However the aggressive stance on *Kultur* taken by Haider and others in the 1990s was an example of the extent to which the reactionary right wing of the party was steering aspects of FPÖ policy. The content of this *Kulturpolitik* was based on the paranoid and conspiratorial belief that Austria had to be delivered from the grip of a 'left-wing cultural mafia'.   While this stance became unsustainable in government, it was evidence of a fault-line within the FPÖ, involving an irreconcilable tension between the traditional *Kultur-Deutsch* faction of the party and the neo-liberal pragmatists, a tension that also led to the collapse of the ÖVP/FPÖ coalition in autumn 2002.

Notes

[1] Andre Zogholy, *Kulturpolitische Strategien der FPÖ und die Hegemonietheorie nach Antonio Gramsci*, Universitätsverlag Rudolf Trauner: Linz, 2002, p. 7.

[2] Claus Tieber, *Die Letzten von Gestern: Die Rechten und die Kunst*, Picus Verlag: Vienna, 1996, p. 41.

[3] Magda Bleckmann, 'Kulturpolitik in einer dritten Republik', in *FPÖ-Jahrbuch*, Politische Akademie FPÖ: Vienna, 1996, p. 386.

[4] Robert Menasse, *Überbau und Underground: Die sozialpartnerschaftliche Ästhetik*, Suhrkamp: Berlin, 1997, p. 176.

[5] Andre Zogholy, *Kulturpolitische Strategien der FPÖ und die Hegemonietheorie nach Antonio Gramsci*, p. 53.

[6] Müller in Yves Mény and Yves Surel, eds, *Democracies and the Populist Challenge*, Palgrave: New York, 2002, p. 155.

[7] Jörg Haider, *Befreite Zukunft jenseits von links und rechts*, Ibera Verlag: Vienna, 1997, p. 67.

[8] Hermann Nitsch in Hans-Henning Scharsach, ed., *Haider: Österreich und die rechte Versuchung*, Rowohlt: Reinbek bei Hamburg, 2000, p. 249. Original text contains no capital letters.

[9] Walter Marinovic, *Diktatur des Häßlichen: Kulturpolitik heute*, Leopold Stocker: Graz, 1995, p. 60.

[10] Marinovic, *Diktatur des Häßlichen*, p. 71.

[11] Matthias Konzett, *The Rhetoric of National Dissent in Thomas Bernhard, Peter Handke and Elfriede Jelinek*, Camden House: New York, 2000, p. 95.

[12] Jelinek in Hans-Henning Scharsach, ed., *Haider: Österreich und die rechte Versuchung*, p. 239.

[13] Allyson Fiddler, 'Staging Jörg Haider: Protest and Resignation in Elfriede Jelinek's *Das Lebewohl* and other Recent Texts for the Theatre' in: *The Modern Language Review,* Vol. 97 No. 2, April 2002, 353.

[14] Marinovic, *Diktatur des Häßlichen*, p. 7.

[15] Haider in J Berchtold, *Das Kunst Buch*, Ferdinand Berger GmbH: Horn, Austria, 1998, p. 71.

[16] *Profil*, February 2000.

[17] Marinovic, *Diktatur des Häßlichen*, p. 51.

[18] Brigitte Bailer-Galanda, *Haider Wörtlich: Führer in die Dritte Republik*, Löcker Verlag: Vienna, 1995, p. 123.

[19] Claus Tieber, *Die Letzten von Gestern*, p. 60.

[20] J. Berchtold, *Das Kunst Buch*.

[21] Freedom Party Manifesto, 1993.

[22] Jörg Haider, *The Freedom I Mean*, Swan Books: New York, 1995, p. 28.

[23] Müller in Yves Mény and Yves Surel, eds, *Democracies and the Populist Challenge*, p. 160.

[24] Jörg Haider, *The Freedom I Mean*, p. 95.

[25] Hans-Henning Scharsach, *Haiders Kampf*, Orac: Vienna, 1992, p. 83.

[26] Cornelia Klinger, 'Faschismus - der deutsche Fundamentalismus?' in *Merkur*, Heft 522/3, 1992, 782.

[27] Marinovic in Claus Tieber, *Die Letzten von Gestern*, p. 73.

[28] Ernst Hanisch, *Der Lange Schatten des Staates: Österreichische Gesellschaftsgeschichte im 20. Jahrhundert*, Ueberreuter: Vienna, 1994, p. 210.

[29] Anton Pelinka, *Austria: Out of the Shadow of the Past*, Westview Press: Colorado, 1998, p. 9.

[30] Andrea Hummer, ed., *Kulturstürmerei in Österreich*, IG Kultur: Vienna, 1995, p. 2.

[31] Wodak in Hans-Henning Scharsach, ed., *Haider: Österreich und die rechte Versuchung*, p. 180.

[32] Magda Bleckmann, 'Kulturpolitik in einer dritten Republik' in *FPÖ Jahrbuch*, Politische Akademie FPÖ: Vienna, p. 390.

[33] Haider in J. Berchtold, *Das Kunst Buch*, p. 84.

[34] Jörg Haider, *Befreite Zukunft jenseits von links und rechts*, p. 70.

[35] Melanie Sully, *The Haider Phenomenon*, Columbia University Press: New York, 1997, p. 44.

[36] Haider, *The Freedom I Mean*, p. 110.

[37] Robert Menasse, *Überbau und Underground*, p. 177 and p. 179.

[38] Haider in J. Berchtold, *Das Kunst Buch*, p. 92.

[39] Magda Bleckmann in *FPÖ-Jahrbuch*, 1996, p. 388.

[40] Peter Sichrovsky, 'Wie frei muß Kunst sein?' in: *FPÖ-Jahrbuch*, Politische Akademie FPÖ: Vienna ,1997, p. 344 and p. 347.

[41] Hans-Henning Scharsach, *Haiders Kampf*, p. 81.

[42] Lorenzer Kreis, from C. Gratzer, *Der Schoß ist fruchtbar noch...NDSAP (1920-1933) - FPÖ (1986-1998) Kontinuitäten, Parallelen, Ähnlichkeiten*, Grünalternativ Jugend: Vienna, 1998, p. 107.

[43] Andre Zogholy, *Kulturpolitische Strategien der FPÖ und die Hegemonietheorie nach Antonio Gramsci*, p. 29.

[44] Benoist in Andre Zogholy, *Kulturpolitische Strategien der FPÖ und die Hegemonietheorie nach Antonio Gramsci*, p. 34.

[45] Haider, *The Freedom I Mean*, p. 73.

[46] Christa Zöchling, *Haider: Eine Karriere*, Econ: Munich, 1999, p. 156.

[47] Isolde Charim, 'Die Rolle der Opposition ist bereits besetzt' in: *Kulturrisse*, January 2001.

[48] Andre Gingrich in Ruth Wodak and Anton Pelinka, eds, *The Haider Phenomenon in Austria*, Transaction: London, 2002, chapter 5.

[49] Haider, *The Freedom I Mean*, p. 21

[50] Haider, *The Freedom I Mean*, p. 22.

[51] Marinovic, *Diktatur des Häßlichen*, p. 135.

[52] M. Wassenair, Interview with Anthony Murphy, January 2002.

Ian Foster

The limits of memory: Christoph Ransmayr's journalistic writings

Christoph Ransmayr's volume of journalistic prose *Der Weg nach Surabaya* (1997) places him in an Austrian context. Like many of his famous predecessors from the 19th century to the present day, Ransmayr is interested in the way the past plays out in our present. He places himself explicitly in this tradition when writing of Austria's Imperial legacy, but a similar approach may also be observed in his work dealing with Austria's more contentious recent past.

The 19th century Austrian *Novellendichter* and dramatist Ferdinand von Saar summarised his own preoccupation with the events of his own lifetime and the immediate past in the following memorable lines:

> Ich bin ein Freund der Vergangenheit. Nicht daß ich etwa romantische Neigungen hätte und für das Ritter- und Minnewesen schwärmte - oder für die sogenannte gute alte Zeit, die es niemals gegeben hat, nur jene Vergangenheit will ich gemeint wissen, die mit ihren Ausläufern in die Gegenwart hineinreicht und welcher ich, da der Mensch nun einmal seine Jugendeindrücke nicht loswerden kann, noch dem Herzen nach angehöre.[1]

For Saar at the turn of the 19th to 20th centuries and for many fellow Austrian writers in the succeeding generation who grew up in the final days of the Habsburg Empire, the recent past held a peculiar fascination; yet this was not determined purely by nostalgic sentiment, but more by the 'reach'of the past into a more mundane present. In dealing with the lived past as a subject here, there will inevitably come a point at which living witnesses begin to fade.

Christoph Ransmayr is among the most celebrated German-language authors of the past decade, yet his image is that of a recluse. He gives relatively few interviews; his rare TV appearances have been more or less restricted to readings from his own work. Compared with his contemporaries, he has said very little in public about his writing. His speech on receiving the Anton Wildgans Prize in 1989 began with a quotation from Luciano De Crescenzo, who puts these words into Socrates' mouth: 'Das Dümmste, was man über irgendein dichterisches Werk sagen konnte, kam stets von seinen Dichtern'.[2] This text was later published under the puzzling title 'Hiergeblieben!' - which refers to the fact that not only does Ransmayr share De Crescenzo's Socratic scepticism concerning the value of writers' comments on their own writing, he also regards the very act of making a 'thank-you' speech as a concession to the seductive limelight of publicity.

All that being so, Ransmayr is no J. D. Salinger. He is conscious of the apparatus of the book market, but chooses to keep it at a distance. Since the worldwide success of *Die letzte Welt*[3] in the early 1990s he has not needed to court public favour. He has also assiduously cultivated an international image. The cover text biographies of all his most recent works note 'Christoph Ransmayr 1954 in Wels / Oberösterreich geboren, studierte in Wien und lebt zur Zeit in Cork, Westirland' - the temporal reference underlining his status as a traveller in this world, a kind of Austrian Bruce Chatwin. Indeed, his 1997 collection *Der Weg nach Surabaya* promises exotic travel in its very title.[4] There is a tension between Ransmayr's would-be postmodern rootlessness and the visible rootedness of this writer that concerns me here. By this I do not mean to refer to the literary rumour-mongering in Austria that Ransmayr's residence in Ireland is purely a piece of unpatriotic tax dodging. I propose to turn Ransmayr's public image on its head to investigate this writer not as a purveyor of travel literature on faraway places like Surabaya, or West Cork for that matter, but as a specifically Austrian writer on Austrian themes in what I will suggest is a characteristically Austrian mode. In Ransmayr's journalistic writings we find an archaeology of his monolithic third novel *Morbus Kitahara*, whose oblique and challenging treatment of the past has caused much controversy.[5] I shall argue that the strategies that caused readers and critics so many difficulties in *Morbus Kitahara* can be better understood if we take into account the same author's treatment of related subjects elsewhere in other genres.

Let me begin by noting that six of the sixteen pieces collected in *Der Weg nach Surabaya* concern Austria directly and, arguably, a further two deal with closely related matters. Of the six texts on Austrian themes, three deal with the Imperial heritage, two with the more recent Nazi legacy, and one with a tourist site.

When it comes to the decline and fall of the Dual Monarchy, the term 'Habsburg Myth', coined by the Italian Germanist Claudio Magris, springs readily to mind.[6] Philip Manger has offered a succinct definition of the term:

> In the Habsburg myth the transformation of reality that belongs to every poetic creation is grafted onto a particular historical-cultural process. The intuitive memory of the world of yesterday combines with a partly conscious, partly

unconscious process of sublimation of a concrete society into a picturesque, secure and ordered fairytale-like world.[7]

What Magris, Manger and those who follow this line of interpretation suggest is that writing in Austria about the Imperial era is prone to a particular set of assumptions that amount to more than mere nostalgia; rather they represent a political agenda beginning in the First Austrian Republic and continuing after 1945 with baleful consequences for cultural, political and social progress.

One of the earliest items collected in *Der Weg nach Surabaya* is entitled 'Die Neunzigjährigen. Fünf biographische Notizen', first published in 1980. This consists of five portraits of 90 year-olds - four women and one man born in 1890. The texts are one-and-a-half pages long, and each is accompanied by a photograph of its subject by Willi Puchner. They were originally published in the *Extrablatt* as 'Geburtsjahr 1890. 90 Jahre Einsamkeit'. The first text, on Therese S., begins as follows:

> Die Nachricht von der Ermordung des Thronfolgers Franz Ferdinand in Sarajevo hatte sie auf einem Jahrmarkt im oberen Waldviertel erreicht, vom Ausbruch des Ersten Weltkriegs hatte ihr der Dorfbäcker im niederösterreichischen Bockfließ berichtet, und viel später war es ein Lautsprecher im Freibad Hietzing, der Hitlers Kriegserklärung nachplärrte - nur an das Feuerwerk in der Silvesternacht zum Jahr 1900 kann sich Therese S. nicht mehr so genau erinnern. (S, p. 187)

Ransmayr underlines explicitly the idea that the five people portrayed here represent a living memory or 'Menschengedächtnis'. All live alone at the end of long lives. The lives of the first four have been marked by the events of the 20th century and all are located socially within the Habsburg system: Therese S. is the daughter of a 'kaiserlicher Zimmeraufseher' responsible for the private apartments of 'die Sisi'; Luise L. lost her business selling artifical feathers and decorative flowers when Imperial fashions disappeared in the First World War; Anton K. was a soldier in the Imperial and Royal Army on 8 Kreuzer a day; Luise M. lost four brothers in the First World War. The final text is a record of an interview that did not take place. The interviewee, Aloisia G., is already beyond reach on her deathbed by the time of the interviewer's arrival.

What these short and unusual texts seem to be suggesting is not just that the personal histories adumbrated are at the boundary of living memory but that they are passing from lived experience and that the 'rest is silence'. The position of the 'non-interview' at the end of the series is no accident. Aloisia G.'s memories will pass with her.

Ransmayr writing as a reportage journalist is far from the cold, bloodless style that was so much criticised in his novels. I am thinking here of the rape scene in *Die letzte Welt* and the clinical descriptions of shootings by various characters in *Morbus Kitahara*. There is a compassion in the journalistic writing that is unexpected, a concern with the destiny of individuals. In the brief space allotted to them they are accorded a degree of respect and dignity they had lacked in life:

> Die Frau am Tisch geht steif zu ihrem Bett zurück - wer dazu imstande ist, darf noch hoffen. Hängt doch am Gehen ein letzter Rest von Brauchbarkeit, von Nützlichkeit. Und darauf ist es schließlich ein Leben lang angekommen.
> (S, p. 196)

The idea of liminal memories passing or on the point of passing into historical record from lived experience is also present in the second of the texts on the Habsburg legacy. This is Ransmayr's account of his visit to the exiled Empress Zita, widow of the last Emperor of Austria-Hungary on the occasion of her 90th (*nota bene*) birthday in 1982. First published under the title 'Kaiserin Zitas Weg in die Kapuzinergruft', at 32 pages it is one of the longest texts in the collection. The tone of the piece is mocking and features a narrator who refers to himself throughout as 'der Untertan'. He accompanies a group of 120 ageing aristocrats and royalists in two coaches on their way to present birthday wishes in Zizers, the convent near Chur in Switzerland where Zita lived from 1962 until her death in 1989. Interpolated within this narrative are observations on the course of Austrian history and interviews with various experts in the field. The socio-political context is all the more interesting when one realises that it was in 1982 that the Austrian Republic first granted Zita permission to return to Austria. The framework narrative is entertaining, not least for the discrepancy between the aristocratic tone of the audience in Zizers and the threadbare reality of the coach party.

The narrative and deliberations on the status of the last Empress are prefaced by a famous quotation from Joseph Roth's *Die Kapuzinergruft*:

> Österreich ist kein Staat, keine Heimat, keine Nation. Es ist eine Religion. Die Klerikalen und klerikalen Trottel, die jetzt regieren, machen eine sogenannte

Nation aus uns; aus uns, die wir eine Übernation sind, die einzige Übernation, die jemals existiert hat...

Ihr habt mit euren leichtfertigen Kaffeehauswitzen den Staat zerstört... Ihr habt nicht sehen wollen, daß diese Alpentrottel und Sudetenböhmen, diese kretinischen Nibelungen unsere Nationalitäten so lange beleidigt und geschändet haben, bis sie anfingen, die Monarchie zu hassen und zu verraten. Nicht unsere Tschechen, nicht unsere Serben, nicht unsere Polen, nicht unsere Ruthenen haben verraten, sondern nur unsere Deutschen, das Staatsvolk. (S, p. 91)

Ransmayr neglects to mention that these words are the reported views of a madman. Despite the attribution of blame to the German-speakers of the Empire, the familiar 'unsere Tschechen' and so on in Roth's text suggest a false harmonious past. Those familiar with Roth's later fiction will recognise a characteristic tension in this extract - as Roth dissects the motivations and manipulations of his German-speaking characters he tends to idealise at least some of the Slavic nations. Ransmayr's text to some extent endorses the point of view suggested in the quotation, particularly in the final interview with the historian Friedrich Heer, who is dying of cancer at the time he delivers a damning judgement on Franz Joseph and the monarchy:

Der Zusammenbruch der Donaumonarchie, haben Sie gesagt? Hier gibt es für mich keine Zweifel. Ich wurde als Untertan Kaiser Franz Josephs, des Herzogs von Auschwitz, geboren, und ich bin zu dem Schluß gekommen, daß dieser ungeheuerliche Diktator und in jeder Weise geistig und seelisch impotente, kleinwüchsige und lebensfeige Mensch, die durchaus umbaufähige Monarchie zugrunde gerichtet hat. (S, p. 119)

Heer's claim is that the Austrian monarchy was blinded by a false view of its German neighbour and of the much-vaunted superiority of the German language and culture, leading it to place Germanness at the apex of an Imperial hierarchy. Alongside Friedrich Heer's historical judgement is set the comic reaction of 'der Untertan' as he leaves the coach party following the audience with the ex-Empress to journey onward by train:

Die Straßen von Chur waren geradezu schamlos belebt. So viel Gegenwart: »Hast du Feuer?... Wo geht's 'n hier zum Bahnhof« Der Untertan war vor einem Zeitungsleser auf einer Parkbank stehengeblieben.
»Geradeaus über die Brücke, immer geradeaus und dann links; ich wünsche Ihnen gute Reise.«

Ihnen? Hatte der Typ tatsächlich *Ihnen* gesagt? Ach so. Der Untertan zog sich die Krawatte vom Hals und stopfte sie in die Rocktasche, öffnete den Kragenknopf, fuhr sich mit der Hand durchs Haar und stellte wenigstens dort das gewohnte Aussehen wieder her. (S, p. 118)

It is notable that Ransmayr does not indulge in rhetorical outbursts against either the survival of monarchist rituals and customs or the toleration of them by the Austrian Republic. The narrator reports at one point on another earlier interview with Professor Ludwig Adamovich, a constitutional expert in the Federal Chancellor's Office. Adamovich had been keen to stress that the 'Habsburggesetz', the National Assembly resolution of 1919 that had banned Emperor Karl and Empress Zita from returning to Austria, could in fact be interpreted under the terms of the pragmatic sanction to mean that Zita, as she could not inherit the Habsburg throne, was in fact permitted to enter the country after all. Allowing a visit by the former Empress might be presented as a sign of maturity and self-confidence in the Republic. That it would also make the same self-confident republic appear both hypocritical and inhumane at once goes unsaid, but Adamovich's comment is telling in its cynicism:

Sie [Zita] soll kommen. Sie ist keine Gefahr. Aber selbstverständlich wäre es uns nicht recht, wenn sie sich hier ansiedeln würde und ihre Anhänger dann jeden Tag mit dem Tomahawk in der Hand um sie herumtanzen würden, das ist klar. (S, p. 118)

One thinks automatically of the pomp and circumstance that attended Zita's funeral in Vienna only a few years later, in which republican Austria deployed monarchist tradition for domestic and tourist consumption with a remarkable degree of cynical self-interest. One image from Ransmayr's text sums up the discrepancies:

In den Auslagefenstern des Café Demel am Kohlmarkt schwebte ein Space-Shuttle-Modell aus Marzipan; auch eine dreistöckige Geburtstagstorte war ausgestellt, daneben eine Fotografie Kaiser Franz Josephs: geboren am 18. August 1830. (S, p. 120)

And where the text has invoked Joseph Roth in its epigraph, another famous passage by the same author will not be far from the reader's mind: towards the end of *Radetzkymarsch* Roth's narrator sums up the anachronistic nature of Habsburg rule by observing that in the age of electricity the palace at Schönbrunn is still lit by candlelight.

The texts 'Die Neunzigjährigen' and 'Auszug aus dem Hause Österreich' are journalistic pieces, at least in origin. The third text that refers to the Habsburg era in *Der Weg nach Surabaya* is of a different character. 'Przemyśl. Ein mitteleuropäisches Lehrstück' is a brief historical allegory. It begins with a striking rhetorical disjunction:

> Am Allerheiligentag des Jahres 1918, zwei Wochen bevor Ludwik Uiberall an einer Schußwunde verblutete, begann auf dem Ringplatz von Przemyśl das Goldene Zeitalter. (S, p. 199)

The combination of a specific date at the end of the First World War and the reference to a Golden Age disorients the reader in itself, but together with the mention in passing of the violent death of Ludwik Uiberall is decidedly odd. The sentence leaves open the question as to the how and why of Uiberall's death and is unclear about the relation between it and the Golden Age. The second sentence at least explains that the local leader of the Social Democrats, the lawyer Hermann Liebermann, declared a Golden Age, announcing:

> die Freie Republik Przemyśl [...] habe die österreichisch-ungarische Herrschaft abgeschüttelt, um endlich in die Welt zu setzen, was in Wien und Budapest immer wieder versprochen, hoffnungslos zerredet und in den Ländern Mitteleuropas [...] niemals verwirklicht worden sei: ein friedliches Miteinander freier, gleichberechtigter Völker in einem vielstimmigen und demokratischen Staat. (S, p. 200)

Liebermann's utopian vision is interrupted by a commotion as a group of Ukrainian carters scuffle with members of his audience. The significance of their sullen dissent only becomes apparent towards the end of the text. There is a cynical reply to Liebermann's enthusiastic proclamation. But it comes in an indirect form. Liebermann has an adversary in the shape of the Czech military doctor Souček, like the 'Nörgler' to the 'Optimist' in Kraus's *Die letzten Tage der Menschheit*. Souček is wont to reply to Liebermann's coffee house tirades from the comfortable preoccupation of the billiard table. His words from the previous week are placed as a reply to the proclamation of a Golden Age:

> Die mitteleuropäischen Völker wollen doch weder einen dynastischen noch einen demokratischen Vielvölkerstaat [...] sondern sie wollen schlicht und einfach ihre eigenen, autonomen, blöden kleinen Nationalstaaten, ihre eigenen

scheppernden Industrien, korrupten Parlamente und lächerlich kostümierten
Armeen. (S, pp. 202-203)

For Souček, the monarchy and its peoples are a menagerie consumed by
mutual hatreds and bound together by particular causes. At the end of
Souček's tirade, the meaning of the death *en passant* of Ludwik Uiberall
becomes clear, for it is antisemitism that is the most potent force in this
particular human zoo:

> Gemeinsam ist den Angehörigen dieser famosen Völkerfamilie doch nur, daß
> sie bei jeder Gelegenheit über die Juden herfallen. Der Pogrom ist aber auch
> schon die einzige Unternehmung, zu der sich die Familie gemeinsam bereit
> findet. (S, pp. 202-203)

The Golden Age of course did not commence in Przemyśl in 1918 - what
follows Liebermann's declaration is a series of power struggles for control
of the fortress town involving only a single death: 'Das Protokoll der
Eroberer überlieferte seinen Namen: Es war der *Pole mosaischen
Bekenntnisses Ludwik Uiberall...*' (S, p. 206). The question here is not so
much one of the passing of memories as of the non-narration of events or
narration in passing. There is an evident structural parallel with *Morbus
Kitahara*. The novel begins with a striking passage whose meaning is
only clear at the end:

> Zwei Tote lagen schwarz im Januar Brasiliens. Ein Feuer, das seit zwei Tagen
> durch die Wildnis einer Insel sprang und verkohlte Schneisen hinterließ, hatte
> die Leichen von einem Gewirr blühender Lianen befreit und ihnen auch die
> Kleider von ihren Wunden gebrannt. Es waren zwei Männer im Schatten eines
> Felsüberhanges. Sie lagen wenige Meter voneinander entfernt in menschen-
> unmöglicher Verrenkung zwischen Farnstrünken. Ein rotes Seil, das die beiden
> miteinander verband, verschmorte in der Glut. (*Morbus Kitahara*, p. 7)

The identities of the two dead men - the two chief male protagonists of the
novel - are unknown to the reader at this point, and the symbolism of the
red rope that links the survivor of the labour camp, Ambras, with the
brutalised son of the perpetrators of the genocide, Bering, is also obscure.
In the same way that the 'dialogue' between Liebermann and Souček is
imagined rather than actually taking place, the surveyor flying a plane at
the beginning and end of *Morbus Kitahara* fails to see the bodies, though
their presence is narrated.

   Although the evidence is perhaps slight - and given Ransmayr's repeated refusals to discuss possible interpretations of his fictional work - the three prose pieces I have examined here that deal with Austria's Habsburg legacy may provide a template for understanding the author's approach to the far more highly-charged questions posed by Austria's more recent history.

   In the essay 'Kaprun oder die Errichtung einer Mauer' Ransmayr opens up a topic more recently covered by other Austrian writers. It is worth noting that the article first appeared in 1985, well before the first rumblings of the Waldheim Affair, the 50th anniversary of the Anschluss in 1988, the performance of Bernhard's *Heldenplatz* at the Burgtheater in the same year, and the numerous other elements that contributed to a shift in the public discourse in Austria regarding attitudes to the Nazi era and Austria's historical role and self-image.

   The dam at Kaprun in the high Taunus mountains and the accompanying power plant was *the* heroic project of Austrian post-war reconstruction. Ransmayr uses Kaprun to expose the layers of mythologising and wilful forgetting that characterise the public discourse on the past:

> Aber wie die meisten Idylle der Zweiten Republik hat auch dieses hier eine Geschichte, deren einzelne Abschnitte das österreichische Nationalbewußtsein mit wechselndem Erinnerungsvermögen bewahrt [...]. (S, p. 79)

He begins with an incident that features in all accounts of the building of the dam: the drowning of rats when the valley was flooded. In an interview Ransmayr refers to this opening image and having spent seven days on this section alone.[8] The account moves on to Kaprun in the present, a fully-developed tourist resort that is, according to its mayor, an accidental by-product of the dam project. Behind the tourist idyll of Kaprun lies a grim tale of slave labour used to build the dam and power station. The only memorial to the Soviet prisoners of war who were the victims of the project is a monument that is off the beaten track, not signposted to visitors. It was only erected on the insistence of the Russians during the détente period in the early 1950s. The wording on the monument is unambiguous:

Hier liegen 87 Sowjetbürger
von deutsch faschistischen Eroberern
ins Elend getrieben und fern von der Heimat
ums Leben gekommen. (S, p. 85)

In the alternative world of *Morbus Kitahara* this half-hidden 'Ärgernis' is
transformed into a huge monument carved in stone letters on the
mountain-side.   Its dimensions in the novel reflect its psychological
significance for the inhabitants of Moor.   Interestingly enough, it would
seem that the municipal authorities in Kaprun have become more sensitive
than they once were to the charge that the real circumstances of the dam-
building have been suppressed. If one compares the memorial site now
with the scene described in Ransmayr's article, there are a number of
evident changes.   Not only has the memorial site itself been cleaned, it is
now clearly signposted from the main street.   The recent photograph
below shows the current setting:

© Ian Foster, 2002

The presence of a number of devotional candles also suggests that owning
up to an Austrian role in Nazi crimes is not merely something that the
authorities have been embarrassed into in order to avoid bad publicity and
perhaps also that the public remembrance of the past has not become quite
as cynical and formulaic as has been claimed.   As was the case following
the unveiling of Alfred Hrdlicka's memorial sculpture, the 'Mahnmal
gegen Krieg und Faschismus', on the Albertinaplatz in Vienna in 1991,
where it was feared that the statue would become the object of neo-Nazi
vandalism, it is the gestures of individual visitors that give meaning to the
memorial itself.   The day after the unveiling of Hrdlicka's monumental

structure, an anonymous visitor left flowers on the kneeling figure in bronze of an elderly Jewish man scrubbing the pavement that forms the focus of Hrdlicka's design.

The text 'Kaprun' is not just about the suppression of the Nazi past. Ransmayr points here to a more generalised phenomenon. For all that is past disappears with living memory. In the building of the Kaprun dam complex after 1945 a further 52 workers died and they too are now fading from view:

> Auf dem Kapruner Friedhof gab es früher einmal eine eigene Gräberzeile für diese Arbeiter [...]. Aber dann hat sich niemand mehr um diese Gräber gekümmert. Sie wurden aufgelöst. (S, p. 90)

A marble stone with the names of the dead is placed next to the town's official war memorial with the hypocritical words: 'Wir gedenken ihrer und aller anderen, die beim Bau verunglückt sind in Trauer und Dankbarkeit' (S, p. 90). Among the descriptions, there are a number of other telling contrasts. Ransmayr describes the pomp of the local 'Wehrmachtsmuseum' – mentioned in all the tourist guides – with its euphemistic references to '[das] große Sterben, das über unser Volk kam' and the vacuous injunction 'Tote Helden mahnen: Seid treu und stark, wie wir es waren' and contrasts these with the overgrown gravestone marking the resting place of 14 Mauthausen prisoners murdered, thrown into a ditch and reburied in a common grave (S, p. 59).

In the last of the texts on the Austrian past in *Der Weg nach Surabaya* - 'Die vergorene Heimat' published in 1989 - Ransmayr comes closest to the subject matter of *Morbus Kitahara* and finds a series of names and images for the relevant social and historical processes. 'Die vergorene Heimat' describes an area of rural Lower Austria that is in slow decline: losing its traditional skills as its traditional apple and pear orchards are grubbed up. This general portrait is woven together from a series of individual life histories (a development perhaps of the technique of 'Die Neunzigjährigen'). The principal theme is announced in the first lines in the figure of the master baker Karl Piaty, who has photographed his community for over 50 years and collected his images in 8600 slides. These stand against 'der vernichtende Lauf der Zeit'. Absent from Piaty's collection of images are any reminders of the Nazi period: 'In der Heimat war es immer schön: es wurden dort Brautbäume und Maibäume errichtet, aber keine Galgen' (S, p. 58). Yet if records are partial (in both senses), if memories fade, and if some choose not to remember, Ransmayr also suggests in a striking image that he will reuse in *Morbus Kitahara* that the truth will out:

> Ein Freund des Konditors, der Maler Reinhard Klaus, verwandelte sich in diesem Jahr vom Heimatliebhaber in einen Professor für Deutsches Brauchtum in Wien und malte Waidhofen im Fahnenschmuck und ganz so, wie der Führer seine Städte gern sah. Das Werk hängt immer noch groß und prächtig im Waidhofener Rathaus; nur die Hakenkreuze wurden, wie so vieles in der Nachkriegsheimat, rot-weiß-rot übermalt und mußten seither von einem Restaurator mehrmals abgedeckt werden, weil sie im Lauf der Zeit trotz des kräftigen Auftrags der Nationalfarben wieder und wieder durchschlugen. (S, p. 60)

Ransmayr's texts on Austria's past are encounters with witnesses and traces. In the Habsburg texts and their treatment of the complex legacy of the monarchy we can discern an acute sense of loss, as knowledge of the past disappears from living memory. The texts on the Austrian Nazi heritage are more complex and particularly revealing of their author's techniques and the origins of many of the images that are reworked in defamiliarised form in *Morbus Kitahara*. The author will go on to explore the themes of forgetfulness, fading memories and the reluctance of the perpetrators of appalling crimes and their witnesses to confront the truth much more fully in the novel. It is precisely through the articulation of these themes within the framework of an alternative history that the novel achieves its effect.

There is one other piece on Austria in *Der Weg nach Surabaja*. 'Die ersten Jahre der Ewigkeit' describes the burial practices of Hallstatt in the Salzkammergut, where the bones of the locals rest in the ground in the tiny graveyard for only a short time before being transferred to the ossuary of the church. Remarkably though, they are not merely left, but painted and decorated and carefully labelled:

> Seit fast vierhundert Jahren ist es in Hallstatt Brauch, die für den Karner bestimmten Schädel zu bemalen: Eichenlaub und Efeu auf die Stirnen der Männer, Blütenzweige und Blumenkränze auf die Stirnen der Frauen […]. Und in solche Zierbeete sind in elfenbeinschwarzen gotischen Lettern die Namen der Toten zu setzen. (S, pp. 64-65)

The significance of this practice lies not just in the decoration of the skulls and the process by which they have become a tourist attraction, drawing

250,000 visitors a year, but in the fact that the skulls retain the identities of their living owners.

What Ransmayr's slender collection of journalistic prose would seem to suggest, then, is that not only is human memory a frail vessel for the preservation of the past and that it is bound to fail as those with direct experience of particular times and places grow old and die, but that the only chance of preserving the past lies in its being transformed into an aesthetic artefact. The delicately painted skulls in Hallstatt command our attention and force us to reflect on our own mortality. In this sense, it seems appropriate to place Ransmayr in a long line of Austrian writers whose most intimate and urgent concern is the way in which the past reaches into the present.

Notes

[1] Ferdinand von Saar, *Die Geigerin*, in: Jakob Minor, *Ferdinand von Saars sämtliche Werke in zwölf Bänden*, Max Hesses Verlag: Leipzig, 1912, vol. 7, p. 157.

[2] Christoph Ransmayr, 'Hiergeblieben! Rede zur Verleihung des Anton-Wildgans-Preises 1989', *Neue Rundschau* (1990), Heft 1, 169-171 (here: p. 169).

[3] Christoph Ransmayr, *Die letzte Welt*, Fischer: Frankfurt a.M., 1991. First published 1988.

[4] Christoph Ransmayr, *Der Weg nach Surabaya*, Fischer: Frankfurt a.M., 1997. Hereafter cited in the text as S.

[5] Christoph Ransmayr, *Morbus Kitahara*, Fischer: Frankfurt a.M., 1995.

[6] Claudio Magris, *Der habsburgische Mythos in der österreichischen Literatur*, Müller: Salzburg, 1966.

[7] Philip Manger: '*The Radetzky March*: Joseph Roth and the Habsburg Myth', in: Mark Francis, ed., *The Viennese Enlightenment*. Croom Helm: London, 1985, pp. 40-62 (here: pp. 47-48).

[8] Christoph Ransmayr, '"…das Thema hat mich bedroht". Gespräch mit Sigrid Löffler über *Morbus Kitahara* (Dublin 1995)', republished in Uwe Wittstock, ed., *Die Erfindung der Welt. Zum Werk von Christoph Ransmayr*, Fischer: Frankfurt a.M., 1997, pp. 213-219 (here: p. 217).

Nicole L. Immler

'Gedächtnisgeschichte' – Ein Vergleich von Deutschland und Österreich in Bezug auf Pierre Noras Konzept der *lieux de mémoire*

Since the nineteen nineties there has been an observable renaissance of the term 'memory'. Everywhere there are ongoing discussions about museums, memorials and monuments. Pierre Nora called these representations of a national memory *lieux de mémoire*. By now, many European countries have taken over his popular concept, creating their own 'sites of memory'. This fashion makes it challenging to look at the different approaches in Germany and Austria and set them into a present-day context. As the broad public attention shows, it is not only a historical but also a political project. The shared interest of science and society in the theory and politics of memory has to be regarded in the process of re-orientation after 1989.

Der historische Kontext des Projekts *Les lieux de mémoire*

Die Gedächtnisgeschichte hat in den letzten Jahren erfolgreich die Brücke zwischen Wissenschaft und Öffentlichkeit geschlagen. Seit Anfang der neunziger Jahre ist die Renaissance des Begriffs 'Erinnerung' zu beobachten. Das Gedenken wird beschworen und bemüht, kommerzialisiert und instrumentalisiert, oft bis zum Überdruss. Wird das 19. Jahrhundert das der Geschichtsschreibung genannt, wird das 20. Jahrhundert in der Zukunft möglicherweise als das der Erinnerung bezeichnet werden. Dieser Trend verhilft der Geschichtswissenschaft in jene Position, die Politikwissenschaft und Soziologie in den sechziger und siebziger Jahren inne hatten: Sie betritt verstärkt die Bühne der Öffentlichkeit;[1] gemeinsam mit ihren Diskussionen um Heimatmuseen, Gedenkstätten und Denkmäler.

Eiffelturm, Jeanne d'Arc, 14. Juli – diese Repräsentationen eines nationalen Erinnerns nennt der Soziologe Pierre Nora *lieux de mémoire*, Orte, an die sich das Gedächtnis lagert. Individuen und Kollektive greifen im Prozess von Identitätskonstruktionen auf solche Orte zurück. Nora schuf eine siebenbändige Topographie des französischen Kollektivgedächtnisses, *Les lieux de mémoire* (1984–1992),[2] eine Selbstvergewisserung, die in Zeiten ihrer Auflösung im EU-Prozess die Nation neu auf die Agenda setzt. Insbesondere in Folge der Umbrüche von 1989 haben zahlreiche Länder das populäre Konzept übernommen und modellieren nun ihre eigenen nationalen Gedächtnisorte. In den Niederlanden, Dänemark, Spanien, Israel, Kanada und Russland wurde das Konzept bisher realisiert. Dieser Trend zur Gedächtnisgeschichte signalisiert ein gesellschaftspolitisches Projekt – insbesondere weil es 'nicht um die Vergangenheit als solche (geht), sondern nur um die Vergangenheit, wie sie erinnert' wird.[3] Ein Vergleich der verschiedenen Konzepte, wie die in den letzten beiden Jahren publizierten Werke in Deutschland und Österreich, zeigt: Pro oder contra Nora lautet die neue Glaubensfrage. Vorworte und Nachworte gerieren sich dabei als eigenes Genre der vergleichenden Wissenschaft. Hier wird Position bezogen, werden mehr Abgrenzungen vorgenommen als Parallelen genannt, was jüngste Positionen in der Geschichtswissenschaft europäischer Nachbarländer deutlich offenbart. Hier initialisieren die Arbeiten von Pierre Nora, Hagen Schulze und Etienne François sowie Mario Isnenghi eine neue französische, deutsche und italienische Geschichtsschreibung, über welche es kritisch heißt, sie sei eine Fortführung der Nationalgeschichtsschreibung des 19. Jahrhunderts.[4] Sind es tatsächlich Beispiele einer neuen Nationalgeschichtsschreibung mit Blick nach innen, oder wie es Nora postulierte, eine Nationalgeschichtsschreibung mit 'erweitertem Horizont'? Vor der Folie Frankreich sollen das deutsche und das österreichische Projekt in Bezug auf die jeweilige nationale Geschichtsschreibung sowie das Verhältnis zu Europa verortet werden. Anschließend wird unter dem Eindruck des europäischen Integrationsprozesses nach der Möglichkeit von *europäischen Gedächtnisorten* zu fragen sein.

Eine Skizze der *lieux de mémoire*-Projekte in Deutschland und Österreich vor der Folie Frankreich

Frankreich

Jedes Land hat seine 'geschichtliche Logik' und sein spezifisches 'Verhältnis zur Vergangenheit', schreibt Nora und betont, sein 'Modell der lieux de mémoire […] bietet keine Geschichte Frankreichs im herkömmlichen Sinne, sondern eine Geschichte wie sie Frankreich heute braucht'.[5] Es ist von französischen Historikern für die französische Öffentlichkeit geschrieben, um das Bewusstsein für die eigene Nation zu stärken; denn die achtziger Jahre in Frankreich waren geprägt von rasantem wirtschaftlichem Wachstum, dem Streben nach Dezentralisierung, europäischer Integration und den Folgewirkungen des Algerienkrieges. Diese genannten Irritationen sind zwar Motivation, doch nicht das Thema. Frankreich präsentiert sich im Werk Noras als eine ungebrochene Nation; mit einem unproblematischen Verhältnis zur Nation und einer bis ins Hochmittelalter zurückführenden Tradition, einer dynastischen und territorialen Kontinuität, unterstützt durch eine kontinuierliche Geschichtsschreibung seit dem 13. Jahrhundert. Nora betont die Einheit des französischen Staates, als Beherrscher der Wirtschaft (Colbertismus), Schutzherr der von Paris aus dominierten Kultur, Einiger der Sprache und damit Erzieher der Gesellschaft; Bereiche, die hingegen in Deutschland 'aus sich heraus das Bewusstsein einer Gemeinschaft und das Nationalgefühl geschaffen haben'.[6] Hier konstruiert Nora aus einer nationalstaatlichen Perspektive Kontinuitäten eines 'natürlichen' französischen Zentralismus, und eine Differenz zum Nachbarn, wenn er betont, dass der deutsche Staat nie in dem Maße das 'Instrument der nationalen Einheit' war wie in Frankreich und die Gleichsetzung von Staat und Nation in Deutschland ein Phänomen der jüngeren Geschichte sei.

Deutschland

Diese Zuschreibung des 'anderen' Erbes findet sich wieder in der deutschen Debatte darum, ob dieses Unternehmen à la Nora für Deutschland möglich sei. Das deutsche Projekt erklärt dann gerade das brüchige Erbe (und dessen Überwindung) zum Gründungskonzept. Der Kontinuitäten brechende Nationalsozialismus und die innerdeutsche Teilung, insbesondere die Ungleichzeitigkeit von deutscher nationaler Einheit und europäischer Integration, werden als die Herausforderungen des 19. und 20. Jahrhunderts gesehen. Deswegen konzentrieren sich die Herausgeber der *Deutschen Erinnerungsorte*, Etienne François und Hagen Schulze, auf das Ausverhandeln einer gemeinsamen deutschen Geschichte zwischen Ost und West und auf den europäischen Blick zu den Nachbarn hin, was die deutsch-französische Zusammenarbeit unterstützt.[7] Das Resultat: Ein dreibändiges, umfangreiches Kompendium von Schlüsselbegriffen zur deutschen Geschichte mit feuilletonmäßigem Touch und ungewöhnlicher Struktur: 18 Oberbegriffe typisch-deutscher Gedächtniskultur ('Bildung' bis 'Zerrissenheit') subsumieren einhundertzwanzig Erinnerungsorte, die in Essayform ein buntes Sammelsurium deutscher Identität bieten.

Die Kritik in den deutschen Feuilletons zeigt, wie sensibel die Öffentlichkeit auf solch ein angekündigtes Jahrhundertprojekt reagiert.[8] Was sind die verbindlichen Erinnerungsorte der Deutschen und ist so kurz nach der Teilung von einem gesamtdeutschen Gedächtnis zu sprechen? Und helfen die europäischen Bezüge das beargwöhnte 'Diktat der

nationale Wende' (Alfons Söllner) in der deutschen Historiographie zu
entkräften?

Ulrich Raulff spricht von einer 'zeitgemäßen Form der
Geschichtsvermittlung', auch wenn er den Fokus auf die letzten zwei
Jahrhunderte und die Vernachlässigung von Literatur- und
Kunstgeschichte bemängelt.[9] Als wertvolles Kompendium von Schlüssel-
begriffen, doch darin fast museales Projekt und 'Arche Noah in den
Fluten' kritisiert Michael Jeismann die fehlende Gegenwartsrelevanz der
Bände, begonnen zu einem Zeitpunkt als die Nation mit Maastricht und
Euro-Planung bereits historisiert war. Die alte Bundesrepublik habe sich
aufgelöst und es sei darüber nachzudenken, was übrig und zukunftsfähig
sei, der Zeitgeschichte aus ihrer Krise zu helfen.[10] Hans-Ulrich Wehler
dagegen betont die zeitgeschichtliche Relevanz des Unternehmens, in der
Intention der Autoren, 1989/90 zum Beginn des deutschen 'normalen
Nationalstaats' zu erheben. Doch er mahnt, dass sich jene Normalität
gerade im Umgang mit der Vergangenheit und Erinnerung zeige, und
erkennt in der fragwürdigen Selektion der Orte eine eindeutig
antirepublikanische politische Haltung.[11] Friedrich Wilhelm Graf sieht die
Auswahl der Orte als zu fröhlich postmodern willkürlich, vage auch die
Zuordnungen der Essays zu den jeweiligen Oberbegriffen.[12] Die Bände
seien hierin konzeptionell unkonventionell, aber doch dem 'höheren
Kulturbegriff' verpflichtet.[13] Populäre Massenkultur und Arbeiter-
bewegung kämen zu kurz, ebenso fehlten Judenemanzipation,
Nationalsozialismus, Völkerfreundschaft, Antifaschismus und auch die
neuen Herausforderungen Globalisierung, Migration, Informations- und
Gentechnologie seien 'insgesamt unterbelichtet', bemängelt Christoph
Jahr. Er problematisiert, wie viele andere auch, das Übertragen des
französischen Konzepts, denn die deutsche Erinnerungslandschaft sei sehr
'viel heterogener, kulturell, konfessionell und regional gebrochener als im
zentralistischen Frankreich'.[14] Auch Ulrich Speck sieht das ganze Projekt
als 'misslungenen Import' eines speziell französischen Modells, das dort
aufgrund einer 'zentralisierten Bildung' und einer 'recht homogenen
Nationalgeschichte' durchführbar sei, doch die föderalistische Struktur
sowie die Teilung Deutschlands lassen 'nur schwer' ein gemeinsames
'Erinnerungsbildungsgut' erkennen.[15] Statt Gemeinsames zu suchen wäre
den Unterschieden mehr Rechnung zu tragen. Gerade das aber werde
verabsäumt, so Claus Leggewie, 'ein und denselben Ort wenigstens
exemplarisch im Licht der "zwei Vergangenheiten" [zu] betrachten'.[16]
Johannes Willms ist das Projekt zu lexikalisch angelegt und er sieht die

lange für den Nationalstaat oder den Nationalsozialismus konstitutiven Feindbilder zu 'kursorisch abgehandelt'.[17] Auch Thomas Maissen sind die Bände zu historiographisch, 'statt über Kanonisierungsvorgänge aufzuklären' blieben sie der Kanonisierung verhaftet. Nur selten gelinge es, den Kult um historische Figuren zu dekonstruieren (wie bei Bach) statt ihn konventionell historisch zu würdigen.[18] Auch Frank Böckelmann kritisiert die Geschichtslastigkeit und fehlende Gegenwartsrelevanz, lobt aber doch, dass eine Verschiebung vom nationalen zum regionalen nachvollziehbar sei, ebenso der Verlust und die Verlagerung von Erinnerung, wie bei der 'Hausmusik' oder der 'Völkerschlacht bei Leipzig'.[19]

Das Feuilleton kritisierte einhellig den bildungsbürgerlichen Charakter des Projekts,[20] delegitimiert aber die eigene Kritik mit der Diskussion über die Auswahl der 'falschen' und 'richtigen' Orte. Hier wird ein Bedürfnis nach Eindeutigkeit und fest umrissenem Kanon formuliert, gerade im Geiste des zuvor so vehement kritisierten hegemonialen Bildungsbürgertums des 19. Jahrhunderts. Diese lineare Gerichtetheit einer normierten nationalen Meistererzählung wollte das deutsche Projekt mit seiner Multiperspektivität – Beitragenden aus In- und Ausland, innerhalb und außerhalb des Wissenschaftsbetriebes – bewusst vermeiden; angestrebt war ein 'Spiegelkabinett' von Selbst- und Fremdwahrnehmung, als Korrektiv und Ergänzung, weil die Fremdwahrnehmung die Selbstwahrnehmung stets geprägt hat.[21] Aufschlussreich sollten deshalb auch weniger die Orte selbst sein, als vielmehr die wechselnden Erinnerungen, die an jene geknüpft sind; damit wäre auch die Auswahl nachrangig. Doch die oftmals deskriptiven und damit normativen Beschreibungen beleben eher alte Mythen (wie z.B. Hitlers Ableben im 'Führerbunker' von Joachim Fest), wiederholen statt zu analysieren und reproduzieren Kultgeschichten statt zu dekonstruieren. Die Nähe zum historischen Detail verhindert oft die Chance den Bedeutungswandel eines Erinnerungsortes (z.B. Hagen Schulzes Darstellung von Versailles als Spiegel des deutsch-französischen Verhältnisses) und die Änderung von Identifikationsmustern deutlich zu machen. Hier wäre eine stärkere Herausarbeitung der Gegenwartsrelevanz dieser Erinnerungsorte sowie die Neu-Positionierung alter Freund-Feind-Verhältnisse aufschlussreich gewesen. Manch ein Essay gleitet ins Klischee ('der Weißwurstäquator'), ins Antiquierte ('Walhalla'), ins Beliebige ('Karl May') ab. Die Ortsbeschreibung 'Reichstag' (Bernd Roeck) als 'Clearing-Stelle' Mitteleuropas ist hingegen zentral für die grundlegende Problematik des Nationalen und des Umschreibens von Erinnerungen im Interesse der Gegenwart. Denn aus der Perspektive der Nationalgeschichtsschreibung hatte das Heilige Römische Reich deutscher Nation einen abschreckenden Charakter. Ganz anders ist die heutige Sicht – nach den Erfahrungen des 20. Jahrhunderts und dem Erleben der Etablierung und Erweiterung der Europäischen Union.

Wird das Projekt von Hagen Schulze auch als Beitrag zur Identitäts*findung*, nicht Identitäts*bildung* deklariert, die neuen Normen – europäisches Ziel und Zentrum Nationalstaat – werden klar formuliert.[22] Die Ausrichtung des Projekts geriert sich europäisch, durch die Bandbreite der Mitschreibenden und die Aufnahme von zahllosen 'geteilten Erinnerungsorten'; solche, die für Deutschland und die benachbarten Nationen (insbesondere Frankreich, Russland, Polen, Österreich) gleichermaßen bedeutsam sind, wie das Straßburger Münster, Versailles, Tannenberg/Grunwald, Rom, Karl der Große/Charlemagne, Rapallo oder der Wiener Heldenplatz. Doch das nationale Element ist dennoch das zu Grunde liegende methodische Prinzip, ein ausschließendes und angreifbares, in Zeiten, wo Globalisierung und die Realität einer Migrationsgesellschaft zusehends ein Wandel des Wissenschaftsverständnisses einfordert. Die diversen Subgruppen im 'pluralen Handlungsraum' (Lutz Niethammer) der Nation bleiben unberücksichtigt; die Realität einer 'Migrationsgesellschaft' ignoriert; wie die Erinnerungskultur von Minderheiten, die seit den fünfziger (Italiener), sechziger (Türken[23]) und achtziger Jahren (Afrikaner) Bestandteil des deutschen Gedächtnisses sind; ebenso die spezifische Erinnerungskultur des ehemaligen deutschen Ostens. Und damit bleibt auch die Intention unerfüllt, eine gemeinsame Geschichte zu verhandeln. Hier formuliert die Einleitung der *Deutschen Erinnerungsorte* Vorsicht, statt Aktualität anzustreben: Schwierig sei diese Balance zwischen dem, was sich auflöse, was Bestand habe und was erst im Entstehen begriffen sei. Hier wurde die Gelegenheit verabsäumt, mit wissenschaftlicher Wahrnehmung von Randgruppen und Minderheiten, Vorreiter gesellschaftlicher Emanzipation zu sein.[24]

Diese Kritik findet sich wieder in einer vielfach geforderten Pluralisierung der deutschen Geschichtsschreibung, jüngst und prominent seitens Karl-Heinz Bohrer in seiner Heidelberger Rede. Das, was deutsche Geschichte bedeute, müsse pluralisiert und zeitlich vertieft werden, um nicht im Kurzzeitgedächtnis des Holocausts zu verbleiben.[25] Auch der Gedächtnisgeschichte wird nun vorgeworfen, was jahrzehntelang bereits als 'Nabelschau' der deutschen Gesellschaftsgeschichte kritisiert wurde: der reduzierende Blick der Sozialgeschichte auf die sozialen, regionalen und europäischen Dimensionen von Nation, und auf die zwei Diktaturen des Nationalsozialismus und der SED-Zeit.[26] Jene Gesellschaftsgeschichte sei inhaltlich zu ausschließlich und vergesse die Pluralitäten in Vergangenheit und Gegenwart. Dan Diner nennt es die Neutralisierung der Erinnerung durch die Sozialgeschichte, 'social history neutralized memory'; man habe stets von *einer* Vergangenheit und *einer* Gegenwart gesprochen, statt die vielen unterschiedlichen Schichten von Erinnerung zu berücksichtigen.[27] Erkennt Diner auch im Jahr 1989 einen Paradigmenwechsel durch die Ablösung der Gesellschaftsgeschichte von der Kultur- und Erinnerungsgeschichte, sieht Nora seine Kritik an der deutschen Geschichtsschreibung in den *Deutschen Erinnerungsorten* bestätigt, wo 'jede Vergegenwärtigung und Neuinterpretation der gesamten nationalen Vergangenheit unter dem Zeichen der zwölf schrecklichen Jahre des Nationalsozialismus' stehe. Gleichzeitig kritisiert Nora den unspezifischen Charakter dieser Erinnerungskultur. Es seien dort all die wirkmächtigen Orte 'zwar alle deutsch, aber gleichermaßen national wie europäisch [...]. Als ob, um es mit Jürgen Habermas zu sagen, der Erinnerungsort, der alle deutschen Erinnerungsorte bestimmt, Auschwitz wäre'.[28]

War die Bundesrepublik Deutschland tituliert als eine postnationale Demokratie unter Nationalstaaten – und mit 'Auschwitz als Gründungsmythos' (August Winkler) eher einem Negativnationalismus verfallen – hat die kurzlebige Preußen-Diskussion sowie die Martin-Walser-Debatte gezeigt, dass sich auch das Verhältnis einer Mehrzahl der Deutschen zu ihrer Vergangenheit entkrampft hat.[29] Zugleich ist es der Augenblick der Historisierung der Nation, der es zahlreichen namhaften Historikern erlaubt, unbescholten über *Deutsche Erinnerungsorte* zu reflektieren, und nicht nur Details der *Machbarkeit,* sondern das Projekt als Ganzes in seiner *Konstruktion* zu hinterfragen.

Österreich

Pluralisierung ist das Motto der österreichischen Projekte: institutionell und inhaltlich. Dezentral wird an verschiedenen Instituten zum 'österreichischen Gedächtnis' geforscht, mit widersprüchlichen Ansätzen und damit ergänzend. Das Projekt *Österreichs lieux de mémoire* am Institut für Wirtschafts- und Sozialgeschichte der Universität Wien (Ernst Bruckmüller, Hannes Stekl) arbeitet in Anlehnung an Nora an einer

anthropologisch-kulturwissenschaftlichen   Studie   über   nationale
Selbstbilder und den heutigen 'homo austriacus'; gestützt auf empirische
Umfragen à la: 'Was assoziieren Sie mit Österreich?'[30]

Weniger Nora und mehr Theorie charakterisiert das Projekt *Orte
des Gedächtnisses* an der Akademie der Wissenschaften in Wien. Das
zeigt der Tenor der seit März 1999 jährlich tagenden internationalen
Konferenzen, wie die Buchreihe *Orte des Gedächtnisses*.[31] Statt das
Bewusstsein einer österreichischen Nationalkultur zu festigen wird der
komplexe Gedächtnisort betont. Historische Orte werden weniger als
Schlüsselbegriffe *einer* nationalen Vergangenheit untersucht, als vielmehr
eindeutige Konnotationen des Nationalen dekonstruiert und die
Vielschichtigkeit und Widersprüchlichkeit diesen Orten zurückgegeben.
Die Dekonstruktion wird potenziert, indem die Medien der Erinnerung
selbst – Gedächtnisspeicher wie Bibliotheken, Archive, Museen oder
Computer – mitreflektiert werden und auch auf der Ebene der
Erinnerungstheorie, von Maurice Halbwachs bis zu Jan und Aleida
Assmann, rekonstruiert wird, wie Gedächtnis *gemacht* wird. Projektleiter
Moritz Csáky stellt die Vorstellung von einem geschlossenen kulturellen
System in Frage und betont den gesamtregionalen Charakter von
'kulturellen Codes'. Hier werden die Phänomene von Assimilation,
Akkulturation, die Prozesse der Aneignung und Ablehnung, sowie das
Umcodieren von Erinnerungsbezügen analysiert, um komplexen
Identitätsbildungen auf die Spur zu kommen – welche auch heute unter
dem Einfluss von Globalisierung und Migrationsbewegungen ähnlich
vielschichtig sind. Schon Jean-François Lyotard nannte deshalb diesen
heterogenen Raum Zentraleuropa in der Epoche der Modernisierung das
'Laboratorium' der postmodernen Lebenswelt, und Moritz Csáky sieht in
Anschluss daran in der Habsburgermonarchie mit ihrer supranationalen
Staatsidee, den Konflikten und Konsensstrategien der Völker, das
'Laboratorium gegenwärtiger Problemlagen'.[32]

In der Ausländerpolitik zum Beispiel könnten diese Erkenntnisse
über die Mechanismen kultureller Hegemonie mit gleichzeitiger
Anerkennung von Differenz zu einer 'Sensibilisierung gegenüber
gegenwärtigen Aporien einer "Politik der Anerkennung"' beitragen.[33] Hier
werden Perspektiven aus den *Postcolonial Studies* auf Österreich
gerichtet. Mit der 'Hybridität' als Leitbegriff – welcher das auch
krisenhafte Nebeneinander von Kulturen und ihre Differenz beschreibt,
die Dichotomie von Zentrum und Peripherie aufhebt und die Grenze als
Übergang und die Vielheit als Differenz denkt – wird das Wechselspiel

Homogenisierung (einheitliche Sprachpolitik und Administration, Barockstil in der Architektur) und Differenzierung (angestrebte Nationalstaatlichkeit) innerhalb der Habsburgermonarchie neu bewertet. Aus Sicht der *Postcolonial Studies* zeigt sich das Projekt der Gedächtnisorte als ein Kampf um die Monopolisierung von Gedächtnis, denn 'die Bedeutungsgebung liege außerhalb des historischen, archäologischen oder geographischen Feldes eindeutig im politischen'.[34] Das postkoloniale Anliegen hingegen sei es, so Anil Bhatti, die Hierarchisierung von bedeutsamen und unbedeutenden Erinnerungsorten aufzulösen, sowie die Machtverhältnisse und Abhängigkeiten auf realhistorischer wie symbolischer Ebene radikal neu zu formulieren. Die postkoloniale Theorie biete hier neue, kritische Perspektiven auf ein altes Thema.

Die Habsburger Monarchie und Zentraleuropa sind schon seit den siebziger Jahren populäre Themen der Geschichtswissenschaft. Doch statt der 'rückwärtsgewandten Utopie' (Heidemarie Uhl) eines harmonischen Mitteleuropas, wie sie in Form eines nostalgischen Habsburg-Mythos bis in die siebziger Jahre gepflegt wurde, werden seit den achtziger Jahren die Pluralitäten, Brüche und Diskontinuitäten betont und Österreich zum 'imaginäre(n) Gedächtnisort der europäischen Identität' erklärt.[35] Diese Anerkennung von Habsburgs Erbe und der Pluralität im Inneren eröffnete nun auch 'ambivalentere Zugänge' für die Wissenschaft.[36]

Auch auf politischer Ebene fand seit den neunziger Jahren eine ähnliche Umdeutung des politischen Fremd- und Selbstbildes, vom Harmoniebetonten hin zur Akzeptanz von Differenz, statt. Das harmonisierende Bild der *Brücke* war innenpolitisch *die* Metapher der Zweiten Republik: Die Brücke zwischen Sozialisten und Christdemokraten, Wien und den Bundesländern, Katholiken und Sozialisten, basierend auf den Erfahrungen des Bürgerkrieges (1934) und des Austrofaschismus (1934–38). Der Metapher inhärent ist der Wille des Überwindens von Hindernissen, einer Verbindung von Gegensätzen und Widersprüchen.[37] Im Zuge der Europäisierung mutierte das Selbstbild zum Fremdbild, als Österreich von außen die Funktion als *Brücke* zu den Balkanstaaten und den südosteuropäischen Ländern zugeschrieben wurde. Doch gerade in den neunziger Jahren, mit der Auflösung der Blockgrenzen, erfährt dieses Bild von der *Brücke* in Zentraleuropa (so noch die Repräsentation auf der letzten Expo) eine Ablösung, und das Bild der *Schnittstelle* rückt ins öffentliche Bewusstsein, welches mehr den *Netzwerk*-Charakter von Österreich, insbesondere von Wien, betont: die Kommunikation, Aufgeschlossenheit und Offenheit nach allen Seiten, sowie die Verbindungsfunktion nach West und Ost. Dieses veränderte politische Selbstverständnis findet sich *inhaltlich* in der Gedächtnisgeschichte wieder, in der die zentraleuropäische Vielfalt und Differenz als ein identitätsstiftendes Merkmal österreichischer Identität betont wird; aber auch im *Begrifflichen.* Hier operiert die Gedächtnisgeschichte seit jüngst mit der Metapher des *Netzwerkes* und signalisiert damit einen Paradigmenwechsel. Nach Bibliothek oder Archiv als Speicher des kulturellen Gedächtnisses, wird nun das Netzwerk, 'eine entsinnlichte, ausgehöhlte Metapher' für ein 'externalisiertes globales Nervensystem'[38] – korrelierend mit dem neuen Anspruch des Übergreifenden und Wechselseitigen. Das könnte eine neue Perspektive für die europäische Gedächtnisort-Forschung sein, die weniger das Trennende oder das Gemeinsame, als die kommunikativen Austausch-prozesse darüber selbst zum Thema macht.

Im Vergleich

Noras methodisch diszipliniertes, analytisches Konzept zur symbolischen Vermittlung von kollektiver Identität hat sich im Zuge seiner Popularisierung 'verflüssigt' und an die jeweiligen Gegebenheiten historischer und politischer Natur angepasst. Jedes dieser Projekte ist zweifellos politisch motiviert.[39] Doch wie es scheint, verhandeln Österreich und Deutschland eher im Bereich der Kultur und der Historiographie, während das Konzept in Frankreich eindeutig politisch ausgerichtet ist, was die Gliederung nach Politik-Epochen verdeutlicht.[40] Auch wird dort stärker unter dem Aspekt der Gegenwart verhandelt, öffentlichkeitswirksame neben alternativen Gedächtnisorte aufgegriffen, die das Gedächtnis des *heutigen* Frankreich bewusst und unbewusst geformt haben. Gemeinsam ist dem österreichischen und deutschen Projekt auch der Fokus auf die Vergangenheit des 19. Jahrhunderts. Doch während im Sinne einer neuen deutschen Nationalgeschichtsschreibung nach der Wende, dort u.a. das Gemeinsame von Ost und West gesucht wird, wird die Habsburgische Vergangenheit zum Vorbild für ein europäisches Österreich. Jene heterogenen, pluralen, hybriden Identifikatoren, die überlappenden Legitimitäten und Solidaritäten, die insbesondere den geopolitischen Raum Zentraleuropas prägten, scheinen vergleichbar mit der heutigen Situation von Europäisierung und Globalisierung, Migrationen und Diasporen. Die nostalgischen Gefahren des Habsburg-Mythos als harmonische Völkergemeinschaft im Kopf behaltend und die konträre Reduzierung auf ein 'Schlachtfeld nationaler

Chauvinismen' (Jacques Le Rider), werden hier wissenschaftliche Fragestellungen und theoretische Ansätze entwickelt, die helfen sollen den begrenzenden Rahmen des Nationalen zu sprengen und mehr transnationale Perspektiven zu entwickeln, um damit auch ein 'Modell' für die Erklärung außereuropäischer kultureller Phänomene zu schaffen. Aus dieser Perspektive kommt auch der Verdacht auf, mit dieser Art der Gedächtnisgeschichte eine neue Nationalgeschichte zu schreiben.[41] Eine, die mit ihrer nationalen Fokussierung Konzept und Inhalte auf eine historische Sichtweise des 19. Jahrhunderts verkürze und damit wenig Aussagekraft habe für Gegenwart und Zukunft, da hier die Bezugssysteme für Identitätsbildung viel komplexer und widersprüchlicher seien. Das österreichische Projekt versucht deshalb übergreifenden zentral-europäischen sowie postmodernen Realitäten gerecht zu werden, während die *Deutschen Erinnerungsorte* angesichts dem Ruf nach Öffnung, Pluralisierung und zeitlicher Vertiefung der deutschen Historiographie vielen nicht zeitgemäß erscheinen.

Ähnlich wie in Deutschland sind es die Brüche des 19. und 20. Jahrhunderts, die die gegenwärtige österreichische Erinnerungskultur prägen. Das illustrieren die Umwälzungen in der Historiographie, ebenso die Feierlichkeiten zum 'Millennium'. Verlief in Frankreich die Tausendjahrfeier zum Gedenken an die Karpetinger 1987 integrativ wie das Projekt der *lieux de mémoire*, waren Konzeption und Diskussion um die Millenniumsfeier in Österreich im Jahr 1996 von distanzierender Ironie und der Rede über Diskontinuitäten gezeichnet.[42] Beispielhaft für diese kollektiven Traumata und Identitätsbrüche der letzten hundert Jahre, welche die österreichische Denkmallandschaft präg(t)en, ist der Wiener Heldenplatz, der den Wandel einer europäischen Weltmacht in einen mehrheitlich ungewollten republikanischen Kleinstaat 'wider Willen' (1918), den Bürgerkrieg (1934), vier Jahre Diktatur des christlich-sozialen Ständestaates (1934–38) und die Kapitulation vor dem Nationalsozialismus (1938–45) paradigmatisch repräsentiert.[43] Gerade diese Erfahrungen einer 'permanenten politischen Identitätsbeschädigung und kollektiven, wie auch je individuellen Verunsicherung' führten nach Peter Stachel zu einem für Österreich charakteristischen 'Streben nach Harmonisierung von Gegensätzen und die überdeutlich bekundete Scheu vor jeglicher Art von offen ausgetragenen Konflikten'.[44] Diese Haltung in Politik und Gesellschaft erfährt in den achtziger Jahren einen Wandel, für welchen der 'Heldenplatz' Symbolcharakter bekommt. Als Kapitel in den *Deutschen Erinnerungsorten* und den österreichischen *Orten des*

Gedächtnisses vorhanden, bietet er sich an, das Konzept der *lieux de mémoire* zu beleuchten, auch als ein Kristallisationspunkt des deutsch-österreichischen Freund-Feind-Verhältnisses.

Der Wiener Heldenplatz, ein *geteilter* Erinnerungsort

Der Wiener Heldenplatz – die monumentale Anlage zwischen Hofburg (der ehemaligen kaiserlichen Residenz) und Ringstraße, welche das innere Stadtzentrum umschließt – ist ein *geteilter Erinnerungsort*, zwischen Österreich und Deutschland, wie auch innerhalb Österreichs.

Der Heldenplatz ist ein traumatisches Symbol für den 'Anschluss' Österreichs an Hitler-Deutschland im März 1938 und damit ein *außenpolitisches* Kapitel. Hier erklärte Hitler vor einer jubelnden Masse den 'Anschluss' seiner Heimat an das Dritte Reich. Deshalb ist er nicht zufällig auch Bestandteil der *Deutschen Erinnerungsorte*, jahrzehntelang wurde die Erinnerung an den Nationalsozialismus dorthin abgeschoben und verdrängt, bis 1986 mit der Waldheim-Affäre – der Medien-Skandal um die Verstricktheit des österreichischen Bundespräsidenten Kurt Waldheim in den Nationalsozialismus – der Opfermythos personifiziert, skandalisiert und ins Licht der Öffentlichkeit gerückt wurde. Medienwirksam erschütterte auch das Theaterstück *Heldenplatz* von Thomas Bernhard, von Claus Peymann 1988 am Burgtheater inszeniert, diesen Erinnerungsmythos der Zweiten Republik. Das Jahr 1986 und das Erinnerungsjahr 1988 (50 Jahre Anschluss) haben mitgewirkt, den in der Geschichtswissenschaften längst vollzogenen Wandel vom Opfermythos zum Täterbewusstsein, in eine breitere Öffentlichkeit zu tragen. Nahezu gleichzeitig wies die Wende 1989 Österreich eine neue Rolle in Europa zu, was nun auch im politischen Bereich dazu führte, vom Thema der Nation Abstand zu nehmen und die historische und politische Perspektive zu europäisieren.

Der Heldenplatz wird damit zur steinernen Metapher eines neuen Umgangs mit Erinnerung, der auch ein *innenpolitisches* Drama offenbart: Das politische Lagerdenken hatte nicht nur die österreichische Politik seit dem Bürgerkrieg 1934 in Sozialisten und Christdemokraten gespalten – in Gegensätze, welche mit der Metapher der 'Brücke' lange überspielt wurden –, sondern auch die Erinnerungskultur geteilt.[45] Der Heldenplatz ist hier ein Beispiel dafür, wie nachhaltig Symbole wirken und sich Überschreibungen widersetzen.

Der Heldenplatz, historisch mit Kaiserforum und Habsburgmythos kodiert, blieb lange eine Herausforderung für bürgerliche und sozialistische Gruppierungen. Bürgerliche und Arbeiter besetzten die angrenzende Ringstrasse mit ihren Zeichen, und das Rathaus wurde dort in der Ersten Republik das Zentrum des Roten Wiens. Ernst Hanisch betont, dass trotz mehrmaligen Bedeutungswandels, sichtbar anhand der Symbolik der Architektur, an Festkultur und literarischen Bezugnahmen, der Heldenplatz lange eine 'altertümliche Starrheit, eine gleichsam "gefrorene Erinnerung" (behielt) [...]. Denn die imperiale, militärische, autoritäre, katholische Kodierung des Raumes verweigerte sich fast durchgehend liberal-demokratischen Repräsentationen'.[46] Diese Erinnerung an den Heldenplatz als Ort monarchisch-österreichischer Inszenierung ist heute durch den Anschluss (1938) vollkommen überlagert. Hanisch und Stachel schildern die oft widersprüchlichen Versuche einer Gegenkultur, den Platz nach 1945 neu zu kodieren wie zum Beispiel sozialistische Kundgebungen oder das Lichtermeer gegen Ausländerfeindlichkeit 1993. Im Jahr 2000 waren es die Demonstrationen gegen die letzte ÖVP-FPÖ Regierung, die mit diesem symbolträchtigen Protest ein Wiederaufleben des alten politischen Lagerdenkens sichtbar machten, welches das Land – wie den Ort Heldenplatz selbst – jahrzehntelang geprägt hat. Der Heldenplatz wurde somit erneut Ort der Auseinandersetzung, um eine Diskrepanz zwischen Selbst- und Fremdsicht (kreisend um die unterschiedliche Wahrnehmung von Jörg Haider innerhalb und außerhalb Österreichs), was in der Frage nach der problematischen 'Wesenhaftigkeit' des Österreichers zu einer Wiederkehr des Nationalen führte und zum Nachdenken über die gemeinsamen europäischen Werte.[47] Insbesondere wegen der Mitinitiative der deutschen Regierung für die Sanktionen gegen die ÖVP-FPÖ-Regierung, wehrt man sich nun gegen die 'Eingemeindung' des Wiener Heldenplatzes in die *Deutschen Erinnerungsorte*, ohne diese jüngsten politischen Diskurse über das Feind-Freund-Verhältnis der Nachbarn näher erläutert zu finden.[48]

Für die Topographie der Identitätspolitik ist auch interessant, dass es bis heute auf dem Heldenplatz kein Denkmal der Zweiten Republik gibt – nach Peter Stachel Resultat der 'übermächtigen Erinnerung an den März 1938'.[49] Das könnte als Versäumnis bewertet werden, geht man davon aus, dass dies die Praxis jeder Politikergeneration war und ist, alte Orte neu zu kodieren oder sich mit neuen Denkmälern zu repräsentieren. Es könnte aber auch als ein Zeichen eines selbstbewussten Umgangs mit der Vergangenheit gesehen werden, den Ort einfach als 'Nazidenkmal' zu belassen, wie das 'Russendenkmal' am Schwarzenbergplatz. Denn wie es Aleida Assmann betont, habe unter 'dem Firnis offizieller Sinnstiftungen' schon längst ein Ende politischer Eindeutigkeit zu Gunsten der Vielstimmigkeiten von Erinnerungen eingesetzt, mit der Einsicht: 'Der Ort ist all das, was man an ihm sucht, was man von ihm weiß, was man mit ihm verbindet. So gegenständlich konkret er ist, so vielfältig präsentiert er sich in den unterschiedlichen Perspektivierungen'.[50] Es ist die Gedächtnisgeschichte, die sich bemüht, den Kampf um diese mehr oder weniger gern 'geteilten Erinnerungsorte' und die 'richtigen' Aufmerksamkeiten, zu *re-* und *de*konstruieren.   Hier könnte diesen Einsichten ein sozusagen unsichtbares Monument gesetzt werden.

Nationale Gedächtnisgeschichte und Europa

Das Projekt der Gedächtnisorte zeigt allgemein, das Thema *Nation* darf wieder erwähnt werden.   Die Wende 1989/90 hat zu veränderten Inbezugnahmen im nationalen Diskurs geführt, der Prozess der europäischen Integration zu Neuentwürfen nationaler Identität sowie zu Veränderungen in der Historiographie.   Wie verorten sich nun das französische, deutsche und österreichische Projekt der Gedächtnis-geschichte in Bezug auf den Integrationsprozess der Europäisierung: Sind sie Beispiele einer neuen Nationalgeschichtsschreibung mit Blick nach innen oder, wie es Nora für den Fall Frankreich postulierte, eine Geschichtsschreibung mit einem erweiterten Horizont?

Nora selbst verwehrt sich dem Vorwurf eines Rückfalls in einen 'intellektuellen Nationalismus' mit dem Argument, seine 'Erneuerung der nationalen Geschichte' resultiere in einer 'vergleichenden Sicht in einem erweiterten Horizont'.[51] Mit 'erweitert' meint Nora jedoch lediglich den Horizont anderer Nationalgeschichten, keineswegs eine europäische Perspektive.   Noras 'europäisches Unbehagen' zeigte sich deutlich auf der Londoner Konferenz,[52] auf der nicht nur die *lieux de mémoire*-Nachfolgeprojekte der europäischen Nachbarländer vorgestellt wurden, sondern auch die Möglichkeiten, Grenzen und Chancen eines europäischen Gedächtnisorte-Projekts diskutiert wurden: Kann es in der Zukunft ein europäisches Gedächtnis geben oder nur eine Vielzahl von Nationalstaaten, wo sich einzelne europäisch imaginieren, oder das Europäische als Zusatzidentität pflegen?

Nora sieht in der Vergewisserung des Eigenen die Voraussetzung, seine Rolle in Europa gut spielen zu können, und plädiert für das Kennen der Unterschiede, um europäische Gemeinsamkeiten zu erkennen: '[…] das genaue Wissen um die einzelnen Erinnerungskulturen (schärft) den Blick für das […], was das Gemeinsame an Europa ausmacht' und betont, 'dass nur aus einem vertieften Verständnis der Unterschiede das Gefühl einer echten gemeinsamen Zugehörigkeit erwachsen kann'. Noras Weg nach Europa führt über die nationale Rückbesinnung. Wenig zielführend sieht Nora die Analyse von europäischen Erinnerungsorten, die eine Idee Europa verkörpern, aber wenig zum Verständnis oder zur Bildung eines europäischen Gedächtnisses beitragen würden.[53] An Noras Skepsis anschließend ist zu fragen, kann es überhaupt ein europäisches Gedächtnis geben, das nicht national vermittelt, nicht global und nicht beliebig ist?

Das Projekt der *Deutschen Erinnerungsorte* plädiert für einen Blick zu den Nachbarn, bleibt aber auf sich und auf die französisch-deutsche Achse eines westeuropäischen Projekts konzentriert, während das österreichische Akademieprojekt die europäische Fahne hisst. Theoretisch und empirisch (Beispiel Prinz Eugen oder der internationale Vergleich der Heldenplätze) liegt der geopolitische Raum Zentraleuropa im Zentrum, institutionell ist man stark vernetzt, mit regelmäßigen internationalen Tagungen grenzüberschreitend kommunizierend, wenn auch mitunter mit methodischen und theoretischen Differenzen zu den östlichen Nachbarstaaten.[54] Doch das österreichische Projekt widersetzt sich der 'Wiederkehr des Nationalen' nicht nur indem es das pluralistische Zentraleuropa als Region ins Zentrum rückt, sondern die vielfältigen ambivalenten widerstreitenden Bedeutungsschichten der Erinnerungsorte sichtbar*er* macht. Denn es ist die Suche nach Eindeutigkeiten, die vor allem in geographischen Überschneidungsgebieten zu den zahllosen 'Erinnerungsschlachten' führt(e).[55] Aber auch die Debatten um den Begriff 'Zentraleuropa' zeigen dort, wo man ihn geographisch zu fassen versucht, statt ihn wie oben genannt kulturell zu begreifen, dass jener selbst neue Grenzen und Abgrenzungen zum Osten schafft und nicht als offener pluraler Gegenbegriff zum Nationalen verstanden werden kann.[56] So schafft der Westdiskurs einen reaktiven Ostdiskurs, der sich in seiner Selbstsicht der Marginalität bestätigt fühlt, in seiner Sehnsucht nach Zentralität und dem Wissen, der Westen imaginiert sich als Europa und den Osten als sein europäisches Anderes.[57] Europa habe demnach als Erinnerungskultur nie existiert und nie funktioniert.[58] Auch das westliche Mitteleuropa, als eine Form von Annäherung seit dem 18. Jahrhundert, sei nie über eine kulturelle Definition erfolgreich gewesen, sondern nur als ökonomische Vereinigung. Das viel beschworene europäische Kulturmodell und seine Prämisse, die kulturellen Unterschiede als Chance und nicht als Hürde anzuerkennen, scheint demnach vielmehr Ausdruck eines sozialromantischen Verlangens zu sein, mit der Gefahr damit kulturelle Unterschiede zu fundamentalisieren und erneut Abgrenzungen und Hierarchisierungen vorzunehmen. Das reflektiert auch Noras Ansatz, nach dem es unmöglich sei, Erinnerungsorte zu schaffen, die mehr das Gemeinsame als das Trennende betonen.

Insgesamt wurde auf der Londoner Konferenz bei der Diskussion um die Möglichkeiten europäischer Gedächtnisorte ein Demokratiedefizit vermerkt und von Michael Jeismann für ein 'stärker horizontales statt vertikales Gedächtnis' plädiert – um die Gefahr zu bannen, dass Deutschland und Frankreich in einer neuen hegemonialen Geste definieren, was europäisch sei. Hier gehöre der westeuropäische Blick um die zentraleuropäischen Länder erweitert, ebenso die Realität von Globalisierung, Migrationen und Minderheiten anerkannt, die das nationale Gedächtnis untergraben. Dennoch, der Tenor ist Zweifel darüber, dass es spezifische *European lieux de mémoire* geben kann; Topoi, die – wie der 'Westfälische Friede' von 1648 – nicht nur in den Köpfen einiger Historiker Schlüsselcharakter haben, sondern für ein breites Publikum heute relevant sind. Das Beispiel des geplanten 'Europäischen Museums' in Brüssel zeigt, dass in der Frage nach qualifizierten Ausstellungsobjekten noch Ratlosigkeit herrscht. Mancher sieht alleine im Nachdenken über Europa die Möglichkeit, einen europäischen Gedächtnisort zu schaffen;[59] was sich in der hier dokumentierten Debatte um die *European lieux de mémoire* bereits realisiert hat.

Resümee

Die *lieux de mémoire* sind bereits selbst zu einem Erinnerungsort geworden, Erinnerungsort einer genau datierbaren Diskussion über die 'postmoderne conditio' (Jacques Le Rider), realiter, die Angst vor dem Verlust der Nation. 'Man feiert nicht mehr die Nation, sondern studiert ihre Feierstunden', lautet Noras nüchterner Befund.[60] Europäische Integration und Migrationen würden die 'Grundlagen von Geschichte und Nation' untergraben,[61] da die neuen Minderheiten (sexueller, religiöser, sozialer, ethnischer Art) zunehmend ihr Gedächtnis einfordern. Somit reflektiere *sein* Projekt der *lieux de mémoire* den Transformierungsprozess zwischen Geschichte und Gedächtnis, 'den Übergang von einem nationalen Geschichtsbewusstsein zu einem sozialen Geschichts-bewusstsein'.[62] Nora sieht die Auflösung selbstverständlicher Gedächtnis-gemeinschaften als Ursache für die Entstehung von Gedächtnisorten und nennt es die Entwicklung vom *milieu de mémoire* zu einem *lieu de mémoire*, wenn mit der Auflösung kultureller Rahmen und gesellschaftlicher Kontexte, Orte, Gegenstände, Einstellungen, Handlungen oder Erfahrungen 'aus dem Zusammenhang lebendiger Aktualität heraustreten und zu Erinnerungen werden'.[63] Nora schreibt diesen Transformationsprozess in kulturpessimistischer Manier dem beschleunigten Wandel durch die Modernisierung zu, der zugleich eine Musealisierung nach sich ziehe. Aleida Assmann weist jedoch daraufhin hin, dass die allgegenwärtige Präsenz von Gedenk- und Erinnerungsorten an den Zweiten Weltkrieg nicht der Modernisierung, sondern vor allem dem Gewaltregime der Nationalsozialisten zu verdanken sei – und damit auch eine deutsche Spezifität sei: Insbesondere das jüdische Gedächtnis sei von Hitler fast vollständig ausgelöscht worden und nur mehr in Denkmalform vorhanden. Das ist nur ein Beispiel für die Entwicklung von einem Gedächtnis der *Orte* zu einem der *Monumente*, losgelöst vom eigentlichen Ort und dessen Aura, ein nur mehr überall wirksames Symbol und Zeichen.[64] Auch hier ist es die abhanden gekommene lebendige Erinnerung, die den Denkmalkult generiert.

Diese topographische Nichtpräsenz, doch symbolische Allgegenwart spiegelt sich in den *Deutschen Erinnerungsorten* wieder. Weder dem Nationalsozialismus noch Auschwitz ist ein Essay gewidmet, doch die Problematik zieht sich quer durch (fast) alle Beiträge. Damit zeigt sich das deutsche Projekt durch die Verluste der Vergangenheit motiviert, während es in Frankreich die Verlustängste der Gegenwart sind, die das Projekt prägen. Die französische Befindlichkeit dürfte erheblich von der einflussreichen Arbeit Jean-François Lyotards, *Das postmoderne Wissen*, eine Kritik an den 'großen Erzählungen' der Moderne (eine davon der Nationalismus), beeinflusst und irritiert worden sein, welche zeitgleich mit Noras Gedankengut in Frankreich entstand.[65] Bei Nora unerwähnt, wird in den *Deutschen Erinnerungsorten* insofern darauf Bezug genommen, als die Herausgeber anmerken, *keine* neue 'Meistererzählung' anzustreben. Dennoch geht es beiden Projekten, dem französischen und dem deutschen, kaum um die Darstellung innerer Differenz, als die der Differenz nach außen. An diesen Grenzziehungen würde auch ein europäisches Gedächtnisprojekt scheitern, sowie am Konzept 'Erinnerungsort' selbst, das die Reflexion einiger theoretisch innovativer Ansätze vermissen lässt.

Unthematisiert bleibt in der Diskussion beispielsweise das Vergessen. Bereits Ernest Renan plädierte im Dienst der Zukunft für Gedächtnishygiene, ein kreatives Gleichgewicht zwischen Erinnern und Vergessen.[66] Sparsam zitiert werden insbesondere die zeitgleich mit den *konstruierenden* Projekten der Gedächtnisorte entstehenden *dekonstruierenden* Reflexionen über die Nation als 'imaginierte' oder 'erfundene' Einheit.[67] Negiert werden auch subversive Überlegungen zum Konzept des Ortes, wie Michel Foucaults Gedanken über *Andere Räume*. Die sogenannten 'Heterotopien' (in Anlehnung und Umkehrung von der Utopie als unwirklichem Raum) sind tabuisierte Räume (wie Bordelle, Kolonien, Schiffe, Gefängnisse, Friedhöfe, Feriendörfer etc.), die als 'Gegenplazierungen oder Widerlager, tatsächlich realisierte Utopien', wie Illusionen und Kompensationen in einer Gesellschaft verkörpern – (noch) nicht gesellschaftsfähige Orte sozusagen, die ein Recht auf Aufmerksamkeit einklagen, auch wenn sie keine Mehrheiten, Unakzeptiertes oder in manchen Augen Irrelevantes repräsentieren, zugleich jedoch auch Teil und Ausdruck der Gesellschaft sind.[68] Hier ungehört bleibt auch der Diskurs über *Nicht-Orte*, Marc Augés 'Transiträume' wie Flugplätze, Wartehallen, Metros, die 'zu Möglichkeits-Orten einer provisorischen und riskanten Identität werden können'[69] – Individualismus pur statt kollektiver Aneignung von Raum. Jene Ansätze fordern zumindest mehr Ironie ein für die Strategiespiele um nationale Konstruktionen auf dem postmodernen Schlachtfeld der Erinnerung.

Anmerkungen

[1] Vgl. Jacques Le Goff, *Geschichte und Gedächtnis*, Ullstein: Frankfurt a.M., 1999.

[2] Pierre Nora, Hg., *Les lieux de mémoire*. 7 Bände, Gallimard: Paris, 1984–92; auf dt. Ders., *Zwischen Geschichte und Gedächtnis*, Wagenbach: Berlin, 1990. Der Begriff 'lieux de mémoire' wurde von Nora geprägt. 'Lieu' (frz) ein gemeinsamer Platz. Das Projekt basiert auf dem Konzept des 'kollektiven Gedächtnisses' von Maurice Halbwachs aus den 1920er Jahren, nach dem nicht nur Einzelne, sondern ganze Gesellschaften ein kollektives Gedächtnis entwickeln. In Anschluss daran bildet sich der Zusammenhang von Identitätsbildung und kollektiver Erinnerung als Schwerpunkt der jüngsten Gedächtnisforschung heraus.

[3] Jan Assmann, *Moses der Ägypter. Entzifferung einer Gedächtnisspur*, Fischer: Frankfurt a.M., 2000 (hier: S. 26f.).

[4] Ich beziehe mich hier auf Diskussionen, stattgefunden im Rahmen der Konferenz 'European lieux de mémoire', organisiert vom Deutschen Historischen Institut London, Cumberland Lodge, 5.–7. Juli 2002.

[5] Pierre Nora, 'Nachwort' in: Hagen Schulze, Etienne François Hg., *Deutsche Erinnerungsorte*, 3 Bände, Beck: München, 2000/2001, Bd. 3, S. 681–686 (hier: S. 681, 684).

[6] Nora, ebda., S. 682.

[7] Vgl. Schulze/François, 'Einleitung', in: *Deutsche Erinnerungsorte*, Bd. 1, S. 9–24; Vgl. zur Fragestellung: Etienne François, Hg., *Lieux de Mémoire, Erinnerungsorte. D'un modèle français à un projet allemand*. Les Travaux du Centre Marc Bloch, Bd. 6. Berlin, 1996; Ders., 'Von der wiedererlangten Nation zur "Nation wider Willen". Kann man eine Geschichte der deutschen "Erinnerungsorte" schreiben?', in: Ders./Hannes Siegrist/Jacob Vogel, Hg., *Nation und Emotion. Deutschland und Frankreich im Vergleich. 19. und 20. Jahrhundert*, Vandenhoeck & Ruprecht: Göttingen 1995, S. 93–107; Constanze Carcenac-Lecomte u.a., Hg., *Steinbruch. Deutsche Erinnerungsorte. Annäherung an eine deutsche Gedächtnisgeschichte*, Peter Lang: Frankfurt a.M., Wien u.a., 2000.

[8] Vermarktung und Verkaufszahlen zeigen, der Verlag C.H. Beck knüpft an den Erfolg des französischen Modells an: Bereits 2002 ist die 3. Auflage der *Deutschen Erinnerungsorte* erschienen.

[9] Ulrich Raulff, 'Heil Dir im Kaffeekranz', in: *Frankfurter Allgemeine Zeitung*, 20.3.2001; vgl. die zusammenfassende Rezension von Jan-Holger Kirsch http://hsozkult.geschichte.hu-berlin.de/REZENSIO/buecher/2001/KiJa0601.htm.

[10] Vgl. Diskussionsbeitrag auf der Konferenz 'European lieux de mémoire', London, Juli 2002.

[11] Hans-Ulrich Wehler, 'Was uns zusammenhält', *Die Zeit* , 22. März 2001.

[12] Friedrich Wilhelm Graf, *Frankfurter Allgemeine Zeitung* , 6. November 2001.

[13] Wolfgang Kruse, *Frankfurter Rundschau*, 17. Dezember 2001.

[14] Christoph Jahr, *Neue Zürcher Zeitung*, 11. Juli 2001; Ders., *Die Zeit*, 15. November 2001.

[15] Ulrich Speck, 'Gediegener Hausschatz', *Frankfurter Rundschau*, 2. April 2001.

[16] Claus Leggewie, *Die Tageszeitung*, 10. Oktober 2001.

[17] Johannes Willms, 'Museum der Ungewissheiten', *Süddeutsche Zeitung*, 17. März 2001.

[18] Thomas Maissen, *Neue Zürcher Zeitung*, 13. März 2002.

[19] Frank Böckelmann, *Süddeutsche Zeitung*, 2. Oktober 2001.

[20] So wird die Populärkultur zwar thematisiert, doch statt jungen Identifikationsmustern Rechnung zu tragen, bleibt der bildungsbürgerliche Griff in den Bücherschrank (Bsp. Felix Dahns 'Kampf um Rom') obligat und die intendierte Bezugnahme auf die historische Problematik des deutschen Kulturbegriffs misslungen.

[21] Schulze/François, 'Einleitung', in: *Deutsche Erinnerungsorte*, Bd. 1, S. 20.

[22] In der Eröffnungsrede als Veranstalter der Konferenz 'European lieux de mémoire', London, Juli 2002.

[23] Erwähnung finden allerdings die Türken vor Wien im 17. Jahrhundert (Mathieu Lepetit).

[24] Dieses Manko sei sichtbar an fehlenden Repräsentationen in Museen, Schulbüchern, Archiven, in den Medien und der Literatur. Deshalb wurde im Sinne einer 'pluralen Geschichtskultur' – Tagungsthema im November 2001 im Haus der Geschichte in Bonn – auch ein 'Erinnerungsort für Zuwanderer' (Jan Motte) eingefordert.

[25] See www.uni-heidelberg.de/presse/unispiegel/us3_2001/bohrer.html.

[26] Vgl. Jürgen Osterhammel, 'Transnationale Gesellschaftsgeschichte: Erweiterung oder Alternative?', in: *Geschichte und Gesellschaft*, Jg. 27, 2001, Heft 3, 464–479.

[27] Die Gesellschaftsgeschichte (das Pendant einer BRD, die ein föderales Gebilde aber kein Staat mehr war) sei von der Kulturgeschichte, das Paradigma Gesellschaft von jenem der Erinnerung abgelöst worden. Nun würden Kultur und Geographie in die Geschichte zurückkehren, so wie die jüdische Geschichte in die deutsche Geschichte integriert würde statt als etwas Externes behandelt zu werden. Vgl. Dan Diner, 'Europe and the Jews: A new Perspective', Vortrag am Leo Baeck Institut London, 4. Februar 2002.

[28] Nora, 'Nachwort', in: *Deutsche Erinnerungsorte*, Bd. 3, S. 684.

[29] Das entspricht dem Ergebnis von Jörn Rüsens Analyse des unterschiedlichen Umgangs der deutschen Nachkriegsgenerationen mit dem Nationalsozialismus. Er diagnostiziert 'Historisierung und Aneignung' dieser Vergangenheit in der Enkel-Generation. Erstmals werde ein 'genealogischer Zusammenhang mit den Tätern' anerkannt, was die zunehmende Rhetorik eines 'Wir' in den Medien beweise. Die 'verstörende Negativität' werde integriert, aber auch historisiert, so Rüsen. Vgl. Jörn Rüsen, 'Holocaust, Erinnerung, Identität', in Harald Welzer, Hg., *Das soziale Gedächtnis. Geschichte, Erinnerung, Tradierung*, Hamburger Edition: Hamburg, 2001, S. 243–259 (hier: S. 254).

[30] Die Publikationen sind in Vorbereitung.

[31] Moritz Csáky, Peter Stachel, Hg., *Die Verortung von Gedächtnis*, Passagen: Wien, 2001; Dies., Hg., *Speicher des Gedächtnisses. Bibliotheken, Museen, Archive*, Bd. 1, Passagen: Wien, 2000; Dies., Hg., *Speicher des Gedächtnisses, Die Erfindung des Ursprungs, Die Systematisierung der Zeit*, Bd. 2, Passagen: Wien, 2001.

[32] Zit. n. Heidemarie Uhl, 'Zwischen "Habsburgischem Mythos" und (Post)Kolonialismus. Zentraleuropa als Paradigma für Identitätskonstruktionen', in: *Newsletter Moderne, Spezialforschungsbereich Moderne – Wien und Zentraleuropa um 1900*, Graz, 2002, Heft 1, 2–5 (hier: S. 4).

[33] Wolfgang Müller-Funk sieht im postkolonialen Ansatz die Chance für die Rückgewinnung der Kategorie des Politischen in die Forschung. Vgl. ebda., S. 4.

[34] In diesem Sinne kritisiert Anil Bhatti die 'Hermeneutik des Eigenen und Fremden' (Peter Niedermüller), welche dem 'romantischen Kulturmodell' entspreche, und plädiert für neue, dem modernen Leben angemessenen Begrifflichkeiten. So sei der Begriff der Wurzel im unsäglichen Heimatdiskurs abzulösen von dem des gewebeartigen 'Rhizoms' (in Anlehnung an Gilles Deleuze, Félix Guattari, *Rhizom*, Merve Verlag: Berlin, 1997) und statt von Authentizität sei von einer 'hybriden' Identität auszugehen, entsprechend der ortsungebundenen Form moderner Lebenspraxis, charakterisiert durch die Verflochtenheit des Einzelnen in mehrere kulturelle Kontexte, in ein anerkanntes Nebeneinander von Differenzen. Ebenso plädiert er für die Bezeichnung Indiens als einer 'Palimpsestkultur', als eine Kultur, deren Text stets neu überschrieben wird und wurde. Statt den Rückgriff auf das Authentische zu suchen, sei der Prozess des Überschreibens zu reflektieren. Vgl. Anil Bhatti, 'Plurikulturalitäten? Indien und die Habsburgermonarchie aus vergleichender postkolonialer Sicht', Vortrag auf der Tagung der Kommission für Kulturwissenschaften und Theatergeschichte der Österreichischen Akademie der Wissenschaften in Wien 'Die Habsburgermonarchie: Ein Ort der inneren Kolonisierung?', 19–21. September 2002, Palais Schlick, Wien.

[35] Jacques Le Rider, 'Mittel- bzw. Zentraleuropa und Österreich als imaginäre Gedächtnisorte der europäischen Identität', in: Moritz Csáky, Peter Stachel, Hg., *Die Verortung von Gedächtnis*, Passagen: Wien, 2001, S. 139–150.

[36] Vgl. Uhl, in: *Newsletter Moderne*, 2002, Heft 1, S. 2.

[37] Vgl. Hans-Christian Heintschel, 'Brücken, leergefegt', in: Walter Hufnagel, Hg., *Querungen. Brücken – Stadt – Wien*, Sappl: Kufstein, 2002, S. 11–38.

[38] Aleida Assmann, *Erinnerungsräume. Formen und Wandlungen des kulturellen Gedächtnisses*, Beck: München, 1999, S. 178.

[39] Vgl. Nicole Immler, 'Wie gemacht für eine schöne Erinnerung. Europa, seine Orte, sein Gedächtnis: Eine Tagung vor den Toren von London zog Bilanz', in: *Süddeutsche*

Zeitung, 11. Juli 2002. – Vgl. Lit.: Mario Isnenghi, Hg., *I luoghi della memoria*, 3 Bde, Laterza: Bari–Roma, 1996/97; Pim den Boer, Willem Frijhoff, Hg., *Lieux de mémoire et identités nationales*. Amsterdam University Press: Amsterdam, 1993; Peter Mandler, *History and national life*, Profile Books: London, 2002; Keith Robbins, *Great Britain: Identities, Institutions, and the Idea of Britishness*, Longman: London, 1998.

[40] Dem am ähnlichsten ist das gleichfalls dreibändige italienische Projekt, strukturiert nach Personen und Daten, Symbolen und Zeichen, Strukturen und Ereignissen.

[41] Vgl. Moritz Csáky, Peter Stachel, 'Vorwort', in: Dies., Hg., *Speicher des Gedächtnisses. Bibliotheken, Museen, Archive,* Bd. 1, Passagen: Wien, 2000, S. 11–13 (hier: S. 13).

[42] Vgl. Jacques Le Rider, 'An Stelle einer Einleitung: Anmerkungen zu Pierre Noras *Lieux de mémoire*', in: Moritz Csáky, Peter Stachel, Hg., *Speicher des Gedächtnisses*. Bd. 1, S. 15–22 (hier: S. 19f.).

[43] Vgl. Peter Stachel, 'Der Heldenplatz. Zur Semiotik eines österreichischen Gedächtnis-Ortes', in: Stefan Riesenfellner, Hg., *Steinernes Bewusstsein I. Die öffentliche Repräsentation staatlicher und nationaler Identität Österreichs in seinen Denkmälern*, Böhlau: Wien–Köln–Weimar, 1998, S. 619–656 (hier: S. 619).

[44] Peter Stachel, *Der Heldenplatz als österreichischer Gedächtnisort*: www.oeaw.ac.at/kkt/heldenplatz-dt.html. Vgl. auch Ders., *Mythos Heldenplatz*, Pichler Verlag: Wien, 2002.

[45] Vgl. Ruth Wodak, Florian Menz, Richard Mitten, Frank Stern, Hg., *Die Sprachen der Vergangenheiten. Öffentliches Gedenken in österreichischen und deutschen Medien,* Suhrkamp: Frankfurt a.M., 1994, S. 20.

[46] Ernst Hanisch, 'Wien, der Heldenplatz', in: *Deutsche Erinnerungsorte*, Bd. 1, S. 105–121 (hier: S. 111).

[47] Jacques Le Rider, 'Mittel- bzw. Zentraleuropa und Österreich als imaginäre Gedächtnisorte der europäischen Identität', in: Moritz Csáky, Peter Stachel, Hg., *Die Verortung von Gedächtnis*, S. 142.
[48] Zu Peter Stachels Kritik am Heldenplatz-Essay von Ernst Hanisch vgl. 'Rezension der *Deutschen Erinnerungsorte*', in: *Newsletter Moderne,* Graz 2001, Heft 2, S. 35 (Rezension der nachfolgenden Bände: 2002, Heft 1, S. 36f.).

[49] Peter Stachel, www.oeaw.ac.at/kkt/heldenplatz-dt.html.

[50] Vgl. Aleida Assmann, *Erinnerungsräume*, S. 330.

[51] Nora, 'Nachwort', in: *Deutsche Erinnerungsorte*, Bd. 3, S. 685f.

[52] Organisiert vom Deutschen Historischen Institut London waren die Vertreter von sechs Nationen (Deutschland, Österreich, England, Niederlande, Italien, Frankreich) vom 5.–7. Juli 2002 versammelt, um 'ihre' Nation unter dem Blick auf Europa neu zu verhandeln. Vor 10 Jahren wurden in Amsterdam die Gedanken zum Projekt der *lieux de mémoire* erstmals formuliert. Aus dem 'holländisch-französischen Versuch' wurde Establishment (Pim den Boer).   In diesem Sinne war es auch eine Jubiläumsveranstaltung.

[53] Nora, 'Nachwort', in: *Deutsche Erinnerungsorte*, Bd. 3, S. 696.

[54] Der kulturtheoretische Ansatz der Gedächtnisgeschichte wurde erst in den letzten Jahren von der jungen Historikergeneration aufgegriffen.

[55] Vgl. 'Die nationale Wende und das kollektive Gedächtnis in Osteuropa nach 1990', Konferenz in Brünn am 15./16. März 2002. Organisiert von der Österreichischen Akademie der Wissenschaften mit dem Austrian Science and Research Liaison Office Brno.

[56] Vgl. Debatte im Einleitungspanel der Konferenz 'The Contours of Legitimacy in Central Europe', St. Anthony's College, Oxford, 24. –26. Mai 2002.

[57] Vgl. ebda. George Schöpflin, 'Reading Central Europe: Defining a Thought-Style'. Vortrags-Abstrakt.

[58] Le Rider, 'Mittel- bzw. Zentraleuropa und Österreich als imaginäre Gedächtnisorte der europäischen Identität', in: Moritz Csáky, Peter Stachel, Hg., *Die Verortung von Gedächtnis*, S. 144.

[59] Diskussionsbeiträge von Michael Jeismann, Heinz Durchhardt, Kryzsztof Pomian, Michael Werner u.a. auf der Konferenz 'European lieux de mémoire'.

[60] Nora, *Zwischen Geschichte und Gedächtnis*, S. 18.

[61] Nora, 'Nachwort', in: *Deutsche Erinnerungsorte*, Bd. 3, S. 685.

[62] Ebda.

[63] Aleida Assmann nennt es den 'Schritt vom Generationen- zum Gedenk- und Erinnerungsort'. Vgl. zur Systematisierung verschiedener Formen von Gedächtnis-orten und Erinnerung: Aleida Assmann, *Erinnerungsräume*; insbes. zu 'Gedächtnis-Orten': S. 298–339 (hier: S. 326).

[64] Aleida Assmann, *Erinnerungsräume*, S. 338f.

[65] Jean-François Lyotard, *Das postmoderne Wissen*, Passagen: Wien, 1986, S. 122.

[66] Vgl. Renan, Rede über die Nation, im Jahr 1887 an der Sorbonne, in: Hagen Schulze/Etienne François, 'Das emotionale Fundament der Nation', in: Monika Flacke, Hg., *Mythen der Nationen. Ein europäisches Panorama.* Koehler Amelang: Leipzig, 1998, S. 33–52 (hier: S. 35).

[67] Benedict Anderson, *Die Erfindung der Nation. Zur Karriere eines folgenreichen Konzepts*, Campus: Frankfurt a.M. / New York 1988; Eric Hobsbawm, 'Das Erfinden von Traditionen', in: Christoph Conrad, Martina Kessel, Hg., *Kultur & Geschichte. Neue Einblicke in eine alte Beziehung*, Reclam: Stuttgart, 1998.

[68] Vgl. Michel Foucault, 'Andere Räume', in: *Documenta Katalog*, Kassel, 1997.

[69] Stefan Hesper, in: Nicolas Pethes, Jens Ruchatz, Hg., *Gedächtnis und Erinnerung. Ein interdisziplinäres Lexikon*, Rowohlt: Hamburg, 2001, S. 200f.; Vgl. Marc Augé, *Orte und Nicht-Orte. Vorüberlegungen zu einer Ethnologie der Einsamkeit*, Fischer: Frankfurt a.M., 1994. Nach Augé ist ein Raum durch Identität, Relation und Geschichte gekennzeichnet, was dem Nicht-Ort fehle, ebenso wie die emotionale Qualität.

Ricarda Schmidt

Albanische Bräute, Monokeleffekt und montenegrinische Barbarei: DDR-Erfahrung in der Fremde und Subjektutopie in Irmtraud Morgners *Hochzeit in Konstantinopel*

This essay explores the unfolding of the contrast between the values of a group of GDR package holiday-makers in Yugoslavia and those of their host country, along different axes (north-south, occident-orient, patriarchal-feminist, competitive principle-passion, reality-fantasy). It is argued that, through superposition of these axes, differentiated, radically critical and witty images of, above all, the home culture emerge. The essay examines, further, how the exotic holiday inspires the fantastic formulation of a subjective utopia of living life to the full, and explores the complex aesthetic structure of this utopia, its fascination and its limitations.

Als Irmtraud Morgners Roman *Hochzeit in Konstantinopel*[1] 1968 veröffentlicht wurde, nachdem der Verlag drei Jahre zuvor Morgners Romanmanuskript *Rumba auf einen Herbst*[2] nicht nur zur Veröffentlichung abgelehnt, sondern sogar einbehalten hatte, wurde der Roman als politisch belanglos empfunden. Der Autorin wurde angeraten, sich doch in Zukunft den großen Themen des Lebens in der DDR zuzuwenden.[3] Morgner hatte also ein Ziel - Tarnung ihres Romans vor der Zensur, um dieses Mal zur Veröffentlichung zugelassen zu werden - so gut verwirklicht, dass ihr anderes Ziel - eine literarisch anspruchsvoll gestaltete Kritik am Status quo in der DDR - nicht nur von der DDR-Zensur, sondern auch von Rezensenten (und vielleicht Lesern) lange nicht wahrgenommen wurde.[4] Denn der Roman bewegt sich scheinbar nur im privaten Bereich von Urlaub am Mittelmeer und Liebesgeschichte. Doch unter dieser Camouflage wird in *Hochzeit in Konstantinopel* der Status quo in der DDR scharf kritisiert, und 21 nächtliche Erzählungen machen die persönlichen Sehnsüchte, die Wünsche nach dem Musilschen 'anderen Zustand' sichtbar, die die Protagonistin und Erzählerin Bele an den utopischen sozialistischen Epochendiskurs knüpft. Die persönliche Subjektutopie und der öffentliche Epochendiskurs befinden sich in *Hochzeit in Konstantinopel* in einem praktischen, nicht aber in einem grundsätzlichen Widerspruch. Die späten 60er und die frühen 70er Jahre waren in der DDR wohl der letzte Zeitpunkt, an dem es für Teile der literarischen Intelligenz noch einmal möglich war, zumindest in der Imagination wie in der Aufklärung 'ein harmonisches Bündnis zwischen subjektiver Zukunft, meiner Lebenszeit, und objektiver Zukunft, der Zeitenfolge der Welt, [zu] knüpfen'.[5]

Denn dass hinter der geographischen Realität des unaussprechlichen jugoslawischen Ferienorts und hinter der durch seine Umbenennung in Konstantinopel evozierten phantastischen Märchenwelt der Scheherezade ein dritter politisch signifikanter Ort liegt, wird durch die kreisförmige Struktur des Romans hervorgehoben, dessen erster und letzter Satz lautet: 'Eigentlich hatten sie nach Prag reisen wollen' (S. 5 und S. 190). Damit wird den Lesern deutlich, dass Beles Begehren auf etwas gerichtet war, für das selbst das märchenhafte 'Konstantinopel' ein unzureichender Ersatz war. Im Prager Frühling schien - für einen kurzen historischen Moment - die sozialistische Utopie auf politischer Ebene zusammen mit den an sie gebundenen Sehnsüchten nach einem persönlich erfüllten Leben in den Bereich des Möglichen gerückt zu sein. Im Ersatzziel des Urlaubs, im sogenannten Konstantinopel aus Märchenzeiten, scheint Bele ein Prag auf privater Ebene anzustreben. Sie scheitert, ohne jedoch ihren Widerstand gegen den Status quo aufzugeben, wie sich vor allem an ihren nächtlichen Geschichten ablesen lässt, in denen sich ihre Subjektutopie vom erfüllten Leben artikuliert - witzig, sprachspielerisch, erfinderisch, satirisch oder elegisch, realistisch oder phantastisch. Es würde den Rahmen dieses Aufsatzes sprengen, alle 21 bisher von der Forschung noch immer nicht ausreichend interpretierten Erzählungen hier zu analysieren. Ich muss mich hier auf diejenigen konzentrieren, die von den Erfahrungen im jugoslawischen Alltag motiviert sind oder selbst orientalische Motive verwenden oder in der phantastischen Atmosphäre der Fabulierkunst von *Tausendundeiner Nacht* wurzeln.

Zunächst jedoch möchte ich untersuchen, wie die Rahmenerzählung den Status quo des real existierenden Sozialismus darstellt, von dem sich Beles Subjektutopie absetzt. Primär soll es hier um solche Kritikpunkte gehen, die sich aus der Situation des Urlaubs im Ausland ergeben, denn ich will die Frage nach der DDR-spezifischen Kritik in *Hochzeit* mit der Frage verbinden, was vom Urlaubsland wahrgenommen wird, wie es bewertet wird und welche Funktion die Fremdwahrnehmung für die Selbstwahrnehmung hat. Die drei in Tagebuchnotizen aufgezeichneten Ferienwochen mit dem arbeits- und erfolgssüchtigen Paul belehren Bele, dass ihre Geschichten nicht den gleichen Erfolg gehabt haben wie die von Scheherezade aus *Tausendundeiner Nacht,* die bekanntlich durch ihr Märchenerzählen den Sultan veränderte. Bele beschließt deshalb, Paul bei der Rückkehr nach Berlin nicht zu heiraten. Doch Paul ist es nicht allein, der Beles Utopie vom besseren Leben entgegensteht. Es sind auch die eingefahrenen Denk- und Verhaltensmuster in ihrem Heimatland, die durch Beles Blick auf das Verhalten der DDR-Urlauber im sonnigen Süden in das Licht der Kritik gerückt werden.

Am Verhalten der Gruppe der Pauschalreisenden aus der DDR wird deutlich, dass die leistungsorientierten Werte, die Paul vertritt, in der DDR weit verbreitet sind. Statt eine Erfahrung intensiv auszukosten und in der Gegenwart zu leben, wird vielmehr archiviert, denn: 'Wöllner reiste, um zu photographieren' (S. 69). Seine Ausrüstung mit Apparaturen hing in Etuis und Riemen, 'die querten die Brust vergleichbar dem Bandelier eines preußischen Dragoners' (S. 69), d.h. dass Disziplin und Pflichterfüllung, nicht etwa Genuss, ihn umtreiben. Von dieser trockenen Pflichterfüllung hebt sich das spontane Verhalten eines montenegrinischen Hochzeitsgastes ab, der im 'schwarzen Anzug, Nylonhemd, Krawatte und Lackschuhe[n]' (S. 69) ins Wasser springt, um dem mit dem Schiff abreisenden Hochzeitspaar zuzuwinken.

Während Paul selbst in den Ferien intensiv arbeitet und Angst hat, Zeit zu versäumen, um seine Karriere voranzutreiben, fällt Bele an einem jugoslawischen Verkäufer auf, dass er einfach Spaß an der Interaktion mit seinen Kunden hat, auch ohne Verkaufserfolg (vgl. S. 17f.). Die Heimat, in der Leben mit Arbeitsethos gleichgesetzt wird, wird durch das Konkretisieren der Metapher, die dieses Ethos beschreibt ('im Schweiße seines Angesichts sein Brot verdienen'), karikiert, besonders weil es sich in der folgenden Beobachtung gar nicht mal um das Verdienen, sondern bloß um das Essen des Brotes handelt, das mit hässlicher Anstrengung vollzogen wird. Die mit dem sentimentalen Heimatbegriff geweckte Erwartung wird grotesk destruiert:

> Der rechte Nebentisch, an dem das Ehepaar Wieseke, Wöllner und der Chauffeur Diepolt frühstückten, verbreitete Heimatatmosphäre. Beim Essen brach Wöllner regelmäßig der Schweiß aus, vorzugsweise auf Stirn, Nase und Oberlippe, an Nase und Oberlippe wuchsen Perlen, bis sie abstürzten, die von der Nase abstürzenden Tropfen fielen auf den Teller oder in die Kaffeetasse, die andern wurden abgeleckt, Bele saß Wöllner gegenüber. (S. 29)

Die Erzählerin Bele hält die scheinbar banalen Begebenheiten in der Urlaubsgruppe weitgehend kommentarlos fest, hat jedoch ihre Tagebuchnotizen auf Wunsch des Verlags in die 3. Person transponiert. Damit erfüllt der Roman die in der DDR geforderte ästhetische Norm von Objektivität, thematisiert sie jedoch als Zwang und unterläuft deren Sinn.

Denn die Erzählerin der Rahmenhandlung ist weder allwissend noch formuliert sie eine Meinung vor, die die LeserInnen bloß rezipieren müssten. Das Mitgeteilte ist so kunstvoll komponiert, dass aus dem scheinbar objektiven, kommentarlosen Bericht über das Verhalten der Urlauber bestimmte Werte und Normen ihres Handelns sichtbar und zugleich durch den Blick der Erzählerin darauf für die Leserin fraglich werden. In der Aufeinanderfolge der Beobachtungen der Erzählerin ist nämlich ein unausgesprochener Kontrast zwischen der Selbstwahrnehmung der Reisenden und der Wahrnehmung durch die Erzählerin eingebaut, und damit die Frustration von aufgebauten Erwartungen der Leserin, die das Wesen des Komischen ausmachen.

Die angeblich klassenlose Gesellschaft der DDR wird als eine von Privilegien, Restriktionen, Standesdünkel und Unterwürfigkeit strukturierte kenntlich. Die Privilegien betreffen vor allem Reise-möglichkeiten in den Westen, die zur Zeit der Romanhandlung in der DDR nur für höhere Parteimitglieder sowie parteitreue Wissenschaftler, Künstler und Schriftsteller möglich waren - eine Gruppe, zu der der Protagonist Paul gehört, der am Reisen überhaupt kein Interesse hat (vgl. S. 44). Westliche Auslandsaufenthalte werden in einer solchen Gesellschaft zu gerne vorgezeigten Statussymbolen. Ihr Prestige wird jedoch komisch unterhöhlt, wenn selbst in der Vorkriegszeit stattgefundene Reisen noch als Statussymbole herhalten müssen:

> Der Rektor in Ruhe hatte mit einer amerikanischen Appartementbewohnerin englische Worte gewechselt und anschließend einen Bericht über seinen Englandaufenthalt im September 1924 gegeben. Paul hatte sich mit einem Bericht über Berkely, Brookhaven und Chicago revanchiert, Bele hatte vom Prenzlauer Berg berichtet. (S. 133)

Beles Ostberliner Hinterhofperspektive unterminiert den Prestigewert von Westerfahrungen noch weiter, denn durch sie dokumentiert sie ihre Weigerung, das in dem Gespräch der Männer enthaltene Wertsystem anzuerkennen.

Selbst Ferien in Jugoslawien sind für viele DDR-Bürger nicht erschwinglich: so reist Bele sozusagen stellvertretend für ihre Mutter, die 'mal unter Pinien sitzen und Zikaden hören möchte' (S. 17), während die Tatsache, dass ein Chauffeur '1750 Mark für eine Reise' (S. 8) zur Verfügung hat, zusätzliche Einnahmequellen (aus Stasi-Tätigkeit) vermuten lässt. Mögen die DDR-Touristen in Jugoslawien auch DDR-Privilegien genießen, auf internationaler Ebene sind sie dennoch zweitrangig. Sie sitzen in einem großen Speisesaal zweiter Klasse, während die westdeutschen Touristen mit ihrer frei konvertierbaren Währung einen kleineren exklusiveren Speisesaal zugewiesen bekommen (vgl. S. 15).

Auch andere Restriktionen ihres Landes folgen den DDR-Bürgern im Urlaub. Sie dürfen im Ausland nicht so viel Geld ausgeben, wie sie wollen, sondern bekommen ein Taschengeld zugeteilt (vgl. S. 8). Für Bedürfnisse, die über den zugeteilten Betrag hinausgehen, müssen sie ihre Kleidung verkaufen (vgl. S. 173).

Viel schwerer als die äußeren Restriktionen, denen DDR-Bürger unterliegen, wiegt jedoch die Tatsache, dass die gesellschaftliche Ungleichheit auch von denjenigen aufrechterhalten wird, die dabei nichts zu gewinnen haben. Diese Tendenz wird durch den exzessiven Gebrauch von Titeln vermittelt, so der wiederholt als 'Herr Dr. Stolp' (S. 7) apostrophierte Reisende, der mit seinen Auslandserfahrungen prahlt (vgl. S. 7, S. 28, S. 29); so der Brief des Sohnes an 'Herrn und Frau Rektor i.R. Vinzenz Wieseke' (S. 29); so auch der Chauffeur und die Pförtner an Pauls Institut, die jede Gelegenheit nutzten, 'um Herr Professor oder Herr Doktor zu sagen. [...] Wenn der Institutshund, ein Boxerrüde, einen Promovierten anbellte, entschuldigten sie sich bei diesem und rügten jenen wegen unstatthaften Benehmens' (S. 174). Die Unterwürfigkeit gegenüber Vorgesetzten hält selbst im Urlaub an: der Chauffeur und der Sekretär eines nicht an der Universität beschäftigten Professors (d.h. also eines Mitglieds der besonders privilegierten Akademie der Wissenschaften) wollen in Konstantinopel für ihren Professor Hemden und Schuhe einkaufen (vgl. S. 87).

Graue Mittelmäßigkeit und das Leben aus zweiter Hand werden karikiert in der Bereitschaft der Wünschenden, ihre Wünsche selber im Innern auf das realisierbare Maß zurechtzustutzen. So werden die mangelnden Reisemöglichkeiten für normale DDR-Bürger mittels grotesker Kompensationsmechanismen nicht einmal mehr als Einschränkungen empfunden. Der Sohn der wissenschaftlichen Lehrerin und des Rektors i.R. schickt einen Eilbrief, in dem er an Hand von meterologischen Tabellen suggeriert, dass ein Aufenthalt an der (DDR-Bürgern nicht zugänglichen) französischen Riviera gar nicht wünschenswert sei, denn:

> Die Tabellen über das Klima der Französischen Riviera zeigten, daß die montenegrinische Küste im Winter die gleiche, im Frühling, Sommer und Herbst aber eine längere Sonnenbestrahlung hätte, von März bis Oktober

schiene hier die Sonne durchschnittlich fünfhundert Stunden länger, "was",
sagte die wissenschaftliche Lehrerin. "Ganz ausgezeichnet", sagte der Rektor
in Ruhe. (S. 29-30)

Jemand, der den Petersplatz in Rom aus Streichhölzern nachgebaut hat, ist
nun an einer Italienreise gar nicht mehr interessiert (vgl. S. 136).

Am brisantesten und vielleicht am besten versteckt ist eine
Kontrastierung des jugoslawischen und des deutschen Verhaltens
gegenüber der Vergangenheit. Ein montenegrinischer Fischer hat in
Eigeninitiative die Zinnen einer alten serbischen Festung einbetoniert,
weil er darauf einen Tennisplatz errichten wollte, ist an dessen Vollendung
aber von der Regierung in Beograd gehindert worden. Sein ethnische
Spannungen anzeigender Mangel an Ehrfurcht dem alten serbischen
Kulturgut gegenüber wird von einem der DDR-Touristen als 'Barbarei'
(S. 127) kritisiert. Doch die Brisanz dieses Kommentars liegt in seiner
Plazierung. Er folgt nämlich nach Herrn Janottes Erinnerung an die
deutsche Nazi-Vergangenheit:

> Einen Genossen hätte die SS nächtelang ergebnislos verhört, seine Freundin
> auch, sie hatte in derselben Widerstandsorganisation gearbeitet wie er, sie
> liebten sich, eine große Leidenschaft, junge Leute, sie hatten sich über fünf
> Monate nicht gesehen, die SS folterte den Mann in Anwesenheit der Frau, ihre
> Schreie hätten Janotte manchmal geweckt, auch ihn hätte man in Einzelhaft
> gehalten, schließlich hätte man die beiden zusammengesperrt und an Händen
> und Füßen aneinandergefesselt. Sie wurden nicht mehr gefoltert. Drei Monate
> später wäre die Organisation aufgeflogen. Wöllner sagte "Barbarei", als er den
> betonierten Platz sah. (S. 127)

Wöllners Kommentar schließt sich so unmittelbar an Herrn Janottes
Schilderung von SS-Verhörtaktiken an, dass die Leserin zunächst denkt,
der Kommentar beziehe sich darauf. Dass ein Deutscher aber die
kommerzielle Nutzung alter Kulturstätten in Jugoslawien als barbarisch
kommentiert, nicht jedoch das Verhalten seiner Landsleute unter den
Nazis, ist das sich - hinter einem Komma verbergende und nur genauem
Lesen erschließende ('Wöllner sagte "Barbarei", als er den betonierten
Platz sah') - Skandolon: Es überführt den zur Staatsideologie erhobenen
Antifaschismus in der DDR als Propaganda, die im Empfinden der DDR-
Bürger leider keine Wurzeln geschlagen hat.

Konkurrenzdenken wird in Pauls Zwang, sich ständig als überlegen
zu profilieren, karikiert: er 'erobert' (S. 6) für Bele ständig Fensterplätze,
obwohl diese von seinen Eroberungen wegen Bewölkung oder Dunkelheit

gar nichts hat. Er achtet beim Schwimmen darauf, dass er schneller ist als Bele, obwohl er bereits den Vorteil hat, 19 cm größer zu sein als sie (vgl. S. 23). Er kann nicht einmal vom Rigorosum des Sohnes des Rektors in Ruhe hören, ohne selbst mit seiner in Wirklichkeit noch gar nicht vollendeten Habilitation aufzutrumpfen (vgl. S. 71). Er wird magenkrank vor Unruhe, weil er im Urlaub arbeiten möchte, um einen Kollegen auszustechen (vgl. S. 92).

Für ihre eigenen, von der Mehrheit der DDR-Bürger abweichenden Wertvorstellungen findet die Erzählerin zu einem gewissen Maße Bestätigung im Ferienland. Denn der Funktion von Italien in der deutschsprachigen Literatur des Westens (etwa in Ingeborg Bachmanns 'Was ich in Rom sah und hörte'[6] oder in Peter Schneiders *Lenz*[7]) vergleichbar, steht der bei Morgner aus politischen Gründen notwendigerweise im blockfreien Jugoslawien verkörperte Süden für daheim vermisste Qualitäten wie Lebensfreude, Sinnlichkeit und Leidenschaft, den Augenblick leben. Gleichzeitig lässt sich durch die intertextuelle Anspielung auf *Tausendundeine Nacht* und durch die Betonung der moslemisch geprägten Kultur das Gastland auch als Figuration des Orients lesen.[8]

Was die DDR-Touristin in Jugoslawien wahrnimmt, ist die sinnlich intensive, doch arme Welt eines noch überwiegend agrarischen Landes, in der das Prinzip von Effizienz nicht vorherrschend ist. Bergbauern reiten, 'in reichlich bestickte Trachten gekleidet' (S. 71), auf Eseln und Maultieren in die Stadt, um ihre Produkte auf dem Basar zu verkaufen, und am Honigverkauf an die Touristen ist eine ganze Familie beteiligt (vgl. S. 71). Die Landschaft und die Kultur dieses Landes werden jedoch mehr und mehr vom Tourismus überformt. Ein Bedauern über diese Entwicklung wird spürbar, wenn es heißt, dass Konstantinopel an einer Bucht von zwei Halbinseln flankiert liegt, die 'rechts kastellartig, links hotelartig' (S. 14) bebaut sind und dass das Minarett 'fast so hoch wie das Hotel [war], in dem Paul und Bele wohnten' (S. 16). Die politische Realität des Vielvölkerstaats wird vor allem als Folklore dargeboten: in einem Konzert war 'jede Republik [...] durch einen Sänger vertreten' - in Nationaltracht (S. 53). Auch die 'Tänze sämtlicher föderierter Völker Jugoslawiens' (S. 158) werden in Trachten aufgeführt. Unter dieser farbenprächtigen Oberfläche machen sich ethnische Spannungen bemerkbar, die sich am Umgang mit dem kulturellen Erbe der anderen manifestieren: so etwa in der Absicht des oben erwähnten Montenegriners, auf einer historischen, von Serben errichteten Festung ein Kaffeehaus und einen Tennisplatz zu bauen, was aber von Beograd verboten wird (vgl. S. 127).

Neben Sonnenwärme, fremden Tänzen, Liedern, Trachten und Sitten, blaugrünem Meer (vgl. S. 14), exotischem Essen[9] und exotischer Flora[10] konkretisiert sich die südliche/orientalische Andersartigkeit und Sinnlichkeit in *Hochzeit in Konstantinopel* in einer besonderen Art des Blickens:

> Ein Erdnußverkäufer. Er grüßte englisch und deutsch und hob eine Braue, dem darunterliegenden Auge entfielen Funken wie ein Monokel, das übrige Gesicht blieb unbewegt, Bele kaufte ihm eine Tüte Erdnüsse ab. (S. 16 f.)

Das Feuer dieses Blickes ist, so heißt es schalkisch, 'offenbar nationalcharakterlich bedingt' (S. 42), denn es ist vielen jugoslawischen Männern eigen (vgl. weitere jugoslawische Herren mit Monokeleffekt: S. 6, S. 42), Paul dagegen 'konnte trotz Trainings den Monokeleffekt nicht erzielen' (S. 42). Zumindest kann Paul dieses Feuer nicht im Blick auf Bele entfachen. Erst am Ende des Romans deutet der Monokeleffekt, den Paul plötzlich einem Arbeitskollegen gegenüber an den Tag legen kann, darauf hin, wo seine wahre Leidenschaft liegt (vgl. S. 189).

Obwohl Beles Utopie des sinnlich erfüllten Lebens von manchen Erfahrungen im Süden beflügelt wird (neben dem Monokeleffekt und dem schwimmenden Hochzeitsgast sei an den Verkäufer erinnert, der ohne Verkaufserfolg freundlich ist), lässt eine feministische Perspektive die Erzählerin andererseits manche Aspekte Jugoslawiens auch auf der Achse Okzident - Orient negativ wahrnehmen. Kritikwürdig ist vor allem der alltägliche Sexismus in Jugoslawien. Hier gehen einheimische Frauen nicht unbegleitet auf die Straße (vgl. S. 42), moslemische Frauen gehen verhüllt und hinter Männern (vgl. S. 43), es gibt Vielweiberei (vgl. S. 43 und S. 128). Zu Liebesliedern liefern die Zuhörer Macho-Kommentare (vgl. S. 54). Wie die autoritätshörigen Arbeiter in der DDR sind es auch in Jugoslawien gerade die Unterdrückten, die die ihre Unterdrückung legitimierenden Werte perpetuieren. Wenn eine moslemische albanische Fischersfrau Paul beschimpft, 'weil er Beles Tasche und eine Hand von ihr trug' (S. 43), wird nicht nur ihre Verinnerlichung des Sexismus, sondern darüber hinaus auch religiöser Fundamentalismus spürbar.

Am nachhaltigsten wird die untergeordnete Stellung der Frau in Teilen Jugoslawiens durch die folkloristische Darstellung einer albanischen Hochzeit auf der Bühne deutlich: die Braut ist ein Objekt, das 'abgestellt' und 'besichtigt' wird (S. 158). Dennoch zeigt der Roman, dass gerade an diesem kritischen Punkt eher ein gradueller, statt ein absoluter Unterschied zwischen beiden Ländern besteht. Denn die sexistischen Kommentare beim Liederabend inspirieren Bele zu einer Erzählung über sexistische Anmache in der Berliner S-Bahn, der die Erzählerin mit einer phantastischen Konkretisierung ihrer Verfluchung des aufdringlichen Mannes begegnet. Sie lässt ihn mit den Worten 'Fahr zur Hölle' (S. 57) in der Bahn sitzen, und die Erzählung endet mit der anschaulichen Beschreibung von einem Riss im Himmel, aus dem ein flammenspeiendes Maul erscheint und den ganzen Zug verschlingt (vgl. 'Höllenfahrt', S. 55-58).[11] Der Kontrast zwischen Pauls scheinbar ritterlichem Bemühen einerseits, dauernd für Bele Sitzplätze zu erobern (vgl. S. 6) oder sie über Tuffklippen zu tragen (vgl. S. 22), und andererseits selbst Bele gegenüber ständig seine Überlegenheit unter Beweis zu stellen (indem er etwa beim Schwimmen stets schneller als Bele sein muss, vgl. S. 23), machen deutlich, dass der Größenvergleich des jugoslawischen Reiseführers zwischen dem serbischen Pascha und Paul (vgl. S. 126) nicht zufällig war, sondern eine tiefergehende Gemeinsamkeit beschreibt. In Jugoslawien nimmt Bele eine für sie unakzeptable Tendenz im Verhalten Pauls in Vergrößerung wahr. Wie in Morgners späterem Trobadora-Roman dient auch hier der Vergleich mit dem Ausland (hier mit Jugoslawien sowie Westdeutschland und der Schweiz, vgl. S. 52-53 und S. 70) dazu, einerseits Sexismus als weltweites Phänomen zu thematisieren und zu kritisieren, andererseits die DDR als das Land mit dem relativ geringsten Grad an Sexismus zu preisen.

Dass die Erzählerin Parallelen zwischen dem Gastland und dem Heimatland wahrnimmt, während ihre Mitreisenden Korrespondenzen zwischen den beiden Ländern nicht zu sehen vermögen, erweist sich auch an der Katzengeschichte. In den Tagebuchnotizen berichtet die Erzählerin, wie ein neuer, noch nicht an Touristen gewöhnter Kellner eine Katze trat und dafür von den Touristen mit Nichtachtung gestraft wird (vgl. S. 81). Im Gegensatz zu ihren Mitreisenden reagiert die Erzählerin jedoch nicht mit der Demonstration moralischer Überlegenheit auf diese Katzenmisshandlung, sondern mit einer phantastischen Geschichte. In der Erzählung 'Für die Katz' findet sich der sensuelle, aber unabhängige Charakter der Erzählerin in einer schwarzen Katze konkretisiert. Als Katze behauptet sie sich nicht nur gegen die Domestizierungs-bestrebungen ihres Besitzers, der einen gehorsamen Hund aus ihr machen möchte, sondern auch gegen die Vorhaltungen eines selbsternannten Moralpredigers, der von ihr Rechtfertigungen über den Sinn von

Zärtlichkeit und von Artikulationen des Wohlbehagens fordert. Es sind Aktivitäten, die er offenbar für sinnlose Zeitverschwendung hält, wie es die titelgebende Redewendung 'Für die Katz' ausdrückt. Doch mit Hilfe einer weiteren Redewendung reduziert die Erzählung diesen Vertreter utilitaristischen Denkens zur Maus, die von der Katze als Vertreterin des Lustprinzips gefressen wird. Denn 'den habe ich aber gefressen' ist die umgangssprachliche Formel, um seine Abneigung gegen jemanden auszudrücken. Die Erzählerin wiederholt den Bericht ihres scheinbar mörderischen Aktes als Katze gleich dreimal: 'Und da habe ich ihn gefressen.' (S. 85 und S. 86). Mit dieser Erzählung schlägt die Erzählerin nicht nur eine Brücke zwischen der konkreten Katzenverachtung in Jugoslawien und der Missachtung der in der Katze symbolisierten Charaktereigenschaften in der DDR, sie weist sie auch mit verbaler Komik in ihre Schranken.

Um den Einspruch gegen die in ihrer Gesellschaft fast universal vertretenen Forderungen nach Disziplin, Nüchternheit, Nützlichkeit, Leistung, Erfolgsstreben und Selbstverleugnung - also das, was Horkheimer und Adorno in der *Dialektik der Aufklärung* instrumentelle Vernunft im Dienste von Herrschaft nannten[12] - geht es in den meisten der phantastischen Erzählungen, die Bele ihrem arbeitssüchtigen Geliebten Paul des Nachts erzählt. Hier entwirft sie, von *Tausendundeiner Nacht* inspiriert, ihre Subjektutopie von Lebensfreude, vom Leben als Ekstase voller Sinnlichkeit, Liebe im Bewusstsein von Vergänglichkeit und Tod.[13]

Neben dem in der Katzen-Erzählung zum Ausdruck gebrachten animalisch-sinnlichen Aspekt der Utopie von Lebensfreude kommt auch den explizit sexuellen Wünschen in den sprachspielerisch phantasievollen Erzählungen eine wichtige Rolle zu, die metaphorische Rede in konkrete Handlungen übersetzen. 'Faungesicht' (S. 124-5) ist eine elegisch-witzige Klage darüber, dass die Liebe der Erzählerin zwar vorübergehend einen Stein erweichen konnte, doch die Metamorphose des Geliebten nur von kurzer Dauer war, da ihm mathematische Kurven wichtiger sind als die seiner Geliebten. Zu ihrer Enttäuschung muss sie einsehen, dass sie 'einem Rücken aufgesessen war' (S. 124 und S. 125), d.h. der begehrte Rücken des Geliebten entpuppt sich durch diese Variante der bekannten Redewendung als Irrtum. 'Wie mir ein Orden verliehen ward' (S. 170-2) persifliert die heimische Hierarchie der Werte durch eine Ordensverleihung, die mit allen Wassern bürokratischer Formalität gewaschen ist, aber zwei kleine Unterschiede aufweist. Sie findet nämlich im Himmel statt, und zwar im legendären 'siebten Himmelsgeschoß' (S. 171), und der Orden ist von unkonventioneller Beschaffenheit:

> Im Gegensatz zu den irdischen Orden wurde dieser nicht an der Brust, sondern am Rücken angebracht. In der Mitte des linken Schulterblatts etwa. Er war von rötlicher Farbe, ziemlich groß, elliptisch, entlang der Hauptachse verlief eine Aussparung. Er wurde auf der Haut getragen. Als mir der Prälat den Orden auftätowierte, zählte ich. Zehn Sekunden zählte ich. Der Prälat hatte einen sehr schönen großen Mund. (S. 172)

Diese höchste Auszeichnung, ist - wenn Sie es noch nicht erkannt haben, lesen Sie nach, wie in umgekehrter Rollenverteilung eine Frau einem Mann einen blauen Fleck am Hals mit den Lippen auftätowiert (vgl. S. 125 und S. 190) - eine vergängliche, die nach einigen Tagen verblasst: nämlich der Knutschfleck als Ehrenzeichen sexueller Leidenschaft.[14]

Manche von Beles phantastischen Subjektutopien erschließen sich nicht direkt durch spielerischen Umgang mit der Alltagssprache, sondern erst in einem intertextuellen Verweissystem. Die exotisch märchenhafte Atmosphäre in 'Schattenspiele' lebt aus der Spannung zwischen scheinbar inkongruenten intertextuellen Anspielungen auf die Romantik und auf Brecht. Obwohl die Geschichte einerseits 'in den Schluchten der Stadt' (S. 19) spielt und damit Brechts expressionistisches Stück *Im Dickicht der Städte*[15] evoziert sowie in der Diktion an expressionistische Gedichte anknüpft, folgt die Erzählung auch einem romantischen Muster. Denn bläulicher Rauch in bläulichen Ringen dient als Orientierung für die verirrte Erzählerin auf ein Haus zu, das ihr mit blauem Schornstein und blau-weiß gestreiften Markisen ein Zuhause verspricht (vgl. S. 19). Das Blau der Romantik wird surreal, wenn dem Dichter Franz blaue Blumen auf dem Kopf wachsen, von denen er eine pflückt und sie der Erzählerin reicht (vgl. S. 21). Novalis' Sehnsuchtssymbol der blauen Blume, in der dem werdenden Dichter Heinrich von Ofterdingen das Gesicht der Geliebten Mathilde entgegenleuchtet, wird hier zu einem Objekt weiblichen Begehrens.[16] Dies Begehren ist sowohl sexuell als auch dichterisch zu verstehen, wie noch zu zeigen sein wird. Der Text kontrastiert jedoch romantische Sehnsucht mit drastischer Körperlichkeit. In Franzens Sonett ist 'von Eos, Scheißhäusern und anderen unerhörten Gegenständen die Rede' (S. 20) - das ist eine Mischung, die auch die Erzählung selbst charakterisiert: Eos, die Morgenröte, konnotiert erotische und politische Ansprüche in metaphorisch anspruchsvoller Sprache; Scheißhäuser signalisieren das Recht des Körpers kompromissloser

Direktheit. Karl Heinz Bohrer hat 'an utopisch gesinnten Menschen, vor allem Anhängern von politischen Utopien, [...] eine spezifische Ichschwäche'[17] bemerkt. Von Ichschwäche ist jedoch bei der Protagonistin dieses Romans keine Spur. Sie vereint Tatkraft und romantische Sehnsucht in einer Person, wie etwa in der folgenden phantastischen Baumbesteigung deutlich wird:

> Als ich Müdigkeit spürte, zog ich Mantel, Schuhe und Strümpfe aus, entfernte mich sechs Schritte, nahm Anlauf, krallte Finger und Zehen in die Borke eines Stamms und erklomm den Wipfel des Baumes. Dächer, soweit das Auge reichte. Wo war ich zu Hause? Ich zählte Antennen, schaukelte mich in den Ästen, spuckte runter. (S. 19)

Neben Novalis' Sehnsuchtssymbol der blauen Blume spielt Adalbert von Chamissos Erzählung von *Peter Schlemihl* eine text-strukturierende Rolle.[18] Peter Schlemihl verkaufte bekanntlich seinen Schatten dem grauen Mann und hat erst spät bemerkt, dass er damit etwas Unveräußerliches, einen Teil von sich selbst, von seiner Seele, aufgab. Der romantische Ernst Chamissos wird jedoch hier zu einem an 'Schattenboxen' erinnernden 'Schattenspiel'. Denn statt um den Verkauf des Schattens mit lebenslangen Folgen handelt es sich hier um ein Schenken. Die Frage bei diesem Geschenk ist jedoch: Wer? Wem? Die Erzählerin lehnt Franzens Angebot, ihr seinen Schatten mitzugeben, damit sie nicht länger einsam sei, ab, weil sie ihre Wohnung nicht mehr mit einem Mann, selbst nicht dem Schatten eines Mannes, teilen möchte (vgl. S. 20). Trotz der blauen Blume ist die Liebesvorstellung der Erzählerin also nicht durch Verschmelzung als utopisches Ziel geprägt, wie auch Franzens misogyne Ode (vgl. S. 21) und sein übermäßiges Zigarrenrauchen deutlich machen, die zwar konstatiert werden, doch dem sexuellen Begehren der Erzählerin keinen Abbruch tun. Um so mehr verwundert es die Leserin, dass nach Franzens Besuch 'der Schatten von Franz, dem Dichter, in meinem Sessel' (S. 21) saß und ihr beim Verlassen der Wohnung folgt, doch dass sie mit ihm 'keineswegs' (S. 21) ihre Wohnung teilt. Es handelt sich bei diesem Schatten also offenbar nicht um Franzens Seele, die mit ihr eins wird (oder gar sie erst zum Menschen macht wie in Fouqués *Undine* oder Andersens *Kleiner Meerjungfrau*). Das zeitweilige Verschwinden des Schattens, wenn die Aufmerksamkeit der Erzählerin anderweitig absorbiert ist, sowie seine eigenartigen Dimensionen (nämlich 'kleiner als Franz, so groß wie ich', S. 21) weisen vielmehr darauf hin, dass es sich um das Bild handelt, das sie sich von

Franz gemacht hat. Eine weibliche Appropriation von Brechts Herrn Keuner klingt hier an, der auf die Frage: Was tun Sie, wenn Sie einen Menschen lieben? antwortete, er mache einen Entwurf von ihm und sorge dafür, dass er [der Mensch] ihm [dem Entwurf] ähnlich werde.[19] Die Kreativität, die durch die Liebe hervorgebracht wird, ist dem Anspruch auf die literarische Gestaltung des Objekts der Sehnsucht verwandt: 'Denn ich liebe die Männer, die alle meine Werke sind' (S. 21). Diese weibliche Schöpfung will zugleich als ein Geschenk an den Geliebten verstanden werden aus einer Liebe heraus, die nicht für die Ewigkeit ist, sondern deren Zeitmaß zwischen 'Kurze Zeit' und '[o]ft' verläuft (S. 21). 'Schattenspiel' kehrt also die in der Literatur so fest verankerten Rollen von Subjekt und Objekt der liebenden Projektion geistreich um, ist selbst ein witziges Schattenspiel (ein Negativ) der üblichen Geschlechtsrollen, und schafft aus dem Kontrast von Brecht mit der Romantik einen neuen, modernen Ton von Sehnsucht, vor allem eine Sehnsucht, deren Subjekt die Frau ist. Andererseits jedoch setzt es das Denken und Lieben in Projektionen fort, nun mit 'weiblichem Vorzeichen'. Aus heutiger Perspektive können wir vielleicht sagen, dass damit der Text gleichzeitig eine subjektive weibliche Utopie eröffnet und kurzschließt, weil er den anderen in seiner Eigenart nicht gelten lässt und die Projektion (die Männer als Werke der Frau) über die Anerkennung von Differenz stellt.

Neben der Evokation von Verhaltensweisen, die ihren Landsleuten bedauerlicherweise abgehen, sowie von solchen, die im eigenen Land dankenswerterweise weniger stark entwickelt sind, aber immer noch kritikwürdig sind, nutzt die Erzählerin die Exotik der Auslandserfahrungen auch als Anlass für eine Formulierung von politischer Kritik, die mit dem Gastland nicht ursächlich zusammenhängt. Diese Kritik kann durch Assoziationen ausgelöst werden. So setzt die Erzählerin die Reaktion einer Frau auf den Tod ihres Großsohns in Jugoslawien mit der Reaktion einer Mutter in der DDR auf den Tod ihrer Tochter parallel: 'Nervenschock' hier, Sprachverlust dort (S. 151). Während aber in Jugoslawien ein Badeunfall die Todesursache war, war es in der DDR ein Selbstmord als Reaktion auf politische Repression, nämlich auf die öffentliche Kritik 'Beatgeschmacks wegen' (S. 151).

Zweitens kann die Exotik zur Camouflage einer rein DDR-spezifischen Situation dienen. In der phantastischen Erzählung 'Pferdekopf' (vgl. S. 155-157) - einer Kritik am sozialistischen Realismus und einer Evokation von Phantasie als literarischer Wert - wird der wahre Ort der Handlung aus der DDR nach Konstantinopel verlegt. Am interessantesten jedoch ist der dritte Fall, wo die kulturellen Identitäten der beiden Länder in einer phantastischen Geschichte zu etwas Neuem verschmolzen werden, nämlich in 'Himmelbett' (S. 31-41).

Die Erzählung ist durch das Prinzip des Kontrastes strukturiert. Das tägliche Gespräch von zwei bettlägerigen Krankenhauspatientinnen unterschiedlicher sozialer Klassen wird mit den nächtlichen phantastischen Reisen der Erzählerin kontrastiert. Bele erzählt die Geschichte, nachdem sie mit Paul einen Streit über den Wert des Reisens hatte (vgl. S. 28). Bei Tag erfährt die Erzählerin die groteske Geschichte von Gerda Jepsens Kriegsschwangerschaft und ihrer nachträglichen Trauung mit dem im Krieg gefallenen Verlobten. Traumatisiert durch die Folgen dieser einmaligen sexuellen Erfahrung, sagt die Arbeiterin: 'Einmal und nicht wieder' (S. 38). Die Erzählerin dagegen ist abenteuerlustig und fährt jede Nacht mit ihrem Bett aus dem Krankenhaus hinaus durch Berlin:

> Tucholskystraße, Ziegelstraße, Friedrichstraße, Weidendammbrücke, Unter den Linden, Am Kupfergraben, Monbijoubrücke, Monbijoustraße, Ziegelstraße, Tucholskystraße bis vor die überdachte Eingangstür. (S. 32)

Ihre nächtlichen Reisen sind Theodor Storms Kindermärchen 'Der kleine Häwelmann' nachgebildet.[20] Im 'kleinen Häwelmann' kann der Junge des Nachts in seinem Rollenbett nicht schlafen und möchte von der Mutter unentwegt hin- und hergerollt werden. Als die Mutter einschläft, spannt er sein Hemd an seinem als Mastbaum ausgestreckten Bein auf und bläst in das so entstandene Segel hinein. Voll Ungeduld möchte er fahren und von aller Welt gesehen werden. Auf dem Strahl des Mondes gleitet er durch das Schlüsselloch aus dem Haus hinaus. Vom Mond begleitet, fährt er durch Straßen, Wald und in den Himmel, bis der Mond den unersättlichen Häwelmann verlässt. Morgens wird er von der Sonne ins Meer geworfen, wo ihn der Erzähler und der Leser auffischen. In 'Himmelbett' ist der Mond nicht nur Begleiter, sondern der Motor der Bewegung. Allerdings wird die 'Mondkraft' vermittelt durch eine phantastische Version moderner Technik. Der reale Ostberliner Fernsehturm wird, unter dem Einfluss der Ferien der Erzählerin in einem muslimischen Land, als 'Fernsehminarett' (S. 33) wahrgenommen. Die an ihm befindlichen Lichter werden als 'neun rote Augen' (S. 33) beschrieben, denen noch die beiden blauen Augen eines imaginären Muezzin zugezählt werden, der den Vornamen Robert erhält. D.h. die technische Funktion des Fernsehturms wird märchenhaft personalisiert.

Überdies wird dem somit muslemisierten Berliner Fernsehturm namens Robert Muezzin eine stasiähnliche Überwachungsfunktion zugeschrieben, da 'dessen blauen und roten Augen nichts entging' (S. 33).

In der Fusion von Berliner Fernsehturm und Minarett (oder anders gesagt, elektronischer Kommunikation und dem allsehenden Auge Gottes) wird eine Verschiebung gesellschaftlicher Werte vom Spirituellen hin zum Technischen suggeriert. Dennoch ist diese Erzählung kein Alptraum von der Ersetzung Gottes durch das allsehende Auge des Staats-sicherheitsdienstes, sondern, im Einklang mit der orientalisch-märchenhaften Atmosphäre, eine subjektive Ermächtigungsphantasie. Denn die Ausrüstung des Fernsehminaretts 'mit den empfindlichsten Abhörgeräten japanischer Bauart' (S. 33) dient in phantastischer Verkehrung der Realität der Stasiüberwachung gerade nicht dazu, Bürger mit staatsfeindlichen Gesinnungen dingfest zu machen, sondern umgekehrt zur märchenhaften Wunscherfüllung eines Individuums.

Statt zum Gebet aufzurufen, hat Robert Muezzin die Rolle eines allmächtigen Vaters als Wunscherfüller in einer Welt von Konsumenten inne. Sein Magnettongerät 'spielte vom unendlichen Kundendienstband: "Sie wünschen Sie wünschen Sie wünschen"' (S. 33). Nur drei Sekunden, nachdem die Erzählerin ihre Wünsche flüsternd unterbreitet hat, steht ihr ein Geselle von Robert Muezzin zur Verfügung, in dem sich unschwer der Mond aus Storms Märchen erkennen lässt: 'rotbärtig, kühl, ziemlich alt, sein gelber Kopf, rund bis sichelförmig, war dunkel gefleckt, eigentlich bestand er nur aus Kopf: ein Denker' (S. 33-4). Allerdings ist dieser Mond mit einer technischen Zusatzausrüstung versehen, die ihn vom 19. Jahrhundert des Märchens ins 20. Jahrhundert katapultiert:

> Die Polyesterspulen, pro Geselle eine rote und eine gelbe, liefen im Gegensatz zu denen des Meisters auf Metalldornen, die aus dem Scheitel ragten, Tonabnehmer und Lautsprecher, nicht zu erkennen, waren vermutlich im Schädel untergebracht, auf den Magnettonbändern, im Prinzip dem unendlichen Kundendienstband des Meisters vergleichbar, waren die Lieder konserviert, die in komplizierter Weise den Wind erzeugten, der zur Fortbewegung meines Bettes erforderlich war. (S. 36-7)

Unter Tausenden Patienten der städtischen Krankenhäuser scheint nur die Erzählerin von der Sehnsucht nach nächtlichen Reisen umgetrieben zu werden, alle anderen begehren nicht einmal in der Phantasie gegen ihr trübes Leben auf. Selbst sie jedoch bleibt während ihrer phantastischen Reisen in Ost-Berlin, fährt am Grenzübergang nach West-Berlin nur vorbei, und die Gesellen des Robert Muezzin erlauben ihr nicht, mit ihrem Bett aufs Wasser und aus der DDR hinauszufahren auf den Atlantik (vgl. S. 40-1). Die Maßlosigkeit des kindlichen Begehrens, die Storms Märchen zum Ausdruck gebracht und pädagogisch eingegrenzt hat, wird hier von vorn herein dadurch gekappt, dass Robert Muezzins Gesellen die Bewegung des Bettes kontrollieren. Die Lautstärke der die Bewegung auf phantastische Weise hervorbringenden Lieder des Mondes jedoch wirkt sich störend auf die Leuchtkraft der Phantasie selbst aus. D.h. zwischen der Imagination und ihrer Erfüllung besteht ein unüberwindlicher Widerspruch, wie die durch die hohe Phonstärke abblätternde Himmelsfarbe, bei der der Grund durchkam, andeutet: 'Und auf grauem Grund waren die Sterne, die mitfuhren, schwer zu erkennen, die kleinen Sterne, die großen Sterne und der Mond' (S. 41). Der 'graue Grund' ist sowohl der Untergrund eines farbigen Gemäldes als auch der Grund (d.h. die Motivierung) für Beles nächtliche Ausschweifungen, nämlich das triste alltägliche Leben, in dem es schwer ist, an der Leuchtkraft der Phantasie festzuhalten.

Lassen Sie mich abschließend zusammenfassen: Nicht ihre Kommentare, sondern Beles Blicke, d.h. ihre Fokussierung bestimmter Details, ihre Reihung und Kontrastierung von Realitätspartikeln zu einem Bild, vermitteln der Leserin einen Eindruck von dem, was Bele an ihren Landsleuten vor der Kontrastfolie Jugoslawiens wahrnimmt. Beles eigene Werte lassen sich sowohl aus ihren phantastischen Geschichten als auch aus der Art ihres kritischen Blickes auf die Urlauber an der Adria erschließen. In der Entfaltung ihres kritischen Blicks lässt Bele sich von Jugoslawien inspirieren, ohne jedoch das fremde Land in ein positives oder negatives Stereotyp zu pressen. Vielmehr wird deutlich, dass zwischen den beiden Ländern graduelle Differenzen bestehen, nicht etwa absolute. Sie entfalten sich auf den Achsen Nord-Süd und Okzident-Orient, die wiederum mit Werten wie Leistungsprinzip-Leidenschaft, feministisch-patriarchalisch, Realität-Phantasie konnotiert sind. Obwohl der Roman in Jugoslawien spielt, ist die Erkenntnis der jugoslawischen Widersprüche und Probleme jedoch eher nebensächlich. Der Fokus liegt auf dem Verhalten der DDR-Urlauber und auf Beles Kritik der sich darin manifestierenden gesellschaftlichen Zustände in der DDR.

Auf der Ebene der Liebesgeschichte endet der Roman ohne Happy-End, doch hoffnungsvoll. Bele verlässt Paul auf dem Weg zum Standesamt, weil sie ihrer beider Lebensauffassungen als unvereinbar erkannt hat. Doch dieses Ende ihrer Liebesbeziehung markiert zugleich ihren Vorsatz, weitere 'wirklich durchführbare [...] Versuche' (S. 190) zur Verwirklichung ihrer Subjektutopie zu unternehmen: '"Was hast du vor?" fragte Paul. "Das absolute Experiment" antwortete Bele und winkte einer Taxe mit dem Rosenbukett' (S. 190).

Dass der erste und der letzte Satz des Romans auf Prag verweist, lässt sich als implizite Aufforderung lesen, auch das gesellschaftliche utopische Experiment noch einmal zu versuchen. Dessen real-geschichtliches Scheitern verweist uns heute auf die Notwendigkeit, die Tragfähigkeit der Subjektutopie, die der Roman artikuliert, - nämlich von einem Leben, das nicht bloß als Umweg zu einem Ziel gelebt wird, sondern im Bewusstsein von Vergänglichkeit Erfüllung in der Gegenwart findet, - und die ästhetische Qualität der Gestaltung dieser Subjektutopie in Abwesenheit einer sie übergreifenden geschichtsphilosophischen Legitimation zu testen. Für mich ist die Ästhetik dieses Romans ein großes Vergnügen, das viele Aspekte der darin enthaltenen Subjektutopie anziehend erscheinen lässt, das mir aber auch Raum lässt, mit manchen Aspekten dessen, was ich als die implizite Subjektutopie entziffert habe, auf Distanz zu gehen - mich also produktiv zu verhalten. Denn während auf nationaler Ebene die DDR und Jugoslawien in einer komplexen Beziehung von Parallelen, Unterschieden und Abstufungen existieren, ist der Roman auf personaler Ebene durchaus dualistisch strukturiert: Auf der Seite der Protagonistin Bele vereinigen sich alle positiv konnotierten Eigenschaften, vor allem Witz, Humor, unabhängiges Denken, Lebensfreude, Sinnlichkeit, Unkonventionalität, Kreativität, Phantasie. Auf der Seite des Physikers Paul dagegen vereinigen sich sämtliche negativ konnotierten Werte: exzessives Leistungsdenken, einseitige Entwicklung der Ratio, Konkurrenzdenken, paschahaftes Verhalten. Zwar gibt es Nebenfiguren, die eine simple Zuordnung dieser Pole zu der Achse weiblich-männlich verhindern. Doch die positiven Seiten der Ratio und die negativen Seiten der Sinnlichkeit kommen nicht in den Blick. Vor allem wird Paul hauptsächlich als Erziehungsobjekt von Beles nächtlichen Märchen wahrgenommen, weniger als gleichberechtigter Partner, dessen Andersartigkeit zu achten ist. Dennoch aber hat Morgner mit *Hochzeit* einen nicht nur politisch radikalen, sondern auch ästhetisch so dichten, innovativen, scharfsinnigen, witzigen und die LeserInnen heraus-fordernden Roman geschaffen, dass ich meinen Studierenden seit vielen Jahren diesen Roman als den besten empfohlen habe, den Morgner zu Lebzeiten veröffentlichen konnte.

Anmerkungen

[1] Irmtraud Morgner, *Hochzeit in Konstantinopel*, Luchterhand: Frankfurt a. M., 1989; Erstveröffentlichung: Aufbau: Berlin und Weimar, 1968. Seitenangaben in Klammern beziehen sich auf die Luchterhand-Ausgabe des Romans.

[2] Irmtraud Morgner, *Rumba auf einen Herbst*, Luchterhand: Frankfurt a. M., 1991; repr. dtv: München, 1995.

[3] Vgl. Werner Neubert, 'Zwischen Phantasie und Gespinst', *Neues Deutschland*, 15. Januar 1969: 'Der Rezensent möchte die Hoffnung aussprechen, daß die erstaunliche Fabulierlust der Autorin sich künftig weitaus deutlicher dem Objektiven und Lebendigen unseres neuen Lebens zuwenden wird'. Vgl. auch Erik Neutsch, 'Und wieder einmal: Vom Nutzen der Literatur', *Neues Deutschland,* 26. April 1969: 'Fühlen wir uns nicht als "Kulturbringer", sondern lernen wir von der Kultur der ehemals unterdrückten und heute herrschenden Klasse. Lernen wir von der sechsundsiebzigjährigen Frau, die eine Straße pflastern will [...]. Mit einem Nachdenken über sie ist mehr getan als mit einem Nachdenken über eine Hochzeit in Konstantinopel'.

[4] Lange bestand eine große Diskrepanz zwischen Morgners Bekanntheit und öffentlicher Wertschätzung als Autorin und der Menge an wissenschaftlichen Untersuchungen ihres Werkes. In den letzten Jahren wird dieses Missverhältnis geringer, aber noch immer sind die meisten Untersuchungen Morgners sogenannten Salman-Romanen (d.h. *Trobadora Beatriz* und *Amanda*) gewidmet. Vgl. zu *Hochzeit* besonders: Günter Jäckel, 'Irmtraud Morgner', *Deutsch als Fremdsprache*, (1978). Sonderheft, 49-54; Michaela Grobbel, 'Kreativität und Re-Vision in den Werken Irmtraud Morgners von 1968 bis 1972', *New German Review*, 3 (1987), 1-16; Petra Reuffer, *Die unwahrscheinlichen Gewänder der anderen Wahrheit: Zur Wiederentdeckung des Wunderbaren bei G. Grass und I. Morgner*, Verlag Die Blaue Eule: Essen, 1988; Gabriela Scherer, *Zwischen "Bitterfeld" und "Orplid"*, Peter Lang: Bern, 1992, S. 52-68; Martina Elisabeth Eidecker, *Sinnsuche und Trauerarbeit: Funktionen von Schreiben in Irmtraud Morgners Werk*, Olms-Weidmann: Hildesheim, 1998, S. 94-114; Geoffrey Westgate, *Strategies under Surveillance. Reading Irmtraud Morgner as a GDR Writer*. Amsterdamer Publikationen zur Sprache und Literatur 148, Rodopi: Amsterdam/New York, 2002, S. 93-113. En passant wird *Hochzeit in Konstantinopel* erwähnt bei: Stephanie Hanel, *Literarischer Widerstand zwischen Phantastischem und Alltäglichem: Das Romanwerk Irmtraud Morgners*, Pfaffenweiler: Centaurus, 1995, S. 30-32; Walter Jens, 'Die Tausendsassa Irmtraud Morgner. Laudatio anläßlich der Verleihung des Literaturpreises für grotesken Humor, 1989', in: Marlis Gerhardt (Hrsg.), *Irmtraud Morgner. Texte, Daten, Bilder*, Luchterhand: Frankfurt a. M., 1990, 100-108 (hier: S. 100-104); Eva Kaufmann, 'Der Hölle die Zunge herausstrecken. Der Weg der Erzählerin Irmtraud Morgner', *Weimarer Beiträge*, 30 (1984), 1515-1532 (hier: S. 1517-1519); Alison Lewis, *Subverting Patriarchy. Feminism and Fantasy in the Novels of Irmtraud Morgner*, Berg: New York and Oxford, 1995, S. 26, 82, 89, 104, 111, 112, 114-115, 177, 255, 264-266;

Beth Linklater, *'Und immer zügelloser wird die Lust': Constructions of Sexuality in East German Literatures. With Special Reference to Irmtraud Morgner and Gabriele Stötzer-Kachold*, Bern: Lang, 1998, S. 73-74, 79-80, 81, 113; Beth Linklater, '"Unbeschreiblich köstlich wie die Liebe selber": Food and Sex in the Work of Irmtraud Morgner', *Modern Language Review*, 93.4 (1998), 1045-1057 (hier: S. 1047, 1050-1052); Hildegard Rossoll, *Weltbild und Bildsprache im Werk Irmtraud Morgners: eine Analyse unter besonderer Berücksichtigung von 'Amanda, ein Hexenroman'*, New York: Peter Lang, 1999, S. 10, 12; Ricarda Schmidt, 'Utopia and its Loss: Women's Writing in the GDR', *women: a cultural review*, 3.3 (Winter 1992), 249-258 (hier: S. 252).

[5] Karl Heinz Bohrer, 'Subjektive Zukunft', *Merkur* (Sonderheft: Zukunft Denken nach den Utopien), 55. Jg., Nr. 9/10 (Sept./Okt. 2001), 756-768 (hier: S. 757). Vgl. auch Martin Seel, 'Drei Regeln für Utopisten', *Merkur* (Sonderheft: Zukunft Denken nach den Utopien), 55. Jg., Nr. 9/10 (Sept./Okt. 2001), 747-756; hier S. 754: 'Je weniger eine Utopie politisch intendiert ist, desto weniger muß sie einer Bedingung der Realisierbarkeit gehorchen. Je privater ein utopischer Gedanke ist, desto eher darf er alle Grenzen der Realisierbarkeit überschreiten. Denn dies sind Utopien, bei denen es gar nicht um Annäherung geht. In der Imagination eines anderen Zustands stellen sie das individuelle Leben nicht in eine aussichtsreiche Kontinuität mit zukünftigen Zeiten, sondern vielmehr in eine heilsame Diskontinuität zur gegenwärtigen Praxis. Hier soll überhaupt kein Zielpunkt erreicht werden; vielmehr handelt es sich um Entwürfe, die gerade in ihrer strikten Unerreichbarkeit den Kreis der Möglichkeiten der Existenz bereichern'.

[6] Vgl. Ingeborg Bachmanns zuerst 1955 veröffentlichten Essay 'Was ich in Rom sah und hörte', in: Bachmann, *Werke*, hrsg. von Christine Koschel, Inge von Weidenbaum, Clemens von Münster, Bd. 4, Piper: München/Zürich, 1982, S. 29-34.

[7] Vgl. Peter Schneider, *Lenz*, Rotbuch: Berlin, 1974 (Erstveröffentlichung: 1973).

[8] Vgl. zur Kritik an einem vorschnellen Orientalismusvorwurf, der auf der Basis von Saids Werk so populär ist, Siegfried Kohlhammer, 'Populistisch, antiwissenschaftlich, erfolgreich. Edward Saids "Orientalismus"', *Merkur*, 56. Jg., Nr 4 (April 2002), 289-299.

[9] Sonnenblumenöl, Yoghurt, Erdnüsse, Thunfisch und Knoblauchgeruch waren damals noch etwas Fremdes und Erwähnenswertes, vgl. 14.

[10] Feigen- und Granatapfelbäume, Oleander, Agaven (S. 16); Pinien (S. 17); Olivenbäume (S. 89) etc.

[11] In seinem ansonsten sehr kenntnisreichen und informativen Buch versucht Geoffrey Westgate (siehe Anmerkung 4), die nächtlichen Erzählungen Beles zu klassifizieren, ohne jedoch mehr als eine im Detail zu interpretieren. Da gerade diese Erzählungen ästhetisch sehr komplex und ohne intensive Interpretationsanstrengung unzugänglich

sind, kommt es zu manchen schiefen Zuordnungen. Westgate unterscheidet vier Themenkomplexe: 1. Programmatische Texte zu Themen wie Kunst und Ästhetik, Dichter und Wissenschaftler, die Einschränkungen bürgerlicher Moral und die Freude, dagegen zu rebellieren. 2. Geschichten, die erotische Beziehungen zwischen Männern und Frauen thematisieren. 3. Geschichten, die weibliche Erfahrungen unabhängig von Männern behandeln. 4. Texte, die (auto)biographische Erfahrungen und Familiengeschichte behandeln (vgl. Westgate, S. 94-98). Diese Unterscheidung in vier Klassen von Themen ist an sich bereits nicht haltbar, denn alle nächtlichen Erzählungen sind programmatisch, insofern sie Beles Subjektutopie vom sinnlichen Leben in der Gegenwart zum Ausdruck bringen. Sie tun dies aber auf ästhetisch verschiedene Weise, nämlich realistisch und elegisch (vgl. 'Die Wanne', die drei Großmutter-Erzählungen, 'Sternstunden'), realistisch und satirisch (vgl. 'Saldo'), realistisch-symbolisch ('Wie die Lauben abgerissen wurden'), realistisch-symbolisch und intertextuell ('Weißes Ostern'); phantastisch und elegisch (vgl. 'Das Hotel', 'Faungesicht'), phantastisch und satirisch (vgl. 'Das Duell', 'Höllenfahrt', 'Für die Katz', 'Kopfstand', 'Gericht', 'Pferdekopf'), phantastisch und intertextuell (vgl. 'Schattenspiel', 'Himmelbett', 'Wie die Häuser gebaut wurden'), phantastisch und idyllisch (vgl. 'Wie mir ein Orden verliehen ward'). 'April' ist, wie der Monat, eine wetterwendische Geschichte mit realistischen und satirischen Elementen, aber auch phantastischen Einschlägen. 'Höllenfahrt' wird von Westgate seiner dritten Kategorie von Geschichten zugeordnet. Doch da der Text eine sexistische Anmache in der S-Bahn behandelt, sowie den Wunsch der Erzählerin, der aufdringliche Mann möge zur Hölle fahren (vgl. S. 57), in konkrete Phantasie übersetzt, ist sie kaum als Ausdruck einer von Männern unabhängigen weiblichen Subjektivität zu lesen. 'Weißes Ostern' ordnet Westgate ebenfalls seiner dritten Kategorie zu, vernachlässigt dabei aber die Zweisträngigkeit der Erzählung, die Geburt und Tod in einer sozialistischen Variante der christlichen Ostergeschichte programmatisch zusammenbringt. Bei 'Wie mir ein Orden verliehen ward' übersieht Westgate in seiner Zuordung zur zweiten Kategorie den programmatischen Anspruch der Erzählerin auf eine Kritik an der herrschenden Rangordnung der Werte, denn mit dem ordenverleihenden Prälaten verbindet die Erzählerin keine persönliche Beziehung, auch wenn seine Beschreibung mit der Pauls in der darauffolgenden Tagebucheintragung identisch ist (vgl. S. 177). Wenn Westgate 'Wie die Lauben abgerissen wurden' seiner dritten Kategorie der von Männern unabhängigen weiblichen Subjektivität zuteilt, ignoriert er die symbolische Parallelisierung vom sukzessiven Abbau der Schrebergärten mit der Verschlechterung der Liebesbeziehung der Erzählerin.

[12] Vgl. Max Horkheimer und Theodor W. Adorno, *Dialektik der Aufklärung. Philosophische Fragmente*, Fischer: Frankfurt a. M., 1988, S. 88-127.

[13] Vgl. meinen Vortrag 'Subjektutopie, real existierender Sozialismus und phantastische Form in Irmtraud Morgners *Hochzeit in Konstantinopel*', University of Sheffield, 13.3.2002.

[14] Weder die elliptische Form des Ordens noch die Tatsache seines allmählichen

Verblassens noch die intratextuelle Einbettung seines Auftätowiert-Werdens werden von Martina Elisabeth Eidecker wahrgenommen, die den Orden als 'Einschußstelle' interpretiert. Der von Eidecker imagierte Schuss hat zum Tod geführt, woraus Eidecker schließt: 'Gesellschaftlich allgemein akzeptiertes, korrektes Verhalten geht einher mit dem – im übertragenen Sinne verstandenen – Tod des Individuums'. (Martina Elisabeth Eidecker, *Sehnsucht und Trauerarbeit*, (siehe Anmerkung 4), S. 111.)

[15] Bertolt Brecht, *Im Dickicht der Städte*, in: Brecht, *Gesammelte Werke in 20 Bänden*, hrsg. vom Suhrkamp Verlag in Zusammenarbeit mit Elisabeth Hauptmann, Bd. 1: *Stücke 1*, Suhrkamp: Frankfurt a. M., 1973, S. 125-193.

[16] Novalis, *Heinrich von Ofterdingen*, in: Novalis, *Schriften. Die Werke Friedrich von Hardenbergs*, hrsg. von Paul Kluckhohn und Richard Samuel, Bd. 1: *Das dichterische Werk*, Kohlhammer: Stuttgart, 1960, S. 183-269.

[17] Bohrer, 'Subjektive Zukunft', (siehe Anmerkung 5), S. 766.

[18] Adelbert von Chamisso, *Peter Schlemihls wundersame Geschichte*, in: Chamisso, *Sämtliche Werke*, Bd. 1, hrsg. von Jost Perfahl, Winkler: München, 1975, S. 13-67.

[19] Vgl. Bertolt Brecht, 'Geschichten von Herrn Keuner', in: Brecht, *Gesammelte Werke in 20 Bänden*, hrsg. vom Suhrkamp Verlag in Zusammenarbeit mit Elisabeth Hauptmann, Bd. 12: *Prosa 2*, Suhrkamp: Frankfurt a.M., 1973, S. 386.

[20] Theodor Storm, 'Der kleine Häwelmann', in: Storm, *Sämtliche Werke*, hrsg. von Karl Ernst Laage und Dieter Lohmeier, Bd. 4: *Märchen, Kleine Prosa*, Deutscher Klassiker Verlag: Frankfurt a.M., 1988, S. 21-24. Storm schrieb das Märchen 1849, ein Jahr nach der Geburt seines ersten Kindes. Es lässt sich auch an das Kindermärchen von Gerd von Bassewitz denken: *Peterchens Mondfahrt* wurde 1915 zuerst veröffentlicht und erschien in 4. Auflage 1919 mit Bildern von Hans Baluschek.

Renate Rechtien

Irene Böhme's novel *Die Buchhändlerin*. A Case of Reconstructing the Past in the Image of the Future?

This chapter examines Irene Böhme's novel *Die Buchhändlerin* of 1999 by placing it into the context of memory and identity politics in the new Germany. It argues that the novel's highly positive reception in the new German *feuilleton* has been based not on aesthetic criteria but on the novel's assumed 'truth value' and its political significance. This reflects not only a dominant trend to repoliticise culture in the new Germany for the purposes of identity construction, but is also designed to trivialise Germany's National Socialist past and to place the lion's share of the responsibility for it firmly at the door of East German citizens.

The fall of former dividing lines such as the Iron Curtain and the Berlin Wall confronted many nations in Europe with the task of redefining themselves and their relationship with their neighbours. As national boundaries have been called into question and established allegiances between states have been challenged, nations, social groups and citizens alike have experienced considerable uncertainties over issues of identity and belonging, and they have had to negotiate many conflicting experiences with relation to both the past and the present. In this context, issues of identity and of memory have become predominant in public debates about multiculturalism, nationalism and supranationalism in Europe as a whole, a phenomenon which led John Gillis to observe that memory and identity 'are two of the most frequently used terms in contemporary public and private discourse'.[1] In this regard, Germany constitutes a special case, and the political and cultural turbulences the country has experienced over the past decade have testified to the fact that Germany's swift unification as a nation state has by no means automatically translated into inner unity. As some have observed, East and West Germans are still strangers in many respects, and the process of growing together psychologically as one nation hinges to a considerable degree on the challenges produced by forty years of division and its lasting impact on historical consciousness.[2] While conservative forces in the new Germany have tended to rethink the country in terms of 'normalisation', the debates about the past we have witnessed in the cultural sphere throughout the 1990s[3] have actually pointed to a growing inner struggle over questions of history and memory, with the latter increasingly turning into a site of intense struggle and contention.[4]

Literary representations of the past published over the past decade have sought to contribute to illuminating Germany's 'double past',[5] but they have also frequently been instrumentalised within a socio-political environment that has politicised culture for the purposes of identity construction in the new Germany.[6]

This, I believe, goes some way towards explaining the importance which the new German cultural press has attached to literary engagement with the past in general, and to narratives promising to shed new light on aspects of the former German Democratic Republic's past in particular. As Stefan Neuhaus has noted, the German *feuilleton* has been indefatigable since 1989 in its search for 'the' all-German novel, with just about every 'längere narrative Publikation mit literarischem Anspruch, die in den 90er Jahren auf den Markt kam und irgendeinen Bezug zur Wiedervereinigung oder mindestens zur untergegangenen DDR hatte', being considered a worthy contender for the title 'deutscher Einheitsroman'.[7] The tendency alluded to here by Neuhaus of rating a text's value according to the 'truths' it tells us about life in the former GDR, rather than judging it by aesthetic criteria, has also been noted by Dennis Tate, who subjected representative texts from the genre of autobiography which have emanated from the former GDR in the course of the 1990s and their reception to critical scrutiny.[8]

This chapter examines Irene Böhme's novel *Die Buchhändlerin* (1999),[9] which portrays the everyday experiences of ordinary citizens in a provincial town in Thuringia during the 1950s. It was the novel's treatment of this crucial period in East German history which suggested it to me as an appropriate case study for the purposes of this volume; for this epoch saw not only the transition from fascism under Hitler to the foundation of GDR socialism under the auspices of Stalin's Russia but also the division of Germany along with the demand imposed on citizens to think of each other as strangers and class enemies. The fact that this historical period has hitherto not been extensively explored outside the well-documented constraints inflicted upon writers in the GDR during the 'Aufbaujahre',[10] furthermore, means that it fills an important gap, a factor which will without doubt also have added to its appeal for critics in the German cultural press. The highly favourable reception of *Die Buchhändlerin* in the German *feuilleton*, however, raises questions along the lines suggested by Neuhaus and Tate, namely whether the significance attached to the text may have been based on its assumed 'truth value' rather than on aesthetic criteria and whether the perspective adopted by the author may have met with particular approval because it affirms rather than challenges dominant trends in the context of the new Germany's memory and identity politics. The fact that Irene Böhme left the GDR in 1980 to live and work in West Germany has, in my view, played a role in the critical acclaim the novel has enjoyed; for the author has the ability to look back as both an insider with intimate personal experience of life in the GDR and as an outsider who brings more than merely historical distance to her subject matter, factors which have recommended her as a narrator able to enhance the historical consciousness of readers on both sides of the former border. As the observation of one commentator, who described it as 'Ein Buch, das "Ossis" nachdenklich macht und "Wessis" viel über das Leben und die Entwicklung in der DDR erzählt',[11] illustrates, her novel has been regarded also as a valuable contribution to inner unity in the new Germany. As my discussion proposes, however, a critical analysis of some of the novel's key premises suggests that, rather than raising questions that might prove fruitful in the context of gaining historical consciousness and informing identity construction in the new Germany, *Die Buchhändlerin* looks back on life in the GDR in highly critical terms, whilst the narrative affirms in particular the values of West German capitalism. Amongst the more disturbing aspects of the text, moreover, is its invitation to the reader to draw parallels between the former GDR and National Socialism.

Irene Böhme was born in Thuringia in 1933 and worked as a theatre critic, journalist and dramatist in Leipzig and East Berlin. She left the GDR for West Germany in 1980, having experienced profound disillusionment with socialism after the Biermann affair, whose repressive aftermath had crushed all hope of continuing her creative work in the GDR.[12] In West Germany, she worked as a dramatist and also as a journalist for the *Süddeutsche Zeitung*. Böhme first made a name for herself in the West with *Die da drüben. Sieben Kapitel DDR* (1983),[13] a collection of essays that shed light on central aspects of life in the GDR such as Party politics, national identity and women in GDR socialism. At a time when Germany's division seemed to have become a lasting reality and when East and West Germans' identities and experiences had moved significantly apart, these essays aimed to facilitate understanding between citizens on either side of the common German border by highlighting their differences rather than their commonalities.[14] Although light-hearted and at times ironic in tone, Böhme's message to 'Bundi[s]' and 'Zoni[s]'[15] was a serious one, namely that repressing the realities of the impact of three and a half decades of division would essentially breed resentment and misunderstanding, and that acknowledging '[d]as Eigene und das Fremde'[16] as different rather than right or wrong would be the first step towards an appreciation of each other's strengths and weaknesses. In the early 1980s, then, Böhme takes no sides in the battle for socio-political, economic or cultural supremacy between East and West Germany, but stresses rather that both have their respective *raisons d'être* in post-war Europe.

With *Die Buchhändlerin*, her debut as a novelist, Böhme revisits some of the topics she broached in the volume of essays, and she pursues in particular her interest in the experiences of successive generations of women in socialist Germany. We can only speculate about her motivation to produce this novel at the end of the millennium, but it is not unreasonable to assume that a personal desire to take stock after the demise of GDR socialism and a wish to bear witness as a member of a generation that experienced the ruptures in Germany's history at first hand will have played a role.[17] As the wealth of autobiographical and autobiographically-based material that has emanated from the former GDR since the early 1990s has demonstrated, Irene Böhme is by no means the only member of her generation who has been prompted to do so.[18] According to the categories identified by Karen Leeder, Böhme's novel may be located within the 'second wave' of literary material to have been produced by women writers and intellectuals from the former East Germany. This writing, Leeder believes, has its roots in the documentary 'Verständigungsliteratur' of the sixties and seventies and is written above all with the dual purpose of having a therapeutic function for the authors concerned on the one hand and of intending to '[…] bring information to the public realm, information about lives often unsanctioned, or even unsuspected, in the dominant cultural domain'.[19] Much of this literature, according to Leeder, aims to make the lives of ordinary women visible and thereby to highlight their importance. *Die Buchhändlerin* tells the story of the lives of two such ordinary women and of people around them whose experiences are shaped not by big historical events but rather by the pressures and necessities of everyday existence and survival.

Die Buchhändlerin is the double fictionalised biography of two women of successive generations, both of them strong female figures who fight for survival and independence, although they do so with different means and very different objectives in mind. Gil (Gisela) was born at the turn of the century and educated at a prestigious Munich lyceum, after which she succeeded in taking her *Abitur* as the only girl among 18 boys in her class (BH, p. 51). Raised in materially-privileged conditions and profoundly shaped by middle-class values such as independence, loyalty, hard work and personal integrity, she takes over a bookshop in her native provincial town bequeathed to her by her doting father after his untimely death. Forced by a womanising and self-seeking husband to fend for herself as a woman in a man's world, she devotes all her energies to keeping her business afloat, defending it first against the clutches of the Nazis and later against the grasp of East Germany's socialist regime under the leadership of Walter Ulbricht. Deeply at odds with socialist ideals and the Party's measures to abolish privately-owned enterprises during the early years of the construction of socialism and a planned economy, Gil is increasingly torn between her devotion to her business and her personal legacy on the one hand and the temptation to leave for the West on the other. Having sent her only son to live with relatives in the West during the early 1950s, Gil eventually loses all hope of keeping her business alive and escapes, hidden in the boot of a car, to West Germany just after the construction of the Berlin Wall. Tragically, she suffers a fatal heart attack during the journey and never reaches the West alive.

Sigrid, born in 1932 and thus close in age to the author herself, has been raised by a single mother who, like Gil, stems from a bourgeois background but is forced, without any property to fall back on, to work all hours in order to keep herself and her two children alive. Owing to her mother's ambitions for her younger brother to succeed professionally, Sigrid has to sacrifice her wish to become a journalist and leaves school 'unehrenhaft' (BH, p. 17) with a profound sense of failure as the only person in her class not to take her *Abitur*. Resenting the demands made on her by her mother who leaves not only all daily household chores to her but also expects her to take primary responsibility for the care of her younger brother, Sigrid feels socially excluded from an early age and deeply envies those amongst her peers who enjoy a privileged middle-class life because of their parents' position and status within provincial circles. Forced by her mother to take up an apprenticeship in the 'Landmannsche Buchhandlung' owned by Gisela, Sigrid soon feels thoroughly disillusioned with the middle-class values imparted to her by her mother and learns that the secret to success in the new socialist order is to be found not in hard work and a principled existence, but in adaptability and a willingness to pay lip-service to the ideological convictions espoused by functionaries within the rank and file of the

Socialist Unity Party. Having provided initial proof of her leadership qualities in the local branch of the Party's youth association, the FDJ, Sigrid soon finds professional opportunities opening up for her within the state-owned sector of the GDR's book trade and eventually moves on to become a leading cultural functionary in the GDR's capital, East Berlin. Like Gisela, she has an opportunity at one stage to leave for the West but decides to remain in the GDR not out of inner conviction to the socialist cause, but because of her personal attachment to a young man of middle-class background who, not dissimilar to the bourgeois Gisela, is determined to keep his father's privately owned 'Handwerksbetrieb' afloat against growing odds.

Around these central stories, Irene Böhme's novel sketches the lives of many other people forced during the turbulent years between the end of fascism and the construction of the Berlin Wall to make a fresh start and to decide whether to opt for the capitalist West Germany or to adapt to the demands of the new communist 'Herren' in their native Thuringia. However, this amounts to little more than a waxworks of superficially drawn figures who fall into the easily identifiable bipolar categories of respectable representatives from the middle classes who mostly decide to leave on the one hand and those who, out of weakness of character or sheer opportunism, embrace the opportunities offered them in the new socialist order to earn a decent living or to advance to social positions of status by turning into well-functioning 'Mitläufer' on the other. The only characters to stand out in this respect are the lovingly drawn male figures closest to the two female protagonists, namely Gisela's husband, Herbert Dietrich, and Sigrid's lover, Karl Wiese. The former is a 'Lebenskünstler' and *bon viveur* of the highest order who rivals the rogue Rhett Butler from *Gone with the Wind* when it comes to making personal capital out of any socio-political situation, be this Hitler's war or East Germany under Soviet occupation.[20] Although Karl is likely to appeal to (some) women readers' romantic imagination, as being morally more principled, he is as stubborn in his refusal to support any ideology other than his personal belief in the supremacy of individual freedom and independence at all times. Even though both Herbert and Karl fail in the private sphere of home and marriage to offer the emotional support, reliability and constancy desired by their respective partners, they seem to more than compensate for their failings by providing by far the single most important source of personal happiness, romantic love and sexual fulfilment for them. The qualities they display in the social domain, where they refuse to conform to social pressure or bow to any authority other than their own, furthermore, is clearly designed to endear them to their readers and to invite identification.

While the novel does contain information that permits the experiences portrayed to be located historically, it leaves it entirely to the reader to fit the pieces of the mosaic together into a reconstruction of the wider historical context. This approach of constructing history 'from below', which places the importance of individual memory and of the personal dimension of history above its collective aspects, has gained popularity in dominant discourses in unified Germany during the 1990s. As Helmut Peitsch has pointed out, it is also the approach favoured by leading politicians in the new Germany who have, since the mid-1990s, expressed a clear preference for historical understanding to be transmitted to future generations within the personal realm rather than through institutionalised historiography.[21] Even though, as my discussion below illustrates, this method is clearly one that has found favour also with Böhme's critics in the cultural press, it is by no means unproblematic. As Mary Fulbrook has argued, it runs the risk not only of ignoring or trivialising the larger historical questions, but also of obscuring the fact that (re)constructions of the past are never value-neutral, but are based on an author's particular agenda, and this is a political one.[22] In this regard it is not without significance that, in contrast to *Die da drüben*, where social analysis focused on the working classes, Böhme's novel is set in the world of the provincial East German bourgeoisie, and it charts the struggle for self-assertion and economic survival of private enterprise in the face of growing state control and Party hegemony. Even though this emphasis may have been motivated by autobiographical impulses – the author herself trained in her father's book shop in her native Bernburg – it is not without political significance if one considers the novel's publication at a time when the impact of profound socio-political and economic transformation produced wide-spread disillusionment with the capitalist market economy amongst East German citizens, along with significant nostalgia for the relative certainties enjoyed within the socialist market economy. It may consequently not be entirely unjustified to surmise that the author's intentions go beyond a desire to take personal stock or to bear witness. As Jürgen Schutte has pointed out, 'Ein Autor stellt einen Ausschnitt der Wirklichkeit in einer spezifischen Form dar, um in einer bestimmten historisch-gesellschaftlichen Situation eine konkrete Wirkung zu erzielen'.[23]

Irene Böhme's novel was praised by Andreas Nentwich in *Die Zeit* as a 'Modell[...] von "Wahrheit"', and as a 'bedeutende literarische Leistung' which, together with the autobiographically informed debuts of Caritas Führer and Irene Ruttmann,[24] should be considered as the 'uneitelsten und wahrhaftigsten Kapitel [...] jenes deutsch-deutschen Romans, nach dem das Geschrei nicht verstummt'. Characterised by 'nuancierte Schlichtheit und helle Vernunft', he thought it 'bemerkens-wert [...], ja erstaunlich'.[25] On a similar note, it was described in the *Süddeutsche Zeitung* as 'nicht der geforderte DDR-Roman, aber ein Anfang davon' and as a successful novel that would appeal to East and West German readers alike.[26] The *Berliner Morgenpost* described Irene Böhme's literary debut as the 'Roman einer Epoche [...], eine bittere [...], nie jedoch verbitterte [...] Abrechnung mit all jenen Ideologien, die vorgeben, das Glück auf Erden zu schaffen'.[27] For Thomas Wirtz, of the *Frankfurter Allgemeine Zeitung*, the novel constitutes 'ein Ereignis', which juxtaposes 'Chronik und Bildungsroman, Jahresliste und Charakterwandlung so [...], dass die große Geschichte und das kleine Leben sich erklären'. His unconcealed admiration, furthermore, was based on Böhme's choice of genre, namely on her decision to use the 'totgesagte und wiedergängigste Gattung, weil sie auch eine politische ist. Denn der Bildungsroman ist die bürgerliche Gattung schlechthin, die Erfindung von Individualität mit gesellschaftlichen Mitteln'. According to Wirtz, this is 'zugleich auch die Form ihres Widerstandes gegen den sozialistischen Einheitsbetrieb'.[28] In terms of her literary accomplishment, Böhme was compared by her critics to authors of note such as Horvath, Fleißer, Härtling, Kempowski, and Reimann.[29]

These highly appreciative extracts reveal much about the expectations brought by the German *feuilleton* to literary texts in the late 1990s. What reviewers value is not aesthetic innovativeness, complexity of form or literary imagination but rather the author's intention to tell the truth about life in the GDR in an accessible literary form and with a political message that reflects dominant trends in the new Germany's public discourses of subjecting to critical scrutiny the history of the former GDR whilst leaving West Germany's past after 1945 intact as reflecting the 'right' side of the double German past. The fact that Irene Böhme has produced a rather conventional developmental novel, which, after all, was the very form favoured by socialist realist doctrine in the former GDR, has been regarded not as a reflection of her possible limitations as an author unfamiliar with the more experimental approaches to the novel, but as a politically significant decision to reclaim this genre for bourgeois Western culture. The novel's clear weaknesses, such as the fact that the two central story lines which, though alternating the narrative perspective between chapters, have not been interwoven to any significant degree, with the lives of the two protagonists crossing only briefly in two of the nine chapters, have been ignored. Significantly, the novel's central protagonist, Gisela, is designed to invite the reader's admiration as a rather idealised figure who offers stern resistance to the creation of socialism in East Germany, whereas she was what can only be described as a silent bystander during Hitler's rule of terror. Gisela's only flaw, it seems, is that her 'linkes Auge schielt' (BH, p. 49). Throughout the narrative, neighbouring West Germany looms large as a positive alternative to developments in the East. Gisela's negative counterpart, the younger Sigrid, furthermore, is seen to embrace socialism not out of inner conviction or conversion to the cause, but because of weakness of character and a willingness to conform in order to fulfil her personal ambitions and find a sense of belonging. It appears that Irene Böhme has set out with her first novel to 'right', retrospectively, some of the 'wrongs' done by party politics and cultural functionaries in the GDR during its founding years. Not only does she seek to reclaim the developmental novel from socialist realist doctrine and reinstate it as a political instrument within post-unification German culture, but she appears also to wish to restore to the socio-cultural history of the former GDR central values and ideals of bourgeois culture such as personal freedom, individuality and romantic love. In some respects, Irene Böhme has reversed socialist realist principles, with idealised figures from the middle classes having replaced the idealised socialist personalities, and with the majority of people now lacking essential values of bourgeois society that would place them in a position to offer resistance to the (communist) 'class enemy'. What the appreciation of the novel as a politically significant work by critics such as Wirtz suggests, then, is that the positions adopted by critics in the cultural press during the now infamous *Literaturstreit* of the early 1990s, with its demands for an uncoupling of the concerns of literature from those of politics, were reversed by the end of the decade when literature once again came to be seen as playing a role in the context of identity construction in the united Germany.

Irene Böhme clearly has the interests of women very much at heart, and her novel seeks to foster understanding between different generations of women. *Die Buchhändlerin* contrasts in particular the experiences of the generation socialised before the rise of Hitler with those of the successor generation, that is with women still in their formative childhood years when Hitler came to power. Women like Gisela and her friend Elli Köbbel, a woman evacuated from the city towards the end of the War and assigned to Gisela's household, have acquired solid values as well as a strong sense of self, and during the absence of their husbands in the War they are able to put both to good effect, fending for themselves and standing their ground as independent women who will not be defeated by adverse circumstances. Even though Gisela offers no heroic resistance to the Nazis, she does display considerable courage when she hides an elderly Jewish couple in her house to protect them from deportation (BH, pp. 74-75). Compared to male characters like her brother Carl, who joins the Nazi Party and turns into a fervent supporter of Hitler's war against 'die Judenbrut' (BH, p. 67), and in contradistinction to her husband, who brings home the spoils of war from Eastern Europe without showing any moral reservations ('Die Polen wissen ja ihre Schätze nicht zu schätzen', BH, p. 70), women like Gisela seem rather innocently caught up in circumstances not of their own making, and they appear to be responding merely to the necessities of survival. A time when women like Gisela and Elli really come into their own, furthermore, are the 'rechtsfreie Tage' (BH, p. 87) between the end of Hitler and the arrival of Soviet occupation forces. Without a man-made repressive patriarchal system to curb their true potential and independence of spirit, Gisela and Elli Köbbel experience during this period a rare taste of genuine freedom, and their great initiative and personal bravery illustrates just what women might be capable of if left to their own devices. Whether they succeed in keeping Gisela's business alive by founding a 'Leihbibliothek' (BH, p. 78), whether they valiantly defend house and home against German soldiers who, at the end of the War, are still willing to put ordinary people's lives at risk for the sake of what has become a lost cause (BH, p. 82), or whether they ensure their own and their children's survival by going on foraging trips to local farms (BH, p. 79), Gisela and Elli clearly make a team infinitely stronger and more reliable than their respective marriages ever were, and their 'adventures' are clearly designed to communicate to younger generations of readers that these are women of substance who are a force to be reckoned with. Contrasted in the novel with young women of Sigrid's generation, who lack the strength of character and resoluteness of their mothers when they conform rather comfortably during the founding years of GDR socialism, these women are exemplary figures designed to inspire a female readership.   However, the perspective adopted by the author strongly suggests that women of this generation were victims of National Socialism, who were not responsible for its horrors and who might consequently be exonerated.   About their role as co-perpetrators the novel remains conspicuously silent, and the fact that Gisela is willing to turn a blind eye when it suits her, as when she does not protest about the fact that her father acquired the 'Landmannsche Buchhandlung', owned by a Jewish family since 1895, for a moderate sum of money in 1934 (BH, p. 56), when she has a pair of leather boots made to measure by the inmates of a local concentration camp (BH, p. 71), or when she decides not to ask any questions about the disappearance of the Jewish couple or their fate (BH, p. 76), 'was ich nicht weiß, kann ich nicht ausplaudern' (BH, p. 76) seems virtually to pale into insignificance in comparison to the positive qualities that characterise her at all other times. There is also the implicit suggestion here that women in Germany today should model themselves on the values espoused by women of this generation, a perspective that rather comfortably reaches back to the 'good old days' before Hitler came to power, overlooking the far more complex role these women played in the rise of fascism.

The explicit depiction of female sexuality in *Die Buchhändlerin* might be considered to be amongst the novel's stronger and more radical aspects.   The author is clearly aiming to break social taboos in order to overcome the silence that for so long characterised the relationship between different generations of women.   As one female character in the novel puts it, 'Wir Mädchen wissen viel zuwenig, zuviel wird uns verheimlicht. Wir bleiben einsam' (BH, p. 16).   Gisela, although no prude, had enjoyed sex prior to her marriage to Herbert Dietrich 'als Freundschaftsdienst, als prickelnden Zeitvertreib' (BH, p. 58), and enters a new dimension with Herbert Dietrich who 'kontrolliert sie, spielt mit ihrer ansteigenden Lust, läßt ihren Atem stocken, läßt sie wimmern wie eine junge Katze, hört nicht auf, zu fingern und zu stoßen, obwohl sie erschlafft ist' (BH, p. 58).   In fact, Irene Böhme tells readers of a younger generation more about the sexual experiences of their grandmothers than the latter are likely to have disclosed to them in conversation. Gisela and Elli, for instance, enjoy a 'liebestolle Nacht im Januar 1945 in der Scheune mit zwei kriegsgefangenen Bretagniern' (BH, p. 90), and also know how to give themselves pleasure, 'Ihr Schoss wird warm und naß. Sie nimmt sein Kopfkissen, klemmt es sich zwischen die Schenkel und reitet sich ins Land der Träume' (BH, p. 169).   Her novel depicts the experiences of women of her own generation even more explicitly, as Sigrid's success at deflowering herself after her first boyfriend, who 'kriegt[e] ihn nicht rein' (BH, p. 108), failed to do so, illustrates:

> Nach dem Bad liegt Sigrid im Bett und befühlt ihre aufgeweichte Haut. Sie will mit dem Finger das Loch finden, das Christian verfehlte. […] Der Zeigefinger rutscht tief hinein […]. Sie nimmt den Mittelfinger hinzu, bohrt beide hinein, preßt die Innenhand ans Schambein und ruckelt tiefer, so gut sie es vermag. […] schleicht in die Küche, holt eine Haushaltskerze aus der Schublade, schleicht zurück ins Bett. Die Kerze schiebt sie so tief zwischen ihre Beine, wie sie es aushalten kann. (BH, p. 112)

Irene Böhme also dispels the myth that unwanted pregnancy and abortion are topical issues only for modern readers, imparting knowledge of the home-spun recipes of older women such as 'Großmutter Zettel' whose solution is 'Einen Stift aus Kernseife tief in die Gebärmutter schieben, wenn du mal Pech hast, und nicht gleich zur Engelmacherin rennen' (BH, p. 39), as well as revealing the gruesome details of backstreet abortions that were often the only way for women of her own generation to avoid marrying a man they did not love (BH, p. 138). Without doubt, Irene Böhme, aged sixty-six at the time the novel appeared, deserves some acknowledgement for the candour of her portrayal of women's issues and for her commitment to fostering understanding between generations of women. However, the novel does also suggest that women in the GDR had fewer choices with regard to terminating an unwanted pregnancy safely than was the case for women in the West, a factor underlined by Sigrid choosing to travel to West Berlin for her second abortion (BH, p. 221). Böhme's outspokenness about such issues, furthermore, does not in itself guarantee the literary quality of her novel, and the quotations above substantiate rather than contradict this observation. Finally, the author seems to have underestimated the degree to which feminism, the women's movement and women's writing have, since the mid-1970s, voiced these issues and brought them to public attention. The fact that the sexual partners of the central protagonists are cast in a negative light that suggests they are driven by sexual desire and carnal longing alone, the beast that destroys women's paradise, so to speak, 'Das Paradies hat eine Schlange, und die steckt in Christians Hose' (BH, p. 143), makes the author guilty of crude stereotyping and of providing a perspective on gender relations that lags somewhat behind the far more differentiated understanding politically aware women readers in united Germany are likely to bring to her narrative. What I would suggest, then, is that Irene Böhme's novel in this respect would probably have been regarded as radical by the yardsticks of cultural functionaries in the former GDR who ruthlessly suppressed any discussion of sexuality in literary texts, and it may well appeal also to the tastes of publishers in the new German literary market place who rate it for its sensationalist potential. As a contribution to women's understanding of their different histories in East and West Germany, however, it has limitations, above all because readers learn little about the problems experienced in this respect by women in West Germany. It is also worth noting that Irene Böhme's novel leaves unexplored topical issues of a more explosive nature to women in Germany today, such as the issue of rape of women during the War by the soldiers of the Red Army. Even though she alludes to this when a 'Flüchtlingsfrau' from Gablonz reflects, 'Ich wußte nicht, daß der Mann beim Geschlechtsverkehr einen weißen Schleim absondert [...]' (BH, p. 14), she otherwise remains silent about this subject. As recent studies have shown, however, rape was a serious problem for women everywhere in Germany, including the author's native Thuringia, 'Even in those areas initially occupied by the American and British troops and turned over to the Soviets in late June and early July 1945 [...]'.[30]

The arrival of the Red Army in provincial Thuringia is depicted in *Die Buchhändlerin* in terms that clearly suggest this to be the dawning of a disastrous era for East German citizens. The novel remains faithful to historical fact when it depicts the jubilant greeting of Soviet soldiers by local townsfolk:

> Erstaunlich viele Fahnen mit Hammer, Sichel und Sowjetstern. [...] Über den Straßen, von Fenster zu Fenster gezogen, breite Spruchbänder: "Wir begrüßen die Rote Armee". (BH, p. 91)

Yet Elli Köbbel, a character the reader has by now been prompted to admire, bursts into tears at this sight and, shouting out 'Verräter! Verräter! Verräter!' (BH, p. 91), she embodies resistance to such misguided action. On a similar note, Gisela demonstratively wears her finest clothes, 'den Silberfuchs überm dunkelblauen Kostüm' (BH, p. 93) during a first family outing after the Russian forces have taken control, reasoning that 'an so einem Tag will sie Flagge zeigen' (BH, p. 93). Occupation by American troops prior to this, by contrast, seems to have been an infinitely more amicable experience for Gisela and her household. Not only does the son of the Jewish Landmann family who were so cruelly driven out of

Germany by Nazi terror, return as a GI who bears no grudges against
Gisela or indeed any Germans, but he immediately feels at home and turns
into a friend of the family (BH, p. 85). 'Leopold Landmann junior'
happily rides his old bicycle in Gil's courtyard,

> Fröhliches Gejohle klingt herein. Der Amerikaner jokelt mit dem alten
> Herrenfahrrad aus der Remise auf dem Hof herum. Eng an seine Brust gelehnt
> sitzt auf der Querstange Karlchen, auf dem Gepäckträger, die Arme um seine
> Hüften geschlungen, Hansi. (BH, p. 85)

This symbolises reconciliation and friendship and suggests that Americans
and Germans, in spite of the highly problematic past, have the potential to
build a peaceful and friendly future. This, I would suggest, not only
leaves issues of responsibility for the past entirely unexplored, but it also
rather dangerously trivialises the suffering of countless Jewish families in
Germany during Hitler's reign of terror.

One of the more disturbing aspects of *Die Buchhändlerin* are the
parallels it invites between National Socialism and East Germany under
Soviet Occupation. Sigrid's transition from Hitler youth associations to
the FDJ, for instance, is portrayed as seamless: 'Der Gott heißt jetzt Stalin,
der Führer heißt Arbeiterklasse, der Glaube heißt wissenschaftliche
Weltanschauung' (BH, p. 186); and the slogans designed to secure young
people's commitment to socialist ideology appear to have remained
unchanged as well,

> „Und setzet ihr nicht das Leben ein, nie soll euch das Leben gewonnen sein.‟
> Sie sagt es laut und deutlich, wie früher als Sprecherin der Hitlerjugend-
> Spielschar. (BH, p. 46)

Gisela comes to similar conclusions when she thinks of Walter Ulbricht as
'[den] neue[n] Führer mit dem Spitzbart' (BH, p. 145). The parallels
between the GDR and Nazi Germany as totalitarian systems are drawn
even more explicitly when 'Notar Maiwald' explains his decision to leave
for West Germany:

> Auch im Sowjetparadies sind die Menschen nicht mehr gleich. Vor Gericht
> gewiß nicht. Da waltet die Abstammungslehre. Was früher für Juden galt, gilt
> heute für Studierte, Handwerker, Geschäftsleute, alles Bourgeois, alle
> freigegeben zum Untergang. (BH, p. 151)

Even though his extreme viewpoint, which claims for the bourgeoisie in
GDR socialism a victim status as significant as the suffering of the Jewish

people in Nazi Germany, cannot be attributed unreservedly to the author herself, Maiwald is a character who has been built up in the novel as a highly respectable person whose behaviour under the Nazis has earned him the reader's respect (BH, p. 75). The fact, furthermore, that he is described as 'Kein Schwarzseher, ein aufmerksamer Beobachter' (BH, p. 152), lends further support to the suggestion that this is a man of integrity whose viewpoint is not to be dismissed out of hand. Without a reflective authorial voice that places it in a clear moral perspective, this position invites an equation of the GDR with National Socialism both morally and politically. In West Germany, by contrast, right-wing thought is shown not to be given a chance to take root again. When representatives of a nationalist organisation display their reading matter at a book fair in West Berlin, for example, citizens immediately take action and, in a concerted effort described as 'angewandte Demokratie' (BH, p. 241), throw them out. The contrast made between East and West Germany in *Die Buchhändlerin* in this respect is clearly not merely crass, it is also highly problematic in the context of united Germany's memory and identity politics. As Bill Niven has explained, such perspectives not only trivialise National Socialist history, but also serve to attribute the lion's share of Germany's responsibility for the atrocities committed under Nazi rule to East Germany, thereby fulfilling an exculpatory function for West Germans. As Niven has argued, the function of such a move is to discourage any re-emergence of socialist thinking in the new Germany and to furnish a basis for a 'renationalization' of German identity in the 1990s.[31]

To conclude, then, it is evident that Irene Böhme's perspective on the former GDR has undergone a significant shift since the early 1980s. Whereas her volume of essays had emphasised the differences between the two Germanies without attaching moral judgements or apportioning blame, her novel of the late 1990s draws distinctions between the two societies that are by no means value-neutral. In contrast to West Germany, where the spirit of democracy is shown to have flourished from the outset, East Germany is portrayed as a continuation of National Socialism under totalitarian communist rule. Citizens from the middle classes who were determined to defend their rights to self-determination and individual freedom are cast in an idealised light that makes them appear to be resistance figures that invite positive identification, whilst the majority of citizens are seen to conform as 'Mitläufer' who fall back on behaviour patterns learned in Hitler's Germany. The author assumes a

perspective of bipolarity on complex issues such as class, gender, identity
and history that encourages the reader to judge characters and events in
terms of 'right' and 'wrong' rather than provoking more complex
questions that might challenge assumptions and promote critical
examination of the past by all German citizens. By portraying history
'from below' without providing an authorial moral voice that places
character's experiences into a wider socio-political and historical context,
the author has not only trivialised important historical questions but also
obscured the fact that her novel clearly pursues a political agenda. This,
as I have demonstrated, is one that is based on Irene Böhme's experiences
of West German society and her own identity as a citizen who has
'overcome' her East German background. Retrospectively, it seems, the
author is now justifying her decision to leave the GDR in 1980, and she
appears to invite her East German readers to critically question their
history, without engaging herself in the task of
'Vergangenheitsbewältigung' in any complex or self-critical manner. The
fact that *Die Buchhändlerin* enjoyed such a positive reception in the new
Germany's *feuilleton*, furthermore, confirms that Irene Böhme's novel
affirms dominant conservative thinking that it is no longer the National
Socialist past that needs to be critically examined by all Germans, or West
Germany's recent past that needs to be subjected to critical scrutiny by
West Germans, but rather that it is exclusively East German history which
now needs to be 'overcome' in order for Germany, finally, to achieve
'normality'.

Notes

[1] John Gillis, 'Memory and Identity: The History of a Relationship', in: John Gillis,
ed., *Commemorations: The Politics of National Identity*, Princeton University Press:
Princeton, New Jersey, 1994, p. 3.

[2] See, for instance, Lutz Niethammer, 'The German *Sonderweg* After Unification', in:
Reinhard Alter and Peter Monteath, eds, *Rewriting the German Past. History and
Identity in the New Germany*, Humanities Press: New Jersey, 1997, pp. 129-151, (here:
p. 129), or Ulrike Meinhof, ed., *Living with Borders. Identity Discourses on East-West
Borders in Europe*, Ashgate: Aldershot, 2000, p. 15.

[3] See Bill Niven, *Facing the Nazi Past. United Germany and the Legacy of the Third
Reich*, Routledge: London and New York, 2002, p. 3.

[4] See, for instance, Frauke Meyer-Gosau, 'Outing to *Jurassic Park:* "Germany" in
Post-Wall Literature. An Essay against Tiredness', in: Jost Hermand and Marc

Silberman, eds, *Contentious Memories. Looking Back at the GDR*, Peter Lang: New York, Washington, 1998, pp. 223-246; Helmut Peitsch, Charles Burdett, and Claire Gorrora, eds, *European Memories of The Second World War*, Berghahn: New York and Oxford, 1999, p. xvii; Siobhan Kattago, *Ambiguous Memory. The Nazi Past and German National Identity*, Praeger: Westport, 2001, p. 11.

[5] See Niven, *Facing the Nazi Past*, p. 5.

[6] Examinations of debates relating to identity and memory politics in the new Germany may be found in Niven, *Facing the Nazi Past*; also in Mary Fulbrook and Martin Swales, eds, *Representing the German Nation. History and Identity in Twentieth-Century Germany*, Manchester University Press: Manchester and New York, 2000; Mary Fulbrook, *German National Identity after the Holocaust*, Polity: Cambridge, 1999; Jane Kramer, *The Politics of Memory: Looking for Germany in the New Germany*, Random House: New York, 1996.

[7] Stefan Neuhaus, *Literatur und nationale Einheit in Deutschland*, Franke: Tübingen and Basle, 2002, p. 15.

[8] Dennis Tate, 'The End of Autobiography? The older generation of East German authors take stock', in: Martin Kane, ed., *Legacies and Identity. East and West German Literary Responses to Unification*, Peter Lang: Oxford, Bern, Berlin, 2002, pp. 11-26, (here: p. 21).

[9] Irene Böhme, *Die Buchhändlerin*, Rowohlt: Reinbek bei Hamburg, 1999. All quotations in the chapter from this text will be followed by page references preceded by the abbreviation BH in brackets.

[10] See Wolfgang Emmerich, *Kleine Literaturgeschichte der DDR*, extended new edition, Kiepenheuer & Witsch: Leipzig, 1996, esp. pp. 113 ff.

[11] *Berliner LeseZeichen*, 7+8/99, Luisenstadt, 1999, 1-2, (here: p. 1).

[12] See Emmerich, *Kleine Literaturgeschichte*, p. 257.

[13] Irene Böhme, *Die da drüben. Sieben Kapitel DDR*, Rotbuch: Berlin, 1982.

[14] Wolf Deinert, in *Die Zeit*, praised the volume for its balance of perspective and stressed that the author sought to inform rather than criticise the GDR, 'Kein Hass treibt die Autorin, sondern Nachdenklichkeit, Kopfschütteln, Mitteilungsbedürfnis und Witz.' *Die Zeit,* 13 and 25 March 1983, 13.

[15] *Die da drüben*, p. 10.

[16] Ibid., p. 16.

[17] Assmann and Frevert, for instance, have suggested that the 'Erinnerungsmarathon' German culture has experienced since the late 1980s is attributable to no small degree to a desire amongst the generation which has first-hand experiences of the past to bear witness at the end of the millennium. See Aleida Assmann and Ute Frevert, *Geschichtsvergessenheit. Geschichtsversessenheit. Vom Umgang mit deutschen Vergangenheiten nach 1945*, Deutsche Verlagsanstalt: Stuttgart, 1999, p. 10.

[18] See in particular the essays by Tate, 'The End of Autobiography?', and Karen Leeder, '"Vom Unbehagen in der Einheit": Autobiographical Writing by Women Since 1989', in: Mererid Puw Davies, Beth Linklater, and Gisela Shaw, eds, *Autobiography by Women in German*, Peter Lang: Bern, 2000, pp. 249-271.

[19] Leeder, 'Vom Unbehagen in der Einheit', p. 254.

[20] This allusion is made explicit in the text through Sigrid's idolisation of this figure as the father she never had. The irony implied by the author of *Die Buchhändlerin* when she suggests that the texts which really fuelled the imagination of young people like Sigrid were not the great classics of socialist realism, such as Ostrowski's *Wie der Stahl gehärtet wurde*, but rather the 'classics' of what would have epitomised Western bourgeois culture's decadence and triviality in the GDR at the time is not lost on the reader. However, the author's particularly crass choice of texts to contrast in this manner is telling. See BH, p. 136 and p. 198 respectively.

[21] See Helmut Peitsch et al., *European Memories of The Second World War*, p. xv.

[22] Mary Fulbrook, 'Verarbeitung und Reflexion der geteilten Vergangenheit seit 1989', in: Christoph Kleßmann, Hans Misselwitz, and Günter Wichert, eds, *Deutsche Vergangenheiten – eine gemeinsame Herausforderung. Der schwierige Umgang mit der doppelten Nachkriegsgeschichte*, Links: Berlin, 1999, pp. 286-298, (here: p. 296).

[23] Jürgen Schutte, *Einführung in die Literaturinterpretation*, third revised and extended edition, Metzler: Stuttgart and Weimar, 1993, p. 217.

[24] Caritas Führer, *Die Montagsangst*, Brockhaus: Wuppertal, 2001 (1998); Irene Ruttmann, *Das Ultimatum*, C. H. Beck: Munich, 2001.

[25] Andreas Nentwich, 'Genau sein, bis zum Schmerz', in: *Die Zeit,* 27-28 June 2001, 39.

[26] Konrad Franke, 'Rosinen in Spezi einlegen', in: *Süddeutsche Zeitung*, 99, 30 April/12 May 1999, iv.

[27] Hans-Georg Soldat, 'Lieben und Lachen in schwerer Zeit', in: *Berliner Morgenpost*, 21 March 1999, 25.

[28] Thomas Wirtz, 'Eine Dunkelkammer der Zufriedenheit', in: *Frankfurter Allgemeine Zeitung*, 14 August 1999, v.

[29] Nentwich, 'Genau sein, bis zum Schmerz', and Manfred Jendryschik, 'Unsere kleine Stadt', *Mitteldeutsche Zeitung*, 25 March 1999.

[30] Norman Naimark, *The Russians in Germany*, Belknap: Cambridge, Mass., 1995, pp. 69-140, (here: pp. 84-85).

[31] Niven, *Facing the Nazi Past*, p. 6.

Birgit Haas

Contemporary German Drama as Aesthetic Resistance against Right-wing Radicalism

Following the conservative turn in German politics after 1982, and the increase in right-wing violence after reunification in 1990, many playwrights expressed their concern through their writing. As a result, a wide range of plays addressed the problems of right-wing radicalism in various ways. Whilst the plays of the 1980s mainly focused on the memory of the Holocaust, presenting notorious Nazis and their victims on stage, the plays of the 1990s considered the rise of neo-Nazi crime in present-day Germany. Drawing on plays by George Tabori, Franz Xaver Kroetz, Rainald Goetz, Oliver Czeslik, Gundi Ellert, and John von Düffel, the essay discusses the ways in which the playwrights engage with the debate concerning the faces of fascism and xenophobia in Germany today.

Introduction

In the last two decades of the twentieth century, German dramatists approached right-wing radicalism and the rise of the Neo-Nazis in two different ways. In the 1980s, the flood of commemorations and anniversaries of the Holocaust and the Second World War prompted many playwrights to stage aspects of the Holocaust in order to remind the Germans of their fateful history. By contrast, the plays of the 1990s portrayed the shock of the escalation in violence on the streets following the right-wing riots in which several foreigners were brutally killed.

This essay will briefly consider the plays of the 1980s, focusing particularly on George Tabori's *Jubiläum*, a play which presents us with the viewpoint of a Jewish writer. The second part will give an overview of the plays of the 1990s, showing the wide range of different responses to the attempted marginalisation of those who were considered to be foreign and different.

The 1980s: Between Anniversaries and a Hard Place

The early eighties saw many plays which responded directly to the Nazi genocide by focusing either on notorious individual Nazis or else on the man on the street. These efforts were fuelled by a landslide-victory of the Christian Democrats in the parliamentary elections of 1983, an event which marked a conservative turn in German politics.[1] During a speech in Israel on 25 January 1984, Helmut Kohl employed the phrase the 'Gnade der späten Geburt', thereby absolving the younger generation from any responsibility for the Nazi past.[2] In the *Express*, Alfred Dregger maintained that Germany should finally emerge from the shadow of Hitler and Auschwitz,[3] and according to Franz Josef Strauß, the Germans should practise the 'aufrechte Gang'.[4] Conservative politicians such as Alfred Schikel generally aimed to decriminalise the German past:

> Statt sich mit der Vergangenheit auseinanderzusetzen und die streckenweise kriminalisierte deutsche Geschichte unbefangen aufzuarbeiten, um das eigene geschichtliche Herkommen zu klären, demonstriert man für den Umweltschutz, besetzt Häuser oder protestiert in sogenannten Friedensmärschen gegen die Politik der Regierung. [...] Es wird daher mannigfaltiger Anstrengungen unserer Historiker, Pädagogen und Politiker bedürfen, um den Deutschen wieder einen natürlichen und unbefangenen Zugang zu Geschichte, Staat und Vaterland zu ermöglichen.[5]

Since the 1980s, playwrights have not only produced collages of material dealing with German mass murder, they have also tackled this sensitive and traumatic period of recent German history in order to counteract the common tendency to gloss over the Nazi past. Intellectuals have taken a critical stance towards the popularity of right-wing radicalism and violence. Once again, their aim is to dismantle the myths of the neo-Nazis in order to show how their falsified historiography distorts history and offends its victims.[6] In opposition to the revisionists, who try to belittle the Holocaust and even deny that it ever happened,[7] thus indirectly justifying right-wing violence, playwrights such as Heinar Kipphardt, George Tabori, Thomas Strittmatter, and Volker Ludwig address the multi-faceted Nazi crimes from a variety of angles. Heinar Kipphardt's play *Bruder Eichmann* (1982/83) focuses on the Eichmann trial in Israel in 1961, yet from a perspective which contrasts it with contemporary fascist tendencies.[8] Tabori's farce *Mein Kampf* (1987) presents us with a fictional encounter between the young Hitler and a Jew, Schlomo, in Vienna, during which the image of the politician Hitler is thoroughly deconstructed.[9] Thomas Strittmatter's *Viehjud Levi* (1982), written in the style of the new *Volkstheater*, tells the fate of a Jew in a small village after 1933.[10] The director of the *GRIPS-Theater*, Volker Ludwig, produced a pedagogical play for the young, a musical production of *Ab heute heißt du Sara* (1989),[11] which successfully adapted Inge Deutschkron's novel *Ich trug den gelben Stern*.

George Tabori's *Jubiläum* stands out, for it challenges the notions of good and evil. In 1983, while the official ceremonies, vigils, and inaugurations commemorating the 50th anniversary of Hitler's coming to power continued, Tabori's anti-jubilee focuses on the sad anniversaries of the 'days of death'. He believes that, to keep one's memory fresh, it is necessary to abandon dates, facts and figures:

> Im Theater ist die Wahrheit immer konkret, man kann keine kollektiven Substantive oder Abstraktionen 3. Grades spielen, auch wenn sie sich noch so hübsch auf dem Papier ausnehmen; da gibt es nur einen, diesen Faust, nur eine, diese Medea, nur den einen Du und Ich. Es war schon immer schwerer, einen Menschen zu töten als dreißigtausend.[12]

In Tabori's view, personal experience comes first, which is why we learn from the character Otto that he hanged himself after he was tortured in a clinic, that Helmut took an overdose of sleeping tablets, that Lotte drowns in a brown flood, symbolic of the rise of the Nazis, and that the disabled girl Mizzi put her head in a gas oven after she received a letter from Jürgen saying: 'Warum hat man vergessen, dich zu vergasen?'[13] At the end of the play, Tabori reminds us of the day of Arnold's father's death, when he was killed in Auschwitz:

> ARNOLD Der Schatten hinter ihm bin ich. Bald danach im November wurde er festgenommen. Alle hatten versucht, ihn zu retten. Er wollte nicht gerettet werden. Wer wird die anderen retten, sagte er. Eines Abends kamen ihn zwei Männer aus dem Chor besuchen. Kommen Sie, wir wollen sie verstecken. - Warum soll ich mich verstecken? sagte er. Ich habe nichts getan. - Cornelius, sagten sie, wenn man nichts getan hat, wird man auch nicht totgeschlagen. Er lachte und blieb. Selbst die Deutschen versuchten, ihn zu retten, zumindest einer von ihnen, ein hohes Tier, das seinen Parsifal zweimal gehört hatte. Er sagte zu seinen Häschern, einen Parsifal verhaftet man nicht. Aber als mein Vater dies hörte, zog er das Kostüm an, das er aus der Münchner Oper gestohlen hatte, und ging zur Gestapo. Und er sagte: Hier bin ich. Das war vor vierzig Jahren, noch ein Jubiläum. Die Zeit hat Sinn für Formen, die Zeit hat, wie die Musik, die höchste Form der Eleganz. [...] Seit vierzig Jahren warte ich auf seine wundersame Heimkehr [...]
> LOTTE Arnold, du spinnst, hör auf damit, du machst mich nervös.
> ARNOLD Ich spinne nicht. Du wirst schon sehen. Letzte Woche hab ich in der Zeitung gelesen, daß man in Auschwitz Brot gebacken hat und keine Väter.
> HELMUT Und solchen Dreck glaubst du?
> ARNOLD Dreck kann auch wahr sein. Es ist halt ein wahrer Dreck, die dreckige Wahrheit, aber ich bete jede Nacht, daß man nur Brot gebacken hat.[14]

Tabori picks up the cynical revisionist statement and gives it a different twist. For him, the 'what if?' expresses the wish for a better world, a world without the painful memories of his murdered father.

The 1990s: Solidarity with the Victims

The early 1990s witnessed right-wing extremist riots on such an unprecedented scale that violence became a real problem, particularly in east Germany.[15] As studies have shown, attacks in east and west rose from roughly 300 per month in 1990 to 961 in October 1991, and in September 1992 more than 1100 were registered. In June 1993 the number peaked at more than 1400 attacks.[16] 1995 saw the fiftieth anniversary of the capitulation of the Third Reich, which was remembered by vigils, inaugurations, speeches, and official ceremonies focusing on the Holocaust. Following Helmut Kohl's attempt to 'normalise' Germany by encouraging a new national identity,[17] however, many a debate was waged about whether or not German youth was still to be held responsible for the Nazi past.[18] Both intellectuals and writers agreed that the memory of Auschwitz and the concept of 'normalcy' could not be reconciled.[19] The new complacent attitude which hid behind the mythical smoke-screen of an 'anschwellender Bocksgesang'[20] was just as vehemently opposed in the media, in classrooms and courtrooms, and in the political field as containing hidden fascist undercurrents. In this essay, I would like to focus on Rainald Goetz's *Festung*, Oliver Czeslik's *Heilige Kühe*, Gundi Ellert's *Jagdzeit*, John von Düffel's *Solingen*, and Franz Xaver Kroetz's *Ich bin das Volk*, which reflect these trends.

Festung focuses on the German trauma of the Holocaust, for Goetz believes that memory is no longer taken seriously enough. *Festung* is thus a play about the problematic German repression of the Shoah, and the tendency to push the horrors of mass murder out of collective memory. In numerous short scenes which do not hang together as a conventional plot, but are grouped together according to the principle of postmodern pastiche, Goetz examines the relationship between memory and media culture.[21] In particular, he uncovers the mechanisms behind the desperate attempt to forget, while pretending to discuss the past. The language is abstract and often deliberately fragmented, disrupted and defective, a feature which is highlighted by the layout, the arrangement of words and the line breaks. It could therefore be described as a long poem voiced by a multitude of speakers. As a result of the 'Stimmenkonzentrat' (F, p. 157) philosophy and superficial phrases mix until language becomes meaningless and shallow.[22] True emotions and meaningful conversations drown in nonsensical media communications. Although the need for communication is constantly underlined, no real exchange of opinions, feelings or factual truths takes place. As the metaphor *Festung* suggests, the Germans lock themselves up in the neurotic fortress of their own world-view and are unable to approach history in an open-minded manner. In the play, the trauma is evident in different ways: in part one, the extreme horrors of extinction, the torturing and gassing of millions of victims is expressed through a defective language; in part two, communication deteriorates into small-talk on television; in part three, a old man soliloquises about history and death without even having anyone to talk to.

Festung could be described as a radical postmodernist experiment, in which people and names are largely missing; the location and setting are not given and the characters make reference to their situation in the theatre. Instead of addressing the theatre as a whole, the play focuses on the 'Rampe', which is a highly ambiguous German word, as it denotes both the 'fourth wall' of the stage and alludes to the selection ramp of the concentration camps.

As the deliberately defective language of part one underlines, the Holocaust is still beyond description, and it remains an unspeakable yet naked truth that everybody avoids talking about:

> SCHWESTER
> nicht auszu
> BRUDER
> Stille
> SCHWESTER
> zu verschw
> BRUDER
> und nichts zu
> SCHWESTER
> beschr (F, p. 50)

In this failed dialogue, the second parts of the verbs 'aussprechen', 'verschweigen' and 'beschreiben' are cut off, indicating that the characters are avoiding talking about the Holocaust in even the most basic of ways. Communication about extinction, or 'die klärende Ausspr', the frank conversation ('Aussprache') about the Nazi past, are literally impossible. Both the unfinished words and the missing nouns symbolise the inability to engage in true dialogue with the past, and thus the failure to create a collective memory.

In view of this, it is not surprising that reunification is described as 'die Geburt des deutschen Gaskammergeistes aus dem klassischen deutschen Ideal' (F, p. 148). Here, two famous quotations by Nietzsche and Goethe are intertwined and given a sinister twist. Tragedy does not emerge from a musical spirit (Nietzsche) and neither does humanism result from German idealism (Goethe). According to Goetz, contemporary German writing is influenced by a notorious hunger for power and hegemony. He is painfully aware of the disastrous effects that idealism, namely nationalism and military expansion, had on politics. Reunification is therefore regarded as an excuse for forgetting the Holocaust in order to justify nationalistic feelings. In Goetz's view, the November revolution of 1918, Hitler's failed putsch in Munich on 9 November 1923, the pogrom on 9 November 1938 ('Reichskristallnacht') and the fall of the Wall on 9 November 1989 all speak of a nationalistic continuity.[23]

Oliver Czeslik is one of few playwrights to tackle the problem of skinheads and Neo-Nazis in Germany. His realistic play, *Heilige Kühe*, tells of the misfortune of Karl Klementi, a Jew who is lured into a trap by the two neo-Nazis, Gero von Wilfenstein and his girl-friend Ulrike.[24] It was first published in April 1992, at a time when extreme right-wing violence had reached a worrying peak in anticipation of the anniversary of Hitler's birthday.[25] *Heilige Kühe* was premiered at the *Schaubühne Berlin* in April 1992, and made into a film by Uwe Janson one year later.

Under the pretext of providing him with insider information on the right-wing scene, Gero invites Karl, a well-known journalist and representative of the 1968 generation, to an abandoned slaughterhouse in a suburb of Berlin. Their meeting begins fairly harmlessly with a few takes of the video-camera, but Ulrike then secretly removes vital parts of Karl's car engine, thus forcing him to stay overnight. While he is asleep, Gero makes him a prisoner by securing a chain around his foot. Karl is to be put on trial and sentenced to death. In the days leading up to this, Karl is systematically tortured and humiliated, until his will is broken and he even begins to love his torturer. *Heilige Kühe* deliberately ignores political correctness, and the cruel treatment of Klementi is aimed at shaking the audience out of its complacency.[26]

In *Heilige Kühe*, the film medium plays an important role, as it not only reflects the artificial character of the meeting, but also implicitly criticises the search for evidence, for filmed proof of what is believed to be true. Czeslik's play explores the relationship between the film medium and the 'actors' on the one hand, and the interdependence between film and everyday violence on the other. In the first scene, the verity of Karl's feature film is questioned, for it transpires that he offered five thousand marks for the interview.[27] With what appears to be almost ridiculous pathos, the two skinheads rant about the violence committed by 'black boots' in the streets of Berlin, and talk about the idyllic atmosphere back home, where all the 'brothers in arms' live in peaceful harmony. Both clearly enjoy the presence of the camera, and as Ulrike yawns in a relaxed fashion and gets herself a beer while she indulges in a description of the 'Schnürstiefelidylle', a term which is not only paradoxical but also cynical.[28] This hints at the belief that journalism may actually have a notable knock-on effect, inspiring further violence. Indeed, some researchers even blame journalists for adding fuel to the fire, and according to recent studies, newspaper and television coverage of such crimes often encourages imitation.[29]

In the mock trial, in which Gero acts as the judge, he plays an associative language-game with Karl. For each mistake that he makes, he receives a broken finger, and finally a broken left arm.

> KARL Ich bin müde.
> GERO Und nenn mich Herr Richter
> KARL Ich bin müde, Herr Richter
> GERO Wir fangen jetzt an. Für jeden Fehler oder jede Falschaussage wird dir ein Finger gebrochen, dann die ganze Hand, der Arm, naja und so weiter ... *Gero gibt Ulli ein Zeichen, die Kamera auf Karl zu richten.* Also los: A!
> KARL A?
> ULLI *leise zu Karl* Etwas mit dem Anfangsbuchstaben A! Mach schon! Schnell!
> KARL A? Arschloch?
> GERO *gibt Ulli ein Zeichen, die Kamera auszustellen. Gero geht zu Karl, ergreift dessen Hand. Es wird dunkel.*
> ULLI *spricht ins Dunkel* der Ringfinger der linken Hand. (HK, p. 48)

Heilige Kühe depicts the taboo skinhead scene, in which the perpetrator's schizophrenic frame of mind is revealed while they play a perverted sadistic game with the Jew, Karl Klementi. Czeslik displays the psychological mechanisms driving Gero's behaviour, namely the urge of 'the nobody' to heighten his self-esteem through a game of military grandeur, in which reality is blotted out. During the course of the play, Gero's strong esoteric line of thinking becomes increasingly evident, until, at the end, he describes his own face as the complexion of a 'real satan' (HK, 49).[30] He obviously perceives himself to be an antichrist-figure who, like Hitler, intends to inflict pain on others, if only for the fulfilment of misguided sexual pleasure.

In Gundi Ellert's play *Jagdzeit*, we encounter a young Neo-Nazi who acts like the 'Führer'.[31] Like his real-life model, Hitler, Robert talks and behaves as if he were a messiah whose task it is to open other people's eyes to the greatness of the future.[32] His langage is littered with religious images which are contorted to fit a Darwinian world-view.[33] He therefore tells the group that they are the chosen ones, like Jesus's followers, who should brace themselves against hardship and humiliation. Instead of preaching a considerate social attitude, however, he suddenly turns around, and while lulling them to sleep, tells them that they are knights in a holy war against the evil in the world:

> ROBERT [...]
> Ich zeige euch den Weg
> Folgt mir getrost
> Ich führe euch
> Folgt mir
> Richtet eure gekrümmten Rücken auf
> Geht stolz und aufrecht
> Wir sind die Flamme die das Feuer entfacht (J, p. 36)

Like Hitler, he borrows phrases from the Bible and combines the apocalyptic threat with the promise of a better future. Finally, Robert secretly takes all the looted money and quietly disappears, abandoning the others. The small-town saviour thus shows his true colours. Examining Germany from below, the play offers valuable insight into the dangers of the right-wing potential, showing that neglect and lack of education may create a younger generation which is prone to right-wing extremism.

The drama touches on a variety of key issues which play a crucial role in the rise of neo-Nazism today, such as unemployment, lack of parental care, and broken family homes. It also points to the distressing fact that so-called minor offences, such as stealing and mugging, are played down, and that the majority of offenders do not face any charges at all. All in all, Ellert presents a rather pessimistic view, as the few kind-hearted characters do not survive; Vinzenz, the man who cannot silence his guilty conscience, and informs the fathers of their sons' crimes, slashes his wrists for fear of being 'slaughtered' by Jens, who is the butcher of the town. The sympathetic, yet slightly demented girl Kathi and the foreigner Sophie are buried alive in the bunker, as the others close the doors on them. Xenophobia, or simply violence, smoulders in a dull little town, a town that could be anywhere, with a typical set of characters that could be anybody.

In John von Düffel's *Solingen*, we are presented with two teachers who are always anxious to appear politically correct. This is particularly true of the older man, who is burnt out by the demands of administration, a fact which becomes evident in a scene where he marks essays, wondering whether he should reprimand a pupil for supporting nationalist ideas by quoting the notorious 'Horst-Wessel-Lied':

> LEHRER (*schaut auf*) Heißt es 'heute hört uns Deutschland' oder 'heute gehört uns Deutschland'
> REFERENDARIN Was
> LEHRER Hört oder gehört uns Deutschland
> REFERENDARIN Weder noch, ich meine, was liest du denn da
> LEHRER Klassenarbeiten
> REFERENDARIN Ja aber
> LEHRER 10a
> REFERENDARIN Aber das geht doch nicht
> [...]
> LEHRER Ich bin der Meinung, daß man derlei Gedankengut nicht von den Kindern fernhalten kann; es kommt darauf an, wie man damit umgeht, ob man es in ein richtiges historisches Bezugssystem setzt et cetera
> REFERENDARIN Und, was willst du an den Rand schreiben, Horst-Wessel-Lied, abgesungen von den Nazis, die sechs Millionen Juden vergast haben
> LEHRER Schatz, bitte, nicht emotional werden; wenn wir dem Jungen das Gefühl geben, er könne uns damit provozieren, dann bestärken wir ihn doch nur[34]

It is absurd that the teacher is so caught up in his academic thinking that he wonders whether the pupil has quoted the National Socialist song correctly, instead of being outraged that this has been used at all. As he is no longer fit or intellectually sharp enough to survive the day-to-day harassment of his pupils, he decides not to make a fuss. It is evident that his classes mainly serve the purpose of keeping the children off the streets, and that the possibility of frank discussion is stifled by his stranglehold.

As the example of the teacher shows, latent fascism is still present and tolerated in schools. It is therefore not surprising that neo-Nazi violence increases during the play, at the end of which the couple learns of a fatal arson attack which killed four members of a Turkish family in Solingen on 29 May 1993. However, the news practically becomes part of their bed-time routine, for, in the usual fashion, he comes to tell her about the latest news on television. Thus the arson attack is only casually mentioned, and her questions are silenced by his stale, pseudo-erotic mixture of quotations:

> REFERENDARIN: Daß so etwas heute passieren muß
> LEHRER Pst; denk ich an Deutschland in der Nacht, bin ich um den Schlaf gebracht.
> REFERENDARIN: (*reagiert nicht*)
> [...]
> LEHRER: Die Nacht schuf tausend Ungeheuer, doch frisch und fröhlich war mein Mut, in meinen Adern welches Feuer, in meinem Herzen welche Glut
> REFERENDARIN: Aua
> LEHRER: Halb zog sie ihn, halb sank er hin (S, pp. 85-6)

In this passage, the original meaning of the citations is distorted, such as Heinrich Heine's famous line 'Denk ich an Deutschland in der Nacht'. Heine's intention was, of course, not to stop worrying about Germany in order to enjoy a peaceful sleep, but rather to remain aware of the nationalist developments of the 19th century. Moreover, the teacher does not make a connection between the 'Ungeheuer' of the night and the right-wing radicals. Von Düffel thus presents us with an example of the dull German 'Michel', who was often mocked and ridiculed in the 19th century. The couple behaves in a similar way to the sleepy and brain-dead 'Michel', who was symbolic of the Germans' refusal to engage in political action at that time. Instead of being politically aware, they sleep with one another. Even those who are supposed to educate and enlighten children are not alert to the dangers of neo-Nazism. The play thus shows that in the long run, political indifference will lay waste to the human landscape.[35]

As Franz Xaver Kroetz points out in his introductory remarks to his play *Ich bin das Volk*, the main topics are xenophobia, neo-Nazis, misery and cowardice.[36] Playing on the famous slogan 'Wir sind das Volk', coined at the *Montagsdemonstration* in Leipzig in October 1989 which was later to become 'Wir sind *ein* Volk', thus calling for reunification, Kroetz links reunification to growing German nationalism. The play shows the various ways in which united Germany serves as an 'Ichmacher', a maker of an aggressive national identity (V, pp. 502, 516). Kroetz also explained this in an interview, yet some of his remarks were received with apprehension, for the playwright expressed his sympathy and understanding for fascist tendencies:

> Ich habe sehr viel Verständnis für soziale Verwerfungen und ich habe auch gerade deshalb sehr viel Verständnis dafür, daß Menschen in unserer Gesellschaft immer teilfaschistisch waren und bleiben werden.[37]

However, these controversial remarks, which could easily be misread, were qualified, for Kroetz repeatedly vented his anger with the conservative political climate:

> Aber das gesamte Klima, die Politiker, die Gerichte, die Berichterstattung in der Presse, dieser hilflos feige Staat - all das hat mich so wütend gemacht, daß ich diese Szenen hingefetzt habe.[38]

Although it could be considered to be short-sighted to simply blame the state for the neo-Nazi violence on the streets, Kroetz's anger is genuine. Indeed, some of his statements, outrageous as they might seem, are rather sarcastic. Kroetz, who is familiar with the everyday fascism around him, is certainly opposed to it.

In the scene 'Justiz', for example, we witness a meeting between lawyers and a judge: the case in question is that of a right-wing youth who is accused of killing a foreigner. The judge pleads for a milder verdict according to the 'Jugendstrafrecht', as he has been blackmailed by other extremists who have threatened him with further violence. The state officials, however, demand severe punishment in order to convey the image of a democratic Germany to the world:

> MINISTERIALDIREKTOR Die Welt will von uns Taten und keine Psychologie. Mir ham auswärtige Insvestitionseinbrüche in Milliardengröße, der Ami zieht sich vollkommen verschreckt aus Ostdeutschland zruck, und wenns aso weitergeht, is Made in Germany in da Welt drausn bald so verlockend - *(kollegial)* wia das Arschloch von am AIDS-kranken Stricher - wie der Herr Minister im kleinen Kreis zu scherzen pflegt.
> KAMMERPRÄSIDENT Deutschland braucht ein deutliches Zeichen. Mir miassn klar macha, daß die von Ihnen geschilderten Verhältnisse abnorm san, und ned mit wohlfeilem Psychologismus so tun, als gäbs des an jedm deutschn Straßeneck. (V, p. 489)

In this passage the alternation between dialect and High German marks the change between official governmental policy and private opinion. Official statements are inserted into the dialogue in correct German, but they swim on the surface of muddy waters. It is a highly cynical passage, for the strict penalty is only insisted upon for fear of losing foreign investors, such as the United States of America, which are referred to here in a colloquial way as 'der Ami'. The mere suggestion of any association between Germany and right-wing radicalism must be prevented, by whatever means. It is a paradox that the punishment is not meant as a warning to other criminals, but rather as a safeguard for public relations. As one of the officials emphasises, the harsh punishment will be a signal to other nations that the German state itself has nothing to do with the rise of right-wing extremism. Through the juxtaposition of these two levels of language, Kroetz thus reveals the biased nature of the legal system, and unmasks the hypocrisy of official policy which obscures the origins of the problem in hand.

It is not only lawyers and judges, but also politicians who are more or less directly accused of promoting right-wing ideals. In a scene called 'Gedenktag', a politician works on a speech that he intends to give on the occasion of a non-specified memorial day. Although he will address problems such as unemployment, foreign workers and xenophobia, he believes that they would not exist if the foreigners stayed at home:

> Ausländische Tote sind auch Mitbürger. Freile. Des weiß ich auch, aber ich frage, warum haben sie sterben müssen? Wenn es nach uns gegangen wäre, gäbe es keine toten Türken in Solingen und weiß der Deife wo, keine ausgebrannten Häuser und Geschäfte mit Frauen und toten Kindern, weil in diesen Häusern, wenn es nach uns gegangen wäre, keine Türken wohnen würden. (V, 479)

Towards the end of his speech, the outlook darkens further, for he mentions necessary changes to sections of the basic law (Grundgesetz), such as the paragraph which assures the equality of all human beings ('Alle Menschen sind vor dem Gesetz gleich'). According to him, however, the lazy, the sick, criminals and anyone who is different should fall into a different category. What is also highly dubious is that he calls into question the foundation paragraph of the Basic Law which reads: 'Die Würde des Menschen ist unantastbar'. In his opinion, it is high time to alter this and grant dignity only to those who 'deserve' it. In view of their obvious nationalistic overtones, these opinions make the audience shudder.

Conclusion

Despite its reputation, much German drama is not concerned with aesthetic problems, and ignores the discussion of self-referentiality in order to participate in political debate. Harking back to the Enlightenment, authors employ the stage as the fourth power within the state, voicing their criticism of the way in which foreign citizens, the next-door neighbours of the man on the street, are (mis)treated. With respect to the flare-up of violent neo-Nazi crimes in the early 1990s, playwrights vigorously opposed right-wing tendencies, and demonstrated how neofascist thinking works. As the arson attacks on asylum-seekers caused an outcry among intellectuals, it can thus be said that with respect to dramatic writing, the 'Wacht am Rhein' is generally rather a 'Wacht am Nein'.[39]

Notes

[1] Claus Leggewie, 'Der Geist denkt rechts. Wo Politik vorgedacht wird. Ein Streifzug durch die konservativen Denkfabriken der Bundesrepublik Deutschland', in: *Die Zeit,* 16 October 1987; also: Claus Leggewie, *Der Geist steht rechts. Ausflüge in die Denkfabriken der Wende*, Rotbuch: Berlin, 1987.

[2] The term was coined by the commentator Günter Gaus and later adopted by Kohl.

[3] Alfred Dregger, '17. Juni - sein Sinn gerät in Vergessenheit', *Express*, 11 June 1981.

[4] Franz Josef Strauß's speech in Hof, which was published under the title: 'Mehr aufrechten Gang', *Frankfurter Rundschau*, 14 June 1987.

[5] Alfred Schikel, 'Der Deutsche und sein Vaterland', *Bayernkurier*, 12 May 1982.

[6] On the glorification of the Third Reich in the legends of today's right-wing extremists, such as the 'war as holy mass', the 'pure blood', and the 'Aryan origin' of the German people, see: Rüdiger Sünner, *Schwarze Sonne. Entfesselung und Missbrauch der Mythen im Nationalsozialismus und rechter Esoterik*, Herder: Freiburg im Breisgau, 1999.

[7] See, for example: Karl Heinz Roth, 'Revisionistische Tendenzen in der historischen Forschung über den deutschen Faschismus', in: Johannes Klotz and Ulrich Schneider, eds, *Die selbstbewußte Nation und ihr Geschichtsbild: Geschichtslegenden der Neuen Rechten*, PapyRossa-Verlag: Köln, 1997, pp. 31-64.

[8] Heinar Kipphardt, *Bruder Eichmann. Schauspiel und Materialien,* Rowohlt : Reinbek, 1986.

[9] George Tabori, *Mein Kampf*, in: George Tabori, *Theaterstücke* II, Hanser: München, 1994, pp. 143-204.

[10] Thomas Strittmatter, *Viehjud Levi*, Diogenes: Zürich, 1992.

[11] Volker Ludwig and Detlef Michel, *Ab heute heißt du Sara*, in: *Theater heute,* 3/1989, 42-57.

[12] George Tabori, 'Spiel und Zeit' in: George Tabori, *Betrachtungen über das Feigenblatt*, Fischer: Frankfurt am Main, 1994, pp. 13-23 (here: p. 22).

[13] George Tabori, *Jubiläum*, in: George Tabori, *Theaterstücke* II, Hanser: München, 1994, p. 59. From a subconscious viewpoint, it is also interesting that the slaughtered pet of *Mein Kampf* and the disabled girl of *Jubiläum* are both called Mizzi, indicating a relationship between the two.

[14] *Jubiläum*, pp. 84-5.

[15] This is mainly connected with the fact that denazification played a much less important role in the GDR and that guest workers in the East were kept segregated from the native population; see Marianne Krüger-Potratz, *Anderssein gab es nicht: Ausländer und Minderheiten in der DDR*, Waxmann: Münster, New York, 1991, pp. 6-13; Marcus Neureither, *Rechtsextremismus im vereinten Deutschland. Eine Untersuchung sozialwissenschaftlicher Deutungsmuster und Erklärungsansätze*, Tectum: Marburg, 1996, pp. 36-8.

[16] See the table 'Entwicklung der ausländerfeindlichen Straftaten Januar 1991-November 1993', quoted in Neureither, *Rechtsextremismus im vereinten Deutschland*, Appendix, p. XXI, table 29.

[17] See, for example, Thomas Nipperdey, 'Die Deutschen wollen und dürfen eine Nation sein. Wider die Arroganz der Post-Nationalen', *Frankfurter Allgemeine Zeitung*, 13.7.1990; Christian Meier, 'Wir brauchen Vertrauen. Über die Notwendigkeit eines nationalen Selbstbewußtseins', *Der Spiegel* 5/1995.

[18] See, for example, the interview with Hermann Langbein, the president of the international Auschwitz committee: 'Die späte Geburt ist eine Bürde', *Frankfurter Rundschau*, 25 January 1995.

[19] See, for example: Ulrich Beck, 'Auschwitz als Identität. Gedanken zu einem deutschen Alptraum', *Süddeutsche Zeitung,* 27 May 1995. Beck writes: 'Auschwitz war nicht, Auschwitz ist. Auschwitz ist überall heute in Deutschland gegenwärtig. [...] Die Gnade der späten Geburt ist eine Legende. Die Wunde Auschwitz ist offen'; see also Christian Meier, 'Der letzte Tag. Auschwitz duldet keine Normalisierung', *Frankfurter Allgemeine Zeitung*, 27 May 1995.

[20] Heimo Schwilk/ Ulrich Schacht, eds, *Die selbstbewußte Nation. 'Anschwellender Bocksgesang'*, Berlin, 1994. Botho Strauß's controversial essay 'Anschwellender Bocksgesang' was first published in *Der Pfahl. Jahrbuch aus dem Niemandsland zwischen Kunst und Wissenschaft*. On 8 February 1993, *Der Spiegel* printed a revised version.

[21] Rainald Goetz, *Festung*, Suhrkamp: Frankfurt a.M. (1993), referred to as F following quotations. In Goetz's first novel *Irre*, the critique of media culture also plays an important role; Rainald Goetz, *Irre,* Suhrkamp: Frankfurt a.M., 1984. Moreover, Goetz's intention was to destroy shallow talk by cutting the surface of language; for a discussion of this see: Julia Bertschik, 'Theatralität und Irrsinn', *Wirkendes Wort,* 47 (1997), 398-423; Hubert Winkels, 'Krieg den Zeichen. Rainald Goetz und die Wiederkehr des Körpers', in: Hubert Winkels, *Einschnitte. Zur Literatur der 80er Jahre*, Köln, 1988, pp. 221-59.

[22] Goetz also explored this topic in a text entitled 'Hölle', published in *Manuskripte* 86/1984. In 'Subito', Goetz attacks the meaningless gossip of the so-called 'Kulturbetrieb'; Rainald Goetz, 'Subito', in: Rainald Goetz, *Krieg/Hirn*, Suhrkamp: Frankfurt, 1986, 2 vols. This text received some media attention, as Goetz cut his forehead with a razor blade during the first public reading of 'Subito', thus expressing his despair. For a discussion of Goetz's criticism of the media in his earlier works see Jürgen Oberschelp, 'Raserei. Über Rainald Goetz, Haß und Literatur', *Merkur,* 41 (1987), 170-4.

[23] For both a critical and informative overview of the problematic continuity in German history in view of the 9 November, see Peter Steinbach, 'Der 9. November in der deutschen Geschichte des 20. Jahrhunderts und in der Erinnerung' in: *Aus Politik und Zeitgeschichte. Beilage zur Wochenzeitung Das Parlament*, 22 October 1999, 3-11.

[24] Axel Schalk, 'Vom Voyeur zum Akteur', in: Christel Weiler (ed.), *Stück-Werk 3*, Zentrum Bundesrepublik Deutschland des Internationalen Theaterinstituts: Berlin, 2001, pp. 35-37 (here: p. 35).

[25] It has frequently been pointed out that the year 1992 saw a rise in neo-Nazi crime. See, for example: Richard Stöss, *Rechtsextremismus im vereinten Deutschland*, Friedrich-Ebert-Stiftung: Berlin, 2000, p. 160; Ruud Koopmanns and Dieter Rucht, 'Rechtsradikalismus als soziale Bewegung?', *Politische Vierteljahresschrift,* 27 (1996), 265-287 (here: p. 279).

[26] Sabine Reinhard, '12 Anmerkungen', in: *Stück-Werk 1*, Internationales Theaterinstitut Berlin, 1997, pp. 22-25 (here: p. 23).

[27] The idea that journalists literally bribe neo-Nazis to show the Hitler salute in front of the camera is increasingly openly discussed. See, for example: Thomas Ohlemacher, '"Wechselwirkungen nicht ausgeschlossen": Medien, Bevölkerungsmeinung und fremdenfeindliche Straftaten 1991-1997' in: Frieder Dünkel and Bernd Geng, eds, *Rechtsextremismus und Fremdenfeindlichkeit. Bestandsaufnahme und Interventionsstrategien*, Forum Verlag: Godesberg, 1999, pp. 53-69 (here: p. 54).

[28] Oliver Czeslik, 'Heilige Kühe', *Theater Heute,* 4/1992, 44-49, p. 44. Subsequent references to this work are cited in the text using the abbreviation HK and page number.

[29] See Ohlemacher (1999), p. 56; Hans-Peter Brosius and Frank Esser, 'Massenmedien und fremdenfeindliche Gewalt', *Politische Vierteljahresschrift* 27 (1996), 204-220. Based on empirical data, the study by Brosius and Esser argues that the influence of the media on right-wing extremism can be explained by different theories, for example 1. simulation, 2. social learning, 3. the suggestive and contagious effect of violence, 4. the model of priming which means that news stays in a person's mind for a certain period of time.

[30] Despite the fact that any official link between satanism and Neo-Nazis is constantly played down, the odd exception paints a different picture. See, for example, the article by Kate Connolly, 'German satanic couple held after ritual murder', *The Guardian*, 13 July 2001; John Hooper, 'Blood-drinking devil worshippers face life for ritual Satanic killing', *The Guardian*, 1 February 2002. On the Satanist and neo-Nazi Hendrik Möbius see: 'Töten für Wotan', *Der Spiegel*, 18 September 2000.

[31] Gundi Ellert, 'Jagdzeit', *Theater heute* 9/1994, 30-42.

[32] The parallels between Christian liturgy and National Socialism are examined by Otto Söhngen, *Säkularisierter Kultus,* Bertelsmann: Gütersloh 1950. On the liturgic features of the Third Reich see for example Klaus Vondung, 'Die Apokalypse des Nationalsozialismus' in: Michael Ley and Jochen Schoeps, eds, *Der Nationalsozialismus als politische Religion*, Philo Verlagsgesellschaft: Bodenheim, 1997, pp. 33-52.

[33] In the language of National Socialism, 'Maid' was used instead of 'Mädchen', 'Mark' instead of 'Grenzland', 'Gau' instead of 'Provinz', 'Jungmannen' instead of 'Männer', 'Sippe' for 'Familie'. The biologically coloured anti-Semitism was expressed by phrases like 'Volkskörper', 'Gift im Blutkreislauf des Volkes', Jews were referred to as 'Blutegel' or 'Parasiten'. See Stefan Bork, *Mißbrauch der Sprache. Tendenzen Nationalsozialistischer Sprachregelung*, Francke: Berne und Munich, 1970, pp. 40-45.

[34] John von Düffel, *Solingen,* Merlin: Gifkendorf, 1995, p. 35. Subsequent references to this work are cited in the text using the abbreviation S and page number.

[35] In the 1990s, indifference to political parties and politics became apparent and was hotly debated. See, for example, Hildegard Hamm-Brücher, 'Wege in die und Wege aus der Politik(er)verdrossenheit' in: *Aus Politik und Zeitgeschichte. Beilage zur Wochenzeitung Das Parlament,* 30 July 1993.

[36] Franz Xaver Kroetz, *Ich bin das Volk. Volkstümliche Szenen aus dem neuen Deutschland* (1993), Alexander Verlag: Berlin, 1995, pp. 473-561 (here: p. 473). References to this work are cited in the text using the abbreviation V and page number.

[37] Franz Wille, 'Mit dem alltäglichen Faschismus selbstverständlich umgehen. Ein Theater Heute-Gespräch mit Franz Xaver Kroetz', *Theater heute*, 10/1994, 4-8 (here: p. 7).

[38] Wille, 'Mit dem alltäglichen Faschismus selbstverständlich umgehen', p. 6.

[39] Odo Marquard, quoted in Thomas Nipperdey, 'Die Deutschen wollen und dürfen eine Nation sein. Wider die Arroganz der Post-Nationalen', *Frankfurter Allgemeine Zeitung*, 13 July 1990.

Alexandra Ludewig

'Heimat' in Central European Cinema

Since 1989 Central European film-makers have drawn on the idea of *Heimat* to relate aspects of contemporary identity. There is, however, a considerable contrast in the use of landscape, nature and folk traditions between Czech and Russian film-makers and their German contemporaries. For directors like Jan Svĕrák, Ivan Fila and Nikita Mikhalkov, *Heimat* represents a source of national identity and pride, however problem-laden the present may be. For Germans like Tom Tykwer, Andreas Dahn, Vanessa Jopp and others, the natural scene and in particular the Baltic coast function as a symbol of the desire to find peace within a disturbing and threatening world.

Introduction

Since the fall of the Berlin Wall, re-unification and the subsequent re-invention of the German nation, film makers have revisited Central European cinematic traditions with a view to placing themselves creatively in the context of its intellectual and artistic heritage. One of these legacies that served as a starting point for a new departure has been the *Heimatfilm*.[1] This genre survived the Nazi era, the post-war years and the economic miracle in the East and West alike.[2]

Films from directors like Tom Tykwer, Andreas Dresen, Thomas Jahn, Vanessa Jopp, Peter Welz or Andreas Kleinert, who in their work and autobiographies bring East and West together, discover *Heimat* anew.[3] The same can be said for Czech productions like *Kolya*, the Russian documentary *Anna* or Prague-born Ivan Fila's *Lea* set in Slovakia and Germany. Yet, while eastern European directors rediscover their countries' natural beauty, German directors seem to rediscover lost territory by ascribing symbolic value to the Baltic Sea in particular, as a show-down location in the concluding scenes of their films. Their protagonists take refuge in a countryside that could not be further removed from the associations of Alpine beauty and touristic folklore as seen in the traditional German and Austrian *Heimatfilm*.[4] On the contrary, the Baltic stands for the rough elements of nature on Germany's coastline, and drives home the message that the only certainty in life is change. While Germany as a nation comes to terms with past injustices and future uncertainty, the backdrop of the boundless, timeless forces of nature serves as a corrective to human fate. Thus, we see a re-orientation from the south to the north, a paradigm shift in the *Heimat* genre from the west to the east, and a rapprochement in setting and thinking. However, this could also be misunderstood as an attempt to lay territorial or moral claim to a region rightly belonging to eastern Europe. This paper will probe the political and ideological message underlying this rediscovery of the Baltic region and Sea as part of a renewed surge of Central European *Heimatfilme*.

The Central European *Heimatfilm* Tradition

As a genre the *Heimatfilm* is renowned for its restorative stance. It often uses dialect and renounces topical issues, advocates traditional gender roles, has an anti-modern impetus of rural, pastoral, often Alpine images, and expresses a longing for pre-modern times, for the good old days that supposedly still exist away from the urban centres. The Nazis used *Heimatfilm* in an effort 'to idealise "Bauerntum" as the site of desirable traditions and stereotyped the foreign (most often the urban) as the breeding ground for moral decay. Veit Harlan's *Die goldene Stadt* (1942) is an excellent example'.[5] As a genre, the *Heimatfilm* has certainly seen transformations. Early examples were Leni Riefenstahl's *Das blaue Licht* (1932) that aimed to overwhelm the spectator by the monumentality and sheer massiveness of the Alpine homeland and the popular Louis Trenker films (for example *Der Berg ruft*, 1937). After the Second World War, the genre still resorted to glorifying depictions of *Heimat* such as in Ernst Marischka's *Sissi* trilogy (1950s) which has provoked a series of anti-*Heimatfilme* as the 'cliché-ridden, Agfa-coloured images of German forests, landscapes, and customs, of happiness and security, appeared to be deceitful movie kitsch'.[6] But the genre also showed signs of a renewal as film makers used it for a more realistic presentation of homeland such as Edgar Reitz's *Heimat* (1980-84) and *Die zweite Heimat* (1988-92), which advocates a new form of regionalism. Likewise recent releases like Joseph Vilsmaier's *Herbstmilch* (1988) and *Schlafes Bruder* (1995) or Tom Tykwer's *Wintersleeper* (1997) have successfully reclaimed 'this traditionally reactionary genre' for art house film.[7]

The genre has also been stigmatised by association with National Socialist ideology.[8] Many *Heimatfilme* produced in the second half of the 20th century were indeed remakes of films from the Hitler era and offered the struggling population of Central Europe familiar images and ideals. After all, *Heimat* post-1945 for Germans 'signified an experience of loss, a vacuum that Germans filled with nostalgic memories'.[9] Not surprisingly the *Heimatfilm* genre has therefore been a popular category particularly in Germany and Austria and saw its heyday in the 1950s, with about 300

Heimatfilme made from 1950 to 1960.   Although there was a steady
decline in quantity, the genre has survived in borrowings and adaptations,
and *Heimatfilme* remain the subject of artistic engagement and political
arguments to this day. The latter was aided by variations of the two most
common prevailing plot-structures and the timeless attraction of the rural
setting.[10] The rural setting of course expresses a love of nature, country,
traditions and regional customs, but in the *Heimatfilm* it also comes with
many political and propagandistic overtones ranging from blood and soil
connotations to a pan-European regionalism. Depending on the presence
or absence of issues like community, history, gender roles, and
consumerism, *Heimatfilme* have communicated ideological messages
intertwined with dominant economic and political agendas in both eastern
and western Europe alike, that is to say:

> the land itself is only important to the extent that it facilitates the formation of
> [harmonic] relationships; it becomes a space instrumentalized for the
> attainment of an objective located within the subject. *Where* one is able to
> discover a sense of belonging and security — the Lüneburger Heath, the Alps,
> the Black Forest — is irrelevant […].[11]

as long as it depicted a pristine setting in contrast to negative influences
elsewhere.
        Structurally, most *Heimatfilme* follow the principles of the
Bildungsroman, which favours the integration of an adolescent protagonist
into society. This is usually achieved after a journey that has led a person
from the path of virtue and social acceptance subsequently back into the
safe haven of a microcosm depicting society and order *per se*. In the
context of the post-war years, this has been an ideologically charged
message that 'prioritizes the social practice of finding one's location in a
system over any emotional phenomena located within the subject'. [12] The
ideal has clearly been the social integration of individuals and their
conformist behaviour in society, in a fusion of 'emotional realization and
social regimentation'[13]. While the need for this conformist and appeasing
ideology was understandable after the two world wars, the post-1989
period has provoked a more differentiated engagement. [14]

Eastern European Ethno-History

The appearance of indigenous costumes, motifs and traditions, customs
and the stylisation of native landscape reflect an increased need for films
to assist the process of nation-building. As Benedict Anderson observed,

the nation-state tide reached its 'last wave' after 1945 in the Western world.[15] Eastern European countries only underwent aspects of this process after Gorbachev came to power and the Soviet influence and interference in the Warsaw Pact states was significantly weakened. During this time of disintegration of the overarching systems of order, the re-invention of independent states and a need for internal cohesion were a priority for states facing a climate of international turmoil.[16] In eastern Europe this phase caused unrest and uncertainty.[17] Directors in eastern European countries took on the task of using film as a vehicle to transmit nationalist symbolism and construct national identities in a peaceful fashion by evoking images of their particular homeland that were worthy of support.   Often, these messages were subtle and not immediately apparent, but nonetheless powerful. As Roland Barthes states, 'What the world supplies to myth is an historical reality, defined, even if this goes back quite a while, by the way in which men have produced or used it; and what myth gives in return is a natural image of this reality'.[18] One historical reality these films illustrate was the representation of the beautiful homeland in the *Heimatfilm* tradition.   Reproducing images reminiscent of the good old days, a legacy of this genre, served as a starting point for the liberated film industry in many eastern European countries that was looking for the re-creation of its own myths and traditions. Their patriotic sensibility sparked a series of cinematic releases that focused on rediscovering the respective homeland's worth and beauty. Celebrating the capital cities as well as rural images, they subscribe to a tourist-like image as well as a sense of patriotism that evokes pride in individuals to be part of such a wonderful community and setting. In an attempt to show urban and rural life as being determined by traditions rather than by history, the films were able to gloss over historical discontinuities and focus on a sense of uninterrupted ethnicity, customs, traditions and patriotism.   In films like *Lea, Kolya* or *Anna* this new discovery of one's *Heimat* plays a prominent role.

Kolya is a highly acclaimed film by the Czech new wave director Jan Svěrák. Set in Soviet-occupied Prague in then-Czechoslovakia prior to the 1988 'Velvet Revolution', the film introduces an unlikely couple, a convinced Czech bachelor, Franta Louka, and a cute Russian orphan, Kolya, who come together in a makeshift father and son relationship. The film is about the rapprochement of opposites, of former enemies and strangers. Symbolising the hated Soviet influence over Czechoslovakia, the plot resolves the conflict in a strong humanistic credo for love and peace. Thereby, the film

> effectively marries the metamorphosing political umbrella with the changes in Louka's personal circumstances. Essentially, this is a tale of new beginnings. Louka, who has wandered through life living only for his music and never wondering what it might be like to have a family, experiences not just a rejuvenation of his soul, but a rebirth, [just] as a different country is rising out of the ashes of the former socialist dictatorship.[19]

In his personal change Franta Louka thus mirrors Czech national development that seemed to free itself from

> the legacy of self-doubt that flowed from Czech responses as a small nation to unfavourable geopolitical realities. Twentieth century Czechoslovakia experienced three such defeats: Hitler's conquest of 1938-39, the assertion of Soviet dominance after 1948, and the crushing of the Prague Spring by the Warsaw Pact invasion in 1968.[20]

These setbacks have left their imprint in Czech identity and make the spiritual credo as expressed in the film's musical motif of Dvořák's theme for the 23rd Psalm ('The Lord is My Shepherd, I Shall Not Want...') an ironic statement. It 'both opens the film and serves as a sublime coda, as the boy recites the psalm in Czech'[21] as he flies to be reunited with his Russian mother in Germany at the end. While Franta Louka has warmed to a less selfish life, developed deeper friendships and a keener understanding of the other, Kolya has preserved his childlike innocence and gained an appreciation for the other in the encounter with Czech culture. Franta Louka taught him the language, introduced him to Czech music and to the country-side. An eagle is glimpsed briefly as Franta drives from the city to the country, mirroring the reverence and eagerness with which many Czechs view trips to the country.[22] Fishing in pristine creeks and sitting around a campfire removes both of them from Prague and its political turmoil, as the Czech countryside offers a place and sense of identification for its people. This message is stressed further through its powerful non-verbal communication of ethnic identity and pride. The images of Franta Louka and Kolya on their weekend retreat set to music by Czech composers instil a sense of pride, ownership and longing for nature and a deep and meaningful experience of one's homeland. Here Louka can see his home that thus far seemed the battleground of the superpowers with new eyes.[23] As reviewer Hal Conklin has commented:

'It is obvious that Louka's personal plight represents the plight of all of Czechoslovakia. Its music and soul has been imprisoned behind Russian walls'.[24] Post-1988 sees the liberation and new discovery of self, both in Franta Louka's personal life and in the country's brand new start. Thus *Kolya* is about how love is established; love between strangers, love between nations but also love for one's own country and oneself. In this sense, *Kolya* is a powerful promotion of Czech 'domov' (*Heimat*).

Another eastern European example of a rediscovery of *Heimat* is to be seen in Nikita Mikhalkov's documentary *Anna* from 1993. Anna is the film-maker's daughter, who was born near the end of the Soviet empire and grew up as the Soviet Union was transformed dramatically. The old order was reformed when 'glasnost' and 'perestroika' instilled hope and uncertainty before finally a new chaotic democracy and capitalistic reform meant bitter disillusion for many Russians. Anna's story mirrors politics as private and public spheres are shown as mutually permeable.

Mikhalkov begins his documentary by introducing his ancestors, including a famous pre-revolutionary poet. This serves as a contrast between the political climate of his parents' day, when the family changed the pronunciation of their name in order to distance themselves from the bourgeois poet, and the times in which his daughter Anna was born, who could proudly claim the same poet as kin. Times have changed and to highlight how everything continues to change he begins to ask his daughter annually a series of questions which document her process of growing up starting at the age of six: 'What do you love most, what do you hate most, what do you fear most, what do you wish and what do you expect from life?' Over the years, childish answers referring to witches and crocodiles give way to a more reflective analysis of her personal state as well as national affairs. Mikhalkov annotates Anna's answers with footage of current events. Anna also shows a developing awareness of self. On camera, she checks her reflection in a mirror and instinctively smooths her hair. Each successive year shows her maturing worldview and her sometimes fearful response to it.[25] In the disintegrating world around her Anna feels more and more lost and as if she is losing something very intangible but precious. She displays a strong love of country and family which her father exploits in the final scene for a patriotic commentary. As the film ends, with Russia under Yeltsin in a state of upheaval and signs of things becoming worse before they will get better, Mikhalkov interviews his daughter for the last time. Now 17 years old, she is preparing to move to Switzerland for her studies. Standing in the same field as she did when she was seven, she answers the same questions now as a pensive, timid teenager coming to terms with her country's and her personal past and facing an unknown future. Now the land itself is most important to her, the very field she stands on. Facing her departure, she tearfully insists that she will return to Russia. In his voice-over narration, Mikhalkov asks: 'Why did Anna, a young girl aged 17, in need of nothing, start crying as she talked about her country?'. The question remains unanswered but the key lies in the scenic beauty in – what Mikhalkov calls – 'our great and unfortunate land'. A strong sense of identity and patriotism prevails in the authoritative voice of the father, who promises to uphold these threatened values against all odds.

Anna as well as *Kolya* have provoked deeply emotive responses to concepts of nation, identity and homeland by way of mythologising country, language, religion, and shared history. Film-makers in Central Europe have embarked on the journey of promoting their ideas of a new world order in a post-nationalistic fashion at a time of uncertainty and political upheaval by upholding fundamentalist values and images of homeland. What aids them in their pursuit is the fact that there is mostly a strong correlation between religion, ethnicity, language and nationality that their narration of nation and their ethno-historical pursuits can base themselves upon. Through their mass-medium they contribute 'to a populistic nationalism in a manner that is more evocative than deliberate'.[26] Moreover, in their attempt to secure a recognised homeland, film makers are appealing 'to an hitherto passive *ethnie*' that can recognise itself and its pursuits as 'a culturally homogeneous "organic" nation'.[27] In the cases of eastern European countries this is evident in their use of what Anthony Smith calls 'ethno-history'. Film makers cultivate poetic spaces, that resemble

> identifying a sacred territory that belonged historically to a particular community […]. Cultivating poetic spaces also signified a process of turning natural features of the homeland into historical ones, and naturalising historical monuments. Rivers like the Danube and Rhine, mountains like the Zion and Olympus, lakes like the Vierwaldstättersee and lake Peipius, have become humanised and historicised by their associations with communal myth and endeavour.[28]

These poetic landscapes can be constructed in all art forms, literature, film, music and all other visual and acoustic means:

> For composers, artists and writers, the nationalistic myth of poetic landscapes evoked powerful sentiments of nostalgia and identification, which they amplified and diffused through their art. For Smetana and Dvořák in Bohemia [...] and Borodin and Moussorgsky in Russia, their country's landscapes and changing seasons, legends, and monuments, stirred strong nationalist passions.[29]

Film can instil 'the feelings of beauty, variety, dignity and pathos aroused by the skilful disposition of forms, masses, sounds and rhythms with which [they] can evoke the distinctive 'spirit' of the nation'.[30] All this is seen as a new discovery after years of foreign influence are finally shaken off and the victimised regions embrace a new nationalism and patriotism. At the same time, their protagonists do not stay put. With their empowering new understanding of *Heimat* they set out to travel westwards, Anna to Switzerland and Kolya to Germany, following their minds more than their hearts. Their strong bond with the land seems to promise a connection to their respective heartlands that they will be able to take with them wherever they go.

The German Discovery of a New *Heimat*

In the German and Austrian context, issues of 'German identity' in the light of the recent past (1945 as well as 1989) and 'Vergangenheits-bewältigung', i.e. coming to terms with the past, have dominated the *Heimatfilm* genre.[31] This gave an impetus to the genre after both world wars when there was a perceived need for refugees, returnees and displaced people to identify with a positive image of the new German state.[32] Like the rural *Heimat*, the urban *Heimat* was used as a locus for national soul searching, where ruins were still visible and the economic miracle a brittle façade hiding many scars.[33]

With Germany's unification and its continued European integration, questions 'of German national and cultural identity, the contradiction between economic and military power and cultural feelings of inferiority, racial versus civil definitions of identity and otherness'[34] are as relevant as ever. Thus it comes as no surprise that cinematic traditions that dominated for most of the 20th century are revisited in an attempt to re-appraise them in contemporary cinema. As such, elements of the traditional *Heimatfilm* and issues of past and identity play central roles in many films released since the *Wende*. Yet, a shift of perspective is evident in these recent productions. As a result. new frontiers and nodes of *Heimat* are identified, and these are distinct from eastern European practice. To exemplify this shift, a selection of films from prominent film makers such as Andreas Kleinert and Tom Tykwer, as well as newcomers such as Vanessa Jopp, Andreas Dresen and Thomas Jahn will be examined with regard to their references to *Heimat* as well as the construction of frontiers.

Many younger directors have taken up the discourse of frontiers to explore national perspectives and anthropological behaviour patterns. In recent films, Germany's post-unification generation of film makers show a new understanding of frontiers, which are not treated as a purely geographical, national or supranational phenomenon. Their films push the frontier experience to an extreme, as their pioneering efforts avoid conventional pastoral or Alpine landscapes. Instead, their last frontier is the sea, particularly the Baltic coastline, in Germany's north-east. Examples of recent films that conclude with a flight to the Baltic Sea are Peter Welz's *Burning Life* (1994)*,* Ivan Fila's *Lea* (1996), Andreas Kleinert's *Im Namen der Unschuld* (1997), Thomas Jahn's *Knocking on Heaven's Door* (1999), Andreas Dresen's *Nachtgestalten* (1999) or Vanessa Jopp's *Vergiß Amerika* (2000).

Andreas Dresen's *Nachtgestalten* can be seen as a paradigm for this shift. The film deals with the harsh realities of urban life in contemporary Germany as experienced in post-unification Berlin. In true *film noir* style[35] Dresen focuses on streets and places of transition, such as airports, streets or train stations, where the lives of street kids, tourists and locals intersect. To introduce the complexity of this urban microcosm *Nachtgestalten* comprises three short stories united only by place (Berlin) and time (the night of the Pope's visit to the city). Not unlike Jim Jarmusch's *Night on Earth* the stories unfold in a seemingly unrelated fashion. Hanna and Victor are both homeless and alcohol-dependent, but try to live one night in dignity thanks to a generous donation of DM100. Like the biblical Mary and Joseph, however, the couple encounter many difficulties in the quest for a roof over their head for the night. The second pairing is made up of Jochen, a naïve 30-year-old farmer from the east German countryside, who seeks company and the sights and sounds of the big city and encounters Patty, an underage prostitute and drug addict, whom he tries to save from her downward spiral. Unfortunately for her, his attempt only causes further problems for both. The third couple constitutes Mr. Peschke, a stressed, middle-ranking businessman who meets Feliz, a child-refugee from Angola, at Berlin Tegel airport. Trying to relieve his bad conscience from racist prejudice, he helps the stranded black boy to be reunited with his family. In doing so Peschke has his car stolen by a gang of youths, who have already robbed Jochen and who also crossed the path of the homeless couple. The film's conclusion brings the youths with their stolen car away from the city out into the country, to the Baltic. Heavily guarded, it formed part of the Iron Curtain from 1961 until 1989. Now, Dresen, whose own memory of the Baltic from his life in Communist Eastern Germany would have been that of an impenetrable borderland, uses it as a symbol for liberation and final insight.

The Baltic Sea as the Epitome of *Heimat* and Frontier

Frequented from ancient times, the Baltic was once important for commerce and trade.[36] Its significance has since decreased, reaching a low-point in the 20th century as the backdrop for many war-time tragedies, including refugee movements.[37] Subsequently, the Cold War transformed parts of it into a no-go-zone for the average East German citizen due to their close proximity to the West and the danger of escape attempts. In contrast to the North Sea, which was accessible for everyone in the West, parts of the Baltic Sea were used nearly exclusively by top Communist Party members as a holiday resort, while it was inaccessible to the average citizen under Communist rule. In addition, heavy industrialisation of the countries bordering the Baltic in the 20th century has resulted in massive environmental degradation.

When young German film-makers use the Baltic Sea for a show-down at the end of their films about contemporary Germany, their choice of setting is symbolic. Against this back-drop, they show people overcoming their past and any inhibitions in an attempted 'self-realisation', free from constraints. It is precisely the experience of the sea in many instances that enables the protagonists 'to achieve a different kind of perspective and some kind of moral improvement' within themselves.[38] Vanessa Jopp uses the Baltic Sea as a catalyst for her protagonists' self-realisation in *Vergiß Amerika*. Here for the first time, David, the shy boy caught in a love-triangle, gains profound insight into his situation and identifies a possible solution. In other movies the sea serves as the ultimate escape, for example, for Lisa and Anna in *Burning Life*. They drive over the cliff's edge with their Russian limousine only to repeat this motion afterwards again, by hijacking a helicopter in which they fly over the Baltic Sea, leaving Germany, their past and problems behind. For others it is not so much a point of no return but a point of physical and metaphysical departure. The edge of the continental mainland becomes the place of life's conclusion.   For the two characters in *Knocking on Heaven's Door*, Martin and Rudi, it is a dream come true and the climax and closure to their lives.   To see and feel the elements concludes a life's journey and leads to peace of mind and the acceptance of death reminiscent of Freud's 'ozeanisches Gefühl'.[39] Freud sees this feeling as being grounded in the childish desire to be one with the mother and condemns it as a distortion of reality.   At the same time he acknowledges that there is a human quest and urge for a union with a figure or entity that is experienced as larger than life and as a promise to resolve all of life's irreconcilable differences.   In the case of the protagonists in *Knocking on Heaven's Door* this entity is the sea as Martin is ready to become one with nature, when he breathes in the fresh air in the sands of the dune at the edge of the breaking waves.

The theological dimension in this final scene is not only invoked by the title but also by referring to Martin's and Rudi's mindset.   The deserted coastline of the Baltic Sea evokes within them a sense and appreciation of solitude away from the city and heralds the possibility of introspection and reflection.   The water masses and rock formations, the cliffs and breaking waves communicate the sense of time more infinite than themselves, with the understanding that the water has washed the shores of the Baltic from time immemorial.   The seemingly endless spatial and temporal expanse of the ocean instils a metaphysical reflection on the landscape, thereby expanding their horizon and mind.   Martin's facial expression at the moment of his death heralds his experience of the intuitive presence of a deity, an epiphany. Experiencing the Baltic landscape 'away from the cities, or other man-made objects [...] is conducive to an awareness of God's presence'.[40] Without reference to any one God or religion this transcendental insight can be seen as pantheistic. God is everything and everything is God, as the world is 'either identical with God or in some way a self-expression of his nature'.[41] In the experience of this sublime / epiphaneic moment, Rudi can transcend his status as a human[42] in a 'paradoxical coexistence of assertion of control over one's surroundings and one's loss of control'.[43]

For the youth gang from Berlin in *Nachtgestalten*, the encounter with the Baltic Sea is an experience where they for once see something larger than their lives, greater than their problems and more boundless than their despair, hurt and anger.   They bring their destruction to this part of the world, torch their stolen car and marvel in the sight of the flames rising into the morning sky.   All this happens against the background of the rolling waves of the Baltic Sea, putting the adolescents in their minuteness against the vast sea and land masses. In the final camera angle the elevated perspective promotes an understanding of a person's insignificance against the natural sea, reflected not least by Nietzsche:

> Am bisher theologisch codierten Blick auf ferne Meere, […], schult sich das Auge Zarathustras, bis es die „ganze Tatsache Mensch aus ungeheurer Ferne" unter sich sieht. Denn das Meer lehrt den Menschen aufzuhören, Mensch zu sein. Glänzend, stumm und ungeheuer stellt seine Schlangenhaut, seine Raubtierschönheit eine Rätselfrage und quittiert die humanistische Antwort „der Mensch" mit Gelächter. Am „schönen Ungeheuer" lernt der Mensch, das Maß des Menschen zu vergessen.[44]

The final scene in *Nachtgestalten* provides this Nietzschean insight into human frailty in contrast to the sea with its physical immediacy evoking energy and force as a continuum of boundless power.

The sea also serves as an image of eternity, since the eternal movement of the waves helps emphasise man's mortality.[45] Caspar David Friedrich's romantic depiction of the cliffs and rocks of the Baltic Sea, of overbearing nature with its forces (wind and water) against which human beings are put into perspective, rings true for humans in the 19th, 20th and 21st century alike, leading to a reassessment of self and one's surroundings. Like a fulfilment of the Kantian imperative of 'self-determination' this becomes a principle of being. 'Applied by Fichte, Schlegel and the other German Romantics to groups rather than individuals, the ideal of autonomy gave rise to a philosophy of national self-determination and collective struggle to realise the authentic national will'.[46]

On a personal level, this is evident in Ivan Fila's film *Lea*, as the dunes of the Baltic Sea become a playground for the couple. It is the place where for the first time in their lives they can reveal their emotions. Now all constraints seem to be lifted as their alienation from society and self that had made them outsiders in unified Germany and led them to a process of gradual self-destruction is overcome. On the occasion of their visit to the edge of their new homeland, they discover themselves, one another and the beauty and grandeur of the world. The experience of the Baltic again serves as a short-hand for their liberation, and heralds a new beginning in their relationship.

In all of the above-mentioned films the Baltic is a place of insight and introspection, of surrender and refuge. It is the ultimate destiny in the life-journey as it becomes the defining moment in their lives, but not as a worldly paradise, an Eden or Safe Haven, nor as a tourist destination, but nevertheless like a Holy Grail that aids their final insight.[47] This connotation of the Baltic is not only reflected in recent German film but also in the writing of Baltic people. The early 1990s in the Baltic lands in general have been a time of reclaiming the past, of rediscovering what was once forbidden, of getting acquainted with foreign literature, as much as, if not more than, of experimentation with the new.[48] Thus, the discovery and rediscovery of neighbours yet strangers in the Baltic region is a trend that can be observed in film as well as literature on both sides, yet the echo this rediscovery on the German side has provoked bears witness to underlying concerns.[49]

A Problematic Trend?

In their depiction of the Baltic setting in German film and literature, artists not only evoke images of boundless space, room for expansion, freedom and new beginnings, they move into troubled waters, as the Baltic is associated with territorial losses in the first half of the 20th century.[50] This resulted in the region being seen as a *Heimat* that has been lost and that now stimulates diasporic identities. Shared memories that were fostered by neighbours and strangers alike recall the Baltic region as a witness to human tragedies of unimaginable proportions during the Third Reich and particularly the Holocaust. From 1940 onwards the Nazi occupation was responsible for an era of terror on civilians, especially Jewish settlers in the Baltic states. The Final Solution was first experienced by the peoples in the Baltic countries as Hitler's executioners began their mass genocide there. At the time, the German occupiers were able to exploit ethnic divisions in the region as well as latent anti-Semitism resulting in many willing executioners among the local population. When the Soviet army freed the Baltic from German rule and occupied the region in turn, many ethnic Germans fled westwards in refugee marches that again took a heavy toll on civilian life. Refugees and displaced people tried to flee in constant fear of attack. Günter Grass's latest book documents this through the tragedy of the sinking of the *Wilhelm Gustloff*.[51] His narrative is one of many recent publications that break the taboo regarding remembrance of the German victims of the Nazi regime and of the Allies. Therefore, this shift to the Baltic region has multiple causes, consequences and political ramifications. The change in the notion of *Heimat* could be seen as an unholy political message that this re-discovery may subscribe to consciously or accidentally. This raises certain questions: Are moderate, intelligent and liberal writers and film makers from the East and West alike nurturing sentiments that are only at face-value innocent displays of scenic beauty and nostalgia? Are they preparing the ground for a broader understanding of *Heimat*? Is their rediscovery of the Baltic even possibly subscribing to a policy of expansionism? As their territorial reference might be seen as laying claim to the former eastern German homeland, this raises multiple possibilities for political instrumentalisation. The eastern German border has shifted many times in recent history.[52] Do these films nurture the desire for yet another change?

While the European Union's expansion eastwards is an economic reality and also backed by a strategic alliance (for example, Poland's recent membership of NATO), the cultural expansion as pursued by German writers and film makers in their images of the coastline along the Baltic Sea evoking connotations of a 'promised land' is worth monitoring critically. Are German notions of a 'European identity' and 'global citizenship' blurring national boundaries in a territorial pursuit of lost homeland in the East? History is clearly changing in the re-telling and re-casting of events from several perspectives. Thereby, it becomes polyphonic and fluid. Is postmodernism the fig-leaf for ulterior motives?

As a place of ethnic cleansing or tragedies inflicted on Germans, accusations and suspicions are never far away when the East is discussed. The issue of the lost *Heimat* in general and the Nazi past in particular guaranteed that the topic is 'emotionsgeladen und ideologiebefrachtet'.[53] Might this have prompted historians, writers and intellectuals in Germany for some time to shy away from the Baltic Sea? Recent discussions in the media of Günter Grass's *Im Krebsgang* (2002) or Volker Koepp's *Kurische Nehrung* (2001) have been timely reminders of this as critics highlighted the possibility of their new *Heimat* concepts and understandings of history as being revisionist. Both Grass and Koepp have their roots in the former ethnic German regions of what is now Poland[54] and have revisited personal memories in their works.[55] And both have had to defend their artistic products against bitter accusations of revisionist tendencies. Koepp has been accused of a revanchist and tainted perspective that mythologises the good old days without problematising the fact that the days his ethnic Germans are marvelling about were Nazi Germany's hey-days in the region.[56] Some critics saw the audience in extreme-right-wing quarters and labelled the film 'Ein absolutes Muss für die Vertriebenen'.[57] The left-wing newspaper *taz* ran several articles on his film, all denouncing it as misleading, nostalgic, emotive and politically charged.[58] The claim that such films support political and ideological attempts to 'legitimize territorial expansion is never far away. This policy was resumed in the post-war discussions of 'Recht auf Heimat' – the right to *Heimat* – and motivated the 'Landsmannschaften', the revisionist refugee organizations, to demand that the Silesian, East Prussian, and Sudeto-German home territories be returned to them.[59] Likewise, Grass is said to have overcome the 'Vertreibungstabu'[60] in his works, something which is perceived with very mixed feelings indeed. Critics highlight Grass's insensitivity in lamenting German victims without acknowledging that there were 50 million deaths inflicted on the world by Germans.[61]

Paradigm Shift

These reactions to Koepp and Grass illustrate clearly that Germany is indeed undergoing a 'Mentalitätswandel', a 'Transformation des Bundesrepublikanischen Geschichtsbewußtseins – oder genauer: der Geschichtsmoral'[62] that is being critically monitored by German intellectuals. Koepp's continued interest in the homeland of ethnic Germans in the former eastern territories of Germany was meant as an unbiased documentation following in his own footsteps with this sequel to his highly-acclaimed documentary *Kalte Heimat* (1995). Grass's book is likewise his sequel to the *Danziger Trilogie* for which he received the Nobel Prize in 1999.

But times have changed and their works and points of view are now less accepted than they might have been before the plea for unification became reality. The unease about the topic as such and the point of view in particular expressed in many reviews brings back memories of political as well as cinematic history as the retreat into the province not only coincided with a traditionally strong regional focus of Germans[63] but was also used as an attempt to turn one's back on the centre of power and flee to the periphery. As Boa and Palfreyman have argued, this was initially an escape from the traumas of the First World War and perceived chaos of the Weimar Republic and then as a mode of inner emigration from the Third Reich. After the Third Reich it served as a 'Vergangenheitsflucht', an escapist cinematic mode that allowed demoralised people comfort away from their immediate post-war realities. Close to the surface was also the theme of the lost *Heimat* following the division of Germany and the loss of lands in the East. *Heimatfilme* offered balm but in sustaining the myth of *Heimat* also stoked resentment.   The latter was evident in the instrumentalisation of *Heimat* in political debates between left and right, in which right-wing, revanchist forces and refugee associations appealed to the lost *Heimat* in the East as a revertible status quo.   This phase in post-war Central European history led to a dialectic 'between the escapist *Heimat* films of the 1950s and right-wing claims to the lost lands in the East to which the anti-*Heimat* theatre and film in the 1960s and 1970s [...] were a response'.[64] Fassbinder's anti-*Heimat* films in particular achieved cult status and exemplified the left's suspicion of *Heimat* and other concepts used to form the basis of in-groups.[65] The end of the Cold War era and the disintegration of the Soviet Union's grip on large parts of Central Europe has led to renewed and increasing explorations of *Heimat* and identity.   During this phase, many film makers from former Eastern bloc countries embraced a fresh approach to their rediscovery of scenic beauties and found peace with themselves and the world in their view of their homeland.   In contrast, many young German film makers opted for a symbolic alternative to the traditional *Heimat* images and resorted to the ocean as a supranational, sublime signifier for their mythic re-invention. The mythic images characteristic of the western and earlier German genre of mountain films from the 1920s and 1930s,[66] which saw an artistic highlight with Leni Riefenstahl's *Das blaue Licht* (1932), have found their present-day counterpart in the rediscovery of the Baltic Sea.[67]

Rather than subscribing to a dominant ideology, the flight to the Baltic now signifies a total rejection of the forms of civilisation to which the present Central European region has succumbed.   It resembles a romantic regression into nature, i.e. the desired *unio mystica* with the Baltic Sea stands for a deep regression from a world that has become too difficult.   Similar to what Reitz wanted to express with his series *Heimat*, it is felt 'that an authentic German identity, and a *Heimat*, are only possible at the periphery, far from the official centres of power – in the provinces. Germany as a nation or a state cannot be *Heimat*'.[68] For the most recent generation of German film-makers, *Heimat* means a place outside of history, removed from progress, caught in a cyclical time that seems only subject to seasons and nature.   They express an existential homelessness that makes them take refuge in a supranational environment. as Morley and Robins put it: 'In a world that is increasingly characterised by exile, migration and diaspora, with all the consequences of unsettling and hybridisation, [...] there is no longer any place like *Heimat*'.[69] The search is deeply personal and could not be further removed from an aggressive political stance.   On the contrary, highly acclaimed, wonderfully sensitive and historically mindful films like Dresen's *Nachtgestalten*, Fila's *Lea*, Jopp's *Vergiß Amerika* or Kleinert's *Im Namen der Unschuld,* but also other contributions in the arts[70] might pave the way for a more balanced view of the rapprochement of east and west, history and present, hopes and fears.   They set an example of a successful merger and take the political and ideological instrumentalisation out of the aesthetic depiction of a symbolic backdrop by foregrounding the fact that the ocean in general is a popular symbol in film making, whether it is the Atlantic coast or the Baltic Sea.   Films like Wim Wenders's *Lisbon Story* (Germany, 1994) or Weingartner's *Das weiße Rauschen* (Germany, 2001) bring their protagonists to Spanish and Portuguese shores, while the unifying message is that the only certainty in life is change, and as Germany as a nation comes to terms with the heritage of Nazism and Socialism and many uncertainties, the backdrop of the boundless, timeless forces of nature serves as a corrective to the human plight.[71] And while the cinema that featured the Alpine refuge had at its core the message that society and individual can live in perfect harmony as integral parts of one another,[72] the ocean back-drop seems to promote a place for the individual within and outside of society and civilisation at one and the same time, as an integral part of nature.   Thus, we see a re-orientation from the south to the north of Germany, a paradigm shift in the *Heimat* genre in some of the better film releases from Germany that are far from revisionist and close to a balanced and informed engagement with the highly political cinematic history.   The title of Andreas Kleinert's film *Im Namen der Unschuld* set on the Baltic island of Rügen is therefore programmatic.   The protagonists seek refugee and reconciliation facing the storm-swept water of the Baltic. They are not driven by revenge nor a spirit of conquest.   They seek peace with themselves and the world around them in the shelter of a mental asylum that seems to be the only place of normality in an otherwise seemingly mad world.   Likewise, Lola in Tom Tykwer's *Lola rennt* envisages the Baltic as a worthy place of final rest, although not for ideological or political struggle.   As she says: 'Manni, ich werde Deine Asche auf Rügen in den Wind streuen.'

Notes

[1] The German term 'Heimat' is impossible to translate into English in one word due to its many meanings and associations, its ideological and aesthetic connotations. Therefore, the German term will be used in this essay.

[2] See Rachel Palfreyman, *Edgar Reitz's Heimat. Histories, Traditions, Fictions*, Peter Lang: New York, Bern, 2000, p. 24.

[3] This article will follow the complex definitions of Heimat (home/land) as set out in Elizabeth Boa & Rachel Palfreyman, *Heimat. A German Dream. Regional Loyalities and National Identity in German Culture 1890-1990, Oxford Studies in Modern European Culture*, Oxford University Press: Oxford, 2000, pp.1-30 and Peter Dürmann, *Heimat und Identität: Der moderne Mensch auf der Suche nach Geborgenheit*. Hohenrain-Verlag: Tübingen, 1994, pp. 88-133.

[4] See Martin Walser, *Heimatkunde. Aufsätze und Reden*, Suhrkamp, Frankfurt a.M., 1968, p. 40.

[5] Tedd Rippey, Melissa Sundell, Suzanne Townley, "'Ein wunderschönes Heute": The Evolution and Functionalization of "Heimat" in West German *Heimat* Films of the 1950s', in: Jost Hermand et al., eds, *Heimat, Nation, Fatherland. The German Sense of Belonging*, Peter Lang: New York, Bern, 1996, p. 139.

[6] Anton Kaes, *From Hitler to Heimat: the return of history as film*. Harvard University Press: Cambridge, Mass., 1989, p. 15.

[7] David Morley and Kevin Robins, 'No Place like Heimat', in: *Spaces of Identity. Global Media, Electronic Landscapes and Cultural Boundaries*, Routledge: London, 1995, p. 91. See also Palfreyman, *Edgar Reitz's Heimat*, pp. 19-20.

[8] Kaes, *From Hitler to Heimat*, p. 15.

[9] Ibid., p. 166.

[10] These can be described in their barest structure as follows: Initially, the action usually revolves around a harmonious rural community whose equilibrium is challenged by an outsider. Often this constitutes itself through a visitor from the city, who is seen as an antibody, is eliminated and order thus re-constituted. Secondly, the genre can centre around a youth / young adult, who leaves the peaceful rural community falling prey to the lure of the city. In this case the films end usually with the return of the lost son/daughter with all its religious overtones.

[11] Tedd Rippey et al, "'Ein wunderschönes Heute"...', p. 137.

[12] Ibid., p. 143.

[13] Ibid.

[14] See Anthony Glees, *Reinventing Germany. German Political Development since 1945*, Berg: Oxford, 1996. The Heimat film genre reiterates a positive relationship to fundamental features of national and ethnic identity (national identity: an historic territory, or homeland, common myths and historical memories; a common, mass public culture; and ethnic: a myth of common ancestry, shared historical memories, elements of common culture, an association with a specific homeland and a sense of solidarity for significant sectors of the population). See also Anthony D. Smith, *National Identity*, Penguin: Harmondsworth, 1991, pp. 14 and 21.

[15] Benedict Anderson, *Imagined Communities: Reflections on the Origin and Spread of Nationalism*. Verso: London, 1983, p. 104.

[16] Isaiah Berlin, 'Nationalism: Past Neglect and Present Power', in: *Against the Current: Essays in the History of Ideas*, ed. Isaiah Berlin, The Hogarth Press, London, 1980, pp. 333-355.

[17] The assassination of the Romanian leader of state, Nicolae Ceauşescu and his wife Elena, is to be seen in stark contrast to the Velvet Revolution in Czechoslovakia.

[18] Roland Barthes: *Mythologies*, Trans. Annette Lavers, The Noonday Press: New York, 1972, p. 142.

[19] James Berardinelli, 'Kolya. A Film Review', http://movie-reviews.colossus.net/movies/k/kolya.html, consulted in April 2002.

[20] Carol Skalnik Leff, 'Czech and Slovak Nationalism in the Twentieth Century', in: Peter F. Sugar, ed., *Eastern European nationalism in the twentieth century,* American University Press: Lanham, Md., 1995, pp. 103-163, (here: p. 137).

[21] Eddie Cockrell, 'Kolya', http://www.nitrateonline.com/rkolya.html, consulted in April 2002.

[22] Eddie Cockrell, 'Kolya', http://www.nitrateonline.com/rkolya.html.

[23] Sugar, *Eastern European nationalism in the twentieth century*, p. 263.

[24] Hal Conklin, 'Kolya. A social and spiritual commentary', http://www.cinemainfocus.com/Kolya_4.htm, consulted in April 2002.

[25] Andrea Chase, 'Anna. Movie Review', http://www.shoestring.org/mmi_revs/anna93.html, consulted in April 2002.

[26] Smith, *National Identity*, p. 92.

[27] Ibid., p. 126.

[28] Ibid., p. 127.

[29] Ibid., pp. 127-128.

[30] Ibid., p. 162.

[31] Part of this tradition are the migrant films of recent years, i.e. Turkish-German (Hark Bohm, *Yasemin*, Germany, 1988) or African-German identity (Pepe Danquart, *Schwarzfahrer*, Germany, 1993). See John E. Davidson, *Deterritorializing the New German Cinema*, University of Minnesota: Minnesota, 1999, pp. 48. and 51: 'There is a sense of being robbed of German cultural identity by that very history, often building an identity on the impossibility of German identity in any traditional Western sense. The two culprits tend to be various manifestations of National Socialism and Americanisation. [...] Because of Germany's past, the filmmakers' language had been violated, their subconscious colonized, their ability to develop an identity fully impaired, and their traditions fragmented. In this self-stylization, they became colonised subjects engaged in a "minor discourse"'. See also Barton Byg, *Landscapes of Resistance. The German Films of Danièle Huillet and Jean-Marie Straub*, University of California Press: Berkeley, 1995, p. 39.

[32] See Palfreyman, *Edgar Reitz's Heimat*, pp. 22-26.

[33] Urban *Heimat* is for example pictured in the Berlin films located in a limited familiar district such as *Berlin Ecke Schönhauser* (Gerhard Klein, 1957). 'A group of young people who do not feel part of the GDR socialist dream, identify with their local neighbourhood, Prenzlauer Berg, which forms a base for a young people's urban Heimat. The hero, Dieter, is forced to leave, but is alientated and rootless in the West. Like so many characters in Heimat fims, Dieter returns, and is [...] reintegrated into the socialist urban Heimat...'. Rachel Palfreyman, *Edgar Reitz's Heimat*, p. 42.

[34] Byg, *Landscapes of Resistance*, p. 46.

[35] The film has a strong element of documentary footage, which can be attributed to two facts: firstly, in preparing his latest film Dresen worked closely with organisations for the homeless to get the right feel for life on the streets. In addition, on the completion of filming, Dresen painstakingly retreated the entire negative of *Nachtgestalten*, removing gloss and toning down colour to give the film a raw, unvarnished quality. The result is characters portrayed with respect and without condescension or sentimentality and a Berlin which is not to be found in the travel brochures. Yet, Dresen's film is less an exotic exploration of some interesting fringe characters, but more an examination of powerful tendencies in German (and not just German) society, probing beneath the surface of the 'German miracle'.

[36] See Christopher Moseley, *From Baltic Shores*, Norvik Press: Norwich, 1994, p. 7: 'The days when the Hanseatic League was an agent of cross-cultural fertilization

between cities around the Baltic littoral… are now long gone. […] to such an extent that by the late 20th century a situation has arisen, where the cultures, languages and societies of Northeastern Europe are as diverse as ever, but they know little more about each other's identities than do complete outsiders'.

[37] Herbert Reinoß, ed., *Letzte Tage in Ostpreußen. Erinnerungen an Flucht und Vertreibung*, Albert Langen-Georg Müller Verlag: München, 1983; Herbert Hupka, ed., *Letzte Tage in Schlesien. Tagebücher, Erinnerungen und Dokumente der Vertreibung*, Albert Langen-Georg Müller Verlag: München, 1981; Klaus Granzow, ed., *Letzte Tage in Pommern. Tagebücher, Erinnerungen und Dokumente der Vertreibung*, Albert Langen-Georg Müller Verlag: München, 1984.

[38] Mario John Lupak, *Byron as a Poet of Nature. The Search for Paradise*, Edwin Mellen Press: Lewiston, 1999, p. 7.

[39] See Sigmund Freud, 'Das Unbehagen in der Kultur', in: *Abriß der Psychoanalyse. Das Unbehagen in der Kultur*, Fischer Verlag: Frankfurt a.M., 1953, p. 91.

[40] Mario John Lupak, *Byron as a Poet of Nature*, p. 5.

[41] Huw Parri Owen, *Concepts of Deity*, Macmillan: London: 1971, p. 74.

[42] See Thomas Weiskel, *The Romantic Sublime*, The Johns Hopkins University Press: Baltimore, 1976, p. 5.

[43] Carole Fabricant, 'The Aesthetics and Politics of Landscape in the Eighteenth Century', in: *Studies in Eighteenth Century British Art and Aesthetics*, Ralph Cowen, ed., University of California Press: Berkeley, 1985, pp. 56-57.

[44] Norbert Bolz, 'Die Verwindung des Erhabenen — Nietzsche', in: Christine Pries, ed., *Das Erhabene. Zwischen Größenwahn und Grenzerfahrung*, VCH-Verlag, Acta Humaniora: Weinheim, 1989, p. 164.

[45] See 'element of timelessness', Christopher Moseley, *From Baltic Shores*, p. 16.

[46] Smith, *National Identity*, p. 76.

[47] While the choice of the Baltic coast line certainly adds meaning on the socio-political and historical plane, the ocean *per se* has already many connotations which have become important in the discussion of character developments. Philosophers, writers, painters and many other intellectuals have dealt with the 'sea' as a trope for personal development.

[48] Moseley, *From Baltic Shores*, p. 14.

[49] The Baltic region that saw the emergence of three new state formations in a surge of 'ethno-nationalism' in the 1980s and early 90s is in itself still a developing multi-entity that has to find its place and ways of dealing with Europe as well as the Russian Federation. Anthony D. Smith, *National Identity*, p. 148. See also 'The return to Europe' in: Graham Smith et al., *Nation-Building in the Post-Soviet Borderlands. The Politics of National Identity*, Cambridge University Press: Cambridge, 1998, pp. 108-109.

[50] After the First World War and to a lesser extent after World War Two, Germany lost extensive territories in the East which had afforded it a huge coastline.

[51] Günter Grass, *Im Krebsgang. Eine Novelle*, Steidl: Göttingen, 2002.

[52] At the end of both World Wars Germany lost territory in the East, moving its border further west each time. With the official division of Germany into West and East, the Iron Curtain meant another westward shift leaving only a stretch of approximately one hundred kilometres of coast line of the Baltic Sea for the West Germans. When the German-German division was finally overcome with the fall of the wall in 1989 and the subsequent re-unification in 1990, the location and state of the new eastern border became a sensitive issue. Therefore the unification treaty stated clearly that Germany was to accept the loss of territories to the east as set out in the Treaties of Versailles and Potsdam and 'recognise the external borders as of 1990 as definite'. Too familiar was still the rhetoric of Hitler pursuing the expansion of 'Lebensraum' not only to the south (which ultimately resulted in the annexation of Austria) but also persistently to the east. Similar visions of a greater German territory were re-instated with right-wing and conservative governments throughout the Cold War and more recently again by Neo-Nazi-Groups.

[53] Helfried Seliger, 'Vorwort' in: Helfried W. Seliger, ed., *Der Begriff 'Heimat' in der deutschen Gegenwartsliteratur*, Iudicium Verlag: München, 1987, p. 7.

[54] Günter Grass was born in Danzig, now Gdansk in Poland; Koepp in former Stettin, now Szczecin, Poland.

[55] They are among a large group of writers and artists who lost their homeland in the first half of the 20th century and have thematised their experiences in their works. See Andrea Bastian, 'Heimatverlust durch das Verlassen der besetzten Ostgebiete', in: Andrea Bastian, *Der Heimat-Begriff: eine begriffsgeschichtliche Untersuchung in verschiedenen Funktionsbereichen der deutschen Sprache*, Niemeyer: Tübingen, 1995, pp. 203-217.

[56] 'Man kann in *Kurische Nehrung* revanchistische Züge entdecken. Man kann den Film für seine Auslassungen kritisieren. Es fehlen Darstellungen: des virulenten Nationalsozialismus, der sozialen Missstände, des Alkoholismus und der Arbeitslosigkeit in den Gebieten der ehemaligen UdSSR. Man kann den Film also

ablehnen (oder mögen) für das, was er zeigt oder verbirgt'. Kathrin Peters, '*Kurische Nehrung*', http:///www.nachdemfilm.de/reviews/nehrung.html, consulted in March 2002.

[57] Andreas Becker, 'Zeig doch mal die Deutschen. Ein absolutes Muss für Vertriebene: *Kurische Nehrung* von Volker Koepp präsentiert schönen Revanchismus', http://www.taz.de/tpl.nf/spText.Name,berlinale.idx,61, consulted January 2002.

[58] 'Volker Koepps *Kurische Nehrung* verklärt das Leben der Bewohner in einer historisch aufgeladenen Landschaft. [...] Die Erinnerungen der Älteren erzählen von Heimatverlust [...] Postkartenidylle'. Urs Richter, 'Und sonntags Krähensuppe', *die tageszeitung*, 3 August 2001.

[59] Ina-Maria Greverus, 'The Heimat-Problem' in: Seliger ed., *Der Begriff 'Heimat' in der deutschen Gegenwartsliteratur*, p. 10.

[60] Wolgang Bücher quoted in *Fachdienst Germanistik*, 4/2002, p. 15.

[61] See '...historische Grundwahrheit [...], dass es ein Vorher gegeben hat' whereby the Germans were 'erstverantwortlich'. Ralph Giordano, 'Über Günter Grass', *Die Welt*, 9 February 2002.

[62] Joachim Güntner quoted in *Fachdienst Germanistik,* 4/2002, p. 16.

[63] Celia Applegate, *A Nation of Provincials. The German Idea of Heimat*, University of California Press: Berkeley, 1990.

[64] Boa and Palfreyman, *Heimat. A German Dream*, pp. 9-11.

[65] Rainer Werner Fassbinder, *Katzelmacher*, Germany 1969 or *Wildwechsel*, Germany 1972.

[66] Boa and Palfreyman, *Heimat. A German Dream,* p. 89.

[67] This is not to be confused with recent films in the wake of 'ostalgia' like the film versions of Thomas Brussig's *Helden wie wir* or *Sonnenallee,* which communicate 'a nostalgic regret for past social networks and local values' which 'is creating a sense of loss for many citizens of the former GDR who felt little attachment to the communist regime but have not felt at home in the new Germany either, faced with the imposition of capitalist competition'. Elizabeth Boa & Rachel Palfreyman, *Heimat. A German Dream*, p. 203.

[68] Kaes, *From Hitler to Heimat*, p. 170.

[69] David Morley and Kevin Robins, 'No Place like Heimat', in: *Spaces of Identity. Global Media, Electronic Landscapes and Cultural Boundaries*, Routledge: London, 1995, p. 104.

[70] To name just two outstanding examples from the visual arts and literature: GüntherÜckers's sculptures on the Baltic coast (2001) or Marie-Louise Janssen-Jurreit's *Das Verbrechen der Liebe in der Mitte Europas,* Rowohlt: Berlin 2000.

[71] This is echoed in Marshall Berman's statement that modern 'environments and experiences cut across all boundaries of geography and ethnicity, of class and nationality, of religion and ideology [...] But it is a paradoxical unity, a unity of disunity; it pours us all into the maelstrom of perpetual disintegration and renewal, of struggle and contradiction, of ambiguity and anguish.' Quoted in Morley and Robins, 'No Place like Heimat', p. 86.

[72] See Tedd Rippey et al, '"Ein wunderschönes Heute"...', p. 150.

Notes on Contributors

Anthony Bushell is Professor of German and Head of the Department of Modern Languages at the University of Wales, Bangor. He is the author of *The Emergence of West German Poetry from the Second World War into the Early Post-War Period* and is editor of *Austria 1945-1955: Studies in Political and Cultural Re-emergence*. He is also series editor of *Austrian Studies in Context* and has written numerous articles devoted to post-war Austrian literature.

Ian Foster is Lecturer in German at the University of Salford. He has published numerous articles on Austrian literature and culture from the 1870s to the present day, including contributions on Ferdinand von Saar, Peter Altenberg and Joseph Roth. He has special interest in military themes and the fin-de-siècle. His most recent work includes articles on Christoph Ransmayr and he has edited (with Florian Krobb) Arthur Schnitzler: *Zeitgenossenschaften / Contemporaneities* (Peter Lang, 2002).

Birgit Haas completed her doctorate on "Das Theater des George Tabori" at the University of Heidelberg in 1998. Since 1999, she has taught as a DAAD-Lektorin in England and is currently at the University of Bristol. Her main research interests are drama and theatre of the twentieth and twenty-first century, dramatic performance, and comparative studies. She has published widely on modern drama, and her book *Political Drama in Germany 1980-2000* (Boydell & Brewer) appeared in November 2003.

Brigid Haines is Senior Lecturer in German at Swansea University. Her research interests include nineteenth- and twentieth-century literature, women's writing and critical theory. She is the co-author (with Margaret Littler) of *German Women's Writing and Feminist Theory: Changing the Subject*. She has just completed an AHRB-funded research project entitled *Maritime Bohemias: Representations of "Bohemia" in Libuše Moníková and other contemporary German writers*.

Nicole Immler studied History, German and Media at the Karl-Franzens-University of Graz. From 1999 to 2001 she was an assistant at the Ludwig Wittgenstein Archive in Cambridge. Her PhD (Graz) is on family-memoirs as a strategy of creating identity, using the example of the Wittgenstein family. She has held Research Scholarships at the Hoover Institution at Stanford University, California (2000) and at the German Historical Institute, London (2001). She has published several articles on Wittgenstein and the *fin de siècle*.

Dagmar Košťálová is Senior Lecturer in Modern German Literature at the Comenius University in Bratislava. Her research areas include German-Slovak literary and cultural relations (*Die Slowakei im mitteleuropäischen Kulturraum*, Bratislava 2003), migrant literature, Christa Wolf, and GDR Literature. She is also concerned with questions relating to the curriculum in German Studies.

Mariana Virginia Lăzărescu is Associate Professor for German and Austrian Literature in the Department of German, University of Bucharest. Her main research areas are literature of the nineteenth and early twentieth centuries and German stylistics. She has published articles on Hofmannsthal, Schnitzler and Stefan Zweig, including studies of their reception in Romania; a study of Eichendorff, *Joseph von Eichendorff: Aus dem Leben eines Taugenichts. Kommentierte Auswahlausgabe.* Bukarest 1985; and a translation, *Peter Handke: Der kurze Brief zum langen Abschied.* Übersetzung ins Rumänische mit Vorwort. Bukarest 1998, for which she was awarded the Prize of the Romanian Writers' Union.

Alexandra Ludewig is Senior Lecturer and Convenor of German and European Studies at The University of Western Australia in Perth. She obtained a PhD from The University of Queensland for a study on Jewish Migration to Australia and a Dr.Phil. from LMU-München for her book *Großvaterland* on Thomas Bernhard. She continues to research issues of German and European identity in film and literature.

Anthony Murphy lectures in sociology in the Department of Social Science and Humanities at the University of Bradford. He is writing a PhD on the Austrian Freedom Party.

Julian Preece is Reader in German and Comparative Literary Studies at the University of Kent. He is interested in German-language writers from Central Europe, in particular Grass, Kafka, Canetti. A paperback edition of his *The Life and Work of Günter Grass: Literature, History, Politics* is in press with Palgrave. He is also the editor of *The Cambridge Companion to Kafka* (CUP, 2002) and ghost-writer of a Holocaust memoir, *Nine Lives: Ethnic Conflict in the Polish-Ukrainian Borderlands* by Waldemar Lotnik (Serif, 1999).

Renate Rechtien is Lecturer in European Studies and German at the University of Bath. Her doctoral thesis (1997) dealt with Christa Wolf and in recent articles she has provided a comparative reading of Wolf's *Kindheitsmuster* with Günter de Bruyn's *Zwischenbilanz* as well as engaging in detail with Brigitte Reimann's diaries. Current research interests include an examination of the interplay between autobiographical and fictional self in Wolf's shorter prose pieces as well as in literary engagements by women authors with issues of identity in the new Germany.

David Rock is Senior Lecturer in German at Keele University. He has published extensively on nineteenth and twentieth century German writers, with special emphasis on the literature of the GDR and German writers in Eastern Europe. He is the author of *Jurek Becker: A Jew who became a German* (2000), editor of *Jurek Becker: Five Stories* (1992) and *Voices in Times of Change: The Role of Writers, Opposition Movements, and the Churches in the Transformation of East Germany* (2000), and co-editor of *Gerhart Hauptmann: Bahnwärter Thiel* (1992) and *Coming Home to Germany. The Integration of Ethnic Germans from Central and Eastern Europe in the Federal Republic* (2002).

Ricarda Schmidt, Staatsexamen, Dr. phil. (Hannover), Senior Lecturer in German at the University of Manchester. Her publications are in the fields of 19th- and 20th-century German literature and culture, with a focus on E.T.A. Hoffmann; the relationship between literature, art and music; GDR literature, women writers; theories of intermediality and intertextuality.

Juliet Wigmore is Senior Lecturer in German at the University of Salford. Her research focuses on Austrian writing since 1970 and on women's writing in both Austria and Germany. Her publications include articles on Elisabeth Reichart, Elfriede Jelinek, Marlen Haushofer and Anne Duden and an edition of Peter Handke's *Wunschloses Unglück*. Current interests include literary and cultural relations in the central European area, especially between German and Slavic speakers.

Arthur Williams is Emeritus Professor of Contemporary German Studies at the University of Bradford. Since his retirement in 2002 he has continued to teach in its Department of Languages and European Studies, principally translation for final honours and postgraduate students, and to supervise postgraduate dissertations. His research now focuses on the work of W. G. Sebald on whom he has written extensively. He maintains the Sebald website of the Literary Encyclopedia and Literary Dictionary (http://litencyc.com). He remains a board member of the (formerly: Bradford) biennial International Colloquium on Contemporary German-Language Literature.

The Vanished World of Lithuanian Jews

Edited by Alvydas Nikžentaitis, Stefan Schreiner & Darius Staliūnas
Preface by Leonidas Donskis

Amsterdam/New York, NY 2004. XV, 323 pp.
(On the Boundary of Two Worlds: Identity, Freedom, and Moral
Imagination in the Baltics 1)
ISBN: 90-420-0850-4   € 70,-/US$ 88.-

The Lithuanian Jews, Litvaks, played an important and unique role not only within the Polish-Lithuanian Commonwealth, but in a wider context of Jewish life and culture in Eastern Europe, too. The changing world around them at the end of the nineteenth century and during the first decades of the twentieth had a profound impact not only on the Jewish communities, but also on a parallel world of the "others," that is, those who lived with them side by side. Exploring and demonstrating this development from various angles is one of the themes and objectives of this book. Another is the analysis of the Shoah, which ended the centuries of Jewish culture in Lithuania: a world of its own had vanished within months. This book, therefore, "recalls" that vanished world. In doing so, it sheds new light on what has been lost.

The papers presented in this collection were delivered at the international conferences in Nida (1997) and Telšiai (2001), Lithuania. Participants came from Israel, the USA, Great Britain, Poland, Russia, Belarus, Germany, and Lithuania.

USA/Canada: One Rockefeller Plaza, Ste. 1420, New York, NY 10020,
Tel. (212) 265-6360, Call toll-free (U.S. only) 1-800-225-3998,
Fax (212) 265-6402
All other countries: Tijnmuiden 7, 1046 AK Amsterdam, The Netherlands.
Tel. ++ 31 (0)20 611 48 21, Fax ++ 31 (0)20 447 29 79
Orders-queries@rodopi.nl   www.rodopi.nl
Please note that the exchange rate is subject to fluctuations

Estonia
Identity and Independence

Edited by Jean-Jacques Subrenat
Translated into English by David Cousins, Eric Dickens, Alexander Harding, Richard C. Waterhouse.

Amsterdam/New York, NY 2004. IX, 310 pp.
(On the Boundary of Two Worlds. Identity, Freedom, and Moral Imagination in the Baltics 2)
ISBN: 90-420-0890-3   65,-/US-$ 81.-

In the span of only seventy years, Estonia first proclaimed its independence, was occupied and deprived of its sovereignty, saw many of its citizens deported, and yet managed to recover its independence. How did this small nation keep its language and traditions alive during half a century of occupation, and how did it maintain such a vivid sense of identity? For the first time in English, this book gives a comprehensive view of the events which shaped the destiny of contemporary Estonia. The Editor, Jean-Jacques Subrenat, has called upon an unusually broad spectrum of the best experts (in history, archeology, political science, genetics, literature), but also on some of the leaders who took part in the rebuilding of Estonia, to offer more than a history, rather a unique testimony on a nation reborn. This book, which opens the series on Baltic Studies at Rodopi, the publishing house, provides rare insight into the many aspects of a country whose location in Northern Europe, within the European Union, and as a NATO ally, but also as a close neighbour of Russia, deserves the attention of scholars, journalists, and informed readers today.

This volume includes a thorough chronology of Estonia (from prehistory to accession to the European Union), and a brief c.v. of each co-author.

Estonia: Identity and Independence is also available in three other languages (A. Bertricau is the pen-name of Jean-Jacques Subrenat, the initiator and Editor of this book):
- Estonian: 1st and 2nd edition : A. Bertricau, *Eesti identiteet ja iseseisvus*, published by Avita in Tallinn, 2001 and 2002;
- Russian: A. Bertricau, *Samoopredelenie i nezavissimost' Estonii*, published by Avita in Tallinn, August 2001;
- French : A. Bertricau, *Estonie, identité et indépendance*, published by L'Harmattan in Paris, November 2001.

USA/Canada: One Rockefeller Plaza, Ste. 1420, New York, NY 10020,
Tel. (212) 265-6360, Call toll-free (U.S. only) 1-800-225-3998,
Fax (212) 265-6402
All other countries: Tijnmuiden 7, 1046 AK Amsterdam, The Netherlands.
Tel. ++ 31 (0)20 611 48 21, Fax ++ 31 (0)20 447 29 79
Orders-queries@rodopi.nl   **www.rodopi.nl**
Please note that the exchange rate is subject to fluctuations

Rodopi